Privacy

Privacy: The Frontier of Social Evolution

Privacy

The Frontier of Social Evolution

By

Timothy M. Jurgensen

Midori Press
Austin, Texas

Privacy: The Frontier of Social Evolution

By: Timothy M. Jurgensen

Published by:

Midori Press LLC
2720 Mt. Laurel Lane
Austin, TX 78703 USA

Graphic design and layout design: Miriam Jurgensen

First Edition – Printed in the United States of America

ISBN-13:   978-0-9801821-2-5
ISBN-10:   0-9801821-2-3

Warning and Disclaimer

Dedication

To the ultimate, insular minority

Acknowledgments

This book builds upon the concepts that Bertrand du Castel and I explored in our earlier book *Computer Theology: Intelligent Design of the World Wide Web*. It also builds upon my own lifetime of experiences and observations regarding the processes encompassed by computer systems and their intrinsic relationship to the social processes that we all engage in our everyday lives. To more accurately express those experiences and observations, Bertrand and I agreed that it would be appropriate for me to author this book rather than co-authoring the book together. Had we done the book together, it might well have been a better book. I do know that it would have been a different book. As noted in the *First Principles*: "I have my own white whale to pursue."

It would probably be fair to say that the parts of this book that are well grounded and perhaps even a bit scholarly are the result of our collaborative effort. In concert with that collaboration, I have attempted to follow the practice of referring back to the original works of pioneers in various fields. While I have tried to learn from and apply those works, I am sure that there are instances where I have not drawn the correct lesson or I have not correctly applied the reasoning of those pioneers. So, the places, and there are many, where the book wanders off into the weeds are due to me alone. Certainly, the mistakes that are surely present in the book are due to me alone.

I want to extend my sincere thanks to those who reviewed and commented on early versions of this manuscript. I cannot assume their endorsement of the words in this book, but their oversight cannot help but make the words better. I trust I can continue to count them among my friends: Bill Quinlivan, Curt Barker, Neville Pattinson, Mourad Faher, Jerry Balkcom, and Ron Habitzreiter. My good friend, Bill MacGregor, who recently passed away, provided an excellent review of the earliest thoughts that became this book. I will miss his wisdom.

I want to thank my daughters Miriam Jurgensen and Sarah Throop for their counsel and support in developing this book. Both have exhibited the virtually infinite patience and understanding necessary to work with me for any length of time. Both have been extremely helpful resolving issues of detail in the form and content of the book. They have also served as excellent sounding boards for my more obtuse musings. It there is any good in the book, they helped put it there. The really bad stuff is due to me alone.

My wife Becky has, as always, been the ultimate source of understanding and support!

Contents

Preface

Privacy is a concept encountered quite often in daily discourse. We routinely engage private conversations in the privacy of our homes, and sometimes on public street corners. We often work in private offices where we exchange our labor for means to acquire private property. In certain situations, we have an expectation of privacy; certainly when we lay beside the pool in the privacy of our backyard surrounded by a privacy fence. If someone should invade our private reverie, perhaps by publishing photographs that show our private parts, they might be held legally liable for infringing our privacy. Of course, in questions of liability the law differentiates between private and public persons, even though privacy is not even mentioned in the nation's defining documents. So, though the term is pervasive, a well defined grasp of the concept is illusive.

In formal proceedings, decisions of the courts have held that an individual has a fundamental right of privacy under law. Some courts view this right as derived from the *Fourteenth Amendment* to the *Constitution*. Others suggest it has non-constitutional origins that convey to the individual through the *Ninth Amendment* and the *Tenth Amendment*. From whatever source derived, privacy is a powerful concept that has become a litmus test to differentiate belief systems. Among its chacteristics, privacy affords a woman the liberty to decide to avoid or even terminate her pregnancy. However, many purveyors and arbiters of public policy don't want to recognize this right. Consequently, whether or not such a right exists has become a central theme of the confirmation process of any person nominated to be a Justice of the United States Supreme Court.

It is small wonder then that we find privacy an interesting subject for examination. It certainly is of profound concern, if it exists. Actually, it probably does exist. It seems too integral to our language to not exist. Of course, ghosts and goblins are a part of our language as well. What, then, is the substance of privacy compared to that of ghosts and goblins? Is privacy a manifestation of an individual's excess; something that goes bump in the night of societal supremacy? Is it the base expression of self-indulgent behavior that government is bound to control? Or, is privacy the morning sunlight that chases the apparitions of societal excess back into the shadows of undue process? Does it in fact comprise a fundamental limitation on the power of government? These are questions worthy of consideration.

Our purpose in this book is to explore the concepts that underlie these questions. We'll do so through a series of concise yet moderately rigorous definitions. In particular, we seek to develop an understanding that might bring some clarity to both individual as well as governmental behaviors relative to privacy. The ensuing discussion will suggest some plausible answers to the questions posed above.

We'll begin by suggesting definitions for **identity** and **privacy** that recognize a fundamental relationship between these concepts. Moreover, both can be better understood and reinforced through technical mechanisms developed in the world of digital computers and their networks. These mechanisms are known colloquially as "identity systems" or as "computer security systems." We will develop a more comprehensive designation of Identity, Authority and Attribution (IAA) Systems that encompasses the basic mechanisms of identity and privacy.

Using concise definitions as starting points, we will show that personal privacy can be significantly enhanced through a society-wide deployment and utilization of IAA Systems that are based on a combination of physiological and digital mechanisms. Our thesis is that personal privacy is more than just a characteristic of behavior. Rather it is the fundamental process of individual being, comprising the rationale of government in general, and the American Republic specifically.

The approach we will take might require a bit of accommodation on the part of the reader. One must be willing to seriously consider for purposes of argument the definitions we offer. Only in this way will they lend some credence to the subsequent discussions. If discussion points are found erroneous, the difficulties can hopefully be traced back to the definitions. We'll attempt to aid the reader by compiling the definitions in a Glossary found toward the back of the book.

Our approach presents definitions of concepts that encompass most colloquial understanding of those concepts. However, we may well suggest meanings more expansive yet perhaps more concisely stated than those found in common usage of the terms. The goal is for the subsequent expositions to be coherent, comprehensive and consistent; hopefully, to also be correct. In the end, a reader may disagree with our conclusions, but at least our rationale might be well understood. This should lead to a better framed conversation.

To engage this discussion on privacy, in forming and using the definitions noted we will rely heavily on the mechanisms of recursion and metaphor. We do this because, based on our reading of the scientific literature, we have come to understand that these mechanisms reflect the way we humans are "wired." Quite literally, they form the way we work at a physiological level. Recursion and metaphor are among the simple machines of organic processes. We live by way of such processes, and thus we want to consider privacy as it relates to the way we live.

Recursion means that a process invokes itself in the course of its operation. A metaphor is a concept that can be invoked in place of a different concept in order to enhance the understanding or use of that different concept. If a metaphor is parameterized and then recursively engaged using systematically modified parameters, fractal geometries result. A metaphorical extension of fractal geometry is a *feedback control loop*; a fundamental mechanism of sustainable processes. Organic processes are well described by such geometries. Recursive metaphor is a particularly interesting concept because it offers points of intersection between the physical and philosophical that epitomize the realms of both neurological processes and digital computers.

A metaphor is often grounded in physical actions. A physical expression can frame the metaphors that derive from it. Let's explore this idea by assuming a mechanism that can be set to one of two states: **on** or **off**; essentially, a persistent switch. Next, consider an associated mechanism that can query this switch and determine whether it is in fact on or off. Now we assume another associated mechanism that supports a persistent list of action invocations through which states can be set to on or off and a query made to determine an unknown state. Finally, we posit a branch among the elements of action invocation based on the results of the query of state condition. This simple collection of mechanisms forms the basis of stored-program digital computers.

The state of the original mechanism can be viewed metaphorically as a "bit"; a philosophical representation of information. A bit that is "on" we might understand as a "1" while a bit that is "off" we might understand as a "0". Using the physical mechanisms that we've described, we can create persistent strings of 0's and 1's. If we perceive these strings of 0's and 1's as binary numbers, we enable mathematical computation. If we perceive them purely as symbols, then we enable symbolic logic.

Assuming either perception, we can establish a metaphorical association of specific binary numbers or symbols with certain actions to be taken on other binary numbers or symbols. Thus, we can create a "program" comprised of some sequence of specific actions to be taken on a collection of persistent, yet malleable information. These mechanisms enable the use of recursive metaphors to extend, virtually without limit, the semantic content expressed by these simple machines. Through this extension, the seminal state machine can become the laptop computer, the smart phone or the massively networked browsers and servers of the World Wide Web.

An even greater degree of this same capability extension is found in the world of living things. In humans, the simple machines that are neuron cells, and their association through synaptic connections, ultimately give rise to the general cognitive facility known as the brain and to its philosophical extension known as the mind. Just as the physical substrate of binary machines gives rise to the complex programs of computer systems, so too the physiological substrate of the nervous system gives rise to the cognitive processes of the mind. As humans are "wired" to ultimately achieve enhanced capability through social structures, so also do computers gain enhanced capability through comprehensive networks. Thus we approach the rationale for our specific exploration of the concept of privacy.

One can describe some of the building blocks of basic personal capability through a recounting of employment history. Over the course of my career, I've donned many hats that give some variety to my *curriculum vitae*: grocery store stock-boy, farm-hand, mail-carrier, computer-operator, teaching-assistant, graduate-student, systems-architect, professor, author and so on. However, my most consistent skill over the years is that of a **computer-programmer**. It's something I first learned in high school in 1962, and it's been an underlying facet of just about everything else I've done since. In retrospect, I quite relish the title.

Much of the impetus for my relatively new found respect for this recurring capability comes from a better appreciation for the processes of the mind. I've had the opportunity to read somewhat extensively in this area, and much is brought into focus by the life story of Temple Grandin, a professor of Animal Sciences at Colorado State University. Professor Grandin is autistic.

Temple Grandin has done much to educate the world about autism in its various forms. Equally profound, as a world-renown expert on animal behavior, she has revolutionized the handling of animals in food production; bringing into being a more humane treatment that has proven morally, procedurally and financially sound. She attributes much of what she has achieved to her autism that allows her mind to see things in a different light than most other people. By essentially exploiting the facilities of her autism to achieve extremely noteworthy accomplishments in the world of the non-autistic, Professor Grandin has become something of a *Rosetta stone* linking these distinct domains.

In a television interview, Professor Grandin was asked whether, if we could through science eradicate autism, should we? Her response struck a chord with me; something along the lines of "If we eradicate autism, we will probably do away with most computer-programmers." I have come to believe that what she was expressing was an appreciation for characteristics of computer-programmers that are shared by the autistic; or *vice versa*. Central among these characteristics is the ability to compartmentalize problems and to "see" the essence of the processes necessary to address the relevant solutions in a manner devoid of overt emotions.

I rather doubt that all computer-programmers are autistic, and I doubt that this is what Professor Grandin intended. In a clinical evaluation, I would probably not exhibit most of the characteristics attributed to autism. However, many computer-programmers, whether autistic or not, do see the world in a quite different manner than most other people. The facility for compartmentalization noted above is one aspect of this difference. Invoking a facility of object-oriented programming, I suggest that this characteristic neurological facility is a distinct trait **inherited** within the minds of both programmers and the autistic from some superior source. Hence, if one could eradicate this aspect of autism, one would probably eradicate it in programmers as well. So, let's explore an interesting consequence of this behavior.

Though still rather ambiguously understood, autism seems to accentuate the dichotomy within the human mind of the "fact" of an experience versus the "emotion" of that experience. Within the "normal" human brain, the memories formed of the experiences of the individual have "fact" and "emotion" highly intertwined. A bit later we will suggest that this amalgam of "fact" and "emotion" is perceived as **sensation**, and that the function of memory is to give persistence to sensation. We will define sensation to encompass **bodily states** such as hunger or thirst, **basic emotions** such as anger or disgust, and **complex emotions** such as love or happiness.

Individuals communicate with one another by way of shared experiences; in essence, by way of shared sensations. This facility is fundamental to the formation and functioning of social groups. In the brains of those who are autistic, this tight coupling of "fact" and "emotion" becomes separated to varying degrees. Thus, if experiential memory normally includes an emotional component, then a memory devoid of emotion will offer a very different perspective. One might view this situation as akin to a personal memory devoid of input from at least one of the basic senses; for example, the memories of one who is without sight or hearing. Temple Grandin suggests a variety of mechanisms that she uses to offset the absence of strong emotional assessment within routine memories.

In a paper entitled *Social Problems: Understanding Emotions and Developing Talents* published by the Indiana Resource Center for Autism, Professor Grandin notes:

> I did not know that eye movements had meaning until I read *Mind Blindness* by Simon Baron-Cohen. I had no idea that people communicated feelings with their eyes. I also did not know that people get all kinds of little emotional signals which transmit feelings. My understanding of this became clearer after I read *Descartes' Error* by Antonio Damasio. From the book I learned that, in most people, information in memory is seamlessly linked with emotion. I have emotions which can be very strong when I am experiencing them, but information stored in memory can be scanned at will without emotion. It is like surfing the Internet of web pages in my mind.
>
> ...
>
> Over time, I have built up a tremendous library of memories of my past experiences, TV, movies, and newspapers to spare me the social embarrassments caused by my autism; and I use these to guide the decision process in a totally logical way. I have learned from experience that certain behaviors make people mad.

Professor Grandin then goes on to describe a simple rule system that she uses as a guide to her behavior in social interactions. We can characterize these in the terms that we will develop within this book as: **rules of basic altruism** such as not murdering other people; **social protocols** such as parking between the white lines in a parking lot; **accommodation of poorly expressed policy** such as 55-mile per hour speed limits on the lightly populated freeways of west Texas; and **"Sins of the Systems".**

"Sins of the Systems" encompass behaviors arbitrarily construed as improper and for which the penalty for their use "defies all logic"; for example, long prison terms for smoking marijuana. This rule system provides a very telling connection between the constructs of personal behavior grounded in the human mind and the constructs of policy aimed at the arbitration of such behaviors among individuals. It brings us to consideration of the **rule of law**, and very specifically to dealing with privacy under the rule of law. Hence, we characterize Professor Grandin's experiences and associated decision process as offering an existence proof for mechanisms that simulate sensation based interactions through primarily logical processes. This is a necessary facility of computer-programmers seeking to create programs that function consistently in social interactions. This is also a necessary characteristic of law and jurisprudence.

The concept of the **rule of law** is all about process; more specifically, process grounded in logic and largely devoid of emotion. Law comprises rules for social behavior intended to be clearly understood and adhered to by all who come under its influence, and punished when they don't behave appropriately. The antithesis of the rule of law is the **rule of men**. Under the rule of law, policy is intended to be uniformly applied by, and to, every person in all the situations encountered in life. This suggests that expressions of policy must be consistently interpreted by different individuals who derive from a broad range of development environments and physiological capabilities. Under the rule of men, policy is influenced by individual subjective interpretation which, by definition, is dependent on those very environments, capabilities and the emotions they evoke. So, we make our way to consideration of privacy.

There currently is significant turmoil within United States legal circles as to how to handle the concept of privacy, or even what the concept is. In a statement of *First Principles* which will open the first chapter of this book, we will put forth a concise definition of the concept. It is a more expansive definition than one might discern from contemporary jurisprudence. It is perhaps more expansive than a person would perceive, based on normal behaviors of the general populace. So, during the course of the book we will examine this definition in some detail. Then, we will attempt to understand the concept in light of how society views privacy today, and subsequently speculate on the possible impact of the concept as we have observed its definition.

A few of the observations developed in the course of the book might be perceived as unconventional. First among these is the idea that identity and privacy are intimately linked. We assert personal privacy in order to provision our identity. Moreover, a person's identity is represented as sensation in the minds of others rather than being an internal characteristic of the person. If we assert privacy to provision identity, and each person has a fundamental right of privacy, then what happens when the privacy assertions of two different people conflict? This is the general dilemma that must be addressed if people are to co-exist under some set of rules other than "survival of the fittest."

In considering the desired system of rules, we'll first observe the basic mechanisms through which privacy is asserted and identity perceived. While these mechanisms are more easily stated in the realm of digital computers, we suggest they can be traced back to fundamental physiological characteristics. This leads us to the proposition that personal privacy can be significantly enhanced through technical means, starting with a comprehensive approach in support of the facets of personal identity; specifically, a national identity system.

It seems that the Founders of the American Republic actually thought this also. Examining in some detail the foundations of American jurisprudence found in the *Declaration of Independence* and the *Constitution,* we observe that an expansive concept of privacy is easily recognized. Moreover, solutions to many of the observed problems in current American society such as the undue influence of political parties and failures of the education system would be more readily addressed by a correct interpretation of the concepts.

We can but hope that our perceptions are well conveyed to the reader. Whether the reader is in agreement or not, we trust the conversation about privacy might be advanced. Would that truth is found in the trust we aver.

1 *The Concept of Privacy*

First Principles

Self is the manifestation of a unique person. Self is aware of existence. The aware self engages the surrounding environment through a physiological sensori-motor system. Self uses its motor system for expression to the surrounding environment. Self uses its sensory system to receive impressions from the surrounding environment. The surrounding environment includes others like self. Acting through their respective sensori-motor systems, self and others can selectively form a **polity**; the aggregate self of a social order. Such is the reality that encompasses self; to the extent that senses perceive and actions impact reality.

Through a linguistic construct, self-awareness forms a point of reference for the language that is expressed and received through the physiological sensori-motor system. Known as a **deictic center**, it is the target of other linguistic constructs such as verbs and pronouns that represent specific actions and generic personal designations. Ownership of tangible objects as well as intangible abstractions resides here. It is the place and time where spatial and temporal references find resolution.

> I am self. These are my thoughts. These are my words. I fling them in anger! I sing them in harmony. I perform them with humor and pathos. My place is here. My time is now. You might call me by my name, but I'm not Ishmael or Captain Ahab for that matter. They are others. I have my own white whale to pursue.

The deictic center is the metaphoric focus of self in sensori-motor reality. It allows the differentiation of self from others, with the reality of each impacting that of the others. A metaphor is a more general construct, one of cognition that predates language. It uses one concept in place of a different concept to enhance understanding of that second concept. Metaphor enables a taxonomic interpretation of an unknown concept in terms of a known concept. It affords a model of learning through which a perturbation on known concepts provides an efficient way to assimilate an unknown concept.

Senses flood the brain with more observations than can be interpreted through sequential conscious assessment. Instead, the mind within the brain appears to work at both conscious and unconscious levels through predictive, metaphorical models. Sensory input is scrutinized by multiple neural processes that implement these models. The cumulative application of these processes is termed **cognition**. More generally stated, cognition is the fundamental process of the mind that manifests as observation, assessment, understanding, motivation and action-invocation in sensori-motor reality. Cognition is a neural interaction whose consequence we recognize as **sensation**.

The basic senses of sight, sound, touch, taste, and smell are presented to the brain where, based on the mind's implementation of cognitive models, they are perceived as sensations across a broad and complex spectrum. At the most basic, sensory observations give rise to fundamental feelings such as cold or pain. However, there is both an information-content as well as an aesthetic-content aspect to sensation. Encompassing social constructs, cognitive models that give rise to sensation evoke emotions such as love or hate. Given persistence, cognitive models incorporate experiential memories discerned as comprehensive moods such as complacency, satisfaction, anger or perhaps **happiness**.

Understanding and value-assessment flow from sensations. They enable self to differentiate among the competing demands on the mind. **Provisioning** instills in the mind the fundamental structures, the guiding knowledge and the operational processes of the metaphoric models called upon to interpret sensory observations and evoke motor responses. Through these models, the mind can anticipate the progression of observations over time and attempt to predict the impact of motor system actions on future observations.

Self achieves persistence through **memory**, the physiological mechanism by which sensations are transferred from the present to the future. A persistent sensation is termed an **experience**. Based on experiences, the mind's metaphorical models are refined and optimized by relating current observations to prior predictions. Self is motivated in its expressions by a fundamental drive to achieve sensations it deems desirable based on experience. This recursion forms a model of learning for neural processes.

Much as with neural processes, optimizing social processes is dependent on physiological mechanisms for disseminating sensations among the members of a social aggregate and for transferring sensations from the present to the future. The nature of persistent self awareness is but tenuously understood. It is the subject of ongoing research in the domain of philosophers, psychiatrists and psychologists. In recent years, it has also become the playground of the neurosciences. It is the realm of pure consciousness. However, when self engages others through its physiological sensori-motor system, its nature becomes more measured through physical manifestations that affect others. Using these manifestations, a polity can be created from an aggregate of individuals.

The polity achieves cohesion through personal **expression** and **impression**, the physiological facilities by which sensations are transferred from one person to another. Expression and impression seek to establish a state of **sympathy** between the self and the other. Sympathy presents as a spectrum that ranges from **apathy** to **empathy**. A state of empathy indicates that sensations are well shared; apathy indicates they are not. The sharing of experiences is called **mimesis**, which forms the foundation of shared metaphoric understanding.

When expression is rendered through physical mechanisms, the result is an **art-form**; that is, a tool used to extend expression beyond its physiological motor system source. Art-forms provide external (to the brain) memory and hence the means by which the aggregate experiences of the polity achieve persistence. Art-forms vary in their effectiveness in conveying sensations. The ability of an individual to effectively use art-forms can vary as well.

It's perhaps more difficult to tell a complex story through cave paintings than through a documentary film, but when wielded by a true artist even a poem can paint a compelling picture.

For the more pedestrian among us, even with an optimum art-form we can't all express ourselves as well as William Shakespeare. Neither can we all fully appreciate the expressions of his words. Thus, the distinguishing characteristic of the true artist is one who can successfully evoke sensation via art-form.

The general transfer of sensations among a social aggregate from the present to the future we call **art**. Conveying the sensation(s) derived from a specific experience we term a **composition**. A composition is rendered in an art-form; for example, a painting, a book, a letter, a picture, a movie, a video, a sculpture, or even a fortune cookie. This list matches our colloquial understanding of an art-form. However, the definition we have suggested renders virtually any physical manifestation as a potential art-form, from a safe-pin to a city. If we can establish a common characteristic of art, then the aggregate can be termed a **culture**. For example, the characterization of a social order through the art that it engenders we term its culture.

Sensory observation enables **impressions of** others and motor action enables **expressions to** others. These comprise a means of engagement among self and others. The compositions shared among self and others give persistence to such engagement. This is different from the pure awareness of self, for now others can perceive self through the physical manifestations of shared compositions and thus form their own memories involving self. Sharing experience is an experience of sharing. Social cohesion results when a social order's experiences are rendered as art and well shared among its polity. The strength of cohesion derives from the level of sympathy among the polity established through shared metaphorical models.

Self uses its physiological motor system to effect compositions and hence experiential perceptions by others. A systematic combination of expression based on impression derived from metaphoric understanding can be characterized as a **behavior**. Like self, others perceive interactions and form memories through their own metaphorical models. We understand the concept of **self from the perspective of others** as **identity**. Through evolution derived behaviors, self seeks to control the provisioning of identity as a means to shape the metaphorical models called forth in the minds of others. This is the means by which self seeks to survive, and perhaps to thrive in a social environment.

The **provisioning of identity** we recognize as **privacy**. For multiple others, self appears to each consistently and persistently according to the memories formed through the association of self and each other. Through privacy, self seeks to independently mold its association with each other. The metaphorical model in the mind of another that reflects self's identity is thus established uniquely with each other and may vary from one to another. Ones identity is never exactly the same to all others.

The uniqueness of identity perceived by each other results because self engages others through pair-wise interactions, often pursued through imperfect expression of language and composition, subject to the inexactitudes of sensory observation. Memories of such interactions are based on organic processes and thus can also be inexact. The consequence of any specific interaction can affect subsequent interactions, and thereby the sensations experienced and the memories formed.

The imprecision of art-forms and the situational impact of interactions all serve to affect the perceptions connecting self and others. When self interacts with one or more others, it can perceive this aggregation of individuals as a repetitively recognizable collective. We refer to this collective as **society**, or more specifically, as a **social order**. Formally, we define society as **others from the perspective of self**. Where the self is the manifestation of the individual, the polity is the manifestation of a social order.

Identity and society are reciprocal concepts. In fact, they are reciprocal metaphorical models. Both are social concepts, depending on a multi-individual environment for meaning. A single self can engage many societies. Each society derives from a specific polity. Self and only one other form the most basic polity. As a polity grows in number, the mechanisms which bind the individuals together into a social order become more complex. These binding mechanisms reflect the **provisioning of a society** which we call **policy**. As the self asserts privacy, the polity asserts policy.

Privacy provides a projection to others of the dynamic characteristics of an individual self; that is, the identity of self. Policy provides a projection to each individual self of the dynamic characteristics of the polity of a social order. These reciprocal concepts demark the individual and the collective. Both concepts have resulted from the evolutionary development of the human species. Both are central to the prowess exhibited by the human species among all other species. The boundary between these two concepts is the frontier of social evolution.

Cognition by Metaphors

In 1637, French philosopher René Descartes established what many perceive as a fundamental basis of Western philosophy when he wrote in his *Discourse on Method*, "*Je pense donc je suis.*" The English translation is "*I think therefore I am.*" To reach a more scholarly audience, in his 1644 treatise entitled *Principles of Philosophy* he used the Latin expression "*cogito ergo sum.*" In each case, the speaker has more a philosophical than a physical connotation. In English, we might express the causal statement of being as "*To think therefore to be.*" How then to connect the philosophical concept of being to the reality of the human person?

Philosophical being melds with reality through the introduction of the concept of **the self** as the manifestation of the person. The focus of both expression and impression, a recurring dichotomy presents between self as the actor and self as the object of observation and target of external actions. In his book *From Axons to Identity*, physician and neuroscientist Todd Feinberg suggests that the distinctive nature of self lies in the coherence of consciousness across time. When one utters "*I think therefore I am*", one is establishing a persistent point of causality of the individual. It is a point that blurs the line between conscious thought and objective reality. While self is the reference point for perspective of thought, of observation and of action of the individual, in contrast, the polity as the aggregate self of a social order is purely a product of sensori-motor reality.

The reader will note that the concept of **person** is somewhat ambiguous in the course of the words of this book. The author routinely makes use of plural pronouns; as in, "We perceive this to be the realm of privacy and policy..." The ambiguity is intentional. Sometimes, the term is intended to reference the collection of those responsible for putting this book together; the **editorial we**. Sometimes the term is intended to express a specific group; the co-authors of a previous book for example. Sometimes the term is used to reference membership in a larger, more amorphous collective such as the members of the human species. And, sometimes the term refers to the social collective comprised of the author and the reader. This isn't terribly important, but as we noted in the opening statement of *First Principles*, it is useful to have a linguistic point of reference. Such linguistic constructs form the beginnings of metaphorical thought, allowing the extraction of specific meaning from context.

Our goal is to examine what we perceive to be the material side of the dichotomy between conscious thought and the physical manifestations that we know as sensori-motor reality. There is, or course, a catch. As we will consider in a bit more detail in *Chapter 2*, there are limits to the extent that senses paint a true and complete picture of objective reality. In our considerations, we won't seek to address the issues of conscious self awareness; at least, not to any depth. However, we will try to examine the mechanisms through which a person engages the social world; the realm of privacy and policy.

To understand the concepts of privacy, identity, policy and society we will proceed from two perspectives. Based on human physiology, privacy can be viewed as the aggregate of evolutionary derived behaviors that enable the individual to survive and even prosper in the physical world. Conversely, based on social policy, privacy can be viewed as the primary **nourishment** of social orders; the *raison d'être* from which the social order achieves effective being through personal privacy's administration and manipulation. The first takes us from the individual toward the social while the second takes us from the social toward the individual.

From a physiological perspective, privacy makes perhaps its most basic appearance through the connection of sensory observations to the endocrine system enabled motor facility known as the **fight or flight response to stress**. This virtually reflexive reaction mechanism was first recognized by Hans Selye in a 1946 paper in the *Journal of Clinical Endocrinology* describing the **general adaptation syndrome**. The fight or flight response forms the first stage of this syndrome. It is a mainstay of an individual's ability to counter threats of all shapes and forms; to act overtly or covertly when survival demands.

From a social policy perspective, privacy makes its most profound appearance through the 1973 legal case of *Roe v. Wade* in which the Supreme Court of the United States recognized privacy as a fundamental individual right. It is no quirk of fate that this case deals with a pregnant woman's power to decide whether to have an abortion. Pregnancy sits astride the boundary between the personal and the social. It encompasses the most profound issues of expression and infringement of privacy. It will be our approach to begin with these two rather diametrically opposed perspectives and, from each, proceed toward the other seeking a clearer understanding of the concepts and mechanisms involved.

In our pursuit of a better understanding of privacy, we will attempt to provide relatively rigorous definitions for some of the more important concepts that we consider; collecting them in a *Glossary* found toward the end of the book. We feel this is necessary because much of our discussion will be couched in terms that are in common usage; terms such as privacy, identity, trust and truth. Used in everyday conversation, the words are often tinged with colloquial understanding. In stating rigorous definitions, we will use an approach from the development of international standards. We will equate a specific word with a defining phrase that one should be able to substitute for the word in a sentence and retain the same meaning; perhaps, even to better understand the sentence.

The concepts in question are best understood metaphorically so as to address disparate contexts with more meaningful clarity. We draw justification for this approach from those who suggest that metaphorical reasoning is a fundamental characteristic of the human brain; perhaps, the characteristic that gives humanity its most profound uniqueness. George Lakoff and Mark Johnson observed as much in their book *Metaphors We Live By*, suggesting the basic concepts of thought and action are metaphorical in nature.

A metaphor is most generally understood as a linguistic concept. It involves the use of one term to provide enhanced understanding of another term that may not, at first blush, appear to be related. A more nuanced and profound interpretation of the concept uses an interaction, or even a family of interactions, to convey deeper meaning and understanding to a different set of interactions. Used in this way, a metaphor becomes an algorithm that is readily implemented by the neural processes of the brain. Through this neural algorithm, an interaction can be assimilated by the mind, forming a model that connects sensory impression to motor system expression. Through metaphorical association, the various facets of this interaction can subsequently be applied to ostensibly different interactions; or, to similar interactions with different contexts.

Using metaphorical association, subordinate concepts related to the first interaction can now be applied to the second interaction. For example, we often interpret significant aspects of our lives according to the basic metaphor of **family** that we learn through our early provisioning. We use our understanding of the facets of family to guide our involvement in a variety of other, small social orders. Consider for example, the bonding that occurs between mother and child, between father and child or between siblings. Such bonding is a subordinate concept of family and can be used to calibrate the strength of association among members of more *ad hoc* social groups.

In his play *Henry V*, William Shakespeare used this gauge to great effect in King Henry's address to his troops before the Battle of Agincourt: *"For he today that sheds his blood with me shall be my brother..."* not an associate, not a comrade, but my brother! As with true brotherhood, King Henry suggests that this association will last for the rest of their lives:

> *And gentlemen in England now a-bed shall think themselves accursed they were not here, and hold their manhoods cheap whiles any speaks that fought with us upon Saint Crispin's day.*

Sports metaphors and battle metaphors find their way into a wide variety of situations. Indeed, many sports metaphors encompass battle metaphors, and *vice versa*. Through metaphorical understanding the mind is able to use cognitive models derived from one type of interaction as a way to address significantly different types of interactions. Using an adequate metaphorical model, the results of sensory observations can be derived and thus understood. Correspondingly, the impact of motor actions on future observations can be predicted. With a really good metaphorical model, actions that are obvious in one type of interaction become plausible or even insightful in different interactions.

Using metaphorical reasoning, similar situations constrained by distinct contexts can be more easily understood as simple perturbations on an existent model. Rather than the mind reasoning according to specific instances of interactions, metaphorical reasoning allows disparate interactions to be understood (reasoned about) through a common framework. The general act of throwing something encompasses a set of basic physiological capabilities. **Throwing a baseball**, or **passing a football**, or **shooting a basketball**, or **flinging a spear** are each metaphorical specializations of the same physiological behavior. **Throwing a pot** offers up something of an ambiguous extension of the metaphor! **Throwing a vase** and breaking it fits the metaphor, but **throwing (shaping) clay** to form a containing vessel becomes an insightful extension of the metaphor, giving rise to **throwing a tantrum** or even **throwing a party!**

As we noted in our statement of *First Principles*, from a social perspective the journey to understanding privacy begins with self. While self has been a focus of philosophers since the dawn of recorded history, we find an interesting view presented by Charles Horton Cooley in his book *Human Nature and Social Order*, first published in 1902. While it probably has no strong bearing on the discussion, we note that Charles Cooley was the son of Thomas Cooley, a noted jurist who served on the State of Michigan Supreme Court and was a recognized scholar of constitutional law. A reference to Thomas Cooley will arise in a later chapter through the Supreme Court decision in the case of *Union Pacific Railroad Company v. Botsford.*

Charles Cooley observed that when self is perceived from external to the person, it becomes a social characteristic that gains meaning through the observations of others. He refers metaphorically to this concept as the **looking glass self**; the individual person viewed by another in a social perspective:

> Each to each a looking-glass
> reflects the other that doth pass.

Cooley posits that self viewed from another's perspective encompasses three principal elements:

- the imagination of our appearance to the other person,
- the imagination of his judgment of that appearance, and
- some sort of self-feeling, such as pride or mortification.

The suggestion is that we anticipate the perceptions others have of us, and we derive some value (self-feeling) from those perceptions. Others judge us based on their perceptions of us. This judgment is a part of their assessment of potential interaction outcomes that involve us. Hence, through our engagement of others we seek to manifest a perception in them that evokes a desired sensation of value in us and a desired judgment in them. The perception we recognize as **identity**. The desired sensation of value we call **happiness**. Finally, we recognize the sensation associated with their judgment of us as **reputation**.

A physiological ability to distinguish others is with us from birth. From the earliest interactions between mother and infant, each can distinguish the other. This recognition is central to their forming a bond that becomes a significant aspect of their focus of existence. Similar bonds between a man and a woman, between an infant and father, and between siblings expand in number and become the basis of family; the fundamental social collective. The bonds are uniquely formed and thus identity is established independently for each other person with whom one interacts. These pair-wise encounters are the mechanisms through which one person engages others and thereby experiences society. Social groups, in turn, can manifest the aggregate bonding facilities of their constituent members in the form of policy, the means through which a social order is provisioned.

All interactions have a common form. An interaction is bounded by a context. Initial provisioning puts in place within the context all that's necessary to enable the interaction to begin. The context can then be recursively provisioned as the interaction proceeds. Physical, physiological and social forces constrain sensory observation and physiological motor actions within the context. Participants are authenticated and the authority for their participation is established within the context. Consequences can be attributed to the participants. We might think of a constrained interaction as one with a well defined beginning and end. This is a useful concept when we want to establish a metaphorical reference to a distinguished interaction in the form of some index that provides a shortcut to recalling an experience.

Context is established according to the personal motivations of the participants, each of whom seeks to realize some specific consequence from the interaction. When the context is in place, an assessment can be made by each participant of the probability that specific actions will result in their desired consequences. If they each deem the probability sufficient, the various participants evoke individual actions aimed to achieve their desired consequences. The action proceeds until all consequences are realized. These consequences may or may not be the ones anticipated by the various participants.

The interaction's tangible consequences, also known as compositions, and individual memories of sensations formed among the participants derive from the interaction. An interaction committed to memory we call an **experience**. As part of the formation of memories, using cognitive models what was anticipated is compared to what was achieved through the interaction and both manifest as sensations. We call the sensation of anticipation **trust** and the sensation of achievement **truth.** Compositions and memories of a uniquely discernable experience contribute to a **forensic wake**.

If one views driving an automobile into a tree as a distinguished interaction, then the wrecked car is a tangible consequence of that interaction. It is in fact a composition, to use the term we have defined. The driver's broken leg is another tangible consequence; also a composition. The two compositions plus the driver's memory of the wreck comprise a forensic wake. At the time of the accident, it is clear that this forensic wake came from a single interaction. However, a few days later when an investigator looks at the wrecked car and a physician looks at the broken leg, it's not necessarily obvious that they both derived from the same interaction. The two consequences still contribute to a forensic wake, but their connection through a common interaction is far less obvious. The truth of their connection is questionable, particularly if the driver's memory is not believed. If it's necessary to objectively establish the connection after the fact, how is this done?

Interactions, like operas, "ain't over 'til the fat lady sings." In the case of social interactions, some form of post-action adjudication may be required to affirm that consequences conform to the effective social policy under which the interaction occurred. Social processes are invoked to systematically assess the truth derived from the forensic wake. This set of recursive interactions allow the social order to weigh the allowed versus the actual consequences as a means to affirm the rules were correctly followed. In this way, the social order can affirm the relevant memories and compositions from the forensic wake.

In summary, through interactions, we express ourselves to others and conversely they express themselves to us. Within an interaction, our expression to others and our impressions of others flow through our sensori-motor systems to and from the physical world. Based on these mutual impressions and expressions, we and they seek specific results according to our personal motivations. As the participants assimilate the actual consequences, all are better able to anticipate the consequences of future interactions. The complementary concepts of trust and truth connect action to consequences. **Trust** is the probability that a specific action will result in the anticipated consequence. Conversely, **truth** is the probability that a consequence resulted from a specific action.

The evaluation of trust is an integral part of every interaction. It is the gating function for the actual invocation of action(s). In a highly trustworthy situation, there is a greater perceived probability of correctly anticipating the outcome than in a less trustworthy situation. In an earlier book co-authored with Bertrand du Castel entitled *Computer Theology - Intelligent Design of the World Wide Web*, we suggested two mechanisms for establishing a basis for trust: causality and process. Only through a common sharing of trust, however grounded, can policy be effectively mandated by a polity and thereby impact the degree to which each individual in the social order accommodates personal privacy to social policy.

For some arbitrary interaction that involves another person, we set the context while envisioning some specific perception of ourselves by that other person. We evoke some action constrained by this context in an attempt to achieve the consequence that will anchor the perception by the others that we desire of them. This perception is our identity. We provision our identity by engaging in successive interactions. Our motivation for engaging these interactions through which we provision our identity is a search for desired sensations; sensations that we have generically referred to as **happiness**. This provisioning we refer to as privacy. Hence, privacy is the means through which we **pursue happiness**.

Through our expression of personal privacy we can constrain and focus specific aspects of our identity as perceived by other individuals, including groups of other people. Through such focus, we can establish a **persona**; a subset of our true or complete identity. When we engage other people through interactions, they will base their involvement in the interaction on sensations derived from our identity as they perceive it; that is, on the persona that we have previously presented to them. We have defined this sensation derived from a subset of identity, or a persona, as **reputation**. We can now connect back to the words that Cooley used by observing that this sensation of reputation is the actual realization of what we had originally only imagined. Reputation is a sensation that provides a measure of the truth one perceives in another's identity.

If the success of social orders results from the coherent participation of its members, then the group must first bind its participants together through a common basis of trust. In turn, coherent participation requires that policy manifestations of the group mandate how the members should act when the group is stimulated to individual or collective action. The coherence of each person's participation in the group's policy is a direct reflection of their common devotion to the basis of trust for the group. This suggests that the members of a group must understand and implement the policy of the group according to a shared metaphorical model.

The physical ecosystem in which all living things exist presents its own basis of trust. This trust is grounded in the ability of individuals to survive interactions with the physical world and with other living things. It is the trust manifested by the "survival of the fittest." The truth that confirms the causal basis of trust is the actual survival of individual interactions that extends over the very long term. In the course of multiple interactions, natural selection ultimately judges whether our trust is wisely construed; whether there is sufficient truth in the metaphorical models that we use to understand sensory observations, and pursue actions accordingly.

If our models are correct, then we're more likely to live longer and pass our genetic characteristics on to our progeny. Among humans, the individual experiences involving one person can enhance the provisioning of others. We can learn by observing others as well as by our own actions. When humans go beyond individual actions, and seek to engage social forms, the species has demonstrated a capability to arrive at a common basis of trust across the members of a social order. As judged by natural selection, this basis of trust can yield collective actions substantially beneficial to the group, if not to specific individuals. Hence, through evolutionary processes humans have learned to forge societies and thus gain natural selection benefit through **altruistic** actions.

For social interactions within the physical ecosystem, the point of causality that establishes the basis of trust is often the sensation derived from an emotionally charged, yet cognitively analyzed event. We term this sensation **ecstasy; the emotionally perceived truth derived from an ecstatic experience**. Ecstasy forms a cognitive feedback loop which can radically alter the value system through which we gauge future interactions.

For some, the sensation of ecstasy might derive as a consequence of a **religious experience** and result in extraordinary devotion to a perceived supernatural deity. For others, ecstasy might result from a ritual induced, altered state of consciousness such as many achieve through meditation or other forms of ritualized expression and impression. In the extreme, ecstasy might be experienced as a consuming fear that overwhelms other personal desires and becomes the basis of trust that guides our actions. Assessing trust is ultimately a reflection of a person's guiding metaphorical model of the world, which in turn is the result of an individual's provisioning. One might wonder how trust by an individual translates into shared trust among a social aggregate.

Mechanics of Polity

As the early settlers moved into the pristine lands of what we now know as western Pennsylvania, Ohio, Indiana and Illinois, they were early adopters of a new social order; a truly disruptive social technology to the native tribes found there. The areas into which they moved were not uncharted wilderness. Besides the indigenous populations, a number of pioneering explorers had gone before. Sometimes the settlers encountered the forensic wake of the meanderings of John Chapman, more popularly known as *Johnny Appleseed*. During his journeys of exploration, he planted apple trees. Once grown and bearing fruit, they provided a welcome bit of almost exotic nourishment to those seeking to establish a homestead in a new land. So it is with forays of personal exploration into fields foreign to those to which we have become accustomed during our individual provisioning.

When one wanders off the paved path while considering people functioning within social constructs, one often finds evidence that Merlin Donald, Professor Emeritus at Queen's University, has been there before. Sometimes his presence is subtle; as though he merely disturbs a leaf or breaks a twig. Sometimes he leaves solid footprints giving evidence of his prior reconnaissance into this particular undergrowth. Sometimes, he fashions a stand of thoughtful and instructive illustration; perhaps not a full orchard, but at least a tree whose fruit might provide nourishment for a pilgrim in the woods. If we can be excused for carrying the metaphor at least "... *a bridge too far*", sometimes he constructs a magnificent tree-house from which we can survey the forest beyond the immediate underbrush.

In developing *Computer Theology*, we found significant guidance in Professor Donald's books *A Mind So Rare: the Evolution of Human Consciousness* and *Origin of the Modern Mind: Three Stages in the Evolution of Culture and Cognition*. These offered valuable insights that we explored in some detail in *Chapter 8 – Enlightenment* of the *Computer Theology* book. For the present work, we find a marvelously positioned tree-house in a chapter entitled *The Definition of Human Nature* that Professor Donald authored for the book *The New Brain Sciences: Perils and Prospects*, edited by Dai Rees and Steven Rose. While we certainly don't claim that our expressions in this current book faithfully follow the author's footprints, we gratefully acknowledge the view of the encompassing forest.

Professor Donald offers a rather concise perspective on human nature, finding it grounded on "...flexibility, not rigidity..." of cognitive capability. He further suggests that the human species has evolved a truly unique facility for cognitive processes; what he characterizes as "...distributed cognitive-cultural networks." These networks are evidence of human-nature's "...flexibility, malleability and capacity for change." One can thus infer that a significant aspect of human cognitive capability is grounded in social structures; in fact, a multitude of social structures. This alludes to a more powerful facility for advancement of the species than can be found in purely physiological evolution of the individual. Because of this profound ability, Professor Donald suggests that humans are the "...cognitive chameleons of the universe."

Merlin Donald presents an evolutionary journey from the Miocene epoch primates to modern humans marked by three distinct stages. Denoting the beginning of the journey, he describes the early apes as having:

> ...a significant capacity for social attribution, insight, and deception, and great sensitivity to the significance of environmental events.

We interpret this description as matching well the constituent characteristics of social interactions that we discussed in the preceding section. The implication being that the basic circuits of neural processing were in place long before the evolutionary path diverged and ultimately gave rise to modern humans.

The first stage of divergence culminated with the speciation of *Homo erectus*. The period from the time of the Miocene apes to *Homo erectus* was one of significant physiological change presented as a series of derivative species. These species had progressively larger brains that consumed more energy than earlier species. Given that the size of the supporting body did not increase proportionally to brain size, this established food-gathering capability and energy efficiency of neural processing as characteristics subject to natural selection's judgment. The truly significant aspect of the emergence of *Homo erectus* was not just their larger brain, but how they used that brain. Professor Donald suggests that the most relevant change derived from the larger brain was the ability to access and dwell on experiential memory without the stimulus of its originating environment.

The apes remembered things episodically. Experiential memories were only recalled by replicating the environmental conditions under which they were formed. This changed when hominids evolved the ability to access memories through other than pure environmental stimulation. Merlin Donald termed this facility **autocueing**. He suggests that this gave rise to the true contribution of *Homo erectus*: **mimesis**, the ability to observe, understand and react to reality by adopting and adapting how others observe, understand and react to similar situations. Individuals became able to use their entire sensori-motor systems to express themselves to others and to receive impressions of others.

The second major transition occurred with the emergence of *Homo sapiens*. The brain of this new species was larger still, but the major physiological change was in the ability to support spoken language. Language is a tool that humans use for highly enhanced expression and impression. Augmented by all the facilities of the sensori-motor system, language allows expression with far more nuanced aesthetic content. Building on mimetic skills enhanced through the use of language, expanded metaphorical understanding allowed the species to effectively engage larger and more complex social orders.

A third major transition occurred perhaps only 40,000 to 50,000 years ago. This transition is marked by the forensic wake of an incredible expansion of social facilities. Donald attributes this transition to the use of external memory; that is, mechanical memory facilities external to the human brain that present as art-forms. In *Computer Theology*, we considered various research suggesting that among the earliest of art-forms was cave painting. A multitude of art-forms followed, and the creation of new art-forms is proceeding even to the present day. Consider that **texting**, a compact yet highly dynamic and expressive art-form, wasn't even part of the vocabulary 15 years ago.

As we have previously noted, sensori-motor expression and impression allow the sharing of sensations among people. This in turn allows the sharing of complex metaphorical models. When this facility is given persistence through art-forms, *Homo sapiens* is better able to utilize larger and more enduring social orders. This seems the embodiment of the "distributed cognitive-cultural networks" that Professor Donald suggests.

In today's world of social engagement, the primary social order is **the state**. So, we seek to better understand the basis of trust, the formulation of policy and the sanctions employed by the polity of the state as it administers the personal privacy of the individual. As we have suggested, interactions in general and social interactions specifically follow a common form. Development of policy, and its subsequent enforcement, manifests as the general management by the polity of social interactions. To pursue our quest in a moderately rigorous manner, we will adopt a definition of **jurisprudence** as a **system of interaction management by the state**. Hopefully, our rationale for this definition will become clearer as we delve further into the mechanics of interactions.

There currently is significant turmoil within United States legal circles as to how to handle the concept of privacy, or even what the concept is. In the statement of *First Principles* earlier in this chapter, we put forth a concise definition of the concept. It is a more expansive definition than one would discern from contemporary jurisprudence. During the course of this book we will examine this definition in some detail. Then, we want to better understand the concept in light of how society views privacy today, and subsequently to speculate on the future impact on jurisprudence of the concept as we have observed its definition.

In contemporary American jurisprudence, privacy is an amorphous and occasionally ambiguous concept. Sometimes, it appears well defined. Other times, it is opaque, if not obscure. Privacy gained an early foothold as a legal concept through an 1890 Harvard Law Review paper entitled *The Right to Privacy* in which Louis Brandeis and Samuel Warren, the future Supreme Court justice and his Harvard Law School classmate came to recognize that many disparate instances of case law offered glimpses of something they could perceive collectively as "privacy."

The impetus for their paper came from a concern for intrusion by the newspapers of the day into the private lives of the well known. The advent of the new art-form offered by easily portable cameras brought the emergence of the first paparazzi seeking impromptu and often unflattering photographs that became the sensation fodder for the papers. From this beginning, Brandeis and Warren ultimately concluded that there was a broader concept in play, but that it was still ill-defined. They referred to it somewhat tenuously as "the right to be let alone". Still, they held out hope for the precipitation of a more concise statement of concept as passing time brought:

> a recognition of man's spiritual nature, of his feelings and his intellect.

The current high water mark in understanding and recognizing privacy as a legal concept is fixed by the case of *Roe v. Wade*. In this 1973 landmark ruling, the Supreme Court recognized a **right of privacy** under which a woman has the power to decide whether to terminate her pregnancy. The period between Brandeis' and Warren's paper and the *Roe v. Wade* decision encompasses the aggregate development of the jurisprudence of contemporary privacy. During this period, the Supreme Court had to deal with the general concept of rights**.**

A **right** is a **behavior precluded from abridgement by the state**. While a number of rights are noted in the defining documents of the Republic, the succinct nature of their mention leaves ambiguity in their treatment by the legal system. For example, are they grounded in a legal source beyond the defining documents? What is their detailed constitution? In general, the defining documents speak only to the infringement of rights, not to establishing rights in the first place. How then does jurisprudence deal with the dilemma arising from the conflicting intersections of individual rights with each other, and with the perceived needs of the state? The *Roe* decision represents the current culmination of those considerations.

Many people were involved in this long march. A central figure was Justice William O. Douglas, who helped derive the concept of unenumerated rights; privacy being a prime example. As we will review in more detail in a later chapter, Justice Douglas provided guidance through a series of decisions that ultimately led to *Roe v. Wade*. Since privacy isn't mentioned directly by the foundation documents of the Republic, he was instrumental in melding the principles that were mentioned into the amalgam that privacy has become. Where we begin with human physiology, Justice Douglas began from legal principles, first considering the concept of rights.

Almost a century after Brandeis' and Warren's paper, Justice Douglas, in his concurring opinion in the *Roe v. Wade* case, observed:

> *Many of them [rights] come [410 U.S. 211] within the meaning of the term "liberty" as used in the Fourteenth Amendment.*
> ...
> *First is the autonomous control over the development and expression of one's intellect interests, tastes and personality.*
> ...
> *Second is freedom of choice in the basic decisions of one's life respecting marriage, divorce, procreation, contraception, and the education and upbringing of children.*
> ...
> *Third is the freedom to care for one's health and person, freedom from*

> *bodily restraint or compulsion, freedom to walk, stroll, or loaf.*
> ...
> *These rights, though fundamental, are likewise subject to regulation on a showing of "compelling state interest."*

Justice Douglas' observations form an interesting connection between legal principles and the form of an interaction that we perceive to be the basis of all social engagement. First, his rationale conflates **liberty**, a concept we relate to the precipitation of actions, with **rights**, a concept we relate to the establishment of policy that constrains actions and to the consequences of those actions. In his reference to the *"...expression of one's intellect interests, tastes and personality."* he also brings **motivation** of actions into the mix. We suggest that all of these concepts derive from a physiological facility of privacy that one might relate to Brandeis and Warren's allusion to

> *... a recognition of man's spiritual nature, of his feelings and his intellect.*

The Supreme Court did not ground its decision in the *Roe v. Wade* case in the concept of liberty. Rather, the Court's decision, in the name of privacy, afforded women virtually unfettered access to an abortion during the first trimester of pregnancy. This suggests that in the eyes of the court, the concept of privacy subsumes the concept of liberty. As a result, it encompasses the consequence of having an abortion, the liberty to have an abortion, and a purely personal motivation as the grounds for making the decision. This is a significant way station on the road to understanding the concept of privacy, but not quite the end of the journey.

In his book *Understanding Privacy*, legal scholar Daniel Solove examines a variety of efforts to conceptualize privacy. He finds lacking all those that he considers, but in categorizing the various attempts he paints a thumbnail sketch of a much larger picture. The six categories that he identifies include:

- the right to be let alone,
- limited access to the self,
- secrecy or concealment,
- control over personal information,
- protection of one's personality or personhood, and
- control over one's intimate relationships.

Professor Solove finds none of these conceptualizations individually compelling, being either too narrow or too broad, and in some instances tinges of both at the same time. However, he seems to find sufficient merit in each to suggest it is part of a larger whole. Indeed, we find that this list comprises a set of subordinate concepts that can each be derived from that of "...privacy is the provisioning of identity."

Focusing attention, not so much on the concept of privacy itself, but on nagging issues emanating from the concept, Professor Solove presents an interesting illustration of the current legal dilemma by suggesting a taxonomy that references privacy problems consisting of four types, divided into sixteen different sub-groups. The problem areas are generally concerned with information; specifically information collection, information processing, information dissemination and invasion. Indeed, much of current discourse treats privacy as mainly concerned with the shielding of information from general scrutiny; with keeping information secret or at least out of the public eye.

Chapter 1 – The Concept of Privacy

From this quite limited perspective, privacy very often conflicts with enumerated rights such as freedom of speech or expression. Consequently, it is viewed as inferior when pitted against such enumerated rights. The court's opinion in the *Roe v. Wade* case deals with an infringement of a woman's privacy in choosing to have an abortion, a problem that Solove categorizes as decisional interference; a form of invasion. This goes well beyond the mere concerns of information management. Thus, while the enumeration of the problems approach to privacy unfortunately fails to offer a clear and concise formulation of concept, it does offer illumination of the ensuing conflicts, both with enumerated rights as well as the enumerated powers of government.

The concept of privacy that we have characterized forms a general basis for the involvement of individuals within social aggregates. As such, one can view privacy as the fundamental concern of social order. With privacy as the foundation, social order has two basic goals: to provide policy for the arbitration of the intersection of personal privacy of multiple individuals within interactions, and to provide policy for the arbitrage of the infringement of personal privacy of an individual to benefit the social order. The first of these forms the bonding cornerstone of collaborative effort while the latter introduces the concept of altruism, which we can perceive as being unique to the domain of social order. Hence, these two goals are ultimately the focus of policy of any social group.

The expansive concept of privacy that we have suggested should encompass all of the classification types identified by Solove. From the concept, one can derive a more consistent understanding of the problem areas; points we will consider in more detail in the fourth chapter. From this concept of privacy, all of the enumerated rights characterized in the foundation documents of the Republic can be derived as logical, subordinate constructs. This will be the subject of the sixth chapter. However, to get to that point we must proceed through a more thorough examination of the mechanisms by which identity, and subsequently privacy, actually manifests.

To delve the inner workings of privacy, we will consider the current understanding of physiological, psychological and sociological characteristics of the human species; characteristics that we view as illustrative of **the human condition**, to paraphrase the rationale of Brandeis and Warren. Much of this consideration deals with current scientific discourse. However, significant insight is obtained from the historical record. Over the full breadth of human evolutionary development, the social systems to which people have given birth suggest remarkable consistency in structure, which in turn suggests consistent cause and effect.

A person might engage many different social orders. Exercising personal privacy, one might seek to join or be involved in various groups whose policy attracts their participation. However, the emergence of the concept of a nation-state has emphasized social orders that assert mandatory subjugation, if not active participation in the interactions of its constituent polity. If you find yourself within the domain claimed by a nation-state, whether or not you are allowed to be a full member of its social order, you are subject to its policy.

Sometimes referred to as a **sovereign** or a **sovereign power**, in general only the state claims **police powers**. The concept of police powers has varied over time. In the seventeenth century, William Blackstone's *Commentaries* described the police power as:

> *...the due regulation and domestic order of the kingdom, whereby the individuals of the state, like members of a well-governed family, are bound to conform their general*

> behaviour to the rules of propriety, good neighborhood, and good manners: and to be
> decent, industrious, and inoffensive in their respective stations.

On a more modern note, the *Britannica Concise Encyclopedia* includes this definition for police power:

> Power of a government to exercise reasonable control over people and property within its jurisdiction in the interest of general security, health, safety, morals, and welfare.

Adopting a slightly different perspective, we suggest that police powers are the rationale under which the state insinuates itself into general interaction contexts, even if it is not a direct participant. The rationale includes the ability to apply mandatory sanctions in any force domain for violation of policy. The police power is a function of the trust infrastructure and hence has outward looking (extrospective) and inward looking (introspective) components: the **military** and the **police**.

The military is outward looking and its function is to enforce the trust infrastructure in the physical ecosystem. That is, for any foreign social order that is not encompassed by the trust infrastructure, it is the purpose of the military to effect control over interactions among policy infrastructures derived from the foreign trust infrastructures. The police is inward looking and its function is to enforce the policies of the dominant policy infrastructure within the trust infrastructure.

A social order with police powers can fight wars with social orders subject to other trust infrastructures. A social order with police powers can arrest people and put them in jail when they don't obey the laws of the encompassed policy infrastructures. This is the distinguishing facet that sets social orders with police powers apart from social orders without police powers. Without police powers, a social order can only effect sanctions within its own social context. Of course, through conditional covenants it can address sanctions through the encompassing policy infrastructure that can assert police powers.

Given the complementary natures of policy and privacy, the structure and functioning of any social order is fashioned from the privacy of its members. The ultimate success of a social order is measured by the degree to which policy can be defined allowing the social order to benefit from actions taken in response to the self perceived desires of the person. Thus, it is in the nature of social orders to subjectively manipulate personal privacy to benefit the group at the possible expense of the individual. In concluding his *Definition of Human Nature*, Merlin Donald expressed somewhat optimistically that found in the technical and social complexity of modern cultures is the possibility of "extreme individuality".

To delve the inner workings of policy, at least among the preeminent social orders of the day, we will consider the mechanics of governance. The founding principles of United States governance provide keen insight into the dichotomy of policy and privacy. The Founders reflected their understanding of this dichotomy through the structure of government they defined. The *Declaration of Independence* and the *Constitution*, as the two primary sources of governmental structure, are almost totally dedicated to defining the basis of trust of the state, the mechanisms through which policy of the state is developed and expressed, and delineating the boundary between personal privacy and state policy.

In their establishment of the principles and structures of government, the Founders used the terms, metaphors actually, of their current understanding of social interactions. These metaphors establish the framework of the great social experiment that was and is the United States. As we will see, the form and functions are products of the Founders' metaphorical understanding of the concept of privacy. Much has been learned in the last few hundred years that gives greater rigor to this understanding. However, it seems apparent that the concept as we perceive it was well ingrained in the minds of the Founders.

Frontiers and Evolutionary Processes

We observe that humans are preeminently social animals, yet like all creatures we have evolved as individuals. The mechanisms of evolutionary development are embodied most directly in the physiology of the person. However, both developmental biology and developmental psychology observe that people progress from conception to adulthood in similar manners, both physiologically and socially. This suggests subtle yet consistent and effective mechanisms at work within each of us that address our structure, not just as biological beings, but as components of social aggregates. These mechanisms, we believe, are the embodiment of the distributed cognitive-cultural networks that Professor Donald recognizes.

The power of these physiologically based, social mechanisms becomes apparent when observing that significant prowess of the species comes from the ability for individuals to assemble and act through social order. All social structures, from two guys on the street, to the family, to the tribe, to the religious congregation, to the polity of the nation-state exhibit similar characteristics that determine their respective form and effectiveness. Social order is grounded in an environment of trust shared by members of the aggregate. Policy is established within the aggregate under the auspices of this trust infrastructure and the level of individual devotion to this basis of trust is fundamental to the ultimate success of the social order.

Through effective policies, social facilities enhance our ability to deal with the physical world. They magnify our individual physiological capabilities to respond both to everyday hazards as well as the more subtle, sensation derived pressures posed by the subjective stimuli of social constructs. But, social engagement provides much more than enhancements to our defensive posture. It is the means by which we seek and achieve that which satisfies our inner drives. The Founders of the American Republic expressed this as our unalienable right to:

...life, liberty and the pursuit of happiness.

Contemporary psychology finds a similar formalism in the stimulation of action responses to sensory input, characterizing such stimuli as deriving from a **hierarchy of needs**. To satisfy our primal needs, individuals have evolved an innate involvement with social structure. It is literally in our nature to seek out, and to act in concert with other people. The resulting duality of existence, first as individuals but then as constituent members of groups, has led to profound tension between the two domains. This tension defines a **frontier** between individual behavior and group dynamics. As we have noted, it is at this juncture that the concept of privacy manifests.

The term frontier is used advisedly. It is a concept equally applicable to the purely physical realm, to physiological capability and to social structure. A frontier generally demarks distinct domains of processes. Those on one side of a frontier will often seek to dismantle the frontier by assimilating the domain on the other side. Conversely, on the other side, processes will often seek to buttress the frontier to allow independent evolutionary development; in a sense, speciation. This is the constant tension across the frontier; assimilation versus speciation.

To one born and raised in the United States, the frontier takes on special significance by addressing not just physical separation, but social confrontation as well. Historian Frederick Jackson Turner introduced his *Frontier Thesis* as a basis for the aggressive, fiercely independent characteristics of American culture. In his subsequent essays published under the title *Frontier and Section*, he expounded the idea of **sectionalism**, a policy of neutralizing the frontier through a systematic, section by section process of encompassing, acculturating and assimilating the domains, including their social orders, which lay beyond the frontier. What Turner described, and intentionally so, was what can best be perceived as a process of evolutionary assimilation.

In evolutionary biology, the frontier between the main population of any species and isolated segments of that species demarks the distinct domains where stability endures and those where evolutionary change occurs. This thesis was given early voice by Ernst Mayr in his work *Systematics and the Origin of Species*. When a sub-group becomes relatively isolated from the main species body, typically through geographical separation, it may be subjected to forces distinct from those experienced by the main body. In such cases, if the environment is significantly different, then over time natural selection will favor specific choices from among the divergent group's total genetic makeup. This has the effect of driving the new group's dominant characteristics apart from those of the original collective; a process that can ultimately result in the emergence of a new, derivative species.

When this process is viewed in retrospect, when we examine the fossil record of history as it were, we can often observe long periods of stability interspersed with the sporadic appearance of new species. Stephen Jay Gould and Niles Eldredge termed this effect **punctuated equilibrium**. The central population of any species remains in a relatively static state while evolutionary progression within isolated sub-groups gives rise to new species through a shift in the characteristics best suited to deal with the new environment.

It's important to note this shift in characteristics usually results through natural selection's preference for different, yet already existing characteristics. Genetic diversity is essential in providing effective, albeit dormant, characteristics that can come to the fore in the new environment. However, sometimes a completely new characteristic arises through mutation; in some cases, mutations induced by specific mutagens. The situation is similar in the technical domain.

In the digital realm of computer systems, the concept of interfaces is highly developed as a means of simultaneously allowing for the connection of disparate components yet giving each the freedom of independent development. An interface is a frontier. A significant aspect of the development of complex technical systems is the establishment of standard interfaces. Such interfaces, be they hardware, software or firmware allow for interchangeable components. They also allow for the competing processes of speciation and assimilation.

When faced with a large technical problem, a typical design technique is to adopt discrete interfaces that effectively sectionalize the problem into manageable pieces. This, in turn, allows for continued development, evolutionary progression as it were, behind the façades of the many interfaces. In some instances, such development can lead to a new species, albeit one whose members can continue to function at an intimate level with those of older species. Witness the emergence of the smart phone as iconically characterized by the iPhone from Apple. This is a class of device, a new species of computer actually, that is equally at home in the **old world of telephony** and the **new world of the Web**.

The iconic illustration of a frontier, particularly as it pertains to privacy, is found in the physiological domain. It is the placental interface between mother and fetus. Formed from the same sperm and egg constructs that give rise to the embryo and subsequently to the fetus, the placenta provides a mechanism through which all the surfaced needs of the fetus are met by the mother. The placenta connects the uterine wall of the mother, and hence the mother's physiological system, directly to the fetus through an umbilical cord. This connection allows food, oxygen and immune system support to be provided from the mother to the fetus. It also allows waste removal from the fetus into the mother's body.

The placental barrier hinders some materials from flowing between the mother and the fetus, but not all. As the fetus develops, more and more direct physiological support is taken on by its own body. At the moment of birth, the fetus emerges from the mother as an infant and, in a timeless **physiological ritual** the presence of a new, unique person is established by the severing of the umbilical cord. Therein lies the rub in the jurisprudential consideration of privacy; at what point does this new, unique person fully emerge in the social domain? This illustrates the iconic juxtaposition of privacy of the person versus policy of the social order.

In the realm of humans, evolutionary development has favored each person with the facilities to anticipate, assess and respond to sensory input arising from the surrounding environment. Simply put, our senses are stimulated by the world around us and we react to those stimuli in reflexive and cognitively determined ways. It is the manner of this reflexive and cognitive determination that is at the heart of privacy and the "...distributed cognitive-cultural networks" suggested by Merlin Donald. Often, our senses convey an awareness of threats that must be addressed socially if we are to individually "live long and prosper", as *Star Trek's* Mr. Spock suggests in a succinct rendition of Charles Darwin's evolutionary theories.

Our senses warn us about danger from purely physical causes as well as threats that emanate from other people. Sensory observations are presented as sensations that we might interpret as feelings of fear, pain, pleasure or satisfaction. The facilities to successfully respond to such sensations, given emphasis based on interpretations ranging from fear to satisfaction, are judged as **good** by natural selection when the corresponding consequences of the responses accruing to the individual leads to enhanced opportunities for progeny. Unfortunate for our understanding, when people act through social structures, the situation becomes considerably more complex.

Privacy and Altruism

Functioning as members of groups, people have learned to engage threats through collectively resolved action, which inherently requires an abridgement of personal privacy. To move away from the physical ecosystem concepts of "survival of the fittest" and "might makes right", some means is required to provide a measure of trust in the abridgement. Two mechanisms seem to best lead to abridgement **fairness** in the guise of equality of opportunity if not of outcome; conditional covenants and stochastic processes. A **conditional covenant** is an **agreement to exchange things**

of comparable value; consideration offered for consideration received. It can range from very informal agreements for common action among individuals to a highly structured and formal agreement among disparate parties.

A **stochastic process** is an **activity viewed through random observations that reflect recognized probability distributions**. A stochastic process is not a deterministic system that behaves exactly the same way in repetition, nor is it a totally random occurrence. Real world interactions are virtually always stochastic processes at some level. Understanding such processes through analysis by synthesis begins by assuming a model of the system being studied. This defines a set of probability distributions for observations of the variables of the model. A sensory system must allow observation of some aspects of the process in question. The results of random observations can then be interpreted within the context of the model.

Conditional covenants and stochastic processes provide a first-order approximation of fairness for individuals functioning within social aggregates. Using these mechanisms, individuals enhance the group's prospects for surviving while ensuring an equitable chance at their own prospering in that survival. For a group to be judged by natural selection as successful, it is necessary for some significant number of individuals to benefit from the group's collective actions. However, if collective actions are systematically harmful to specific individuals, those people are less likely to contribute to the actions.

Progeny is a direct function of two individuals; a mother and a father. The mother is physiologically necessary following conception, while the father is socially necessary. Therefore, natural selection bestows at least some of its judgment at the social level, not just at the physiological level of the individual. However, for group actions to actually have an evolutionary impact, their benefits must accrue to individuals through secondary effects. This suggests that the impetus for an individual to react to sensory input as the group would desire is also due to secondary effects; or, as we will come to understand it just a bit later, to higher order needs.

Sometimes the results of actions that a group deems beneficial are actually detrimental to isolated people or subordinate collections within the group. Let's consider a squad of soldiers huddled together in a foxhole on the battlefield when a hand grenade lands among them. One soldier immediately, virtually instinctively, flings his body on top of the grenade. His body absorbs the explosion, killing him, but saving the lives of his comrades. One is sacrificed for the benefit of the group.

Now, suppose that there are only two soldiers; not a squad. Often the same consequence plays out. One will sacrifice himself for the other. When one saves many, evolutionary benefit can be at least qualitatively discerned. When one saves one, the evolutionary benefit is questionable, but the action is applauded within the greater social order.

> Greater love hath no man than this; that he lay down his life for his friend.

The actions of an individual giving rise to such results are termed *altruistic*. From a cursory perspective, they are often viewed as contrary to successful evolutionary behavior since they may diminish a specific individual's chances for progeny. If one's sacrifice saves many, then evolutionary benefit does accrue to a larger collective. But, it makes us wonder whether such quantitative reasoning is factored in to the individual's reaction?

If it were simply a question of numbers, perhaps one soldier could force another on top of the grenade. Thus, an act of potential altruism becomes an instance of predator versus prey. The hero becomes the pariah and diminishes individual devotion to the social collective. The group will not look kindly on such an action. It requires significant anticipation and conditioning within a group for an individual to properly align altruistic actions with personal needs and desires. To instantaneously choose death to save another, to act contrary to the anticipated consequences for personal safety and security in order to achieve benefit beyond one's self, is an iconic illustration of altruism.

Altruistic acts are the cornerstone of successful human social orders. In general, they arise from a social compact between the individual and the social order; consideration offered for consideration received. It is through the stimulation of actions potentially detrimental to the individual yet beneficial to the group that successful groups continue. However, if everyone in the foxhole flings themselves on the grenade, then probably no one benefits; everyone is killed. Conversely, if no one absorbs the explosion, everyone is killed as well.

Social success comes from just the right amount of altruism. A successful altruistic act should really be the only viable option in the given situation. If one could simply pick up the grenade and toss it out of the foxhole, then falling on it is probably an unwarranted sacrifice.

While a social order feeds off of the altruism of individuals, it is a bit tricky to bring about. If there were a designated person in each squad whose responsibility it was to fall on the occasional grenade, it is questionable whether that social structure would long endure, or whether it would be particularly successful in its endurance. Those designated to sacrifice themselves might choose to avoid grenades.

So, the question is how the social order designates who is to fall on the grenade. Conditional covenants which call for certain death for one party are difficult to sell. They can be made more palatable by invoking stochastic processes through which death, if required, derives from some random selection of the party who must make the supreme sacrifice. The probability distribution for the process should reflect just the right amount of altruism.

This selection process is critical to evoking devotion to a social order. It revolves around how the context of the potential interaction is addressed by social provisioning such that the pending grenade explosion will be effectively accommodated? How is an individual provisioned such that she will view it as desirable to throw a grenade at the faceless **enemy**, and yet find it worthy of the supreme sacrifice to save the faceless **friend** from a thrown grenade? What is the nature of the social compact engendered by and engendering of altruistic sacrifice? How is the effective policy derived and from whence comes devotion to it?

Thus, we return to the frontier of individual behavior versus group dynamics. Do we as individual members of the social order exist for the benefit of society? Is our ultimate purpose the group's happiness without regard to our own? Should we all fling ourselves on the grenade? Or, taking a contrary view, does society more properly exist for us, as individuals? How do we differentiate the desirability of acts of individual altruism versus acts of individual exceptionalism? An effective social order creates an equivalency among them.

In the presence of conflicting situations throughout our lives, how are we individually provisioned to make the correct decisions in a near instinctive reaction to threats or danger? Privacy manifests at this frontier. What then is this manifestation?

We have suggested this definition.

Privacy is the provisioning of identity.

Identity we have recognized as self from the perspective of others. Provisioning refers to the development of metaphorical models through which our minds interpret sensory input and evoke motor action responses. We can provision ourselves; self from the perspective of self. We can provision others; self from the perspective of others. The first establishes how we think of ourselves while the second establishes how others think of us. Both influence how we interact with others.

We define an interaction as the **association of independent entities through constrained forces.** Provisioning of identity entails the engagement of interactions through which is provided information about an individual along with the understanding, calibration and adoption of processes that interpret and make use of that information. The esteem that we hold of ourselves and the reputation that others perceive of us is crucial to the conduct of interactions involving us and others.

Privacy is the means through which a person establishes reputation in the eyes of others through the shared memories of sensations derived from interactions and their consequences. Through reputation grounded in identity, all participants have a basis for the establishment of trust in pending interactions. Identify is recursively derived. It is cumulative. Hence, evoked by privacy we engage interactions through which we impact the basis for our participation in future interactions.

On the other side of the frontier from privacy is policy. Policy encompasses the effective will of social orders. Writ large, policy is the formally constructed basis of a social order. The original documents of governance of the United States of America are the *Declaration of Independence* and the *Constitution*. The style of government put forth in the words of these documents establishes the means through which the social order can effect policy. A careful reading of the documents suggests that the Founders were well in tune with the concept of privacy that we observe. Indeed, the interface between privacy and policy is well established.

The manner in which a social order balances policy with privacy defines its inherent character, forming a manifestation of culture. Such character spans the spectrum of social systems that we can discern from history. At one extreme, totalitarian dictatorship stresses the complete infringement of personal privacy for the benefit of the state as manifested in the controlling dictator. State socialism, also at nearly the same extreme, entails complete infringement of personal privacy but is ostensibly balanced by an arbitration of personal privacy intersection among individuals that is based on egalitarian principles.

In general, pure parliamentary systems also totally infringe the privacy of individuals. However, grounding a parliamentary system on representative democracy such as a republic as the means to effect policy can lead to some degree of privacy being maintained by the individual. Infringement of that privacy is at the whim of the polity. This is the theoretical environment through which a social order could establish what Karl Marx referred to as the "dictatorship of the proletariat."

The proletariat majority infringes the privacy of the minority bourgeoisie. Ostensibly, such infringement would ultimately dissipate any class distinctions among the polity. History suggests a potential threat to the social order can arise if exceptional instances of privacy that can benefit the social order are minimized or eliminated. Such policy will certainly mitigate the benefits of personal accomplishment. Typically, the policy is justified as a way to diminish perceived excesses of the extraordinary at the perceived expense of the ordinary. The issue then becomes how to value the extraordinary versus the ordinary.

Constitutionally limited government, with the United States as the iconic example, seeks to address this issue by providing a system through which to equitably arbitrate the intersection of personal privacy among individuals based on equality of opportunity. The arbitrage of the infringement of personal privacy to benefit the state involves a similarly equitable distribution across the general polity and is intended to be limited in scope. The processes of constitutionally limited government should then allow each individual to benefit from their own abilities, with the state getting a piece of the action. How big a piece is the obvious question in the arrangement?

Certain characteristics of personal privacy enumerated as explicit rights are ostensibly removed from the purview of the state as potential infringement targets. In practice however, such rights are never absolute, and policy that infringes them at some level virtually always occurs. Actually, both the processes of arbitration and of arbitrage result in at least some infringement of privacy. It is impossible to arbitrate the intersection of personal privacy of two individuals and still maintain completely uninfringed privacy for both.

At the extreme of emphasis on personal privacy lies anarchy in which the only rules are those of the physical and physiological domains. In this case, the personal privacy of the individual reigns supreme. When the privacy of multiple individuals intersects, the manner of arbitration to derive an effective policy of *de facto* social groups is prejudiced by the personal privacy of the fittest. Hence, in a society of anarchy social interactions tend to degenerate into primarily physiological and physical interactions, with the stronger assimilating the weaker. It's rather easy to view this spectrum as a closed loop since in effect it seems but a short distance between totalitarian dictatorship and pure anarchy.

The spectrum is continuous. There are few examples of pure social systems, even among the simple illustrations that we've mentioned. Implementations usually fall short of theoretical intent. For example, more compassionate totalitarian systems typically provide some limited benefit to the common individual. Without accommodation of the individual, instances of completely totalitarian systems in which all personal privacy is confiscated by the state have proven susceptible when placed in competition with systems that show greater reliance on personal privacy. At the very least, in truly repressive totalitarian systems clandestine, subordinate social orders often emerge within which members achieve some semblance of privacy.

Human slavery, the iconic illustration of total infringement of personal privacy, is a recurring theme throughout history. It always appears as a subordinate social structure, a subculture that is subject to a stronger social order whose character can range across the entire spectrum. While we might usually want to associate it with totalitarian states, in more recent times slavery has been found not infrequently in ostensible democracies and republics as well. Slavery is a direct descendant of the predator versus prey environment; the predator's privacy is the prey's slavery. Or course, the predator in this case might be an individual or it might be the social order of the nation-state.

At the other extreme, complete reliance on personal privacy without any social oversight often appears to degenerate as the arbitration of personal privacy intersection tends toward anarchy. Within contemporary society in the United States, there is great tension between social goals; some favoring the individual while others favor the collective. Great tension manifests if the infringement of personal privacy of some accrues to the benefit of others. Conversely, tension can also result from a reliance on personal privacy that offers satisfaction of individual motivations for some but asymmetric outcomes for others.

Privacy favors consequences based on individual capabilities and efforts. Social aggregates succeed by harnessing a part of such consequences. How big a part becomes the question? The balance establishes the culture of the social order. It is the classic dilemma of symbiotic relationships. How do society and the individual exist in mutually beneficial balance? At what point does symbiosis degenerate into parasitism, or even into predator versus prey?

Syllabus

Privacy is a facility of the individual. It is the means through which a person establishes an external manifestation of self allowing her to function and even excel within social aggregates. Personal privacy is fundamental to societal evolution. It provides the metaphorical equivalent to genetic diversity and mutation found in the physiological and physical domains. As social systems engage new environments, the unfettered personal privacy of their constituents offers a powerful mechanism through which the social order can accommodate the new environment. To more fully examine these aspects of privacy, in the course of this book we will take the following systematic approach.

This first chapter establishes the foundation on which the succeeding chapters are constructed. It begins with a succinct statement of first principles defining the basic taxonomy of interaction mechanics through which privacy manifests. Based on the premise that human cognition is essentially metaphoric in nature, the taxonomy addresses the means of individuals functioning in and through social aggregates. This gives rise to the self as the deictic center of a person and the polity as the aggregate self of a social order. Consideration of the mechanisms through which the individual and society interact in sensori-motor reality sets the stage for a more rigorous exploration of privacy and policy in succeeding chapters.

In the second chapter, we will examine an interaction model through which one can more rigorously understand physiological and social processes. These are processes with a significant subjective component. Understanding subjectivity in an objective way is challenging. To do so, it is necessary to form a rudimentary understanding of subjective decision making as an objective protocol. This requires insight into the concept of provisioning, which is a complex process in its own right. We have suggested that privacy is the provisioning of identity. To understand this provisioning, we need a good handle on identity.

Seeking this better understanding, in the third chapter we will explore the concept of identity. Identity is a physiological manifestation comprised of two components: distinguishing people, as in telling them apart, and forming memories of interactions with people. Through these two facilities, we are able to establish our identity with other people by choosing what interactions to engage and what we do in that engagement. In this way, we influence what memories are formed by these other people. As others perceive these experiences and their memories, our identity presents to them as the sensation of reputation. The sensation of reputation is central to the subjective decision making process through which one chooses to engage interactions with other people and how to proceed in the course of the interaction.

We will start by examining the physiological characteristics of identity. These are perhaps best understood through the basic needs recognized by human psychology. Identity is a social characteristic. It evolved as an intrinsic facility necessary for forming successful groups. These physiological characteristics make use of mechanisms that are only effective in relatively small social orders. We then need to examine how to realize these same facilities in the digital domain, thus allowing their extension into larger social orders. This is the subject of the next chapter.

In the fourth chapter, we take a more detailed look at the concept of privacy as it sits astride the interface between the individual and the group. As with identity, we will start from a consideration of the physiological and social mechanisms used to effect privacy in small groups. Then, we will consider mechanisms of the digital domain that allow the realization of privacy throughout larger social orders. We will illustrate some of the tension between privacy and policy and suggest means to maintain some semblance of stability between the two.

Privacy is the means by which the individual asserts herself into social order. Policy is the means that the social order uses to impress itself on the individual. Under the auspices of its police powers, the state manifests policy as law and the resolution of conflicted consequences within this law derives from adjudication. The facilities of making policy and adjudicating consequences according to that policy are aspects of jurisprudence. We will examine the interplay between privacy and policy as it manifests within American jurisprudence in the remaining chapters.

In the fifth chapter, we will consider the contemporary view of privacy found in existing case law. This view is continuing to evolve because contemporary jurisprudence is still searching for the definitive concept of privacy. We will examine the progression of case law as it seeks the concept. Viewing this process in the abstract, the search for privacy illuminates the concept of **due process**. Recognition of this concept and establishing it as a foundational component of American jurisprudence is something of an aesthetic masterstroke by the Founders of the Republic. We will conclude this chapter with an overview of due process.

In the sixth chapter, we will speculate on the impact of privacy as we understand it as a forcing function on the fundamental structures of American jurisprudence. Our rationale is that the Founders were well in tune with this concept of privacy. They stated it a bit more obliquely, but it's rather straightforward to recognize privacy's principles in the basic trust and policy infrastructures that the Founders defined. We'll pursue this speculation as an exercise in applying a systematic methodology to the analysis of social infrastructure. We will include in this consideration the foundation of altruistic demands by the state. Altruistic demands derive from compelling interests of the state expressed through due process. We will conclude this chapter with an overview of the rationale on which are based compelling interests of the state.

In the seventh and final chapter, we will consider the complementary concepts of privacy and policy with an eye toward how their changing equilibrium has affected, and could affect going forward, society in the United States. We suggest that the formal foundation of American jurisprudence is the *Declaration of Independence*. In this foundation, we recognize an expansive concept of privacy as the basis of the trust infrastructure and nascent policy infrastructure of the American state. This formulation of an expansive concept of privacy has profound implications for the American social order, forming as it does the essence of American culture. We will examine the impact of this culture on the provisioning of the polity of the state and the provisioning of the policy infrastructure.

A significant rationale for this book is the potential role of technological facilities in advancing the cause of personal privacy. We have suggested a causal connection between privacy and identity. Technology offers the prospect of a ubiquitous and effective identification system. While generally viewed with suspicion, we suggest that a national identity system could provide a solid foundation for enhanced personal privacy. To this end, we will conclude with a modest proposal for such a system.

2 *Motivation and Mechanics*

Some people grow up to be killers
....
Some people grow up to catch them.

In the television series *Criminal Minds,* the character Special-agent Aaron Hotchner, leader of a team within the FBI's Behavioral Analysis Unit, makes this assessment of serial killers and those who pursue them. It is a daunting illustration of the scope of personal identity derived through privacy's provisioning.

Offering perhaps a more rigorous perspective, we find in the compendium volume *Theory and Research on Human Emotions*, edited by Jonathan H. Turner, the paper *Integrating Emotion into Identity Theory*. Here, sociologist Sheldon Stryker approaches the concept of identity from the perspective of group processes and arrives at much the same point. Recounting current identity theory as intimately associated with human emotions, Stryker observes:

> ...the paradigmatic question identity theory seeks to answer is: why, on a free weekend afternoon, does one man take his children to the zoo and a second choose to play golf with his buddies?

We suggest that the answer again tracks to personal privacy's provisioning of identity; albeit in this case with a bit less dramatic flair.

Basics of Provisioning

Growing up is a colloquial term applied to the seminal provisioning of the person. This early provisioning is fundamental to establishing the metaphorical models through which the mind's neurological processes function. It establishes the fundamental weights and measures that give rise to the motivation of actions. It forms the base from which a person's identity is cast. While growing up we don't always exert complete control over these expressions of our being; but, it is in our nature to try. Various pathologies of our physiology can sometimes overwhelm provisioning, but for the sake of these discussions we will focus on the normal provisioning of the person; to the extent that we can discern normalcy from the social and scientific discourse.

Evolution has instilled in each of us mechanisms with which we observe the world and through which we attempt to manipulate ourselves, and the world, in an effort to establish an identity to our liking. These mechanisms encompass our most profound intellect coupled to our most primitive biology. Consider that our bodies emit adrenaline as impetus for living, pheromones to anchor bonding, and endorphins to ease dying. The secretion of these chemicals can arise from stimuli emanating from the highest levels of our mind, yet their affect is realized at the most basic levels of our physiology. Such mechanisms, through which privacy is pursued, are guided by the motivations that express our most intimate desires. In the extreme, they are mechanisms through which social policy can find its way to the body's autonomic nervous system and even the arcane communication pathways of the endocrine system. Thus it becomes an act of personal physiological fulfillment when one falls on the grenade.

Childhood finds the control over privacy's provisioning often taken out of our own hands and instead residing in those of society; most profoundly, our parents, but also our friends, the bully down the street, our childhood sweetheart, our school teachers and classmates, the clergy and church congregation, the policeman on the beat, the business where we find our first job and perhaps even the monsters under the bed. Some grow up in abject poverty; their provisioning molded by the needs of survival. Some grow up in homes of privilege; their provisioning engendering a sense of entitlement.

Some children are abused; their provisioning gone terribly awry. However, privacy is complex, as are the identities and ensuing reputations that result. The downtrodden can emerge as paragons of generosity, perhaps even easier than the privileged. Unfortunately, the downtrodden can also demonstrate that the privileged have no monopoly on malice and greed. The abused might grow up to be serial killers, or those who catch them.

With the passage of time, we each grow up following nature's provisioning pathway; a rather common path that most follow. Studies of human psychology and sociology suggest remarkable consistency in how the individual person engages and assimilates their provisioning. A similar consistency is found in the motivational mechanisms that impel the individual in so doing. It is a consistency that finds one child growing up to be a killer while another grows up to catch killers. Personal privacy encompasses this breadth of logical outcome. While it derives directly from human physiology it lends its primary affect in the social domain.

We're not all born to be killers, or even to be those who catch them. Rather, we each seek a relevant sensation that we know generically as happiness by establishing unique identities through provisioning of our own design. Privacy is manifestly an expression of our individual being, realized through recursive and cumulative processes. Recursion means that our future identity is a function of our past provisioning. The identity we established in the past affects the privacy we assert in the future. Cumulative aggregation of experiences suggests that the privacy expressed by the adult begins with the physiological grounding of the infant and continually evolves through the provisioning of the child, and the adolescent. Adulthood does not terminate provisioning, but it does deliver control of it into our own hands.

Our perceptions of the concepts related to the psychological motivations and physiological mechanisms by which privacy manifests come to us through the fog of human myth, legend and undocumented history. Seeking firmer ground, we look to the contributions of early pioneers in a number of relevant fields of study for a basis of our considerations. For example, in pursuing the foundational concept that the mind works by way of metaphorical models, we find early guidance in the work of Hermann von Helmholz from the late-nineteenth century. Coupled with his discoveries in thermodynamics, his proposals in the domain of developmental psychology form a basis for many of the paths of current research in the neurosciences.

In their paper *The Berlin School of Thermodynamics founded by Helmholtz and Clausius*, Werner Ebeling and Dieter Hoffman noted that Hermann von Helmholz was first trained as a physician. In 1847, while serving as a military surgeon he published his first work examining the conservation of energy. His earliest experiments considered the relationship of matter and heat production through biological processes. Subsequently pursuing a formal education in physics, in 1871 he was awarded, among other titles, that of Professor of Physics at the University of Berlin; at the time, ostensibly the leading university in the world of physics and other disciplines as well.

Helmholz achieved lasting notoriety for his work in solidifying the basic laws of thermodynamics. These have great import in the considerations of optimizing the efficiency of physiological energy systems. Perhaps as interesting from our perspective, he postulated an approach through which the human sensory system observing stochastic processes might function; something that almost a century later became known as **analysis by synthesis**, when the concept was given a more rigorous grounding by Ulric Neisser in his book *Cognitive Psychology*. The approach asserts that neural processes are implementations of metaphoric models.

Using a model to periodically assess the process, the time progression of sensory observations can be predicted. This allows fine tuning of the sensory observations so as to enhance their applicability to the model. Observations can be focused on the most important anticipated aspects of the process as predicted by the model. We call these **models of learning**. Through their systematic application, interaction contexts can be personalized, providing a calibrated framework for subjective decision making.

Central to the working of this adaptive approach is the decision making process through which neural circuits can determine that somehow changing a sensory view or revising the predictive model makes for better understanding. It is rather natural for us to view such decision making from a cognitive perspective; that is, decision making has a significant subjective element that we have to consciously think about. For relatively low-level mechanisms, too numerous for us to consciously consider individually, it is much more natural for each mechanism to make decisions through **adjustable feedback loops**; a significantly more mechanical approach.

To realize a feedback loop, some causal parameter of a process must be identified. If it can be discerned that changing this parameter influences the functioning of the process, then the parameter can be used as the basis for providing controlling feedback to the process, assuming that there is some available sensory observation of this parameter. Discernment means it must be possible to observe, in fact to measure, some consequence of the entire process.

By relating a desired change in consequence to a change in the input control parameter, a feedback loop can be created. The observed consequence is used to cause some modification of the input control parameter. In this fashion, either the consequence can be maintained within some range through a negative feedback loop, or the consequence can be driven in a given direction through a positive feedback loop. Either approach results in some optimization of the desired consequence by providing a way to differentiate **better** from **worse**.

The general field of neuroscience concerns itself with understanding the functioning of the nervous system in general and the mind within the brain specifically. Building on analysis by synthesis as a paradigm for the way the mind works, it is surmised that the acquisition of sensory input is guided so as to give the best information on which to validate the model. This, in turn, allows the mind to anticipate future sensory observations based on predictions from the model as impacted by physiological motor system expression controlled by the mind. Thus, a metaphorical model of learning forms the basis of a predictive model of interactions. The prediction of anticipated outcome forms the basic concept of trust which is foundational to all personal interactions.

Geoffrey E. Hinton, *et al*, in a 1995 paper entitled *The Helmholtz Machine Through Time* described the use of such a

> *...hierarchical, top-down generative model of an ensemble of data vectors* as a way to implement a *wake-sleep algorithm* using *a multilayer, unsupervised, stochastic neural network.*

Expressed very simplistically, a hierarchical set of neural processes such as those found in the brain can work in two ways to derive understanding from sensory observations. In a bottom up **wake** phase, the view of the relevant senses is focused on the aspects of the stochastic process being observed such that observations best fit the predictive model. The senses can be focused to observe the process better. Alternatively, in a top down **sleep** phase the mind alters the predictive model to better accommodate sensory observations. The model can be modified to better explain the sensory observations. Mechanisms that work in this fashion are termed by the paper as **Helmholtz Machines**.

Being is the expression of a body comprised of organic, interconnected systems, ranging from the nervous system centered on the brain, to the skeletal system marked by a skull which supports and shields the brain. A variety of associated systems provides means to observe the world and to respond with specific actions within that world. Through the concerted operation of these physiological systems, being achieves a connection between observation and action. While culminating in the functioning of people, this paradigm finds applicability across the full range of living organisms; sensory impression elicits motor expression through cognitive interpretation.

Using metaphorical reasoning, the human mind interprets sensory observations by viewing them as the same, or similar to, observations of systems that it has previously encountered. This enables a process of derivative provisioning. Once a model that describes some situation is known, only ostensibly minor variations in sensory observations must be accommodated; the variations that make this experience unique from previous occurrences. This greatly simplifies the neural processing required of the brain. It is a characteristic of the species that we can easily adopt the metaphorical models developed by others. This process that we earlier recognized as mimesis means we learn by observing the actions of others. With the development of language we acquired more robust facilities of expression, allowing us to learn indirectly as others convey to us the metaphorical models that explain their own, or others, impressions and expressions.

Only when a model is unable to successfully explain relevant interactions does the mind have to exert itself to find a more correct interpretation of sensory input. Probably, this is why we find it more challenging to learn things the first time. Once we have learned a thing, perhaps how to ride a bicycle, it is easier to do on a recurring basis. Our ability to learn a thing is a function of our provisioning; including our individual cognitive and sensory capabilities. Our individual physiology forms the foundation of our subsequent provisioning.

In the early days of the twentieth century, Albert Einstein was able to discern the general theory of relativity. At the time, he was one of a very few individuals appropriately provisioned to quantitatively extract such a non-intuitive explanation for a number of obtuse observations. It seems highly likely that he had an exceptionally capable brain; definitely, he was smarter than the average person. However, after he showed the way, while perhaps not everyone could grasp the nuances of time dilation at relativistic speeds, even the most pedestrian of people came to appreciate the relationship between mass and energy when presented the evidence of a nuclear bomb exploding.

For most personal endeavors, with practice we can improve our performance; assuming, of course, that we can differentiate the good from the bad and surmise the direction toward improvement. Long before humans thought deeply about the concept of metaphor, nature had provided means to weigh the adequacy of our metaphorical models. In the large, this assessment is made by natural selection. If the predictive models of the world in which we live are good, then the actions we engage under their auspices more likely enable us to live long enough to have progeny and pass our experience to them. Otherwise, our genetic line will disappear.

Viewed in the small, for individual interactions, natural selection isn't a particularly good measure of interaction outcome. For example, how can we best respond to a tiger on the prowl? In this case, the immediacy of living or dying requires a much more rapid response than waiting to see if we have great, great, great grandchildren. Fortunately, evolutionary development has provided some very useful tools for assessing the utility of our metaphorical models in the very short term. Paramount among these facilities is **sensation**.

Sensation is an aspect of our physiology. It allows the mind, through its conscious and unconscious facilities, to take the measure of sensory input and respond appropriately. Sensation enables the mechanisms of feedback loops that allow processes to modify their actions to better address specific sensory stimuli. We use the term sensation to encompass all that the mind discerns as impressions derived from basic senses; as feeling, as emotion, or perhaps even as moods. The mind registers sensation related to the outcome of interactions. It is the memory of these sensations that helps define what is desirable as an outcome for future interactions.

Consider a young child wandering in the cold forest at night. Made aware of a campfire by the sensation of visual shock caused by the bright light in the dark night, the child is drawn to the flame. On closer approach, she feels the sensation of light and warmth registering as a pleasant alternative to the cold and dark. Smelling and even tasting the smoke in the air, the child is reminded of past pleasures of food that satisfied the pangs of hunger.

Lacking a firm grasp of the concept of fire, the child might put her hand into the flames; first feeling warmth but then searing heat and then pain. Shortly thereafter, perhaps a feeling of some chagrin creeps in as understanding that it was probably not a good idea to stick ones hand in the fire. The visual shock, the warmth, the smell, the taste, the heat, the pain, and the chagrin are all distinct sensations. Sensations connect the cause and effects addressed by the mind's metaphorical models with the evaluation process that allows the mind to discern appropriate responses. Sensation is the basis for optimization of neural processes. Indeed, the pain and chagrin that result from once having stuck ones hand into a fire enhances the metaphorical model surrounding fire such that it is likely to register this as a bad idea in the future.

Sometimes causes and effects are displaced in time or location such that it's hard to connect them. More important, sometimes we don't have a good sensory observation for a specific causal effect. We've all heard the old admonition of being "mad as a hatter." It took a long while before it was understood that one whose occupation was making hats, that is, a hatter's nervous system was damaged by the vapors of mercury which he used in the course of working with felt fabric. There was no immediate, recognizable sensation that connected the danger of mercury vapor to impaired mental function. Rather, the only observable was of the damage after it was done.

This illustrates the limitation of sensation derived from sensory observation. In the formal representations of analysis by synthesis models, the real world is perceived to be comprised of **hidden states**. A truly hidden state derives from a characteristic for which no sensory observation is available. For characteristics that senses can actually perceive, sensory observations are translated into **internal states** that form the framework in which the mind's metaphorical models operate. Sensation is a manifestation of this translation.

In general, living organisms derive benefit when sensory observation impacts routinely encountered situations; particularly if they bear on the continuation of individuals and thus collectively on the continuation of the species. However, in many instances evolutionary progression has not yet had the opportunity, or perhaps the impetus, to connect sensory observation to motor response in more subtle situations. Our senses don't always paint the full picture of these hidden states, so our metaphorical models sometimes don't fully reflect reality. It helps that humans have an evolved facility to at least partially compensate for hidden states and the means to manipulate them; tools.

The most basic and intimate of tools is language. We consider this a tool because it is used to amplify the individual sensori-motor system such that it more readily impacts other people. It's rather important to realize that language is a tool that requires a social environment for its development. Merlin Donald termed this the capacity for **lexical invention**.

There are precursors to natural languages; gestures, mannerisms, facial expressions, basic sounds and so on. These are used to convey meanings of varying complexity from one person to another. Natural languages extend this facility such that more complex meanings and sensations can be conveyed. The human brain seems naturally tailored through evolutionary processes to be particularly facile with language.

Complementing language, people are quite adept at creating more mechanical tools to enhance the capabilities of their physiological sensori-motor systems; tools that we previously characterized as art-forms. Art-forms impact both the sensory and the motor side of the equation. Current technology is replete with art-forms to amplify our senses: microscopes, telescopes, light amplifiers, radar... and the list goes on and on. Equally profound are art-forms that extend the human physiological motor system: knives, spears, arrows, guns, bombs, saws, hammers, milling machines, lathes ... and this list goes on and on as well. The creation and use of art-forms is so fundamental to human evolutionary progress that they are generally perceived as an integral aspect of the human sensori-motor system.

Perhaps the next most complex of human tools beyond language are computers and their derivative devices. At the present time, the ubiquitous interconnection of computers and their offspring has created a virtual parallel to the normal sensori-motor world; a creation sometimes referred to as **cyberspace**. Taking a recursive perspective, cyberspace is an art-form that is addressed through other art-forms. An overarching goal of this book is the consideration of the physiological capability of privacy as it extends into cyberspace.

This brings us to a point where we can recognize a rather interesting question posed by neuroscientists: Is there an organizing principle that allows the processes of the body, including the mind, to optimize the gathering and interpretation of sensory observations and the formulation and evocation of motor action responses? Research in the field suggests just such an organizing facility termed the **free-energy principle**. It is fractal in the sense that it seems to present in various neural processes that operate over a wide range of scales, from the microscopic to the macroscopic.

Free Energy Principle

The metabolic energy requirements of the human body have cast significant constraints on its evolutionary development. Finding food shaped the form and function of the sensori-motor system of the early hominids. However, unlike the apparent progression toward size and power taken by many other top-predator species, the evolution of humans seems to have taken a course towards efficiency of operation of various physiological systems. As we noted earlier, the positioning of the primary sensors that humans use to locate and gather sufficient food-stuffs may have been driven by observational effectiveness. This positioning also has a significant impact on neural architecture. In essence, the first rationale is enhanced by the second.

There is apparent evidence that similar strides toward metabolic energy efficiency have played a significant role in shaping the form and function of the brain, and the mind within it. Merlin Donald, in his *Definition of Human Nature*, noted that *Homo erectus* presented a larger brain size than earlier primates. This expansion came at the cost of reduced gut size. This placed a premium on metabolic energy efficiency in the operation of this larger brain. It also placed a requirement for greater pre-processing of food-stuffs, which in turn placed a demand for greater cognitive ability in finding and preparing food. Evolutionary pressure emphasized the importance of the free-energy principle as a mechanism for optimizing the operational efficiency of neural systems.

The free-energy principle and its application to cognitive processes stems from the work by Hermann von Helmholtz that we considered earlier. In the field of thermodynamics, Helmholtz defined the concept of **free energy** as being that **energy within a complex system which is available to do work**; essentially the energy within a closed system not consumed by entropy. **Entropy** defines **energy that can no longer do useful work**. The energy is still around. It's just distributed across a system. In general, it exists as ambient levels of heat throughout the system.

Energy cannot be destroyed. Think of burning a log. The energy stored in the log in the form of various sugars, once burned, is distributed as heat among a variety of byproducts of the fire. We cannot recreate the log from the byproducts without introducing additional energy into the system. The distribution of energy across the byproducts is an expression of entropy. In naturally occurring systems such as plants, additional energy is reintroduced through sunlight. Thus, many of the byproducts of burning can be reused in the next cycle of plant growth. We just can't reuse the *"old"* heat released when the log was burned.

In thermodynamic analysis, a closed system is also termed an **adiabatic system**. This is a **bounded system in which no energy can flow through the constraining boundary**. If we put a plant in a box where sunlight can no longer get to it, we have created an adiabatic boundary. The laws of thermodynamics apply to such systems when they are in a state of thermal equilibrium. Energy stored in such systems can change form, for example a log can be burned to generate heat.

However, the end result of changing the form of energy within the boundary of the system is to more evenly distribute that energy across all the material within the system. This we recognize as an increase in entropy.

Within the confines of an adiabatic system, optimizing the use of free-energy for one mechanism leaves the maximum amount of free-energy available for other mechanisms. Once increasing entropy has rendered energy no longer available to do useful work within an adiabatic system, the ability of the system to respond to new situations is limited. One might anticipate that natural selection rewards the most efficient application of free-energy to a specific issue. This allows the maximum number of issues to be addressed by available energy stores.

In a paper published in *Nature Reviews Neuroscience* entitled *The free-energy principle: a unified brain theory?* neuroscientist Karl Friston observed that a key component of any successful theory of the operation of neural systems (that is, brain theories) was an ability to optimize the systems. Derived originally from thermodynamics, its recursive application suggests that the optimization of free-energy utilization forms a coherent progression of feedback mechanisms across the full expanse of human physiological processes.

One might wonder whether the human body, or simply the brain within the body, is actually an adiabatic system. Technically, the answer is no; however, the effective answer depends on the time-frame of the interactions considered. The body can replenish the energy that it uses, but at a rate limited by its physiological condition. The time the body needs to convert foodstuffs or stored fat into energy available to the brain and other parts of the body is typically long relative to the time-frame of neural processes. For near instantaneous control of the sensori-motor system, there is a premium due to optimization of free-energy utilization.

In his review, Friston notes that much of modern research is based on **agent models** of human interaction with the physical world. Agent models are specific instantiations of the analysis by synthesis metaphorical models that we view as central to neural processes. In such models, entities in the natural world can be perceived as agents within a sensori-motor environment that proceed through time and space according to the influence of forces that act upon them. Their movements are assumed to follow a path described by **equations of motion** couched in **state variables** that ultimately define the systems. Since only some of these state variables may be subject to sensory observation, the full set of equations of motion may be only partially visible and predictable by the relevant model. Consider a couple of examples.

With our eyes, we can see things in **visible** light, but not in the infrared or ultraviolet. As a result, we can't readily determine that the pan we're about to pick up is very hot. Based on what we can see at visible light wavelengths, we can discern the pan and even its handle. However, when we grasp the handle, we might be in for a surprise when we burn our hand. In other cases, we can observe shapes of objects at a distance, but not the mass distribution within the object. We don't have a natural sense that detects mass at a distance. Therefore, we might not recognize that the mass within the heavy box on top of the stack is asymmetrically positioned, making it easy to tip the stack over. True forces and characteristics of the resulting motion of objects subject to these forces can be hard to discern because our sensory perceptions are limited.

Like most concepts dealing with the body and mind, the concept of force and its influence can be viewed metaphorically as well as physically. Thus, we can perceive forces that act on the mind as well as the body, bringing into play the interactions among individuals and giving rise to the confluence of social policy and personal privacy. The mind accommodates the potential discrepancy between what is actually real and what is merely observed by continually seeking to interpret observations through predictive models. When reality can be better discerned, perhaps through secondary effects beyond direct observation, then the mind refines the models accordingly.

We can observe the principles of entropy and free-energy at work all around us. As a rather simple minded illustration, consider the power adapter that recharges the battery of a laptop computer. A power adapter changes the form of electrical energy from the alternating current, high voltage form found in a wall socket to a low voltage, direct current form used to recharge a battery.

A laptop computer is typically powered by a battery; a device which can convert chemical energy to electrical energy. As electrical power is drawn from a battery, it depletes the chemical reservoir of power causing the battery to discharge. If external electrical energy is supplied to a rechargeable battery from a power adapter, the process can be reversed and energy can be stored within the chemical elements of the battery. This is a bit like providing sunlight to a plant; it's a way to counter the effects of entropy by bringing in energy from a new source. Thus, the battery is re-charged, ready once again to convert the replenished chemical energy reservoir into electrical power.

The electrical components necessary to construct power adapters have evolved over time. Their evolution has been primarily driven by a desire to make them physically smaller and to generate less heat during the recharging process. Heat is an expression of entropy; the manifestation of an inefficient process. Producing a lot of extraneous heat indicates high entropy, a measure of energy no longer available to do useful work. If recharging a battery throws off a lot of heat it implies an inefficient process. As a secondary effect, it can also be uncomfortable to the user; perhaps even unsafe.

The generation of heat suggests that too much free-energy available from the wall socket is being used to recharge the battery. If the electrical components can be optimized to perfection, then essentially no heat is generated in the power adapter. All the power drawn from the wall socket flows directly into the battery. Then there is more power left in the electrical circuit that powers the wall socket; power that can be used by other appliances plugged into that circuit on other sockets. To be sure, we all know that physical systems don't work this perfectly.

Power adapters typically get warmer when they're actively recharging a battery. As we noted earlier, batteries work by converting energy through reversible chemical processes into electrical current. This process can throw off heat as well because the chemical process can generate or absorb electrical current at some optimal rate. By providing more power to the recharging operation than the battery can optimally consume, the recharging can be made to proceed more quickly. This creates excess heat in the power adapter and in the battery. As the construction of power adapters has evolved, a measure of the excess heat generated gives us a good handle on the efficiency of the recharging process; lower heat, more efficient process.

This presents a rather interesting illustration of communicating efficiency of operation of an electrical device to the human brain. Measuring the efficiency of operation of any mechanism is non-trivial. To optimize efficiency in general requires indirect inference from observation. As an example of using such an indirect approach, consider four different power adapters that can fully recharge the same battery, starting from a totally discharged state, in the same interval of time.

One can judge the efficiency of each power adapter's operation by feeling how warm each device gets during the recharging operation. In general, if one device is cooler than a different device, then it is probably operating more efficiently. It has been optimized by minimizing the consumption of free-energy available at the wall socket and this is conveyed to the brain through the sensation of touch derived temperature.

Within the mind, sensations offer means to indirectly gauge the efficacy of physiological processes. Natural selection provides a long term perspective on such efficacy by reinforcing the propagation of processes that prove useful to the continuation of the species. We speculate that sensation provides a high level optimization measure by urging our actions in directions that have historically proven effective. We further speculate that all of the processes of the mind, including their relationship to sensation, are subject to individual and societal provisioning. Through our individual provisioning, we come to associate specific sensations with the **goodness** or **badness** of recognizable consequences of processes, thus allowing our cognitive responses to have a basis for anticipation.

Relative to developmental psychology, Helmholtz suggested a model for learning that is applicable to such situations. Humans observe the world through their senses and then interpret those observations through a predictive model. From this model, the brain anticipates what the observations should be. Thus, to the extent that prediction corresponds to observation, the model is determined to be correct. If prediction does not correspond well to observation, then the mind seeks to refine both the prediction and the observation in an effort to achieve better agreement. At the highest levels of the mind, sensation provides the measure of satisfaction between observation and the predictive model.

The contexts within which observations occur are usually difficult or impossible to duplicate exactly. A predictive model will then present as incorrect because changing context gives rise to different observations. As observations change over time, the brain seeks to adjust the model such that it predicts the new observations. In making that adjustment, through its cognitive processes the brain makes use of available free-energy to formulate a new model. In so doing, it further seeks to minimize the use of free-energy in the formulation. In this way, evolving the predictive model involves a process of minimizing the use of free-energy. A model that satisfactorily predicts behavior and uses less free-energy is a better model.

This presents a somewhat esoteric view of the functioning of neural processes. At the most basic level, it suggests mechanisms that are grounded in the purely physical realm can describe rather well the subjective processes as perceived at much higher cognitive levels. The terms used in neuroscience to discuss the free-energy principle are heavily oriented toward making this objective to subjective connection. Consider the variance of observations due to subtle differences in context.

The human senses observe the world as stochastic processes. For any sense, there are huge numbers of discrete sensors involved. Each sensor makes observations in some repetitive process. These observations form a statistical distribution. The brain performs an analysis of these statistical distributions and subsequently functions by utilizing the parameters of this analysis. It perceives the results of sensory observation in terms of statistical distributions and variances of these distributions.

The predictive models that the brain constructs are couched in the resultant distribution parameters. In discussions of the free-energy principle, the deviation from the statistical norm is termed the level of **surprise** of the observation. A narrow distribution of observations is cast as low surprise; a broad distribution is cast as high surprise.

For pending interactions, a person will typically seek to establish context that forms an effective sensori-motor boundary for the interaction participants. By constraining sensory observation, the level of surprise registered can be moderated. This simplifies the adoption of appropriate metaphorical models through which to interpret sensory observations. If the context is improperly established it can result in increased surprise and more difficulty in arriving at the most appropriate model. This, in turn, increases the ambiguity in the evaluation of trust for the pending interaction.

The human sensory system is an evolution derived facility that was largely shaped by the individual's quest to control interaction contexts. Through the ages-long proving ground provided by the recurring struggle between predator and prey, the senses of the predator seek a context offering offensive advantage while those of the prey are usually after a defensive capability. Human senses provide a good bit of both, which is not unreasonable since humans are in the somewhat interesting position of comprising both predator and prey. If the interaction context establishes an effective sensori-motor boundary, then human senses cannot perceive impressions from beyond the context boundary and human motor systems cannot express themselves beyond this boundary. Conversely, expression and impression cannot cross this boundary from the other side. At least, this is the theoretical goal of interaction context.

Context establishes constraints on actions, including: **physical constraints**, **physiological constraints** through establishing limits based on capabilities, **logical constraints** through the application of social policy, **participation constraints** through identity authentication and authorization, and **process constraints** through trust evaluation, including reputation assessment. This sets the stage on which the subordinate interaction mechanisms will play out.

The context might encompass others as participants. At the discretion of the various participants, one or more actions constrained within the context can be engaged. The interaction is set in motion with each participant seeking some specific consequence to result from the action. Ultimately, a set of consequences resulting from the action(s) is realized.

Consider the role of context in a simple case of visual acuity. When we walk into a room with subdued lighting, our visual senses rather quickly reach a state of moderate equilibrium. The light levels don't change much. In a typical environment, we may not perceive a lot of motion in the room. The continuing observation of the room presented by our senses shows little surprise.

From a statistical evaluation standpoint, little surprise suggests that the observation samples remain close to the statistical norms. If we walk outside into the bright sunlight, we receive a great visual surprise; we might even characterize it as an optical shock. The surprise can be so great that it takes a while for our eyes to adjust to the bright light.

When we walk outside into the bright sunlight, our brain has to modify the predictive model that it uses to understand the sensory observations being presented to it. The brain can make this adjustment based on its prior provisioning. To move from a dimly lit room to the bright sunlight outside is a significant shift. If we're rather used to moving from darkness into bright light, it may well be within the experiential memories of the brain to smoothly adjust the predictive model accordingly. In fact, the brain probably has a predictive model in reserve that can deal quite nicely with the great outdoors. But, if the shift from dark to light is unanticipated, it can require significant effort for the brain to settle on the correct adjustments.

Based on experiences over time, the brain develops a number of relevant models, each by minimizing the consumption of free-energy necessary to arrive at a satisfactory explanation for the changing observations; optimizations driven by sensation. Many of our physiological systems adjust accordingly, some without conscious cognitive involvement. Our pupils become smaller, we squint our eyes, our capillaries expand or contract and we draw our coat more closely to our body because we know it is cold outside.

We observe optimizations across a broad range of neural processes; some are conscious and some unconscious. In all cases, sensation drives the optimization. At the highest cognitive level, the sensation can be complex such as anticipation of the uncomfortable sensation of being cold. It can urge us to pursue a motor action response of drawing our coat more closely to our body in anticipation of being warmer. At a much lower cognitive level, the pupils in our eyes continually adjust to deal with slight changes in ambient light levels. We usually don't even register that change at a conscious level.

When we were young and hadn't been outside much, our brain probably learned some new adjustment to make each time we went out. Through this provisioning process, our mind continually optimized its predictive models. As the models became more reliable at anticipating what our behaviors should be, we **felt better**. This sensation of feeling better is part of the feedback loop that lets our brain know that it's on the right track with the new model. The precise sensation that registers as feeling better will obviously vary from situation to situation; the world and the mind are complex that way. As we noted earlier, for purposes of our discussions we will perceive the encompassing sensation as one of **happiness**.

We might assume that the first time one voluntarily jumps out of an airplane, it is a new and surprising situation that the brain has to accommodate. We might further surmise the second jump to be more profound than the first because the distribution of observations present in our memory is quite broad and the brain doesn't yet have a good set of statistical characteristics; that is, of the sensations derived from sensory observation of the free fall environment.

We can anticipate that on the fiftieth jump, the brain is perhaps better able to take it in stride. There may well be less reticence on our part to jump out of the plane than was the original case because the anticipated exhilaration is sufficient to cause acceptance of the short term apprehension. Here we have actually illustrated the use of a metaphorical model to assess the development of a new metaphorical model, suggesting that mental optimization processes are recursive.

The free-energy principle suggests that the many recursive processes of the brain that become involved in the action of jumping out of an airplane behave in a similar fashion. In each process, observation reflects the state of the environment. These observations register as sensations. The brain interprets these sensations through a predictive model which allows it to understand the cause of the sensations and use that understanding to formulate what to do next.

The predictive model gives rise to a recommendation for action to perfect ones situation within the environment. These actions then impact the environment and the subsequent observations. In optimizing the predictive model and in optimizing the desired actions taken in response to the predictions of that model, the brain seeks to minimize the consumption of free-energy. Sensations perceived in the mind drive this optimization process.

An existing predictive model within the brain can accommodate sensations beyond its comfort zone by perturbation of the model. This process is likely more efficient in the consumption of free-energy than would be the construction of a completely new predictive model. This matches well with our experience in learning. It also matches well the use of metaphors as a means to extend our understanding of the current environment.

As infants, we possess brains with a minimal set of predictive models. It is the function of our provisioning to establish such models. We begin with the most basic processes of sensory observations. We must learn to see, to hear, to feel, to smell, to talk, to reason, to express and interpret information aesthetically. Such are the early stages of the process of growing up.

A Heuristic Model of Human Motivation

Sensation provides the measure of motivation for human actions. In very low level neural processes such as optimizing the size of the eye's pupil for the ambient light level, the perceived sensation can range from the subliminal to the visual shock of walking from a dark room into bright sunlight. In very high level neural processes such as the cognitive activity of pursuing a mathematically elegant explanation of the photoelectric effect, the sensation of **satisfying intellectual curiosity** perhaps motivated Albert Einstein to his Nobel Prize winning revelation. Understanding human motivation across this wide range of processes is a rather daunting exercise that spans research from physics and chemistry to basic neuroscience, to psychology, to sociology, to political science and to theology.

In a pioneering paper entitled *A Theory of Human Motivation*, which he subsequently expanded to book form in *Toward A Psychology of Being*, psychologist Abraham Maslow observed a pattern of sensory input motivating motor response that he perceived to be consistent across the members of the human species. He characterized this pattern as a hierarchical presentation of *needs* according to the ascending order: physiology, security, belonging, esteem, cognition, aesthetics, self-actualization and transcendence. The degree of need is roughly proportional to the cognitive activity necessary for its fulfillment. Physiology is perceived as a low-level need while transcendence is a high-level need.

Unlike many earlier psychologists who developed their own theories of human behavior based on animal experiments and the study of pathologies, Maslow observed the actions of well adjusted people that he termed **self-actualized**. His theory posited that such people engage in activities according to the dictates of their specific needs and that these needs are a normal part of the functioning of the person. Maslow's observations offer profound insight into an extremely complex domain, but their validity often requires subjective assessment. In a 2007 survey of research on human motivation, educational psychologist William Huitt observed that while there was a lack of hard evidence supporting the hierarchy, it was nonetheless widely accepted.

In the computer world, we would characterize Maslow's theory as a **heuristic model**. It is grounded in observation and interpretation, but not necessarily expressed in a rigorous formalism subject to experimental confirmation. Offering a consistent, overarching model relative to analysis by synthesis, its suggestion of a hierarchical organization comprised of subordinate systems forms a compelling interpretation of complex sensations driving human actions. The model offers an interesting introduction to the relationship between physiological mechanisms and digital mechanisms, even if lacking rigorous confirmation.

We can view the expression and servicing of human needs as a recursive series of neural processes through which sensory input stimulates sensations in the form of **appetites** according to the hierarchy. These appetite sensations are then addressed through responsive actions stimulated according the heuristic model. An appetite is a modulated manifestation of need that the mind, the culmination of the nervous system, can perceive and thus react to. This perception is another way to describe sensation.

The body's physiological sensors, observing both internal and external processes, detect conditions that are relayed primarily through the peripheral nervous system; in most cases, ultimately finding their way to the brain. Initial processing of these sensory indications can give rise to modulated sensations that form the stimuli for action. In response to such stimuli, the facilities of the brain evoke various motor system actions in a directed effort to sate the causal appetite and fulfill the basic need. In this view, appetites can arise across the full range of needs, either in isolation or in complex combinations. The sensations to which the mind responds can range from the simple to the exceedingly complex. The responses can range from the autonomic unconscious to the subjective conscious.

The most easily recognized needs are those from the lower levels of the hierarchy. Thirst is an appetite for water while hunger is an appetite for food. In response to the sensation of thirst, we engage in actions to obtain water. In response to the sensation of hunger, we seek food. A sensation of thirst, derived from a low level physiological need for water, can manifest a higher level motor action; a directed search for water motivated by the anticipated sensation of the sating of thirst.

We pursue a complex, motor action response to achieve a desired sensation based on a metaphorical model of the world that suggests that the action will lead to the desired sensation. We know that when we're thirsty, getting a glass of cool water from the kitchen and drinking it will satisfy the thirst. Alternatively, when we become thirsty during a trek across the prairie we head toward the row of green trees on the horizon anticipating that there may be water there.

Maslow observed that **physiological needs** form the base of a hierarchy in which more cognitively demanding needs build upon more basic needs. This order is often the inverse of the urgency associated with the fulfillment of the need where the urgency is indicated by the perceived sensation. The response to physiological needs often involves less cognitive assessment and yet generally manifests as more urgent.

Needs are related. The appetites induced by lower order needs must be met, at least to some degree, before those of the higher order needs present sufficient urgency to be addressed. On the other hand, sating the appetites engendered by higher order needs can serve to ameliorate those of lower order needs as well. Thus, humans learned to grow food in proactive anticipation of sating the appetite to be caused by future hunger.

Subjective provisioning derived from higher order needs may constrain the means of meeting lower order needs. We might kill and eat the cow, but perhaps not the pig. A high order need perhaps tells us that pigs are unclean and not to be consumed. On the battlefield, we toss the grenade at the socially characterized enemy, but we fall on top of the grenade to save the personally characterized friend. This is the way that altruism manifests.

Building on physiological need is that of **security**. The sensation through which a deficiency of security is expressed we'll call **apprehension**. This emotional response is indicative of real or perceived threats. When the appetite that engenders the sensation arises, the response evokes measures intended to alleviate the apprehension. In nature's interaction domain of predator and prey, security is often achieved through the practice of stealth. The predator uses stealth to approach prey and the prey uses stealth to hide from predators. One uses the mechanism to obtain food while the other uses it to obtain security.

In the physical environment where predator and prey interact, a significant premium is due to individuals who can effectively address real and perceived threats. As we previously noted, the fight or flight response to stress is central to this capability. When presented with sensory input that suggests a threat, perhaps a loud noise or a bright flash of light that is perceived **out of context**, the human body undergoes a set of almost instantaneous physiological changes that prepare it either for battle or for a dash away from danger. As a context altering event occurs, actually an act of provisioning, the mind forms an emotion modulated cognitive response based on a contextual appraisal of the specific sensory stimuli. The response answers the question, "Do I run or do I fight?"

In certain instances, the determination might actually be "Maybe it would be best if I stay real still!" In this case, stealth is the order of the day. The evoked response can determine the continuation of the person, or at least their immediate well being. If one is surprised by a bear, it may be best to run; either to get away from the bear or to seek available defensive shelter. If one is cornered by an assailant in a back alley, fighting may be the only option for survival. If one is surprised by a skunk, it may be best to stay very still and hope that the skunk continues on its way.

The general adaptation syndrome can be viewed in greater detail as a sequence of events, in essence a protocol, beginning from the context of an individual's day-to-day routine activities. Within that framework, when a stress inducing situation arises, the fight or flight response is triggered. After the situation is resolved, the body resets such that the response can be triggered again. If the response and reset events are engaged excessively, the individual becomes too fatigued for the fight or flight response to be effectively engaged. A period of rest and recuperation is then required before it can again be called upon successfully. During this period, the individual is in a significantly more vulnerable state. However, if the individual is successfully reenergized, then the response can once again be called to action.

The fight or flight response stems from physiological and security needs. However, in anticipation of its alarm, higher order needs can impact provisioning of the context through which the action response is stimulated. We can be trained to anticipate loud noises or bright lights in certain situations. In that case, we react through more orderly actions. We may not engage the fight or flight response.

In suggesting that the fight or flight response first stems from the more basic needs of physiology and security, we note that these are typically the most urgent of needs. Responses to them can involve both cognitive and reflexive motor actions. Both the autonomic and the central nervous systems are engaged; perhaps even the endocrine system. It is at this most basic of human levels of sensory input and action response that the concept of personal privacy begins to emerge.

Recognition of a stress inducing situation within a given context is often the first indication that a quick response is needed. To fight, flee or freeze comprises the most basic of actions that a person can engage within this context. Lack of effective action can mean death. As we will observe, we are judged by others from their perspective of our experiences. Successful engagement of the fight or flight response can be a profound experience. It comprises a significant event in the provisioning of our identity and is a primal expression of personal privacy.

Successively higher order needs enhance the fight or flight response. Through them, a person might perceive a more comprehensive context, a wider range of effective actions and more nuanced anticipation of consequences. Indeed, the needs of belonging and esteem which build upon that of security form the foundation of what we will come to more fully understand as identity. They form the foundation of social aggregates. The even higher order needs of self-actualization and transcendence bring personal privacy, and subsequent altruistic action, to full emergence.

At the more basic levels, one discerns two distinct yet complementary facets of identity; how do we tell people apart and how do we associate and evaluate information pertaining to specific individuals. In particular, how do we attach consequence to information such that it provides a guide to future interactions that might involve specific people? We'll subsequently see that, stimulated by the need of self-actualization, personal privacy yields an identity of the individual that forms a constraint on all subsequent social interactions. Thus, privacy seems a natural characteristic of human evolutionary development.

Maslow referred to the lower order needs as **deficiency needs**. The higher order needs he called **growth needs**. Perhaps, it is more pertinent to note that the needs of order higher than security are all social needs; they require a social aggregate for their fulfillment. Looking outward, from self to other, they contribute to an expression of personal privacy in provisioning our identity for others in the social order. Looking inward, from society to self, they contribute to the understanding and devotion to policy as it applies to the engagement of our personal interactions.

The first of these social needs, and a foundational concept that ultimately contributes to the social environment from which derives identity, is that of **belonging**. This need manifests as the fundamental aspect of social structure by evoking bonding among individuals. Viewing the most primitive of social structures to be the family, we readily see a physiological basis to the need of belonging.

Strong bonding apparently derives from the limbic system, the seat of emotions that has evolved as a general characteristic of the mammals. Bonding between individuals presents as a comforting sensation of attachment. The appetites derived from the need of belonging most often are expressed as some variant of a desire for **love** or **affection**. Fulfillment of this need builds on the assurance that others are identifiable; that the known friend can be confirmed and the unknown stranger can be subjected to categorization.

A pathology known as **Capgras delusion** offers some evidence of the two distinct facets of identity. Those who suffer the delusion become convinced that a loved one has actually been replaced by an imposter. They can remember and appreciate information about the loved one, but the means by which they actually distinguish that person from other people does not function correctly; a physiological pathology known as **prosopagnosia**. To one so afflicted, a person might look like their mother, but they are convinced that it is not actually their mother. This suggests that biometric authentication has an emotional as well as a logical component.

In the normal individual, belonging builds upon, as well as addresses in part, the needs for safety and security as well as physiological support. It forms a foundation for the mechanisms of higher order needs.

The need of **esteem** builds upon that of belonging. In very generic terms, esteem evokes the development of means to establish relative worth or value among the members of a collective. In the world of goods and services, esteem correlates with value in a marketplace, forming the basis of conditional covenants; consideration offered for consideration received. In the context of self, esteem allows for comparison of the appetites evoked by needs across the entire hierarchy, thereby allowing the conscious self to choose among potentially overlapping or competing appetites. In the consideration of higher order needs, one sees in esteem the potential basis of altruistic action.

Esteem generally flows from this categorization of and by others. It evokes appetites indicative of **recognition**, **appreciation** or **value**. Esteem is the basis for the concepts of attribution and ownership. Another person warrants esteem in our eyes due to a reputation based on their ownership of actions and accomplishments of which we are aware. Conversely, we warrant esteem in the eyes of others based on reputation derived from our ownership of actions and accomplishments of which they are aware. Esteem in either case flows from, or can be viewed as an integral aspect of, the provisioning of the various perceptions of self. Esteem is foundational to the subsequent assessment and application of trust.

In *A Theory of Human Motivation*, Maslow posited a five level hierarchy. The first four, as we have considered them, are classed as deficiency needs of the individual. The top level need, Maslow termed it **self-actualization**, was recognized as a growth need. In later work which was summarized in the *Foreword* written by Richard Lowry for the *Third Edition* of *Toward a Psychology of Being*, Maslow suggested three additional levels in the hierarchy; drawing out nuance originally encompassed by that of self-actualization. He recognized the additional **cognitive**, **aesthetic** and **transcendence** needs as forming a more detailed set of higher order motivational stimuli.

From our perspective, it seems more coherent to view all four of these hierarchical levels as facets of self-actualization. This actually brings Maslow's hierarchy into general agreement with characterizations by psychologists William James, Clayton Alderfer and Gordon Allport who each suggested three-level needs hierarchies that can be roughly designated as **existence**, **relatedness** and **growth**.

Existence correlates well with Maslow's physiological and security needs. Relatedness generally matches Maslow's belonging and esteem levels and growth matches self-actualization. Within these three level hierarchies, a differentiation is made between the outward looking extroversion characteristics of a person and the inward looking introversion characteristics. They bring to bear a more direct consideration of the individual as an element of social order; differentiating privacy from policy. Nevertheless, the higher granularity of Maslow's hierarchy provides a clearer illustration of the mechanisms inherent in realizing privacy that we'll consider a bit later.

Maslow originally presented self-actualization as the highest order human need. It formed the basis of an individual's **being**. In determining the needs hierarchy, he studied people who could be readily characterized as self-actualized; that is, people who were generally perceived to be "... masters of their own fate." These were people who truly lived their lives through peak-experiences; by anyone's assessment. However, he suggested that everyone experienced life through episodes of self-actualization. A quite reasonable interpretation of self-actualization was expressed by the Founders of the American Republic as the **pursuit of happiness**.

Let us then view self-actualization as the primary focus of the higher order needs. Supporting this focus are the distinct facets of cognition, aesthetics and transcendence. Each works in concert with the others to establish the motivation for, and stimulation of, actions aimed at the most general and far-reaching responses to sensory stimuli, both for the individual as well as for the social order. Self-actualization and transcendence manifest as privacy in provisioning identity looking outward while they accommodate the interpretation of, and devotion to policy as it pertains to the look inward toward urging accommodation of personal motivations to group needs. Cognitive and aesthetic facilities are central to sharing individual sensations among a social collective.

Cognitive need evokes the appetite of **curiosity**. It reflects a craving for information and understanding of processes on which to base actions; specifically to evaluate trust and invoke actions. Cognitive need is concerned with the establishment of context and the understanding of the forces at work as a person interacts with the surrounding world.

For natural forces, cognitive need evokes an appetite toward understanding physical laws, physiological capability and social policy. For physiological interactions, it anticipates the likely consequences of the application of physiological capability and social policy. At the most complex, it is concerned with affording an effective response relative to other people, perhaps even across the members of a social group in support of the need of transcendence.

Complementary to cognitive need is aesthetic need. The appetite presented by aesthetic need is a sensation laden variant of curiosity, perhaps well illustrated by the term **passion**. Colloquially, we generally view aesthetics as appealing to the mind's perceptions of beauty. More generally, aesthetics form a general purpose corollary to the need of esteem; a corollary that can be used to differentiate physical objects or abstract concepts. Esteem applies to personal needs while aesthetics applies to general information or processes; to compositions. Our use of the concept of sensation tends to meld both cognitive and aesthetic elements.

Information conveyed to the mind by way of impression is more likely perceived by the mind as emotionally as well as cognitively relevant. Perhaps more in tune with Maslow's hierarchy of needs, aesthetics form a component of self-actualization by enabling the mind to imbue greater significance to information presented in a manner that sates the aesthetic appetite. It is information for which the mind can feel passion; through which the mind can experience ecstasy. Expression is the way one person conveys sensation to another. In our further discussions, we will tend to use the term cognition in a manner that also subsumes both expression and impression.

Further complementing self-actualization, transcendence presents an appetite that motivates individual involvement in social order. Viewed as the need to be a part of something greater than self, it is sometimes referred to as a spiritual need. From our perspective, transcendence evokes the human drive toward social structure. It seems a likely motivation of altruistic behavior.

The policy guided actions of its members imbue the group with greater resilience than is found through isolated, individual efforts. Provisioning of our physiological makeup makes us recognize that prospect. However, successful social groups are those that provide for the needs of their individual members as well, for the group cannot continue unless the individuals that comprise the group continue. Transcendence is where policy and privacy meet.

This consideration of personal motivation in engaging interactions is crucial to our understanding of the interplay between privacy and policy. The human needs hierarchy illustrates that both privacy and policy are dynamic mechanisms. To fully comprehend, and perhaps control this interplay requires an appreciation for the motivations of both. The motivations, in turn, are sensitive to, if not totally dependent upon, the provisioning of both. Personal and social motivation are central to the provisioning of identity and society, just as privacy and policy are central to formulating personal and social motivation.

Physiological Provisioning

We are not born with fully functional minds intact. To achieve the necessary utility, the mind must be appropriately provisioned within the brain. Indeed, our brains do not reach full functionality until some months after birth. Our bodies do not reach full functionality until some years after birth. Our minds at some point reach an adequate level of functionality to qualify us as a normal, fully functional adult. However, through our personal privacy, we continue to provision our individual identities throughout our lives. As we grow and mature we surface appetites that seek the sustenance that a particular need requires. That we appear to do this in a consistent manner, across multiple individuals and across generations of those individual humans, was the epiphany of Jean Piaget.

Trained as a biologist, Jean Piaget was instrumental in the emergence of the field of developmental psychology. He reckoned that children were unable to perform certain tasks until their minds had developed to a level sufficient to support the task. This development occurred through two distinct processes: **assimilation** and **accommodation**. These would appear to be high level corollaries to the lower level concepts that present in a sleep-wake process of sensory adaptation. They also show similarity to the processes of assimilation and speciation that we observed relative to general frontiers.

Assimilation is the manner in which a person accumulates sensory experience. Accommodation is the manner in which the mind, or its metaphorical models, is subsequently changed to adapt to and make use of the assimilated experience. The two comprise central mechanisms in what we have referred to as provisioning; provisioning pertaining to physical, to physiological and to social interactions. The fact that these mechanisms emerge so consistently in most persons suggests that the structure of the brain has a significant impact on the provisioning process.

In his book *La psychologie de l'intelligence*, Piaget observed four distinct stages of human development: **sensori-motor**, **preoperational**, **concrete operational** and **formal**. Other scholars have suggested alternative divisions of activity among different development stages. Indeed, some relatively recent theories suggest each person develops in a unique progression largely dependent on physiological capabilities. What is clear is that from the perspective of recurring social orders, consistent progressive development of the body and mind across a broad population is to be anticipated. This development is central to the form and function of provisioning facilities engaged by the individual and by social orders.

In Piaget's model, during the sensori-motor stage that lasts from infancy until approximately two years of age, the person is essentially calibrating the relationships among sensory input, reflexive reaction, cognitive assessment and considered motor-action responses. Cognitive assessment is further moderated through the establishment of appropriate emotional responses. Through this early provisioning the infant is learning when it is appropriate to laugh, cry, scream or coo. In the early sensori-motor stage, virtually all expressed needs require social engagement for satisfaction. As the stage progresses, the distinct nature, and capabilities, of the individual comes to the fore. An assertion of personal privacy emerges and identity formation begins through interactions with others.

The second of the stages that Piaget recognized is the preoperational stage. The transition from the sensori-motor stage to the preoperational stage seems correlated with the acquisition of language. Learning language is an iconic illustration of the mind forming a metaphorical model based on observations of stochastic processes. In her article *Statistical Language Learning: Mechanisms and Constraints*, Jenny R. Saffran suggests that the structure of the brain's language centers are actually predisposed to deal with the statistical properties of language, and that the structure of languages is heavily influenced by this physiological mechanism.

One possible interpretation of this suggestion is that the metaphorical model for language processing is largely a function of basic brain structure. Perhaps the overall consistency of how people engage provisioning is also at least a partial reflection of brain structure. As the structure of the brain changes with age, the expression of appetites related to needs changes.

Infants learn words, but the toddler learns to construct sentences. This facility is central to an individual's effective functioning within a social order. This stage generally lasts until around the age of seven. During this period, the individual continues the calibration of reaction responses, particularly as they relate to other people. The mind continually engages mimetic expression and impression leading to shared metaphorical understanding.

The following period of pre-adolescence begins the concrete operational stage when the child emerges from a highly self-centered world into the broader expanse of societal existence. During this stage, the person develops the facility for logical thought. Relating the developmental stages proposed by Piaget with the needs hierarchy of Maslow, it might be perceived that the concrete operational stage is more driven by cognitive need. The subsequent state, which centers more on abstract thought, might be perceived as more substantially driven by aesthetic need.

The formal stage lasts from around twelve years to the end of life of the individual. Its onset is typically associated with entering adolescence. In this ongoing stage, the individual first develops and subsequently enhances the ability for abstract thought. At some time relatively early in this stage, the individual achieves the operational state that we might associate with adulthood of the person. In this stage, one has developed the foundations of emotion focused, cognitive assessment of sensory input that gives rise to socially accepted motor action responses. The subsequent life of the individual presents a never ending sequence of interactions requiring a well provisioned mind to determine the socially appropriate actions necessary to achieve the desired consequences, even when the context encompasses new and unknown aspects.

What have these considerations of psychology shown us? That within any given interaction context, we respond through the most appropriate available action as divined by our own mind according to its needs based motivation. We assess the best action through an evaluation of trust according to metaphorical models that our minds use to understand the progression of interactions, derived from the context, the interacting entities and the forces in play.

The evaluation of trust provides a probability determination for the desired outcome versus the anticipated outcome. In an effort to force the anticipated outcome to be our desired outcome, we attempt to impact the interaction context, the forces actually applied, and the manner of participation of the other participants to the interaction. We do all of this in a continually evolving fashion from the time we are born until we die. Some of this evolutionary progression is due to physiological development while some is due to physiological and social provisioning.

At some point we achieve adulthood, a condition in which a normal person should be able to balance the desires of personal privacy and the constraints of social policy. We call out this specific point in the life of each person because this is ostensibly when privacy becomes the dominant personal motivation. Prior to achieving adulthood, others may infringe our privacy and provide direction to the provisioning of our identity.

The work of Piaget *et al* suggests that there is actually a physiological rationale to this dichotomy. Prior to achieving adulthood, while we are still children, our brains actually work differently than they will as adults. This suggests there might well be justification for social policy to infringe the privacy of the child. As we will see in subsequent chapters, the rationale for policy to infringe privacy is very different once we achieve adulthood.

The manner in which we assess trust is based on provisioning achieved prior to, or perhaps during the course of, an interaction. The point being that we don't respond to sensory input with a lockstep action response. Rather, we engage interactions possessing a context for trust assessment that we apply; though not always to perfect purpose. Indeed, subsequent events sometimes attest to the incorrectness of actions invoked in specific instances. The degree to which our actions, predicated on our provisioning, lead to the general satisfaction of our needs is the measure of truth.

Trust and truth are foundational to social order. We observed that the mind, by entering an altered state of consciousness, can impact the context of trust assessment and truth evaluation. Through various means such as cognitive appraisal, expression of profound experiences, including aesthetically enhanced rituals, or perhaps externally applied drugs, the mind can establish through an evaluation of **truth** what actions are **trusted** to achieve desired consequences in future contexts. Maslow's heuristic model suggests that the effective motivation seeking desired consequences is a complex derivative of our entire needs hierarchy.

To provide a gauge for our motivations, we seek to establish at least a causal relationship between truth and trust. Calibrating this relationship might be accomplished through experiencing the sensation of **ecstasy**. To adopt a common metaphor, it can require a **religious experience** to evaluate the truth we find in our assessment of trust. Ecstasy short circuits the objective evaluation of truth.

We characterize a religion as a social order in which trust is established independent of truth; a trait that we refer to as **faith**. Policy in a religious social order is grounded in faith. In general, it does not submit to or require a rigorous evaluation of truth, but rather seeks to evaluate truth through indirect relationships between cause and effect. This becomes a point of significant importance when we seek to establish policy under the auspices of the police powers of the state.

Relative to any social order, our foundation of trust and truth is probably not something we are born with. Rather, it seems more likely that it is something that we establish as a general result of our cognitive provisioning. Since we continually engage provisioning, anything that can be established can also be subsequently reestablished. Thus, our basis of trust and truth can vary over the course of our lifetimes. This contributes to our ability to exploit the wide variety of **distributed cognitive-cultural networks** suggested by Merlin Donald.

The mechanisms through which our internal trust infrastructure is established can be used to refine or even redefine our basis of trust. It is the way that we move among social orders, or how social orders evolve policy to maintain the devotion of their members. It is the hallmark of a successful group to imbue its members with a common basis and level of trust. This portends the individuals in the group responding to common sensory input through coordinated actions as indicated by the policy of the social order. Thus, we see a coherent polity emerge from a loosely associated aggregate.

As we noted earlier, Maslow's hierarchy characterizes two distinct needs that form the foundation of social order: belonging and esteem. The need of belonging evokes the means for person to person bonding, allowing one person to **know** another person. In this context, **to know** means establishing a significant degree of trust that the other can be reliably distinguished repetitively over a long time period. Complementary to this, the need of esteem evokes a means of value judgment that can be used to qualify the bonds established in response to the need of belonging. Taken together, they establish a capability to associate a context sensitive trust assessment with a distinguished person. This capability allows people to evaluate the probability of consequences for social interactions engaged within relatively small social orders.

Both belonging and esteem engage emotions which derive from the limbic system of the human brain. The limbic system appears to have achieved current levels of capability as part of the emergence of the mammals. The production of mother's milk is also a generic feature of mammals. This suggests that the basic physiological bonding mechanism that is grounded in hormone and neurotransmitter action extends into more general social bonding based on emotions. In response to appetites evoked by the need of belonging, people seek associations with other people. Esteem allows such associations to convey a level of confidence that is calibrated by the sensation of reputation.

In order to establish, and then repetitively reestablish such associations, humans make use of **physiological mechanisms** such as facial recognition, tactile sensation, odor recognition, voice recognition, or mannerism recognition. All of these can be categorized as biometric characteristics. We refer to them as physiological mechanisms because they all require sensory input, cognitive assessment, emotional response and memories of past interactions. In establishing person to person bonding, these mechanisms are used in complex combinations. The end result is that among the family or relatively small social orders, we are provisioned to know and to trust (or not) another person.

Once we can know a person in a reliable and repetitive fashion, we can imbue that person with a level of trust, or trustworthiness, based on the value system that we establish in response to our need of esteem. The size of the social order is important to the workings of these mechanisms because of their reliance on physiological characteristics. They work by forming memories of the interaction consequences with the people participating in those interactions; specifically, people that we know.

To know someone in this way, it is necessary to engage them through pair-wise interactions. This is difficult to accomplish as the size of the group gets larger. Consider that in a large gathering of people, it's difficult for each person to have a conversation with every other person in the gathering. We ascribe to this type of activity the term **networking**, a decidedly technical metaphor. In such encounters, we use physiological mechanisms to gauge and remember the strengths of the connections we make.

For small groups, generally centered on the family, we can characterize a recursive, two-faceted protocol for engaging interactions with other people. First, we distinguish a specific person using biometry based recognition mechanisms augmented by an emotional response through which we validate the recognition. In order to refer to this complex biometric authentication process through language, we ascribe names to people.

Names are metaphors for people, allowing us to better index individual identification as we accumulate memories of interactions associated with others. Names also allow us to convey experiential-identity information to other people who were not directly involved in specific interactions. This is the way we transfer metaphorical models through expression and impression. It comprises a form of mimetic learning. As we seek to engage further interactions, from the identification of the person we assess their reputation as a means of establishing a level of trust through which we determine whether or not to engage the new interaction.

We should be clear; within the physical ecosystem there exist only the basic forces of nature. We apply the term **physiological forces** to our individual abilities to manipulate or react to those basic forces through the actions of our bodies and our minds; that is, our sensori-motor system. Consider an afternoon at the Olympic Games when the world record in the long-jump was extended from around 27 feet to well over 29 feet. When we watched the pictures of Bob Beamon extending the record by almost two feet at the 1968 Olympic Games in Mexico City, it was almost easy to believe that gravity had changed values for a short time in the stadium that day.

What had actually changed were the physiological facilities that Beamon called on to manipulate his body's reaction to an unchanged gravitational attraction. His muscles probably didn't get any stronger between the preliminary round and the final round of jumps, but something in the melding of his mind and body did change. The physiological forces which he engaged to effect the action that was his world record jump were obviously unique. Physiological forces are not arbitrarily malleable, but they can be impacted by provisioning; particularly by training applied to the body and the mind; and the establishment of context.

In a similar fashion, we apply the term **social forces** to policy, which is to say the rules, regulations, principles and common mores that we encounter within any social order to which we are subject. Unlike physical forces and physiological forces, social forces are entirely malleable. Consider that since the founding of the Republic, it was held an accepted power of the state to limit, perhaps to completely forbid, the decision and subsequent action of a woman to terminate her pregnancy through abortion. The laws infringing such actions were seemingly as firmly grounded as gravity in the purely physical realm. However, in 1973 when the Supreme Court of the United States delivered its opinion in the case of *Roe v. Wade*, we could feel the tectonic shudder of the change in social force. Virtually instantaneously, the concept of privacy came into significantly greater focus. Not clarity yet, but far less opaque and certainly no longer totally obscure.

Physiological and social forces at work can be a bit difficult to understand. The interaction consequences that derive from these forces can entail the subjective, recursive application of rules before finality is achieved. Thus, provisioning in these domains is highly subjective. Its primary manifestations are **training, teaching, performance** and **experience**. While each of these terms suggests some similarity, the mechanisms to which they refer have significantly different and often orthogonal characteristics.

Training entails physiological conditioning of both the body and the mind in tandem. The athlete does exercises to improve the physiological characteristics of her body; to get stronger or faster. The singer trains to enhance vocal technique. Teaching, on the other hand, entails enhancing cognitive abilities such as learning new processes and how to apply them; also, by learning information about processes and how to impact them.

Performance is an aesthetic form of expression of particular effectiveness in teaching and training; it engages aesthetic facilities of the mind to convey sensation, and trust, along with information and process. Experience entails learning by doing; by engaging in interactions and being better provisioned through their consequences for future interactions. Experience contributes to the provisioning of self and the identity perceived by others, which in turn serves to establish the predictive basis for action stimulation, the concept we have already characterized as trust.

In the physiological realm, the behavior of a living entity is guided by its observation of the surrounding physical world through its sensory system and then affected through the response of its motor system. Different forms of life have vastly different senses through which they learn of their surroundings, and they have correspondingly different motor systems through which they react to sensory input. The climb up the tree of evolution is marked by enhancements to both sensory input and stimulated motor responses. Most profound is the variance in emotional and cognitive ability through which sensation is formulated and subsequently translated into responsive action.

Social Provisioning

The most complex of the interaction domains encompasses engagements among entities responding to forces effected by policies of social order. Within the animal kingdom, there are many species that function within a constraining social structure. Termites, ants and bees form highly regimented organizations. The distinct capabilities of their specialized members form an interlocking structure of mechanical precision in gathering food, providing shelter, defending against threats and supporting the procreation of subsequent generations of the collective. Humans go well beyond such examples in their formation of distributed cognitive-cultural networks.

Using ever more powerful facilities, human societies have risen to the pinnacle of the species chart. Organization structures ranging from the basic family to the nation-state enable people to compete against other species, against other people and against other social orders. We can characterize these structures by the manner in which they balance privacy and policy. This balance can be discerned in their cultures; in the art they engender.

Developing a comprehensive understanding of social interactions is a truly daunting task. As we've noted, in the best of cases growing up takes many years. Even then, the typical person has at best a rudimentary understanding of complex social interactions by the time they become an adult. In adulthood, we're often still learning how to function effectively within groups. Part of the difficulty stems from constraints on provisioning mechanisms.

In general, it is not feasible to establish real world contexts within which large groups can be observed and measured as they engage internal as well as external interaction mechanics. We just don't get many chances to practice profound, real world engagements. It is virtually impossible to elicit true sensations through other than actual experience. To train someone to correctly respond in a life or death situation, without actually putting them in a true life or death situation, stretches the bounds of human expression. Moreover, if you're killed during the training, it defeats the whole purpose. However, all is not lost, because evolution has conjured up a fascinating facility that serves as a social training ground; **play**.

Play is comprised of **spontaneous interactions**; that is, those not motivated by direct, sensory observations but rather by the higher order stimuli of self-actualization. We view play as a metaphorical extension of autocueing into the sensori-motor world. As a concept, it's perhaps easiest to perceive as a behavior that is characteristic of growing up; as a facility of childhood. We tend to first engage play in its most unstructured form. As infants, we play to acquire a calibrated perspective on the physical world in which we exist. We then extend play to encompass physiological provisioning. We enhance our sensori-motor systems to provide a better picture of our surrounding environment. Our most comprehensive use of play is to provision ourselves for the social world.

At each stage, our motivations for the interactions that we spontaneously engage are generally something that verges on pure sensation. Some of our earliest excursions into play deal with almost pure sensory observations. We wonder at the color of the sky. We "listen to the rhythm of the falling rain." We fixate on the smell of dinner in preparation. We engage activities purely for the fun of it!

We play games, totally unstructured games, for the thrill they engender. We make up games. This gives us insight not only into interactions, but trust and policy infrastructures that will prepare us to subsequently engage more formal social orders. Turning the tables a bit, behavioral psychologists learn about children, both collectively and individually, by watching how they play.

Given the utility of play, it is not surprising that as we age, we expand on it as a means of enhancing expression and impression in all the realms of our sensori-motor systems. In *Computer Theology*, we suggested that theatre was perhaps the most comprehensive means of provisioning the individual for social interactions; that ultimately it might be necessary to engage computers in theatrical training if they are to truly mimic human behaviors.

Similarly, sports provide the most comprehensive means of physiological provisioning. Sports derive from unstructured play carried into the domain of formal learning. Thus, we see play itself raised to a high art-form. Let's consider a very large scale interaction that can be viewed as an illustration of provisioning in general, and social provisioning specifically. As children, we might have made the proposition:

Let's pretend it's important that we send men to the moon!

Actually, it was proposed with a bit more rhetorical flourish.

I believe that this nation should commit itself to achieving the goal, before this decade is out, of landing a man on the moon and returning him safely to the earth.
– President John F. Kennedy

On May 25, 1961, in a speech before a joint session of Congress, President John F. Kennedy issued this challenge to the nation. The words were those of an emergent leader seeking to place his imprint upon the United States' position in the world; a position tinged with tension amid the turmoil of a cold war fervently raging between the Soviet Union and America. His challenge, not even the central focus of his oration, is singularly memorable. His words evoked one of the better defined, large scale examples of the spontaneous interaction mechanism, and its provisioning, that we want to better understand.

In our quest to explore privacy, we seek to make connections among privacy as a technological facility, a concept of law, a physiological capability and a manifestation of social evolution. This expansive theme draws upon the concept of interaction to establish the common ground on which to make the connections. To that end, we have tried to provide some perspective on what an interaction is; how it is fashioned, how it is called forth, how it proceeds and how it finds its end? All these elements bear on the model of privacy that we've put forth. In our search for greater clarity, we can use the interaction that progressed from President Kennedy's exhortation since it is a textbook illustration of this most basic of natural processes in its many guises.

The ultimate desired interaction consequence was simply stated; sufficient for a single interaction, albeit of a very large scale. It stressed a time frame which engendered a sense of urgency, a sensation lending impetus to subsequent actions. Deconstructing this single, grand interaction into smaller, more manageable components, the goal was pursued as three sequential interactions; each with its own progression of actions and their anticipated consequences: Project Mercury, Project Gemini and Project Apollo.

Today, we remember mostly the Project Apollo part. From the origins of its precursors in President Kennedy's speech, it was completed on August 10, 1969 in Houston, Texas when three Apollo 11 astronauts were released from quarantine with a clean bill of health. Thus, the anticipated consequence of the original interaction was achieved; the safe return to earth of two men who had landed on the moon. Their safety was not completely assured until it was assessed that they had not picked up any moon or space based pathogens during the trip; a danger not readily recognized in 1961 but a risk factor unveiled by the large scale provisioning of the primary interaction.

It is prudent when stating social goals to choose words judiciously. In the politically charged climate of the day, the wording that President Kennedy used to set the interaction in progress had been carefully crafted. The words, in turn, were quite eloquently stated; an excellent illustration of the power of aesthetic expression. The set objective was to send a man to the moon and return him safely to the earth. What occurred before and what came after were of less, if not little, consequence. It was grand theatre! Perhaps even more appropriate, the interaction had all of the characteristics of a game.

The game was a contest between the Soviet Union and the United States. It had surprisingly little to do with space exploration. Rather, it was more about cultural supremacy within a backdrop of international politics. Prowess in space was simply how we kept score. Herman Wouk, in his book *The Language God Talks*, suggests that Neil Armstrong's first words from the moon should simply have been "We won!" While appropriate, it would have been slightly premature since he wasn't safely home yet, and it was a game fraught with bad plays.

In January, 1967, three astronauts of the Apollo 1 mission were killed by a fire in their spacecraft as it sat on the launch pad during pre-flight testing. Electrical wire insulation had inadvertently worn away, exposing the conductor and thus enabling it to spark. Most everything in the capsule was flammable in the atmosphere of pure oxygen. The spark quickly turned into a raging inferno that killed the astronauts in a matter of seconds, long before they had any chance to open the escape hatch of their vehicle.

Their heart wrenching loss did not invalidate the mission's ultimate success. Three men were subsequently launched in a rocket system that flew them to the moon and returned them to the earth. Three men walked out of the quarantine facility and two of them had actually landed on the moon. The goal was met. Any interim difficulty notwithstanding, the anticipated interaction consequence was achieved.

This grand interaction, engaged through oratorical splendor, subsequently died a lingering death in 1972 with the completion of the Apollo 17 mission. The movie was over in 1969. It took until 1972 for the credits to run and all the bit players to be recognized. The compelling program of exploration fell victim to the more banal concerns of a changing social context. These changes derived, at least in part, from the interaction that spawned the program in the first place. From an interaction mechanics perspective, the context evolved; the motivation for moon exploration was provisioned out of existence.

The goal established by President Kennedy involved all three of the interaction domains that we've mentioned. At the most basic level, sending a man to the moon and then returning him to the earth required an interaction, or a collection of interactions, in the purely physical realm. It required machines and a clear understanding of their capabilities to modulate natural forces. Moving a mass such as a spaceship with a man inside from the earth to the moon requires countering the gravitational attraction between the earth and the spaceship. In 1961, the only practical way to achieve this was using a rocket that derived thrust from a chemical reaction.

The rocket and spacecraft were comprised of a huge number of discrete parts. Some large subset of these parts had to function in a predictable manner, without error, in order to achieve the desired consequence of the interaction. Such large, complex systems have operational characteristics, including failure modes, which are difficult to discern in great detail. Failure modes that are benign in isolation can take on significant ramifications in unforeseen combination. The proper accommodation of natural laws had to be achieved in designing, building and operating the rocket system.

As the Apollo 1 disaster proved all too well, a spacecraft using a pure oxygen atmosphere did not properly accommodate the use of electrical circuits which, in some situations, can spark and thereby ignite a fire. Interestingly enough, natural evolution had provided the accommodation long ages before. It's called *air*. Don't use pure oxygen in the spacecraft. An atmosphere of air, comprised of a mixture of nitrogen and oxygen rather than pure oxygen, was central to the evolution of all land species. It's what kept the first lightning bolt from incinerating the planet. So, just use air in the spacecraft. Problem solved!

There were other problems to be addressed. When the top level interaction was engaged, no rocket system existed to accomplish the physical task at hand. It wasn't known whether people could survive the voyage through space. After all, they would be weightless for a long period of time. In this environment, would they be able to breathe, or swallow? No one had spent a significant amount of time in weightlessness before. Most daunting, the existing social structure had neither the directed will nor the necessary resources to immediately achieve the desired result.

The President's spontaneous expression of a goal provided the impetus for the formulation of a general context, and set in motion a number of subordinate interactions to provision this larger context within which the goal could be met. The National Aeronautics and Space Administration was charged with achieving the goal, while the national will to pursue the effort was expressed by government through the allocation of necessary funding and social structure adjustments.

Sending a man to the moon was more than a technological engineering effort. It was a social engineering effort as well. It wasn't merely that no one had designed and built a moon rocket. The real issue was that no organization knew specifically **how to design and build such a device**. So, the groundwork for the effort went all the way back to putting in place the people who could accomplish the task. It required teaching and training and experience and more than a little bit of aesthetic expression. It required research, much of it involving experiments, to adequately characterize as yet unknown interaction mechanics. The necessary social, physiological and physical contexts had to be provisioned before the final interaction could be properly engaged.

To accomplish this, the overarching interaction proceeded from a social construct, to a physiological construct, to a physical construct. In the United States, many people grew up within the encompassing environment of "the space race." Characterizing the larger social interaction in terms of a game fostered a shared metaphorical model across the social order. Many today are products of that resulting model. It influenced their individual expressions of personal privacy.

Policies that affect the way we think and act as social beings were shaped by the myriad subordinate interactions derived from the deconstruction of the overarching one set in motion in 1961.

The lunar program forms an excellent example of a tightly constrained, albeit extremely complex, spontaneous interaction. The context was established, the action was stimulated and the desired consequence achieved. It was an act of **play**, expressed through policy's provisioning of the social order that was the United States. In a very large way, it contributed to the provisioning of individual identities of the populace and it contributed to a national identity as well, establishing how we wanted other nations to perceive us, collectively and as individuals. How often today we hear in the preamble to any call to social action, "If we can put a man on the moon, we can surely 'fill in the blank'!" However, we must recognize that identity, like society, is dynamic.

The race to the moon was run through an interesting amalgam of public policy and individual personal privacy. The primary effort was managed by a civilian government agency, the National Aeronautics and Space Administration. Auxiliary efforts aimed at provisioning a scientific and technical workforce were managed by the National Science Foundation. The primary goal was established by President Kennedy's proclamation. However, the primary policy mechanism put forth by the government was funding.

Neither people nor companies were compelled to participate in the effort. Rather, on a case by case basis the intersection of privacy and policy was established through explicit or implicit contracts. The astronauts, all experienced military test pilots, worked as civilians on a leave of absence from their military duties. Again, it was an expression of their personal privacy rather than their military duty.

We touch on this aspect of the lunar program to illustrate an instance where there was a perceived compelling state interest to achieve a goal; less so in completely controlling the mechanics of achieving that goal. This will be a recurring theme when we consider the ramifications of a comprehensive concept of privacy as it reflects on public policy expressed in law. There is a significant distinction to be drawn between defining goals that are desirable, and the means of implementing mechanisms to achieve those goals.

Identify is provisioned by what we do, by what we say and by what we achieve. It is provisioned by our successes and by our failures. It is provisioned by our altruism and by our selfishness. The policy of any social order is thus focused on the privacy of its members. We can recognize such policies in virtually every social order of historical record. Privacy in America is paramount. Here, in isolation, it is not the purview of policy to arbitrarily affect the provisioning of our identity. In social orders, it is only the purview of policy to affect the provisioning of our identity to the extent that it impinges on another's privacy, or when there is a compelling state interest in so doing.

The great social experiment that is the United States is perhaps the most obvious example of a move toward addressing the two fundamental processes of policy and privacy in something of a balanced manner. In fact, we suggest the form and function of American society as intended by the Founders should be decidedly preferential to personal privacy at the expense of social benefit. We'll explore that assertion a bit later. First, we must look to the details of identity and then of privacy as they pertain to contemporary society. Only then can we fully examine the policy implications of privacy in the larger social context.

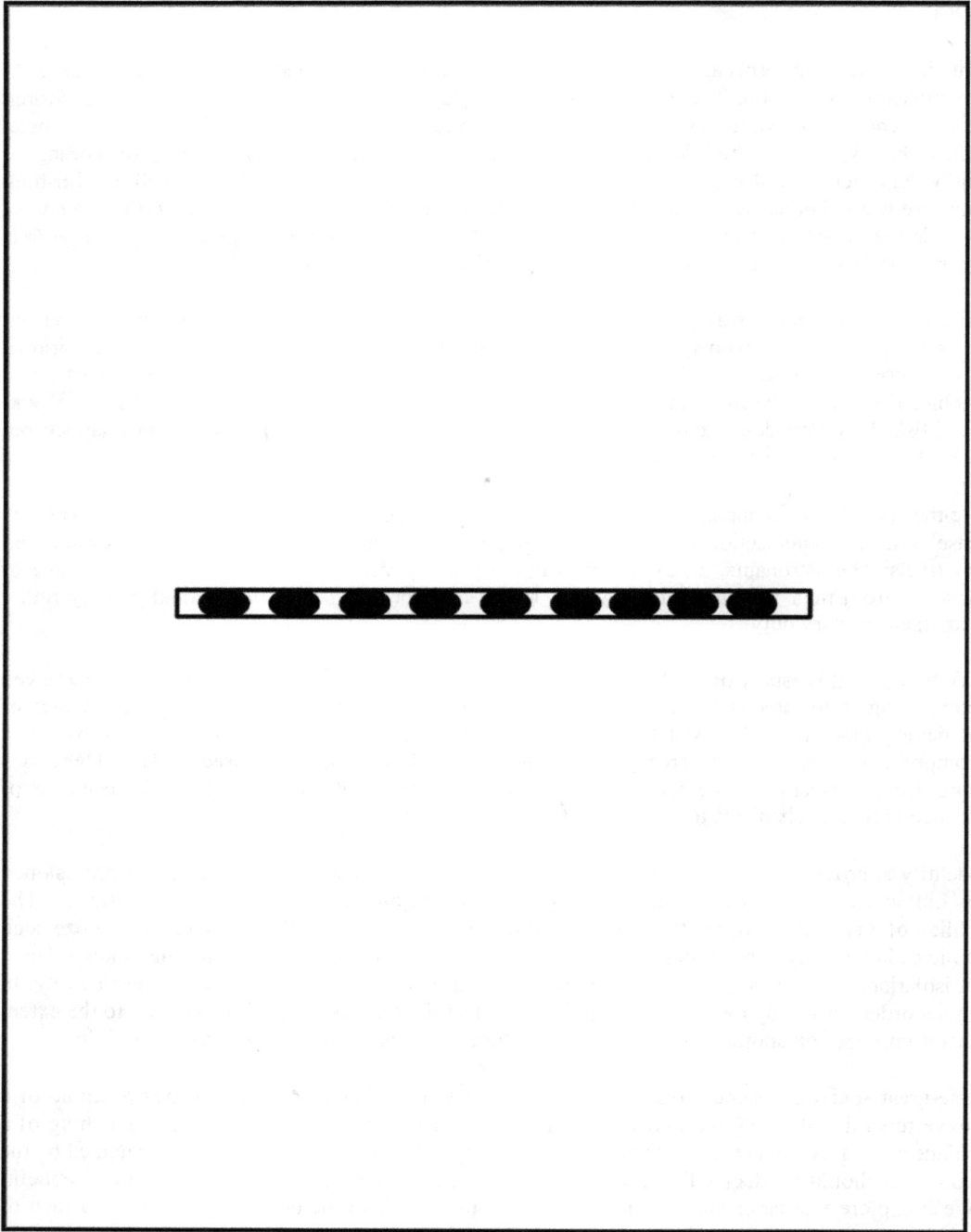

3 *Identity in a Digital World*

Evolution has molded human behaviors to give people a fighting chance in the sensori-motor world. The fighting metaphor is well grounded as evidenced by the fight or flight response to stress. Imminent threats typically register as a sensation of sensory surprise. How a person reacts to perceived threats can be a matter of life and death, depending on the active context. Provisioning is crucial to this reaction.

The fight or flight response suggests that a person must be able to act almost instinctively in moments of profound importance. While one should at least be able to fight or flee, there are often more options. A person needs to be well provisioned for many eventualities. Included among possible courses of action is that of stealth; making the situation or the participants appear different from reality. In some situations, one can present a persona through which they might be able to confuse or to intimidate an adversary. Both real confusion and false intimidation are forms of stealth. Such realization of stealth aids the cause in the ensuing struggle, whether one fights, flees or freezes.

In refining context, it's a distinct advantage if one can discern other individuals as friends or enemies; or at least assess that they're non-threatening. Ultimately, conflict advantage follows when a person is able to act in concert with friends against enemies. This is one great benefit of humans' abilities to act through distributed cognitive-cultural networks. Thus, distinguishing others is a means of establishing trust within the context of an interaction. Evoking a common assessment of trust among members of a social group enhances their ability to act in concert.

As one seeks to enlist friends in the struggle against enemies, the reputations of the friend and the enemy are important in discerning the most appropriate actions. If a person is perceived by another as one who fights adversity, this registers in the mind of the other as a sensation of specific reputation. Likewise, if a person is known to flee from adversity or one who hides under the bed in the face of a serious threat, this reputation is also an exclamation point on the trust imbued that person. If an enemy has the reputation of giving no quarter, then the possible courses of action are better framed.

Physiology of Identity

Identity enables others to experience the sensation of our reputation in the course of anticipating the consequences of pending interactions with us. It is important to us for that identity to be perceived to our benefit. Likewise, it is important to others that their perception of our identity is valid; that they can depend on the sensation they derive from our perceived reputation. This brings us to the intersection of privacy and policy. As a matter of our personal privacy, we seek to shape our identity to our advantage. As a matter of social policy, it is to the advantage of others in the social group that identities are trustworthy; that reputations are in fact truthful.

The mechanics of identity have evolved over the ages. They encompass the facility to repetitively distinguish a person and the facility to aggregate memories of interactions with that person in order to correctly evoke the sensation of reputation. Between one person and another are two sensori-motor systems. The only way to connect the self that is one and the self that is the other is by an interaction conveyed through physical processes. Humans have senses to observe the physical world. They have motor facilities to impact the physical world. Interactions in the physical world require that all who engage them do so through their sensori-motor systems.

Perhaps the most basic of interpersonal interactions are those among the various members of a classic family: mother, father, and siblings. Among these family members, a collection of pair-wise bonds exist that allow the members of each pair to distinguish one another and to sense their respective reputations. Identity finds its beginnings among these pair-wise connections, which in turn form a necessary preface for the extension of identity to large social orders.

The mother to infant pairing is an interesting starting point for the consideration of the mechanics of identity because it includes one party, the infant, that possesses only the most basic cognitive facilities through which to engage an interaction. An infant depends on these early interactions with its mother because they quite literally determine where the infant's next meal is coming from. The manner in which the personal privacy of mother and child, as well as the social policy of both, plays out in these critical interactions forms a degenerate case of the interplay between privacy and policy among more diverse social groups.

From the perspective of the infant, its privacy assertions must derive significantly from pure brain structure. What are the infant's privacy assertions? Well, it wants to be fed, and kept warm, and protected from things that want to harm it. Perhaps it simply wants to know that there are others around. Its stimuli of motor actions in response to sensory inputs are heavily influenced by what we might think of as instinctive behavior. At birth, a human infant hasn't yet had the opportunity for significant levels of social provisioning of its brain structure. Its provisioning largely is brain structure.

As we noted in the second chapter, Maslow's hierarchy characterizes two distinct needs that form the foundation of social aggregates: belonging and esteem. The need of belonging evokes the means for person to person bonding, allowing one person to know another person. In this context, to know means establishing a significant degree of trust that the other can be reliably distinguished repetitively over a long time period. The need of esteem evokes a means of value judgment that can be used to qualify the bonds established in response to the need of belonging. Esteem is the precursor to reputation.

The need of belonging among humans expresses an evolved capability to tell other people apart. Illustrative of the need of esteem, they've also evolved a capability to associate context sensitive sensation with a person so identified. The two facilities work together to allow people to evaluate the probability of consequences for social interactions among relatively small social orders; particularly members of a family. Motivations for interactions derive from the full hierarchy.

Lower order needs such as physiology and security can often be addressed by the individual. Higher order needs are more involved, sometimes engaging social aggregates. The motivations for conception and pregnancy are among the most complex, enlisting much of the needs hierarchy of the mother and father with strong influence from social policy. Connecting mother and infant is perhaps a bit more straightforward.

During pregnancy and birth, physiological bonding occurs between infant and mother. At least some of this attraction seems to derive from oxytocin, a hormone and a neurotransmitter which is secreted in the milk that the mother feeds to her infant. Among its other properties, oxytocin appears to alter the baseline of trust determination that the mother pursues as a prelude to engaging interactions through which she delivers care to her infant. Through oxytocin, human physiology puts a thumb on the scale as the mother's mind seeks to assess the probability of a satisfying outcome of pending interactions. Other bonding hormones and neurotransmitters such as serotonin, which evokes feelings of well-being, are likely influential as well.

Increased serotonin levels in the mother moderate the evaluation of the consequences of interactions with her infant, making it more likely for her to view the potential outcome as desirable; or, at least less undesireable than might otherwise be the case. This establishes a positive feedback loop that enhances the mother's anticipation of a satisfying consequence from pursuing family policy to have and care for an infant. The feedback also reinforces her subsequent assessment that the consequences were in fact satisfying.

We can infer from this that the individual provisioning that the mother might have previously experienced, the provisioning that stressed security through self-preservation or the satisfaction derived from self-actualization, were effectively short circuited, or at least manipulated, by naturally occurring drugs. Their presence within the mother's body affected her interaction mechanics, while their presence in the milk affected the infant's.

Considering other pair-wise associations among family members, the bonding between male and female is largely grounded in physiological need manifested through sexual gratification. The bonding between mother and infant derives from physiological need given a significant provisioning boost from hormones. However, for bonding among the other members of an extended family, indeed for the social cohesion of small groups in general, higher order needs come into focus as well.

Over time, the sexual attraction between a man and a woman can moderate and the connection between mother and infant is subject to the maturation of both. In a polygamous social setting, one could anticipate the formation of somewhat larger social groups based on physiological bonding. However, in establishing policy for a social order based significantly on long-term, monogamous relationships, it seems necessary to realize multi-person bonding based at least partially on social rather than purely physiological stimuli. That brings us to the consideration of experience derived identity, a foundational facility for the formation of larger-scale social groups.

In order to establish, and then repetitively reestablish general pair-wise associations, humans make use of physiological mechanisms such as facial recognition, tactile sensation, odor recognition, voice recognition, or mannerism recognition. All of these can be categorized as biometric characteristics. We refer to them as physiological mechanisms because they all require sensory input understood as sensation derived through cognitive assessment. In establishing person to person bonding, these mechanisms are used in complex combinations. The end result is that among the family or relatively small social orders, we are provisioned to know another person; to distinguish one from another.

Once we can know a person in a reliable and repetitive fashion, we can imbue that person with a level of trust, or trustworthiness, based on the value system that we establish in response to our measurement of esteem. The size of the social order is important to the workings of these mechanisms because of their reliance on physiological characteristics. They work by forming memories of the interaction consequences with the people participating in those interactions; specifically, people that we know.

For small groups, generally based on the family, we can characterize a recursive, two-faceted facility for engaging interactions with other people. First, we distinguish a specific person through biometry based recognition mechanisms augmented by an emotional response through which we validate the recognition. Second, we form memories of experiences involving that person and thereby build a sensation of reputation ascribed to that person. In order to refer to these complex biometric authentication processes through language, we ascribe names to people.

Names become metaphors for other people, allowing us to better index their identity as we accumulate memories of interactions associated with that person. Names also allow us to convey experiential-identity to other people who were not directly involved in specific interactions. We have previously alluded to this as an aspect of mimetic learning. As we seek to engage further interactions, from the identification of the person we can assess their reputation as a means of establishing a level of trust through which we determine whether or not to engage the new interaction. We build up our sensation of reputation by continually assessing the truth of interactions that we engage. As the old adage goes, "Friends help you move; good friends help you move bodies." Reputation allows us to differentiate our enemies from our friends, and perhaps our friends from our good friends.

The more interaction memories we accumulate, the more reliable becomes our assessment of reputation. We tend to assess reputation preferentially from those aspects of identity most closely related to the context of the interaction at hand. Reputation is multi-faceted. It is not just a one-size-fits-all characterization, but rather presents as a sensation influenced by the provisioning of a specific social interaction. Trust flows most reliably from reputation derived from a persona related to the pending interaction context.

Mechanics of Identity

The natural mechanisms of **identification** are primarily physiological. We define the verb **to identify** as **to uniquely distinguish one entity within a set of entities**. Fully provisioning identity, which is aimed at the establishment of reputation, derives from the action. Relative to people, identification and the provisioning of identity evolved within small social orders. We seek to extend these facilities to larger aggregates while achieving similar, or better, results.

Ideally, we seek to pursue processes that give levels of trustworthiness for person-to-person interactions in widely distributed domains comparable to those we realize in small groups. We want the extension to reach into the digital realm of computers and computer networks. The way we will do this is by constructing an identification infrastructure that achieves through a combination of physiological and mechanical facilities the same capabilities realized within small social orders.

Our starting point is the pre-kindergarten curriculum used to teach children to count. Our reasoning is that telling entities apart such that we can count them is the most basic facet of identity. We have defined identity as self from the perspective of others. When establishing identities in an interaction context, the first issue facing both self and other is the differentiation of the one from the other. When other people want to interact with us, how do they distinguish us as being distinct from some other person? Similarly, how do we differentiate the others? This is exactly what we must do when we count a collection of entities.

Counting involves three distinct stages. First, the set of things to be counted must be defined. Then, each of the things in the set must be sequentially placed in a one-to-one correspondence with the positive integers. Finally, some means must assure that each of the things is counted only once. We're interested in counting people, but we can illustrate the procedure a bit more simply by considering in detail how we might count a collection of inanimate objects; for example, a bunch of apples.

The first step is establishing the set of things to be counted. This can be done by putting the apples in a box. Next, we must have means to accomplish the last step; that is, assure that each apple is counted only once and correspondingly that all of the apples are counted. This can be done using a second box. For the counting operation itself, one simply takes an apple from the first box, associates it with a positive integer, and places it in the second box.

Viewing the process in somewhat excruciating detail, the first apple we pick up is associated with "one". Then, this apple is placed in the second box. Another apple is now taken from the first box, associated with "two" and placed in the second box. The procedure continues in this manner until all the apples are gone from the first box. The last number associated with an apple is the total number of apples that were in the first box, and that are now in the second box.

Simple as the process is, the identification aspect of it is quite rigorous; although fleeting. When we have each apple outside of both boxes, while we're associating it with a positive integer, then for a fleeting moment we can distinguish that apple from all the other apples. At that point in the counting procedure, without further detailed analysis we only know enough about that apple to count it. So, within that constraint, we have identified a specific apple.

Once we've put the apple into the second box, we can no longer distinguish it from all the other apples. It is useful to assign a name to this particular facet of identity. We call it **differential-identity**. It is that facet that allows us to differentiate one apple from all the other apples such it can be counted. No further information about any one apple is maintained.

Using two boxes to count a bunch of apples is just one approach. We could use a different mechanism to assure that an apple is counted only once, and that all the apples are counted. For example, we could provide a box in which the storage of apples is structured. We can then use the systematic storage structure to distinguish each apple from all the other apples. To do this we insert a set of dividers in the box that provides a distinct space for each apple.

Using dividers to create twenty-four rows of twelve columns of distinct spaces, we can store two hundred eighty eight apples in a single layer of a box. Creating twelve such layers, a single box contains three thousand four hundred fifty six apples; that is, twenty four gross of apples. We can easily label each space where we store an apple by assigning a naming convention for row, column and layer; a triple of values. When we put an apple into a space, we can reference that apple by the triple that designates its storage location. When all the apples are in a space, we can easily count them because the structured storage fulfills our requirements for counting.

What we've done is associate differential-identity with a physical location. This location is actually the consequence of an interaction involving the apple; that is, the interaction through which the apple was stored in a space in the box. It's an interesting approach to counting, and to establishing differential-identity as an auxiliary facet of counting. For twenty four gross of apples, it's not an unreasonable way to count.

Interestingly enough, this is essentially the approach used every ten years to count the population of the United States. While useful for a bunch of apples, it's not at all obvious that it works well for three hundred million people. The difficulty is that many people tend to move around and not stay at the same address for a long period of time. If we could create a box with a bit more than three hundred million spaces, and get everyone to stay in a space all day on census day, which is typically April 1 of the year of each census, we might get an accurate count.

Of course, in the real world people die and new people are born periodically. During the course of the census day, approximately nine thousand people will be born and perhaps six thousand people will die. Adding to the ambiguity of the count, we have many addresses that don't contain people; equivalent to spaces in the apple box that don't have an apple stored in them. Also, we generally have a significant number of people who don't have an address; equivalent to some number of apples lying on the floor outside of the box.

We try to address some of this ambiguity by keeping a list of names of the people who live at each address. However, across three hundred million people we realize that names are ambiguous for identifying people. Also, people move around, so the address associated with a name can lead to more ambiguity. We need to find additional characteristics that differentiate people in order to accurately count all of them. The greatest problem is simply interacting with each person in order to count them; some people just don't want to be counted. The bottom line is that the census count is always wrong. Unfortunately, there's a also good bit of ambiguity as to just how wrong it is. Estimates of its inaccuracy tend to change every ten years.

One might note that we've strayed a bit from mechanisms aimed purely at differentiating people. When we started to consider ways to associate information about an apple, such as where it is physically located, we entered the realm of establishing persistence of an experience, an interaction that included a specific apple. This illustrates the second facet of identity that we call **experiential-identity**. The two facets of identity that we've now characterized as differential-identity and experiential-identity are social mechanisms that parallel the physiological mechanisms that derive from the needs of belonging and esteem. In order to enhance privacy, we seek to maintain differential-identity and experiential-identity as orthogonal concepts.

To maintain persistence of experiential-identity we must associate a specific differential-identity with a specific experience; with a specific interaction if you will. If we want to use differential-identity as a foundation for experiential-identity, we have to add some form of persistence to differential-identity. In adding this persistence, we need to be cautious and maintain differential-identity in as pure a form as possible. In addition, it is important to remember that with the physiological mechanisms we considered earlier, sensation provides a means of establishing trust in the ensuing recognition and memories. We need to be on the lookout for some means of bringing sensation to the counting.

In developing social processes to establish differential-identity and experiential-identity, we need to have corresponding means for establishing and maintaining trust in the processes. First, we'll examine the identification mechanisms and then we'll consider the issue of trust. We should note this topic was considered in some detail in our earlier book, *Computer Theology: Intelligent Design of the World Wide Web*. We will elaborate on the concepts introduced there in the following discussion.

Let's propose yet a third mechanism to determine if an apple has been counted. This time we'll just have the apples stored in a large bin. We'll start by picking up an apple and associating it with a positive integer. Again, the first apple we'll call "one". We'll now take a felt-tipped marker pen and we'll write the number "1" on that apple. Then, we'll put that apple back into the bin. Now we'll pick up another apple, but this time we'll look to see if it has a number written on it. If it does, we'll just put it back into the bin. If it doesn't, we'll call this second apple "two". We'll write the number "2" on it and put it back into the bin.

Periodically, we'll rotate the bin causing the apples to tumble around and be mixed up; shuffled as it were. This introduces a factor of randomness into the counting, essentially transforming it into a stochastic process. We'll resume counting by continuing this process. Eventually, we expect to write a number on all of the apples in the bin. For an identification system, this process of writing a number on an apple is called **enrollment**. Together with a process called **authentication** which we'll consider just a bit later, these form the basic mechanisms of any identification system.

We recognize that if the bin contains a very large number of apples, it's going to be difficult to know when we've finally counted all of the apples; that is, when all the apples have been enrolled in the identification system. Given that the counting operation is a stochastic process, we can show mathematically that if we continue it indefinitely, we will asymptotically approach addressing all of the apples in the bin. This starts to look a lot like the general census problem of counting people. We can't really know that we've counted everyone, but we can pursue processes that get us close.

If we're a bit more systematic and put the apples into a second bin after we write the number on each, then we've duplicated the very first approach that we used. However, we have added one important new facility. We've remembered the differential-identity of each apple after we identified it. We have associated the number that we wrote on the apple with that apple's differential-identity. We call the number that we wrote a **marker**. This is a most interesting facility because it allows us to associate additional information with a specific apple. This has the downside of taking us into the realm of experiential-identity, but in fact the only experience that is remembered is that of counting the apple.

Another interesting bit of information about an apple that we might seek to maintain is its existence. Let's assert that apples enter existence when they're counted and they exist until they're eaten; then, they no longer exist. Existence in this case is a social characteristic. Therefore, we can give it a highly subjective meaning; one that has a strong social connotation, not a purely physical connotation. An uncounted apple doesn't exist, despite the fact that it grew on the tree, was harvested and is now on its way to the counting house. An eaten apple no longer exists. That part of the definition is more intuitive.

As we count the apples and apply a marker to each one, we can keep a log book with the marker numbers written in it. There is an important distinction to make at this point. When we write a number on the surface of an apple, we establish its differential-identity as evidenced by this marker. When we write the marker number in the log book, we're establishing a credential associated with the marker and hence the differential-identity. The utility of both mechanisms will become more obvious as we work through further illustrations.

The log book is just going to contain a string of numbers. However, each number comprises a credential that attests to the existence of a specific apple. If someone picks an apple out of the second bin and eats it, we can cross off the marker number in the log book. We thus cancel or revoke the credential that attests to the existence of the apple. At any time, if we count the number of entries remaining in the log book, we know how many apples still exist.

Since at any time we know how many apples exist, we have a continuous census of apples in the bin. By writing a marker on each apple, we have established persistence of the differential-identity of each apple. By writing each marker number in a log book, we create a composition that encompasses the credential through which to maintain persistence of experiential-identity.

Suppose there are several different orchards in which apples are grown. All the apples are brought to the central bin for counting. As we write the marker on each apple and record its number in the log book, we can write the name of the orchard beside the marker number in the log book. Now we have in our log book a record of which orchard each apple came from; an **attribution** of orchard to apple. If we want, we can now establish a census of apples from each orchard. At any time, we can determine the number of apples from each orchard as indicated in the log book.

As apples are eaten, we cross off the relevant marker in the log book thus revoking the credential that attests to the existence of an apple. Suppose instead, we had written the orchard designation on each apple as part of its marker? In so doing, we would be intertwining differential-identity with experiential-identity. We would not be maintaining orthogonality between the two concepts. We'll find that such orthogonality is important in facilitating privacy.

We could embellish our apple census a bit if, when we write the marker in the log book, we also write the current date. Assuming the definition that an apple doesn't exist until we count it, our census now gives us the age of every apple still in existence and the orchard from which it came. Suppose, rather than cross off an apple's marker when it's eaten, we simply note in the log the date on which it's eaten. Now, for each apple we know where it came from, when it came into existence and when it was eaten. Denoting the date on which an apple was eaten replaces the operation of crossing off the marker in the log book as a way of indicating the apple no longer exists.

With the log book as it now exists, at any time of our choosing we can determine the number of apples that have been counted and how old each one is. We can also determine the age of any of the apples that have been eaten. We can also determine the age of any apple still in existence. We can also calculate some potentially useful statistics from the information in the log book: average

age of apples that have been eaten, average age of uneaten apples, numbers of apples from each orchard that have been eaten, or not eaten.

When we defined the form of a marker, we thought it good that the only interaction memory found in the designation of differential-identity was the fact that an apple had been counted. Actually, there is slightly more information captured. By using the sequential real integers as marker numbers, relative numbers yield relative ages for existing apples. A lower number was counted earlier, and hence is older, than an apple with a higher number. We can actually correct this by simply creating a random number and using that for the marker number.

Since we're maintaining a log book, for each apple we can generate a random number and compare that to each marker number entry in the log book. If we don't find a match, then we use that number as the next marker and we write that in the log book. By using a random number as a marker, we don't maintain any information through the marker that indicates the order of counting. Our marker truly represents only the interaction consequence of counting the apple.

It is probably useful at this point to offer a bit more detail about what we mean by a random number. Let's assume that in counting apples, we'd like to be able to count up to a million apples. This means that in the course of assigning markers, we're going to have numbers that range from 1 to 1,000,000. If we just use the number of the count in establishing a marker, then we know that Apple 5 was counted earlier, and hence is older than Apple 57. Instead of using the actual count number, let's note that to count a million apples we need a million markers.

So, we could actually use the designations 000000 to 999999 as the markers. Now, each time we count an apple we select a designation in this range randomly. Perhaps, we write these designations on a million ping pong balls and put them in a hopper, like a lottery drawing. Now, when we need a marker we draw out a ball to select a number. For Apple 5, we draw a marker of 881433 and for Apple 57 we draw a marker of 137042. We throw away each ping pong ball after we draw it, assuring that each marker is used only once. In the differential-identity log book, we record these marker numbers in the 5th row and 57th row respectively. On the 5th apple we mark 881433 and the 57th apple we mark 137042.

With this approach to establishing markers, and with the structure of our log book, we now have a differential-identity registry that records each apple that has been counted and what its marker is. In the same log book, we've recorded other information about each apple. The log book is also a credential registry for experiential-identity. For the sake of keeping these two facets independent, or **orthogonal**, it is attractive to think about splitting them into two separate log books. When we make the split, we'll call the new repositories **registries**.

In the **differential-identity registry**, formerly the differential-identity log book, we'll record only the marker; now a random number. Suppose we also add a second random number beside each marker. We can either select this number through a random drawing, just like we did the previously selected markers, or we can compare a randomly generated number against all other "second random numbers" in the registry to confirm that it's unique. We will call this number an **experiential-identity identifier**. Finally, we'll leave a space into which we can write the word "EATEN". Actually, to save space we might just leave a single space into which we can write a single "E". So, a row entry in the differential-identity registry contains two random numbers and an "E", or at least space for an "E".

Let's now create a second log book; the **experiential-identity registry**. In this book, we'll record the experiential-identity identifier, not the marker. Beside each experiential-identity identifier we'll write the date of counting, the orchard from which the apple came, and we'll leave a space to indicate the date when the apple is eaten. Using the identifier and not the marker allows us to maintain orthogonality between the two registries.

When an apple is eaten, we'll use its marker to find its row in the differential-identity registry. There, we'll mark that apple as eaten. Next, we'll remember the experiential-identity identifier and we'll access the experiential-identity registry. There, we'll search for the appropriate row for that identifier and write the date into the space left for indicating when an apple is eaten. Now, in the differential-identity registry we maintain a running count of apples in existence, but nothing else.

Using the experiential-identity registry, we can calculate the age of individual apples, and other statistics. However, we cannot relate any of this information to an actual apple unless we have access back to the differential-identity registry. We have established rather strong separation between the two registries and strong orthogonality between differential-identity and experiential-identity. Separation derives from maintaining two registries. Orthogonality of concepts derives from the fact that we can now extend the experiential-identity registry information to include new interactions without affecting the differential-identity registry.

The two registries that we've created can be quite useful in ensuing interactions. Suppose we learn that all the apples picked from a specific orchard on three successive days have been found to have been inadvertently sprayed with a toxic chemical that will cause illness if eaten. When someone selects an apple to eat, we can track the orchard it came from and the date on which it was counted to determine whether it is safe to eat. If it's not safe, we can discard it and pick another apple. How do we match a specific apple to the registries?

Well, we use the marker number recorded in the differential-identity registry and we compare it to the marker actually found on the apple. **Comparing an anticipated marker with the actual marker** is called **authentication**. The **process through which comparison is done** is termed an **authentication protocol**. Remember, a protocol is just a rather highly structured interaction. A bit earlier, we alluded that together with enrollment, these two operations are foundational to the operation of any identification system. This now raises a couple of additional issues.

If we determine that an apple was picked on a day other than the days when toxic chemicals were present, we can view this as establishing an **authorization** to eat an apple. We might even want to establish a specific experiential-identity registry entry that is an authorization-to-eat; a credential of edibility if you will. Complementary to authorization is attribution. Both characteristics can be established through credentials derived from the experiential-identity registry.

To realize such credentials, we first assume that an apple is counted on the same day it's picked. If this is not the case, then we could add another entry in the experiential-identity registry; an entry for the date picked. Second, we now have a new way to terminate the existence of an apple; we discard it rather than eat it. So, in the experiential-identity registry we need to add another entry for the date of discarding of an apple.

If we're going to use the two registries to detect bad apples, and perhaps to cause apples to be discarded, then we really need to trust the information found in the registries. Trust in this case refers to our ability to project the anticipated outcome of an interaction. If the information about bad apples is correct, then we'll only discard bad apples. If that information is incorrect, that is, not trustworthy, then we may well end up discarding good apples. So, how do we establish trust in the registries?

In this case, consider that we're working within a small social order. One person is maintaining the counting station, which doubles as the place where people come to get an apple to eat. Assume that there is one person who picks apples in each orchard and that person delivers apples to the counting station. Further assume that anyone who wants an apple to eat comes to the counting station to pick an apple. Finally, assume that the person maintaining the counting station and the entire apple picker populations know each other. They've worked together for years and haven't been disappointed to encounter an unrecognized bad apple yet.

In this environment, the person who maintains the counting station is the most likely source of trust. As a causal act, we assume that this person is trustworthy. When a specific apple picker brings some apples to the counting station, the picker is recognized by the counter. The counter trusts that this particular picker is bringing apples from a specific orchard. So, the counter can now count the apples, mark them, enter their markers in the differential-identity registry and create the credential entry for each apple in the experiential-identity registry. A person wanting an apple to eat comes to the counter, selects and eats an apple, and the counter updates the experiential-identity registry and the differential-identity registries accordingly.

Since the counter is essential to the trustworthiness of the system, we could enhance the trust infrastructure by having a second counter to oversee the work of the first. Why would this have an impact on the trust infrastructure? In essence, the counting operation becomes a social interaction. With two people involved in the counting, policy must be determined for the effective social order that they present. This policy will derive primarily from the intersection of personal privacy of the two counters.

Aligning the higher order needs of two different counters in such a fashion as to violate the trust requirements of the counting operation would ostensibly be more difficult than for a single person. In general, it's harder to enlist two people into a concerted devious act than one person acting alone; not impossible, just harder. With this example in mind, let's see if we can apply some of these same principles to identifying people.

Building a Social Order Identification System

Crucial to building an identification system for people is determining how best to establish markers. The approach that we used for apples, placing an indelible number on each apple, elicits an emotional reaction of disgust if we consider using it with people. It reminds us of images of identifiers being tattooed on the arms of people shipped off to death camps. Indeed, it is such images that can strike dread when the mere topic of identification systems is raised. We obviously need something less damning. If we can find a marker that serves its purpose, but doesn't conjure up nightmare images, perhaps we'll be able to alleviate some of the fears; perhaps not.

In current identification systems, the general means of distinguishing people are credentials. A credential is a physical assertion of truth. A very common credential is the driver license. It asserts as true that its bearer is entitled to operate a motor vehicle on public roadways. It is issued by a government agency, usually a state's Department of Motor Vehicles or Department of Public Safety. For our discussion, we'll assume the DMV.

The license is a composition in a physical art-form intended to convey an assertion of truth or credence, hence the term credential. Usually a plastic card, it typically includes a picture of the driver along with their name, address and birthday. It also includes an identifier, a unique number assigned by the agency issuing the credential. The connection between the person and the credential is the picture. The card usually has a hologram or seal of the state to lend further credence that it came from an official and hence trusted source.

If a police officer observes an infraction of driving rules, the vehicle can be stopped and identification of the driver demanded. When presented, the picture on the license is compared by the officer with the face of the driver. If, in the officer's eyes, there is a match, then the driver is authenticated to be the person to whom the license was issued.

When the officer observes the face of the driver, it is to assess the marker for the driver; the facial image. When the officer compares the facial image observed with the picture on the license, an authentication protocol is performed; a biometric authentication protocol to be more accurate. An authentication protocol establishes a single state of **true** or **false**. If the face and the picture match, then the authentication state is true; otherwise it is false.

If the authentication state is true, the license then conveys to the officer a name, a birth date, and thereby the age of the driver, plus an address where the driver resides. It also conveys the unique identifier that allows the officer to differentiate among people with the same name. We note that a routine traffic stop doesn't actually need to refer to the name of the driver at all. Authentication is done biometrically and is made persistent through the identifier on the credential.

Age and certification to drive a motor vehicle derive from the driver license credential. From a process perspective, a ticket for a moving violation could be issued to the unique identifier number. The point of this observation is that a name is not a necessary identifier either for differential-identity or experiential-identity. We also observe that the driver license is used to establish and/or convey both differential-identity and experiential-identity.

Police officers are trained to recognize the license itself as one appropriately issued by a government agency and that the license is currently valid. However, their authentication by facial recognition is a highly personal and subjective process. In addition, over time it has become commonplace for a convenience store clerk to use the same credential to validate the age of a person buying beer. The authentication process used by the clerk is just as personal and subjective as those of the officers. However, the clerk is likely not as well trained as the officers.

In a different venue, a driver license is sometimes used by the folks at the door of your favorite airline lounge to confirm the face of the person seeking entrance matches a name, and the name matches that on the airline's club card, which doesn't have a picture on it. This further illustrates that the driver license has morphed into a ubiquitous identification token. However, the authentication procedures that use it vary significantly in form and accuracy.

To obtain a license, a person goes to the Department of Motor Vehicles office, presents a source document such as a birth certificate and applies for a license. This is an enrollment process. The person will probably have to provide one or two fingerprints and have their photograph taken while in the DMV office. This is a relatively recent addition to the enrollment protocol and is intended to bring biometric markers more fully into the identification procedures.

Capturing the fingerprints and picture in the DMV office enhances their credibility by establishing a baseline for integrity assessment. This offers the possibility of more rigorous authentication procedures. The purpose of the source document is to connect differential-identity with experiential-identity. It accomplishes this by associating an initial experience, for example, being born in Bismarck, North Dakota on a specific date, with the identification information presented on the license and with the biometric characteristics of the person captured while in the DMV office.

Obtaining a license may also require demonstration of knowledge about the state's policy regarding roads and operating a motor vehicle. A person may be asked to demonstrate some facility with actually driving an automobile; either through a driving test administered by the DMV, or by presenting a credential that attests to attending a certified driving school. Satisfactorily meeting this requirement means the license conveys authority to drive.

We observe that these various requirements comingle differential-identity and experiential-identity. They meld the concept of identity authentication with that of authorization and attribution ascribed to that identity. From a societal perspective, requiring a person to carry a driver license is rationalized as being acceptable because it's a voluntary act on the part of the person. After all, it's not a right to drive a car, it's a privilege; or so goes the rationale.

Using a birth certificate as a source document establishes a name and a birth date to be associated with the differential-identity of the license holder. The birth date is important because the penultimate need for a driver license seems to be buying alcohol, for which one generally needs to be 21 years of age. When we consider the trust implied by the derived credential, we must wonder about the trust conveyed from the source document. If it is a birth certificate, what connects the certificate to the person?

How do we know that a birth certificate corresponds to the person presenting it to obtain a driver license? In relatively recent times, a biometric marker such as a footprint is sometimes captured at birth; if a person is born in a trusted facility such as a hospital. Unfortunately, this is not a particularly rigorous requirement. However, when it is available we observe a rather circular argument regarding the level of trust conveyed by the license. Valid driver licenses of parent and doctor, functioning as identity tokens, lend credence to birth certificates, which in turn lend credence to future driver licenses.

The presentation of a driver license to a police officer is an aesthetic ritual intended to convey trusted information from the driver to the officer and trusted information about the driver from the Department of Motor Vehicles to the officer. A reciprocal presentation by the officer can be requested, but it may be more tenuously remanded. Hence, the mutual authentication of officer and driver is often asymmetrically established.

While driver licenses are perhaps the most prevalent means of identification, they leave much to be desired as a foundational element of wide area social interactions. Their greatest deficiencies are first, that those that issue them, the Departments of Motor Vehicles, typically don't want to view them as identity credentials, and second, they are not **digitally enabled.** They can't plug into a digital system and provide identification services.

Curiously, a significant aspect of the process involved in obtaining a license is about identification, not about driving a motor vehicle. So the reticence to call them identity tokens is obviously a societal form of "whistling past the graveyard." The social order absolutely needs some trusted means of establishing the identity of individuals, but people are reluctant to be included in a societal identification system. Also, while current digital interaction systems recognize the importance of establishing identity, the potential legal liability of claiming to provide an adequate identification infrastructure and then having it fail is daunting at best.

None-the-less, we assert that it is highly desirable to have a ubiquitous means of identification in order to buttress personal privacy, especially in the digital domain. Since most driver licenses do not currently have a strong digital capability, they cannot function as a person's token for establishing either differential-identity or experiential-identity in digital social interaction contexts. In the last chapter, we will close with a proposal for establishing a truly ubiquitous system.

Since society needs trusted authentication of identity, let's consider the construction of an identify infrastructure that would rigorously support personal privacy as we have been discussing. It should become clear that establishing differential-identity with a credential like a current driver license is awkward at best. It is inadequate for creating a foundation for strong personal privacy.

In current interaction environments, several mechanisms have evolved for divining markers that are closely associated with a person. These include signatures, pictures, secret passwords and Personal Identification Numbers known as PINs. All are variants of identity establishing credentials. Each is plagued with significant trust deficiencies. Nevertheless, let's consider briefly how each of them fits into an identification system. Actually, we've already considered in some detail the use of a picture as a marker for differential-identity, so we can concentrate on the other mechanisms.

A signature is a marker that is based on the concept that a person's handwriting is unique and reproducible only by that specific person. To enroll in a signature based identification system one merely needs to visit the differential-identity registry and write some words. The usual social convention is to write one's name. Often, a signature, while appearing unique, is actually unreadable. So, a further convention is to print one's name in the registry and write one's signature beside it.

An authentication protocol in a system using a signature as a marker requires that a person present their name and their signature template via a credential issued by some trusted authority. If the signature appears to match that found on the template which derives from the registry, the person is presumed to be the person named in the registry maintained by the trusted authority.

A driver license can serve as a token in such a system. That is, when a person enrolls, in addition to a facial picture and fingerprints, the person can provide a signature. The image of this signature can be printed on the card, along with the picture. The card thus becomes a template to be used in authentication protocols. When a person presents the driver license to an officer, the officer can also require them to provide a signature. This establishes two markers that the officer can verify; the picture and the signature.

Chapter 3 – Identity in a Digital World

Any document bearing a signature can now become a credential indicating physical presence of the person at a certain place and time. If a police officer issues a citation, the person to whom it is issued might be asked to sign a receipt for it. The officer then has a credential that proves to some level of truth that the person received the citation at a specific time and place. The signed receipt is a credential of attribution or non-repudiation that the person acknowledged receiving the citation.

Signatures have been used for hundreds of years and variants of the technique such as signets have actually been used for millennia. Their downside is that signatures are rather easily forged and can be affected by the emotional state of the writer. The level of trust they convey is modest at best. A significant problem with a signature is that it doesn't easily translate to a digital system. It's difficult to obtain a signature and then match it to that found in a registry in a purely digital system. Rigorously determining that two signatures were written by the same person involves rather sophisticated pattern recognition and comparison that derives from complex provisioning of the mind of the interpreter, a process not easily translated to digital algorithms.

Passwords offer another marker mechanism. A password fits rather nicely into distributed, digital systems. To enroll in a password based system, one simply accesses the registry and either provides a multi-character password, or the identification system creates and provides a password to the person. The typical convention is to register an account name and a password. The password is intended to be kept secret by the person. In this system, the differential-identity registry must be kept secret as well; at least the password component.

When a person wants to authenticate their differential-identity they provide the account name and the password. If the password matches that found in the registry, the differential-identity of the account is authenticated. A couple of obvious problems with this approach arise. If someone else learns the password, it is easy for them to impersonate the person in question. A similar problem exists for the system seeking to authenticate the person. The person might allow someone else to impersonate them, without the system knowing. Thus, there are significant risks of trustworthiness on the part of all participants to the interaction.

A Personal Identification Number is virtually the same as a password except that it's all numeric. For a digital system, a keypad through which one enters a PIN only has to support numeric characters. The keypad can be made simpler, smaller and cheaper. Unfortunately, lots of scams can be used to surreptitiously capture passwords and PINs. We're left to observe that differential-identity based purely on credential systems is fraught with opportunities for counterfeiting, fraud, or other forms of identity theft.

The most basic goal of a marker is to allow only the person in question to use the marker to authenticate their differential-identity. How best then to realize such a marker? As a guide to answering this question, let's consider some characteristics that make for an effective marker.

The marker must be unique for every individual. We must be able to define unique markers for the six or seven billion people on the earth at the present time, and for many billions more that will exist in the relatively near future. To be somewhat safe, let's assume that we need at least one hundred billion markers. A marker then must be unique to one part in one hundred billion. An enrollment protocol should then be able to distinguish unique identification to at least one part in one hundred billion.

It is important to be able to consistently divine the differential-identity of a person over their entire lifetime, so a marker must be immutable for that period. The marker must be very closely associated with a person. The marker should only be available from the person to whom it is connected. In fact, it would be best if the marker was actually a physiological characteristic of the person. In this case, the marker would be a naturally occurring credential of differential-identity. A facial image is such a credential, as are finger prints and iris patterns.

When a person enters an identification system, an image of their differential-identity marker is captured and stored in the differential-identity registry for the system. This process is termed **enrollment**. Applying for a driver license is enrollment. In the apple counting system that we considered a bit earlier, the counting and marking of apples constituted enrollment in that system. There, the marker was actually created when it was written or marked on the apple. Authenticating the differential-identity of a specific apple required observing a number written on the skin of the apple. Thus, the marker was closely tied to the apple.

In an identification system for people, the marker image recorded in the differential-identity registry establishes a copy of the marker that can be referenced at some later time as part of an authentication protocol. In some systems, this stored image is called a **template**. At the time a person enrolls, the marker template must be compared to all existing templates in the registry to confirm that the person is only entered into the system once. As we noted earlier, this one-to-many comparison process is termed **identification**.

Any equipment necessary to detect the marker or the value of the marker must be non-invasive to the human body. The blood vessel pattern on the surface of a kidney, while perhaps unique to each person, would require invasive techniques to observe. On the other hand, observing the blood vessel pattern in a finger might be quite innocuous.

Besides being non-invasive, any measurement equipment should be relatively inexpensive, highly reliable and accurate. It should be possible to certify a level of trustworthiness of the equipment and of the capture and comparison operations on which enrollment is based. In any enrollment event, the level of trust conveyed will be dependent on the level of trust inherent in the mechanisms through which markers are captured, a composition of the marker maintained and the comparison operation performed. Remember, a rendering of the marker expressed in an art-form is a composition.

The process of subsequently observing a marker and comparing it to a template that was stored away when the person enrolled in the identification system is termed either **verification** or **authentication**. The marker should be of such a form that a highly reliable comparison of captured marker versus stored template can be made. Since this is a one-to-one comparison operation, it is not unrealistic to expect it to be reliable.

In performing the authentication comparison, the probability should be low that images that should match don't, and the probability should be high that images that should not match indeed do not match. The comparison process should be relatively quick, which typically means well less than a second. If it takes two hours to perform, then the authentication operation will be useless for most interactions.

Chapter 3 – Identity in a Digital World

We can also suggest a couple of characteristics that help us to keep differential-identity teased apart from experiential-identity. First, the marker should convey no information about the individual other than the differential-identity of that person. The marker should offer a minimal or non-existent forensic wake. This suggests that the marker not be amenable to unintended indication of interaction activity which can be perceived as a forensic wake. The casual reader might notice that experiential-identity itself is an example of a forensic wake. Actually, for a person it is the definitive forensic wake.

It's somewhat difficult to create an artificial marker that conveys differential-identity only at a specific time and place. Nevertheless, it is highly desirable that only through an intentionally activated authentication protocol is it possible to establish differential-identity. To subsequently establish physical location corresponding to the point where differential-identity is verified requires a second operation using a trusted location indicator. This result can then be associated with differential-identity to establish a result that falls within the realm of experiential-identity. That is, being able to affirm that this person was here at this location.

At the present time, the most reliable differential-identity marker mechanism that possesses these traits is one or more of the biometric characteristics of the human body. Biometric characteristics are naturally occurring credentials that attest to the uniqueness of a person relative to all other persons. This uniqueness derives from the natural processes through which various parts or patterns in and of the human body are formed. There is a natural randomness to these processes which makes it highly unlikely that duplicate patterns will form on multiple individuals. A biometric characteristic is very much like the random numbers that we used in the apple counting scheme that we considered a bit earlier.

Principal among the useful human biometric characteristics are fingerprints, handprints, facial images, retinal patterns, iris patterns and DNA. We will use the term **biometric** to refer to any such characteristic. Note that we're suggesting that a biometric forms the differential-identity marker, not some card or other token that contains the biometric image. If we establish a trusted and rigorously correct system through which we capture and compare biometric images, then we can repetitively establish the differential-identity of a person to an extremely high degree of accuracy.

The last two marker requirements that we noted illustrate concern for the demarcation between pure differential-identity and using differential-identity as an index for experiential-identity. In counting apples, we arrived at a means to make this separation by creating two registries; one for differential-identity and one for experiential-identity. They were connected through an experiential-identity identifier. We can do the same for people.

Consider that we might use a fingerprint, perhaps from the right index finger, as a marker. We can store a digital image of that fingerprint in a differential-identity registry. By using a random number as an experiential-identity identifier that we store in both registries, the two are coupled. In the experiential-identity registry, only this identifier indexes the information stored there. This registry will not contain fingerprints or other biometric markers. As a means to greater privacy, we might establish many experiential-identity registries, each with its own identifier to link it back to the differential-identity registry. Each registry reflects a specific persona of the person.

To truly respect our set of marker requirements, we might be more inclined to use a fingerprint or an iris scan versus using a DNA pattern as a marker. DNA conveys a lot of health related information that an individual may well want to hold secret, but when we die our DNA typically outlasts the rest of our body. Consequently, it offers prospects of identification after other biometrics are no longer available. Looking back to the apple identification system, if we want to maintain an indication of the state of a person within their life-cycle in the experiential-identity registry, DNA offers the best marker of last resort through which to determine that a person no longer exists.

For an active identification system, we might be more inclined to use an iris scan versus a fingerprint because the iris scan traditionally offers significantly less forensic value than does a fingerprint. Criminal records are largely based on fingerprints. When we handle things, we often leave behind our fingerprints. When we look at things, ostensibly we rarely leave behind our gaze. We typically view fingerprints as leaving a strong forensic wake while iris patterns leave a weaker forensic wake. However, technological advances can affect our choices. Consider a rather famous example of biometric markers involving a magazine's cover picture known as the *Afghan girl*.

In 1984, National Geographic photographer Steve McCurry captured a picture of a young Afghanistan orphan girl in a refugee camp in Pakistan. He didn't obtain her name or any other information about her. Her hauntingly beautiful image was published on the cover of *National Geographic Magazine* in June 1985 and became an iconic representation of the Afghani people.

In 2002, National Geographic mounted an effort to find the girl, certainly by this time a middle aged woman. After considerable effort, she was located in a remote region of Afghanistan. While her appearance was sufficient to convince the searchers that they'd found the correct person, the very real prospect of imposters suggested they confirm the identification by doing an iris pattern comparison with the original picture. This verified that the current mother of several children was indeed the *Afghan girl*. Technology has now reached the point that iris patterns can be captured with surveillance cameras, in some instances from a few meters away. There are more and more instances when we do leave our gaze behind.

Current technologies for marker capture and comparison are generally less accurate than the one part in one hundred billion that we specified as a requirement. Fingerprint capture and comparison is typically accurate over a range of one part in a thousand to one part in a million. To achieve reliable comparisons in the range of one part in one hundred billion requires either more sensitive capture and comparison methodologies, or it requires the use of multiple biometric markers; or both. The accuracy of the enrollment comparisons generally need to be better than subsequent comparisons used to authenticate differential-identity, but enrollment tends to be less time critical than subsequent authentication. Consider an identification system based on iris patterns and fingerprints.

Capture of iris patterns can be accomplished with a high resolution digital camera. Such cameras are cheap and ubiquitous; many cellular telephones have them. Fingerprint capture can be done with pressure sensitive or photographic sensors. This technology is becoming relatively inexpensive, commonplace, and highly compact. Portable fingerprint detection sensors are readily available to be included on computer platforms of all sizes and shapes.

Captured images of either biometric can be quickly examined for quality. The amounts of data involved suggest that an enrollment device with technical capabilities comparable to a smart phone is adequate. Standard 3G or 4G data communication channels can handle transmission of the requisite data volumes within seconds. This means that quite literally a device that is technically equivalent to a smart phone can be used for enrollment in a world-wide identification system. The enrollment process can be engaged from virtually any location in the world.

From a trust standpoint, it is advantageous if a trained and trusted operator is involved in the enrollment of new members of an identification system. Such support will diminish errors in the image acquisition and will diminish uncertainty in the registry due to improperly matched images. A trusted operator is also useful in avoiding outright fraud.

For example, it is useful to make sure that at enrollment the various biometric images come from the same person and that multiple, slightly modified images are not entered to affect the overall quality of the system. Quality testing can be performed automatically on the captured images and they can be reacquired if necessary to achieve sufficiently high quality. The images then need to be transmitted to an enrollment data-base; the large scale equivalent of the differential-identity registry that we discussed for the apple counting system. At that time, a one-to-many comparison is made for each biometric image against the registry data-base to ensure that a person is represented only once in the system.

It is useful from a quality perspective if biometric images can be ascribed to a trusted location indicator showing where the enrollment physically occurred. Similarly, it is useful if the images can be ascribed to a trusted time stamp indicating when the enrollment occurred. Time and location of enrollment attest to the subsequent establishment of experiential-identity. This is all that's necessary to enroll a person. If they're not previously enrolled, then their biometric images are added to the registry along with trusted time and location stamps.

If a person is already enrolled, the new biometric images can just be ignored, or they can be added to the registry in order to track variances in the chacteristics over long periods of time. There's no particular penalty in terms of data storage or computer utilization with attempting to enroll multiple times. The basic differential-identity registry is comprised only of biometric images, time stamps and location stamps. One additional type of information is needed to build a more expansive identification system; unique identifiers to connect each person in the differential-identity registry to entries in one or more experiential-identity registries.

It may seem a bit strange that the differential-identity registry doesn't contain a name, or an address, or a birth date. It certainly doesn't contain a social security number, a bank account number, or any of a myriad other tidbits that we tend to think of as our personal, identifying information. Indeed, a problem that many people have with identification systems in general, particular systems administered by a governmental agency, is the lament, "I don't want them to know all about me!"

Most of the information that really concerns people falls into the realm of experiential-identity. It is quite appropriate for people to be concerned with how this information is defined, stored, protected, and used! It's important! However, in general people don't want to keep this information completely secret. They quite typically want to use it under the auspices of their personal privacy. After all, this information is how contextual and emotional content is provisioned into subsequent interactions. When we've truly exercised our personal privacy, this information conveys the way we want others to perceive us. Our primary concern is with control, not secrecy!

Privacy suggests that we want to use experiential-identity information in a way that benefits us as determined by our personal perception of needs, no matter which side of an interaction we're on. When we interact with others, we also want to use their experiential-identity information to benefit us as we seek to control the context of an interaction; still a facet of our personal privacy.

Conversely, others want to use our experiential-identity information in a way that best benefits them. Policy has to determine the proper mix. We'll consider in the next chapter the mechanisms through which this determination of policy manifests. To prepare the way, let's complete this chapter by considering some of the elements of the experiential-identity part of a general identity framework on which privacy can be based.

Establishing Personas

Based on our earlier discussion, we can now envision a differential-identity registry. It includes biometric images for all the people enrolled in the system. We know that experiential-identity encompasses information derived from the consequences of interactions that determines how other people will perceive us. To the extent that such interactions are products of our personal privacy, we control how other people will perceive us. We've observed that we may seek to have different people or groups of people perceive us in specific ways. We term these different ways as personas. That being the case, let's consider building up distinct experiential-identity registries for the different personas that we choose to project.

A number of **persona types** can be defined. Each type offers different levels of trust to be imparted to a pending interaction. Each contributes to an experiential-identity registry from which reputation can be derived. Through mutual negotiation, different parties to an interaction can agree on the specific persona type to be used by each participant.

We will consider four persona types: **anonymous**, **situational**, **floating**, and **anchored.** These types have been a part of social interactions since the dawn of the species, but the digital domain offers the prospect of a more rigorous definition of each. From this, we can discern something of the levels of trust that can be derived from each type of persona.

The first type, and one that generally conveys a minimal level of trust, is anonymity. In a sense, anonymity is the absence of identity. To project true anonymity in an interaction, one must leave absolutely no forensic wake that can be traced back to the differential-identity of a person. It is a persona that is perhaps easier to achieve in the digital domain.

In the physiological domain, if other people are involved in an interaction their memories form a cursory forensic wake, even if they're interacting with an otherwise unknown person. In the digital domain, there are means to shield the differential-identity of a person from an interaction. It is a useful persona when we want to participate in a single interaction in which we don't want the consequences to be attributable back to us. Perhaps we want to report a crime, but we fear retaliation from the perpetrator if they know we saw them. To be sure, anonymity also affords the possibility to falsely accuse people of crimes and thereby infringe their privacy and adversely impact their identity.

Any trust attributed to information derived from an anonymous persona is heavily dependent on its context. An anonymous tip that "the body is buried there!" can be directly confirmed; if you dig up the body you confirm that the tip was trustworthy. An anonymous tip that "John Smith dropped a body in the middle of Lake Michigan three years ago!" is perhaps less trustworthy. If John Smith is a candidate for public office, one might even suspect an ulterior motive for the tip.

There is a variant on the persona of anonymity that is particularly insidious with respect to personal privacy. We call it **institutional anonymity** or **role based identity**. While it is difficult for an individual to mask the creation of a forensic wake within typical interactions, institutional anonymity engages a social order conspiracy to mitigate even this diminished possibility. Government is particularly adept at allowing its agents to act anonymously and to prevent others from accessing facilities through which to discern the forensic wake of those who are acting anonymously.

Other social orders can act in this manner as well; generally somewhat less effectively. The end result is that institutional anonymity is able to infringe the privacy of individuals, often without incurring any significant consequences. This is the realm of "Big Brother", as described by George Orwell in his book *1984*. Digital systems offer the prospect of greatly diminishing the instances and capabilities of institutional anonymity if they are appropriately constrained by state policy.

A slightly more involved persona is one we call a **situational persona**. This persona is iconically represented by the phrase "What happens in Vegas, stays in Vegas!" The concept centers on being able to establish differential-identity level authentication within some context, but to avoid having any interaction consequences associated with the actual differential-identity of the person. This is the persona of the witness protection program.

Through this persona one seeks to adopt an identity that serves for some period of time in some specific context, perhaps even in multiple interactions, and yet leaves no long-term record of a person's involvement. One's use of such a persona has the goal of interaction consequences being highly compartmentalized within specific experiential-identity registries that are not rigorously connected with the differential-identity of the person. This persona illustrates the dangers present when parties to an interaction cannot accurately gauge reputations.

It is the classic ruse of the predator to present themselves as less of a threat than is actually the case. Likewise, prey may well seek to present a more threatening demeanor than is warranted. In the purely physical domain, both predator and prey have evolved mechanisms to counter the other. In the digital domain, our lack of adequate senses makes detection and application of countermeasures problematic. As part of the framework for digital interactions, we need means to address this problem. For example, in the digital domain we anticipate that the mechanics of presenting any persona should at least be recognized as such in advance of an interaction.

The most prevalent persona in use on the Web, even for ostensibly trustworthy purposes, is the floating persona. This persona provides, or attempts to provide, identification primarily through experiential-identity. The floating persona has only indirect connection to a person's actual differential-identity. When we create an account on a server on the Web, during the enrollment process we may be asked for some set of experiential-identity information; perhaps a personal name, an address, an e-mail address or a telephone number.

In response to our enrollment information, the server allows us to obtain an account name and a password. The account name is the metaphorical reference to the experiential-identity registry formed by the account proper. The password subsequently functions as the differential-identity marker for the account. This persona has an obvious trust issue because the marker is not a strong credential of personal differential-identity. The general problem of **identity theft** is due to the ubiquitous use of personas of this type.

Identity theft is actually something of a misnomer. The act refers to obtaining and improperly using experiential-identity information about a person. It usually does not involve stealing the physiological differential-identity of a person. However, when information about a person allows one to create a new, floating persona in that person's name, then the damage is done. The real problem lies with enrollment in the registry where the floating persona is established. By not being grounded in true differential-identity, the registry allows improper use of the reputation of the person in question. This same improper use allows the experiential-identity of the person to be damaged in the process.

Finally, we come to the anchored persona. This is a persona that is firmly anchored to one's physiological differential-identity. An experiential-identity registry based on this persona has the highest potential level of trust of any of the personas. We say potential because the actual level of trust exhibited by any registry depends on the trust inherent in the authentication and authorization processes used to construct the registry. We'll get into the details of these processes in the next chapter.

Any of the personas that we've characterized can form the basis of an experiential-identity registry. By compartmentalizing our true experiential-identity into different registries, we achieve our greatest degree of personal privacy. The persona that we use in any specific social interaction becomes an issue for arbitration as the policy for the interaction is established. The general process of arbitration we term a **protocol**. We can define formal protocols as a way for entities with potentially conflicting interests to arrive at a common course of action that proceeds from a mutually agreed starting point. In social interactions, we often proceed on the basis of informal protocols that we perceive simply as accepted codes of behavior.

If a stranger stops us on the street and asks for the time, we're probably not too concerned with their presentation of an anonymous persona. If a stranger knocks on the door and asks to test drive the car we have for sale, we might seek to establish a more trustworthy basis for the interaction. If we want to consider actually engaging the interaction at all, we'll probably require a floating or anchored persona. We might even choose to go along for the ride.

We've defined four types of personas. They are types that people have used since the emergence of the species, although probably not under these names. We teach our children to "never talk to strangers", a reference to anonymity. We're cautious of previously unknown people that seek to involve themselves in certain situations. Are they "truly who they say they are"; or, are they merely presenting a situational persona?

If an initially unknown person presents herself repetitively and reliably then we might perceive her as someone we come to know, but that we don't "know everything about her." We perceive the person as a floating persona. Often, it seems that only if someone is charged with a crime do we gain knowledge of their experiential-identity derived from strong coupling to their differential-identity; that is, their anchored persona.

With that connection back to popular convention, let's now consider briefly how to establish such personas in the digital domain. Anonymity is perhaps the hardest to achieve. The major problem derives from the addressing mechanisms used on the Internet. Most networked devices have an address that can be repetitively and reliably determined. For virtually any interaction, a log is maintained somewhere on the network. Within that log is recorded the network addresses connected within the context of an interaction. This allows out-of-band mechanisms to be used to potentially attach a personal differential-identity to the network address used during the interaction.

Suppose you use your home computer to connect to a server on the network. You might create an account on that server with a bogus name, or you might simply use the name "anonymous." Even if the server requires no additional information, a transaction log on the server will typically store network addresses. If required to do so, perhaps by law enforcement, your Internet Service Provider (ISP) can connect an otherwise anonymous persona to the network address. This might lead through further connections to other information related to a floating or anchored persona. The best prospects for anonymity arise if one engages multiple chained interactions presenting an anonymous persona in each.

On the Internet, this facility has historically been provided through "anonymity servers." Such servers, often in a country that provides a social order more difficult for law enforcement to access, allow the creation of anonymous accounts. These services then function as source platforms for further network interactions. An interaction engaged with "someone" from such a source platform is presented with an extremely tenuous forensic wake.

Although it is grounded in analogue processes, we consider telephony to be in the digital realm. There are instances in which one wants to make an anonymous telephone call. Virtually any land-line, even a pay-phone, offers a non-trivial forensic wake. None-the-less, a pay-phone in a well traveled area offers a reasonable prospect for anonymity, at least in the digital domain. Pre-paid cellular telephones are probably the best option, although there is a forensic wake established when they're purchased.

If you want to make a truly anonymous phone call, you might try slipping a typed note and a hundred dollar bill under a solid fence to someone whose attention you attracted by banging a pipe on the fence. The note should ask that person to go into the convenience store down the street, purchase a pre-paid cellular telephone, and slip it back under the fence. Of course, if that actually works, you should perhaps just ask that person to make the phone call for you.

Establishing a situational persona in the digital domain is also somewhat problematic. Probably the most prevalent mechanism used in the digital realm is to steal the experiential-identity of someone else. If you successfully establish a floating persona using someone else's experiential-identity, then the result is a situational persona for you. The consequences of interactions will not become part of your experiential-identity; they will become part of the experiential-identity of the person you're impersonating.

Alternatively, you can establish a floating persona for a fictitious person. Such personas can be created by adopting source documents such as a birth certificate from other people; sometimes a person who is deceased. The issue with maintaining situational personas in this manner is making sure that your biometric characteristics are never associated with the persona. In the telephony realm, pre-paid cellular telephones are still the way to go.

In perhaps a less facetious vein, the most direct way to achieve a moderately effective situational persona is to prepare a laptop with this goal in mind. Don't establish any naming on the computer that provides links to your true differential-identity or experiential-identity. Then, make use of temporary network connections such as through an Internet café. In this manner, you can repetitively establish a level of identification, but a level that does not allow interaction consequences to be easily attributed to you.

Establishing a floating persona is quite straightforward. For anyone making use of legitimate accounts on the web, this is the persona that they engage every day. This is the persona of the credit card, the forerunner of identity tokens. Enrollment in a typical account will require entry of information derived from your experiential-identity: name, address, telephone number, driver license number, credit card number, etc. As a means of establishing greater trust in the account, cross-reference information is sometimes required, ostensibly to establish a more trusted association with differential-identify.

The most common piece of information used to cross-reference such accounts is an e-mail address. An e-mail address establishes an alternate point of network connectivity. In most instances, when you establish such accounts, you're allowed to create your own account name and password. Within this account, an experiential-identity registry may be maintained. Interaction consequences realized through this account will build upon the experiential-identity maintained within the account. Any connection to the differential-identity of a person derives from this experiential-identity. The connection is not established through authentication of the person's differential-identity.

Using a moderately technical process it is possible to establish a more trustworthy persona within the digital domain. This process makes use of a digital identification infrastructure to access differential-identity markers in a more trustworthy fashion. The most effective means today is through the use of computer based tokens such as **smart cards**.

A smart card token looks like a credit card, but with a very small computer embedded in the plastic. Through a metal pad on the face of the card, a computer to computer connection can be made between a host computer and the computer in the plastic card. The host computer has a reader device attached to it. By inserting the smart card into the reader, the computer to computer communication channel can be established.

The card token is intended to be carried by a person. Within an identification infrastructure, this token can be used as a credential to establish the differential-identity of the account, which is the manifestation of a persona that the person seeks to project. In so doing, the computer in the token uses cryptographic mechanisms to authenticate this differential-identity within the context of an interaction that is occurring somewhere within the network. Interaction consequences accrue to the account as experiential-identity of the persona. With that framework in mind, let's consider the most simple use of a digital token; storage of markers that can be used to authenticate differential-identity.

Earlier, we noted the use of credentials such as passwords or PINs as markers through which to authenticate differential-identity. Using a digital token, upon enrollment of an account in an identification system the account name and a password can be stored on the token by the differential-identity registry. When the token is later inserted into a reader attached to some host computer, the host can read the account name and password from the token and thereby authenticate the differential-identity of the account.

A token creates a persona for the card bearer and enhances the trust established through the authentication protocol by allowing the password to be longer and made up of a complex, essentially random set of characters; more than a person could normally remember. The password can actually be kept secret from the token bearer. So, the only way to obtain access to the account is to have the token in one's possession.

With this approach the token is strongly associated with the differential-identity of the account, but it is not strongly associated with the person in possession of the token. It is associated with the account name, not necessarily the person's name. The token containing the account and password information might, in fact, belong to someone else. The account's differential-identity is actually conveyed by possession of the token. So, we recognize this as the domain of the floating persona. When we seek to establish an anchored persona, the situation needs to be reversed. The differential-identity of the token bearer must somehow be instrumental in allowing the token to function on behalf of its bearer.

One way to effect this functionality is to make it necessary to enter a PIN before the token can provide the account and password to the host computer. We sometimes refer to this approach as using a PIN to lock the token. Now the token bearer has to remember the PIN, which might seem quite similar to remembering the password in the first place. In fact, a PIN is typically shorter and easier to remember. The smart card computer can limit the number of attempts made to specify the PIN. So, if the rightful owner of a token happens to lose it, this limitation prevents someone who finds it from trying to guess the PIN. These are mechanisms that we're all familiar with in using our ATM cards.

In the United States, tokens used in ATM machines are typically not smart cards. Rather, they store information such as account and password information on magnetic stripes on the back side of the cards, not in a computer embedded in the card. Unfortunately, if the bit stream between the token and the host computer, for example an ATM machine, can be intercepted, the token itself can be duplicated.

Without a computer platform in the token, information flow cannot be dynamically encrypted. If the PIN can be intercepted through some type of scam or clandestine observation, the duplicated token becomes usable. With a smart card, even if the PIN can be obtained, it is necessary to also obtain the token because the computer based information cannon be readily accessed and duplicated. However, if the token is stolen, even a smart card token can be used by someone other than the actual owner of the token if they have the associated PIN. So, with this as preface, let's move on to the anchored persona.

The anchored persona is the basic means by which the family and small social orders learn to know one another. It is a persona that is grounded in the biometrics of the individual person. In small social orders, provisioning is done through pair-wise interactions involving the members of the group. Experiential-identity accumulates in the memories of the participants and reputation becomes a part of future interactions based on those memories.

The goal of digital identification systems is to extend the anchored persona across the expanse of wide area computer networks. To establish and use an anchored persona, a token utilizing the biometrics of the token bearer to lock and unlock the token is a highly trusted technique. The mechanisms to achieve this capability are central to the realization of privacy in the digital domain. That is the subject of our next chapter.

4 *Privacy in a Digital World*

Personal privacy manifests as provisioning; the development and personalization of the metaphorical models that constitute our identity perceived by others. In the sensori-motor world, stimulated by our individual motivations, we assert privacy utilizing a number of physical, physiological and social mechanisms that form the domain of personal interactions. Tools allow us to extend this domain. Using these mechanisms, and tools to amplify them, we address the distinct facets of interactions.

Privacy's provisioning affords control over interactions. To assert privacy is to assert control over all the facets of an interaction, concluding in the personal ownership of the final consequences. We attempt to accomplish this control using only our physiological and social capabilities. To achieve similar affect in the digital domain of computers and their networks, we bring a variety of technological facilities to bear. Using these facilities, we can implement mechanisms that allow us to establish an environment of trust. In turn, this environment enables us to assert privacy and achieve a more comprehensive level of control of the various parts of an interaction.

Mechanisms of Privacy

The mechanisms through which privacy is pursued include **opacity**, **integrity**, **identity**, **authority** and **attribution**. Each of these contributes to the ability to exert control over interactions and thus guide them toward desired consequences. As preface to examining them in a bit more detail, let's begin by refreshing our understanding of the facets of personal interactions that we introduced in the first chapter: **context**, **cognition**, **action**, **consequence** and **memory**. We'll start by observing that an interaction occurs within a context which encompasses all the other facets.

Provisioning the context of an interaction is often accomplished through other interactions, a function of the inherent recursive nature of interactions. Physical, physiological and social constraints on sensory observation and physiological motor actions are applied within the context. Participants are authenticated and the authority for their participation is established within the context. Policy which defines social forces is established within the context through some form of arbitration of privacy infringement among the participants and any encompassing social order.

Context is shaped by the motivations of the participants, each of whom seeks to realize specific consequences from the interaction. As we defined the term in the first chapter, cognition is the fundamental process of the mind that manifests as **observation**, **assessment**, **understanding**, **motivation**, and **action-invocation** in sensori-motor reality. Thus, motivation derives from past provisioning that established the metaphorical models that cognition embraces and that calibrate our personal subjective decision making. Personal motivations can be impacted by the constraints of policy that elicit altruistic actions.

Once the context is in place, cognition provides an assessment of trust by each of the participants. Trust is the probability that an anticipated consequence will result from a specific action.

Depending on the level of trust individually determined, each participant evokes actions aimed to achieve their desired consequences.

While the interaction begins with the establishment of context, it will not produce observable consequences until actions are invoked. They proceed until consequences are achieved. Integral to consequences are the resulting sensations perceived by the participants. These sensations are then given persistence and disseminated through individual memories and expressions.

Memories of an interaction's progression, including any resulting consequences and derived sensations, are formed individually by the participants. Some consequences have physical form; that is, compositions presented through art-forms. All of these memories and any physical manifestations of consequences comprise a forensic wake. Through a forensic wake, it may be possible to reconstruct some or all the facets of an interaction after the fact. In many situations, social policy can require post-action adjudication to affirm that any derived consequences are valid under the effective social policy. This may precipitate a process to assess truths that can be derived from the forensic wake.

Truth is the probability that a consequence is the result of an action, and hence of a defined context within which the action occurred. To assess truth, one weighs the anticipated versus the actual consequences. Knowing the truth enhances future interaction engagement by building a correlation between trust and truth for a specific interaction. In this manner, one can continually improve the metaphorical models for interactions through which trust and truth are determined. The same holds for social engagements. Societal benefit accrues when shared metaphorical models are enhanced through a valid determination of truth.

Whether personal or social, the recursive invocation of metaphorically similar interactions offers the prospect of enhancing the assessment of probability of achieving desired outcomes. As we are able to relate truth to trust in specific cases, we improve our ability to successfully engage subsequent interactions. Thus, as we do the same or similar things over and over again, we tend to get better at them. With these points in mind, we can now consider the details of the mechanisms used to realize privacy.

We define opacity as the **resolution of sensory observation**. It is a measure of the ability to observe the facets of an interaction. The degree of opacity can range from transparent to opaque; from totally observable to totally cloaked. A cloaked interaction cannot be observed by an entity located outside its context. Opacity is achieved through a variety of means, ranging from physical barriers to social policy that constrains information dissemination. One of the great fallacies in current conceptualizations of privacy is the conflating of privacy with opacity.

In common terms, an interaction is often classified as either public or private. A public interaction is open for the world to see. A private interaction is hidden from public view. The implication is one cannot assert privacy in a public interaction. Even the courts have fallen into this trap by observing "an expectation of privacy", or a lack thereof, in certain situations. In contrast, we observe that privacy is first and foremost about control. Control may invoke varying levels of opacity, but control is not necessarily lost when secrecy is compromised.

Transparency does not necessarily constitute a loss of privacy. A woman who is publicly observed to be pregnant still retains the absolute right of privacy to decide to have an abortion during the first trimester of gestation. Likewise, keeping information secret does not necessarily qualify its concealment as a valid expression of privacy, nor does its publication necessarily mean it is no longer possible to assert privacy's control over it. In the digital realm, it is quite plausible to exert control over widely disseminated information; especially, since control is synonymous with ownership.

The digital realm of computers and their networks, as iconically represented by the World Wide Web and the Internet, allows the establishment of small social orders that are widely distributed in time and space across the network. Through the Web, a collection of people who share some common but perhaps arcane interests can form a coherent community. While there might be only one member of such a community in a city, across a collection of cities the community can be quite substantial. Through digital mechanisms, this community can realize all of the characteristics of personal privacy and social order found in the geographically defined communities that are cities. This particular facility will be of interest in the next chapter when we consider certain Supreme Court decisions that are couched in the concept of communities and the characteristics that they display; particularly as regards the establishment of community standards.

From a personal privacy perspective, an interaction should be structured so as to allow an accurate anticipation of its outcome. Specifically, we seek outcomes that fulfill our personal motivations. The mechanisms that we use in the conduct of interactions are largely about trust. Integrity refers to a set of mechanisms whose purpose is to establish a sound basis for the assessment of trust. Integrity mechanisms are all aimed at the validity of contextual information in an interaction. Looking across the various action domains, integrity encompasses the accuracy of information, the source of information, the immutability of information and the persistence of information related to an interaction.

In the third chapter, we characterized identity in terms of two distinct facets: differential-identity and experiential-identity. There are a variety of mechanisms through which we can address the authentication of differential-identity and the trustworthy attribution of experiential-identity. Trust derives from the ability to distinguish the participants of an interaction through authentication and to experience the sensation of reputation for each based on attribution.

Attribution encompasses the establishment of external memories from a specific interaction; what we earlier termed compositions. Credentials of non-repudiation are trustworthy compositions. They can attribute consequences of an interaction to differential-identity, thereby forming a trustworthy episode of experiential-identity; an externally persistent, trusted memory if you will.

Within a comprehensive interaction context, actions stem from physical, physiological or social forces. The authority to evoke an action derives from the domain specific facilities of **contact**, **capability** and **consent**. Contact is a concept of the natural ecosystem indicating that a specific action is physically possible. It refers to authority realized through physical processes. The concept of supernatural derives from a non-contact basis of action; that is, actions not grounded in well understood natural or physical processes. A supernatural authority defies our usual facilities for assessing trust and truth. Therefore, we view consideration of such authority as primarily religious in nature.

Capability indicates a physiological ability to perform an action; for example, being able to dunk a basketball. This authority is necessary to engage a trusted interaction aimed at dunking a basketball; for example, participating in a slam-dunk contest. Finally, consent encompasses the social facility of being allowed, under the applicable social policy, to invoke a specific action; for example, having an FAA license to pilot a commercial aircraft.

Authority is central to the establishment of covenants. An unconditional covenant is a promise of future consideration. It only has meaning if one has the capability and also consents to fulfill the promise. A conditional covenant is an agreement to exchange things of comparable value; consideration offered for consideration received. It is an assertion that the conditions of the covenant can be met and the covenant thus fulfilled. It is difficult to address failed unconditional covenants through policy since the values of remedial actions are difficult to determine if a promise goes unfulfilled. On the other hand, conditional covenants have remedial value built in.

Value is an external expression of esteem that offers a form of authority. The value of what is offered and the value of what is received are subject to the negotiation of the interaction participants. Some social orders establish a standardized means for stating value; for example, money. Money offers a means to compare the relative value of dissimilar things. It can be used in conditional covenants in which what is offered and what is to be received are dissimilar. One might exchange labor for money and then exchange money for food; or, one might "work for food."

Attribution is the remembrance of interaction processes and consequences through the expression of compositions. Attribution is an indication of truth because it can connect consequences with differential-identity, which manifests as the concept we know as experiential-identity. Attribution is a facet of reputation. In the course of interactions in the absence of tools, attribution is mostly about the memories formed in the minds of interaction participants. If tools are brought into the picture, and we include as tools the physiological forms of language such as speech or writing, then the concept of credentials become important to attribution; particularly, to trustworthy attribution.

Privacy in the Sensori-Motor World

The causes and effects of interactions in the sensori-motor world are born to the mind through sensations derived from sensory observation. We use our physiological motor system to affect the mechanisms of experiences. In this way, we seek to mold the outcome of interactions. While we use senses and motor actions in complex combinations, let's consider them in orthogonal isolation in an attempt to better understand their uses. In general, the human sensory system is largely about understanding interaction context while the motor system is largely about tailoring it to our individual liking.

There are two motivational extremes that have been the forcing functions for evolutionary development of species: that of the predator and that of its prey. While there is a lot of room between the extremes, when we adopt one or the other of these perspectives it serves to guide our approaches to establishing context and to the invocation of actions. It is useful to consider sensory observation from the perspective of offensive needs of the predator or defensive capabilities required by prey and the motor system facilities that each needs to achieve its desired ends.

In humans, the eyes are preeminently offensive in form and function. Positioned at the front of the head, they offer binocular vision from which can be derived depth perception. These sensory facilities enhance the predator's abilities to locate, stalk and attack prey. The eye's location allows huge volumes of sensory input data to be fed into the nearby brain through the optic nerve. Massively parallel neural processing then enables hierarchical analysis of visual images for subsequent interpretation through relevant metaphorical models. Thus, a powerful approach to establishing interaction context is through visually surveying the surrounding environment.

Four of the five primary senses are centered at the head. This offers observation from a location as far off the ground as a human can establish without external tools; a location somewhat removed from observational clutter. The ears, positioned on the side of the head, are well suited for defense. By moving the head while listening, the direction to the source of sounds can be determined. The eyes can move independently of the head, so both offensive and defensive postures can be simultaneously supported. Hearing and seeing are often complementary senses; we might see something in the distance long before we can hear it and we can hear things in the dark that we're unable to see. Used in combination, the ears can suggest to the eyes where to look for either pending danger, or for the next opportunity to find lunch.

The sense of smell provides indirect observation of context. In general, human olfactory facilities are insufficient to approximate the predatory tracking prowess of wolves. Neither is the human sense of smell as good a defensive mechanism as might be found in rabbits as they seek to avoid the wolf. In humans, the sense of smell is often more useful in assessing whether food is safe to eat than in locating the food in the first place; or, in establishing that a predator is lurking nearby. Used in concert with the other senses, smell offers a nuanced assessment of context and it is a powerful index for interaction memories. Distinct odors are often quite effective in recalling certain memories.

For humans, the senses of touch and taste offer very fine grained analyses of context; not only is this food safe to eat, but it's easy to chew and it tastes good. More important from the standpoint of predator or prey, touch and taste offer sensory observations of the surrounding environment within the physiological perimeter of maximum threat or opportunity. In general, they are closely aligned with sensations that engage the fight or flight response. They offer assessment of context at its most profound; when the ultimate consequence of life or death is literally at the tip of the fingers, or at least within arm's reach.

We use the sensations derived from sensory observation in making value judgments on all aspects of a pending interaction. The calibration of the scale of value assessment is based on our prior provisioning. Our goal in any interaction is to achieve a desired consequence; where desirable is defined by sensations that reflect our individual motivations. Our assessment of trust determines whether we think the outcome probability is sufficient for us to invoke action. Our establishment of context is setting the stage for trust assessment.

A second step in our establishing context, and a significant aspect of our ultimate assessment of trust, is the evaluation of options for our possible action(s). In the absence of other people, or a social context for a specific interaction, the forces in play through which we effect action are going to be physical or physiological. As we assess context, the metaphorical models through which we're interpreting sensory observations provides a judgment of actions that are physically plausible and actions of which we are physiologically capable, or at least of which we believe we're capable.

If we engage an interaction with others under the auspices of a social context, then social forces come into play. When context encompasses multiple participants to an interaction, identification of those participants becomes a part of context assessment. To accomplish identification we make use of what we perceive to be the trusted processes of differential-identity authentication and experiential-identity reputation assessment. Keyed to this identification, we also invoke various means of authorization.

If we're faced by a masked person with a gun threatening us in a dark alley, our authentication and reputation assessment is likely to be far more emphatic than if we're faced with a person seeking to provide us with financial investment advice. Authority often flows from the barrel of a gun in the physical domain, while credentials showing a fat bank account or a sterling record of investment success lend greater authority in the social domain; although, guns are sometimes used as authority to make impromptu bank withdrawals. The point to be noted is that authority is one aspect of the constraint on forces within an interaction context. The more varied aspects of authority will derive from the effective policy to be applied to social interactions.

A human life can be perceived as one continuous interaction; we're born, we live, we die. Viewed from a thousand years later the details have been lost. Conversely, a human life can be perceived as a vast collection of minute physical engagements; seemingly random events from which it is daunting to extract meaning. Such is the span from the cosmological to the quantum mechanical. The granularity we seek falls into the more readily conceptualized middle; a granularity that we might perceive as the happenings of everyday life. Consequently, our interests are primarily with social interactions, and at the very least, we'd like to understand interactions at the level of **legal cases**.

In general, interaction context will vary smoothly as we go about our daily lives. This is the result of the mind's application of metaphorical models that seek to minimize surprise in sensory observation. We tend to move from one context to the next with an aim to minimize being surprised. When some observation occurs that is significantly out of context, the mind is forced to reorient its guiding model. In the world of predator versus prey, it is to the benefit of the predator to not force a context transition on the prey. Conversely, it is to the benefit of the prey to have a rather tightly constrained range within which observations do not register as surprising; anything outside this range is an attention grabber.

How we seek to control context is first influenced by whether we initiate an interaction, or whether an interaction is forced on us. To a certain extent, this looks like the dichotomy between predator and prey. Our subsequent behavior is guided by that first step. If it's a bright, sunny afternoon on a well populated street and we see someone we know and approach them, our level of surprise in the interaction is minimal; after all, we started it.

If we're approached by a person that we do not know, we may register a bit more surprise. If that person when still a few feet away, says "Excuse me?" it is still likely within our comfort zone. We allow them to approach us and engage in conversation. However, if it's late at night, on a dark street, we might well attempt to avoid allowing someone to approach too close to us; we might even quickly walk to the other side of the street to avoid them.

Consider another situation; perhaps one that's more typical. We are engaged by someone that we ostensibly know. In this case, again assuming that we don't find ourselves in a surprising context, we will subliminally apply a variety of biometric authentication checks to confirm that this is the person that we think we know. Based on our previous experiences with this person, we will engage an interaction based on our sensation of their reputation.

If the other person wants to chat, we may not be terribly sensitive to their reputation. If they want to borrow money, we'll probably be more circumspect. A bit more extreme, if our past experiences with them suggest that they might choose to attack us, then we'll react accordingly. But, what if we don't directly know the other person?

Suppose we're approached by a total stranger. We don't recognize their face and we don't know their name. So, we start to look for indicators that allow us to bring some particular metaphorical model into play; one that we might use to help in our assessment of trust. We do this through the application of standard protocols. These are collections of behaviors that experience has shown us to be effective at addressing potential threats.

Some behaviors we learned from our family and friends. Some we learned from observing others; a hand-me-down facility from our *Homo erectus* ancestors. Some we might have been taught in school or in special classes. All derive from our past provisioning. A mainstay of such protocols is the credential. Uniforms are useful in this respect.

Uniforms are credentials from which we can derive trust through cursory attribution and assessment of authority. If we're approached by someone in a police officer's uniform, we typically attribute a positive assessment of their reputation and their authority; unless we're in the midst of a criminal act. If we're approached by someone wearing a ski mask, our assessments will likely be more negative.

Unfortunately, it's at this level that stereotypes often come into play. The uniform provided by one's skin color, ethnicity or gender is sometimes used as a credential indicative of a stereotype. Any single or minimal set of characteristics not related to the specific context of an interaction can fall into the realm of stereotypes. Stereotypes are credentials that sometimes offer little actual credence.

In the absence of a uniform, we might engage a different protocol. For example, we might strike up a preliminary conversation in order to obtain a name or other salient information from the person. If a name, we might then seek some indirect connection between this person and someone else that we know. If we have heard an old friend talk about this newly met person, our old friend offers the authentication and authority of a **trusted third party**. "The friend of my friend is my friend; the enemy of my friend is my enemy." The reputation of the trusted third party is indirectly applied to the previously unknown person. Thus, since we have a well established calibration of our level of trust in the third party, by reference we have a better measure of the newly met stranger.

Language and cultural references conveyed through language can also be used as credentials. During the Battle of the Bulge toward the end of World War II, clandestine enemy units dressed in American army uniforms were secreted behind the lines of battle. The enemy units had valid uniforms and they spoke excellent English and played havoc with rear echelons. To defend against this threat, American troops made use of impromptu protocols in the form of conversations related to current cultural characteristics. "Who won the World Series last year?" "What's the City of the Big Shoulders?" In the Pacific Theater, American marines used personnel who were members of the

Navajo tribe to talk on radios on the battlefield. The Navajo language is quite arcane and essentially provided a form of analogue encryption allowing communication in the face of adversaries.

Lacking a known person who can function as a trusted third party, sometimes a stranger can present credentials to us that establish authentication and then authority from some more formal entity that we trust. This brings us into the domain of tools such as tokens; for example, a badge or a driver license. Either can establish credence if issued by a trusted third party and it's a party that we know and can recognize their tokens of credence. In some instances, simply having possession of the token is meant to convey credence; for example, a badge. In other instances, having some biometric image on the token that links it to the specific person is used; for example, a driver license with a picture of the license holder.

A significant credential of authority is money. In purely financial transactions, cash conveys authority from a buyer to a seller. Under the auspices of their personal privacy, one owns currency and the other owns something they're willing to exchange for currency. When they interact, the effective policy that derives from the arbitration of the intersection of their individual privacy is a conditional covenant.

To conclude the covenant, money is exchanged for the item that is for sale. If the amount is substantial, then the seller might give a bill of sale credential to the buyer, indicating a transfer of ownership of the item. The seller can maintain a record of the sale, showing what was sold and how much currency was collected. These become credentials of attribution and non-repudiation of the interaction.

Tokens that establish credence have been used for millennia. Over time, they have evolved to convey identity and attribution as well as authority. Networks of trusted third parties such as banks or legal facilities have enabled interactions among widely distributed communities. The Knights Templar established a comprehensive network of trusted third parties, enabling the organization to provide one of the earliest forms of international banking. In the digital realm, tokens are beginning to take on an enhanced role; that of **avatars**.

In the Vaishnava tradition of the Hindu religion, the god Vishnu sometimes deigns to descend from heaven and walk among men as an avatar. From this perspective, an avatar is an incarnation of a god among men. A more mundane definition says that an avatar is the manifestation of an individual in an environment distinct from her normal realm of existence.

In John Cameron's movie *Avatar*, hybrid individuals are grown by melding human DNA with that of the Navi; indigenous humanoid creatures of the planet Pandora. These avatars are remotely linked to the central nervous system of human avatar drivers. Through this physiological manifestation, *Homo sapiens* can fully engage the world of the Navi. This is a pretty good illustration of what we seek in today's digital world.

Games have long used avatars, either to represent the players or to represent the game itself. In various games of "ball", sometimes the ball iconically is the game. The more representative case for our purposes is the use of avatars as symbols to represent participants. With children playing the board game *Monopoly*, the selection of game pieces to represent each player is often more contentious than the game itself. It seems that someone always wants to be the racecar; god forbids that someone else wants to be the racecar too!

Computer games have long allowed their players to interact with the game's environment, and with each other, through avatars. In many games, the initial activity of the player is to personalize an avatar through which they will engage the digital world in which play occurs. In multi-user games, the various participants interact with each other's avatars.

In many such games, the avatar is simply constructed by the player. An avatar might be formed by player selection of characteristics; somewhat like constructing a sandwich from a table of ingredients and condiments. In other cases, the characteristics of the avatar might evolve through the consequences of players' interactions within the game. In this latter approach, the avatar is a result of provisioning by the player. It is an identity provisioned through the expressions of the player's choices within the context of the game.

Privacy through Digital Technology

To bridge the concept of personal privacy found in the sensori-motor world to the mechanisms of privacy in the digital world, we can use the concept of avatars to personify the digital self. We considered this approach in some detail in our earlier book *Computer Theology*. There we referred to a more general construct termed the **transcendent personal device**; a device able to map the human sensori-motor system into the digital domain. From the perspective of interaction mechanics, several general facilities of personal privacy must be available to the avatar if it is to act as a transcendent personal device.

First, privacy suggests that an individual controls or seeks to control the context of any interaction the individual engages. Within this context, the individual controls or seeks to control the invocation of action and the continuing application of forces for the duration of the interaction. The motivation for provisioning the context and invoking the action derives from what the person perceives to be a desirable consequence. The degree of control that a person has of an interaction contributes to that person's level of ownership of its consequences.

We can view the digital domain of computers and their resulting networks as a recursive extension of the physical ecosystem. While obviously subject to the real world's forces, the digital domain extends that ecosystem on a logical and metaphorical plane to provide a virtual reality comparable, yet subordinate, to purely physical reality. Computers and their networks comprise a collection of art-forms. More than virtually any other tool or system of tools, they encompass societal expressions that are aimed at the persistence and distribution of metaphorical understanding.

Much as roads and highways exist as physical means to support social interactions subject to policy, computers and their networks provide similar support in a digital realm. They are likewise subordinate to the rules, regulations and laws put in place by social order. However, the digital world does not yet offer a comprehensive, ubiquitous basis of support for social interactions, lacking as it does consistent analogues of the physiological mechanisms for the trusted arbitration and arbitrage of personal privacy. Technologies are available, but their application is as yet insufficient for the task. With the goal of correcting this insufficiency, let's consider how to get from here to there.

Only when the relevant mechanisms are grounded in an effective trust infrastructure can the control desired from an assertion of privacy be truly realized. Consequently, a digital framework must first establish a basis of trust. From a technical perspective, this usually proceeds from a point of causality derived from the inherent facilities of one or more computer platforms. The framework can subsequently extend this basis, enabling a trusted domain within which interactions can occur. Erecting the framework from this foundation, trusted processes can provide the means to provision the context for the interaction proper.

Once a basis of trust is established, a digital framework must next put in place a trustworthy place of action; something we'll refer to as the **interaction focus**. This is the metaphorical point at which a digital interaction can be perceived to occur; essentially, its procedural context. We speak of a metaphorical point because computers and networks allow for the distribution of interaction components across a broad expanse, both in physical location as well as in time.

The interaction focus encompasses the art-forms through which distribution is realized. In particular, the registries found at the heart of identification systems are prime examples of such art-forms. The registries are typically realized through the technologies of data-bases and knowledge-bases which support the archiving of complex collections of compositions. Data-bases store the fundamental information of digital interactions. Knowledge-bases also associate the relevant actions applicable to that information.

Data-bases enable the conveyance from the present to the future of "digital sensations", which we recognize as experiences. Knowledge-bases provide means to convey "metaphorical understanding" realized from those experiences; tools of mimesis if you will. The markers, keys and identifiers that we discussed in the third chapter provide the means to relate experiences across distributed registries. By allowing malleable references to such experiences and metaphorical understanding, these technologies can be thought of as culture enablers. They are central to forming distributed cognitive-cultural networks in the digital realm.

Just as with social interactions in the sensori-motor world, within the confines of the interaction focus the mechanisms of privacy must be addressed to exploit the basis for trust on which the application and consequences of the ensuing actions depend. Included are some or all of: **opacity**, **integrity**, **identity**, **authority** and **attribution**. Historically, these facilities have evolved in the digital domain under the guise of **computer** or **network security**. Let's examine them in more detail from a digital perspective as we consider their respective roles in establishing and conveying the trust on which privacy is ultimately grounded.

Opaqueness encompasses the means to shield from external observation the information and processes found within the interaction focus. This enhances control, which is the primary goal of privacy. If the details of a pending interaction are invisible outside the interaction focus, the risk of compromise is greatly diminished. Thus, an interaction can proceed substantially from the information found within the context at the start of the interaction. Similarly, if the integrity or trustworthiness of this information can be assured, including its source and whether it changes during the course of the interaction, then correctly anticipating the outcome of the interaction is more likely.

The framework must support authentication of any of the personas discussed in the previous chapter, thereby providing the means to determine and enforce social policy. It must provide facilities for ownership to be established and then exported beyond the context of the interaction. To bring closure to the interaction, the framework must provide mechanisms to finalize consequences based on the policy under which the interaction occurred. This includes facilities for action control and consequence adjudication. To this end, the participants must be recognized as deictic centers within the interaction focus.

A deictic center is a point of personal, spacial, temporal and policy reference; a point with respect to which we can establish orientation of each of the relevant facets of interactions. It is how we define **who**, **where** and **when**. It lets us differentiate **here** from **there**, **now** from **then** and **one** from **another**. By referencing deictic centers, the interaction focus can establish which rules apply and thus which forces apply. As interactions progress, trusted protocols come into play. Points of reference, along with orientation and directionality from such points, allow the protocols to convey trust among the points.

In deference to the consideration of protocols, it is useful to characterize a couple of the roles to be played by the deictic centers of interaction participants. The first is that of the **sentinel**; the keeper and protector of the interaction. The second is the **supplicant**; one that seeks or succumbs to association with the sentinel through an interaction. There may, in fact, be several supplicants engaged in an interaction. The role of the sentinel is oriented towards policy while that of each supplicant is oriented towards privacy. The sentinel comprises one deictic center while the supplicant(s) comprises the other(s).

In the simplest of social interactions, that involving two individuals, one can act as sentinel while the other acts as supplicant. For a completely symmetric interaction, each individual may have to act both as sentinel as well as supplicant. In this situation, as each takes the role of sentinel, they must establish through arbitration a shared responsibility for the integrity of the interaction. In some instances, a true sentinel may guard the interaction involving two or more supplicants.

This scenario introduces the concept of a trusted third party that can convey trust among diverse individuals. Each supplicant establishes a bond of trust with the sentinel, and through the sentinel they come to find trust in each other. It is the purpose of the sentinel to guard and affirm authority within the context of the interaction. It is also the role of the sentinel to effect attribution of interaction consequences among the appropriate participants.

If information pertinent to an interaction must be imported across the boundary of the interaction focus, the trustworthiness of the importation processes must be established. The authority of the various participants must also be established. The ultimate consequence will be derived within the context and made part of the interaction registry in a fashion that cannot be later repudiated by the participants.

From within the established bounds of the interaction focus, the consequences of the interaction are expressed in a trustworthy fashion within the experiential-identity registries of the participants. Finally, the ownership of interaction consequences is appropriately attributed to the participants within the interaction focus. To convey this ownership beyond the interaction focus also requires trusted processes.

We begin the construction of the interaction focus on the computer platform that supports the presence of the sentinel for the interaction. In order to consider the more general network aspects of interactions in the digital domain, we'll assume that each supplicant is present on a different computer platform. Thus, each participant is represented within the interaction focus by a digital surrogate whose primary purpose is ostensibly to act at the behest of a single participant. The digital surrogate is the computer platform and its salient software that each participant trusts to act on their behalf in the digital realm.

The platforms are connected by a communication pathway, perhaps a network link. We will use the facilities of computer and network security to effect an interaction focus that encompasses all these platforms. As a foundation, we have assumed that the platforms are intrinsically trusted. That is, we affirm as a point of causality that the platforms are under the complete control of the sentinel in one case and the supplicant in the other. We affirm that there are no clandestine monitoring facilities on either platform. One might wonder, on what basis do we make such affirmation? It is certainly not typically true of computer platforms as they are used today for digital interactions.

On a computer platform, as on any machine, the capability to exert total control over the operation of the platform is an issue of architecture and construction. Measuring the validity of construction as a faithful rendition of architecture requires the provision of pervasive, integrated testing facilities. This requires that one must examine the machine from beyond the boundaries of its implementation and operation in order to establish the degree to which it is secure from intrusive observation and control as part of its architecture and construction. Only from this perspective can it be discerned whether there are clandestine means of observation and control embedded in the machine. If observation can only be achieved through **in-band** processes, it is virtually impossible to detect the existence of **out-of-band** mechanisms and to assess their capabilities.

So, we begin with intrinsically trusted computer platforms. We discern their inherent characteristics through trusted third parties that can examine and certify the characteristics and then issue credentials affirming such certification. When any two trusted computers are linked through a communication channel, we always assume that the connection is suspect. In virtually all cases, it is possible, if not probable, for clandestine listeners to observe the information streams that flow between the platforms. The mechanisms employed by these clandestine listeners can be incredibly innovative!

During the cold war, Americans eavesdropped on Soviet telephone traffic through inductive coupling to subsea cables accessible only with nuclear submarines. The Soviets reciprocated by bugging the concrete used in constructing the American Embassy in Moscow. In the case of complex networks, it is considered a virtual certainty that someone is listening. It is in this environment that we want to better understand the mechanisms through which to achieve some level of computer, network and interaction security. Only in this way can true personal privacy be asserted by the participants to the interaction in question.

We continue our consideration of digital security mechanisms with opacity. While we've previously noted that opacity is often conflated with privacy, in fact they are quite orthogonal. Though opaqueness can be used to achieve some aspects of privacy, privacy can be effectively realized without opaqueness. Opacity can be used to subvert privacy and privacy can be used to subvert opacity. As we suggested in looking at basic human physiological mechanics, opacity would seem to derive from the stealth practiced by predator and prey, while privacy seems more akin to the fight or flight response.

The simplest example of an interaction focus is comprised of two secure, trusted computer platforms connected by a suspect communication channel. The sentinel exerts control on one platform and the supplicant exerts control on the other. We want to establish a fully shielded context that encompasses the two. Ron Rivest, a pioneer of security techniques, suggests this is the domain of **cryptography**, which he defines as "trusted communication in the presence of adversaries." By cryptographically processing information that flows between the two, any eavesdroppers on the communication channel are less able to discern any specific information. By sending superfluous information across the channel, it is possible to disguise even the occurrence of the interaction.

One method of cryptographic processing is digital encryption; a means of modulating a coherent stream of information bits to form a stream of essentially random bits. The coherent stream is referred to as plain-text and the random bit stream is referred to as cipher-text. An inverse operation called digital decryption restores the original coherent stream of information bits from the stream of random bits. To accomplish the two complementary operations requires a computational algorithm, a computer program if you will, and a shared key on each computer platform.

A key in this context is simply a set of bits that can be used as a parameter in the encryption and decryption computations. The metaphor derives from that of a locked door in which a key is used to lock or unlock the door. The program on one computer makes use of the key to encrypt a stream of information bits, yielding a random bit stream; a locking operation. The program on the other computer makes use of the same key to decrypt the random bit stream and reconstitute the original information bit stream; an unlocking operation.

By allowing other programs on the two platforms to exchange information through the encrypted channel, eavesdroppers are less able to discern salient information. A shared domain of secrecy is thus established encompassing both computer platforms and the suspect communication channel that connects the two. It sounds high tech, and it is, but the basic concepts have actually been around for a few millennia. The desired results can be accomplished largely with wax and clay. The sealing wax, signet rings and clay bullae used in the earliest recorded civilizations have much the same purpose; to allow trusted communication in the presence of adversaries.

One might wonder how two independent computer platforms can obtain the same key such that they are able to establish this domain of secrecy throughout the interaction focus. As it happens, there are mathematical algorithms that can be engaged by the programs on the two platforms allowing them to determine a shared key, even though they have no intimate knowledge of each other. One such method is the *Diffie-Hellman Key Exchange* protocol. It's important to note that the key derived from this protocol is not suitable for authenticating differential-identity of either of the two platforms. The key changes each time the two platforms engage a communication channel, so it's only useful for establishing secrecy.

The mathematics involved in this protocol is of less interest than is simply its existence. One can consult Bruce Schneier's book *Applied Cryptography* to learn the mathematical details. Suffice it to say, such protocols form the basis of secret communication between Web browsers and Web servers across the Internet. Neither browser nor server knows in advance any specific details of the other and yet they are able to establish a zone of secrecy surrounding them both by arriving at a common key used to encrypt and decrypt the communication channel that connects them.

Shared secrecy among other programs on the two trusted computer platforms enables the enhancement of the interaction focus to the extent that it is distributed across both platforms. The main limitation to this extension is that the highest level of trust that can be established throughout the interaction focus is dependent on the minimum level of trust intrinsic to either of the platforms themselves. So, once a shroud of secrecy can be cast on the interaction focus, it next becomes necessary to look at the trustworthiness of the salient information on which the pending interaction is based. With that in mind, let's consider how trust in information is established and then maintained throughout the interaction focus; a characteristic of computer and network security that we refer to as information integrity.

On computers, we can express information as compositions in an art-form known simplistically as a **string of bits**. The most basic aspect of information integrity is then to confirm that a bit string does not change over time. By maintaining a copy of a composition in an archive, a registry if you will, at any future time we can compare the current form of the composition to its archived copy. If they are different, then the integrity of the information is suspect. Information integrity also involves the accuracy and the trustworthiness of the information itself. Hence, we seek to reliably know the source of the information; its point of causality if you will.

To establish the validity of information, it is often necessary to know its source or to have a third party that we trust vouch for the information in question. This is obviously a requirement that we be able to authenticate differential-identities within the interaction focus and to reliably attribute information to that differential-identity. Then, we must be able to affirm that such information has not been changed since its source was determined.

Affirmation often begins outside of the interaction focus in which it is to be used. It derives as a consequence of an interaction in its own right. Mechanisms to assure integrity allow the trustworthy transfer of information across the boundaries of diverse interactions. The transfer of an entire composition from an archive can be inefficient in terms of consumption of resources and time required to assess integrity. So, let's first concentrate on how we can efficiently detect changes in information and then come back to the issue of authenticating the source of information and the impact of trust established through third parties.

A fundamental technology used to assess information integrity in the digital domain is the same as that used to achieve secrecy; cryptography. In order to efficiently determine whether information changes over time, we use a variety of cryptographic algorithms, including some called one-way hash codes. A hash code algorithm is applied to a digital bit stream of arbitrary length. From this arbitrarily long bit string, the algorithm calculates a much shorter, fixed length bit string; typically 120 bits long. This shorter bit string is called a hash code. It is sensitive to the order and number of information bits in the original string. Hence, a hash code can be used as a quantitative symbol representing the actual composition in question.

Being much shorter than the composition itself, and being of fixed length, the hash code is much easier to use in subsequent operations to determine whether the composition has been altered. For a composition comprised of a string of bits and bytes, once a hash code is established we can subsequently determine whether any of the bits that make up the composition has changed. We simply apply the algorithm again to recalculate the hash code. If it is different from that originally calculated, then the composition has changed. This establishes whether information integrity is intact, or has become suspect. If we can also associate the hash code with trusted indicators of time and location then we're able to attest to the integrity of the composition at some fixed location and at some fixed time.

Implicit in our consideration of information integrity is the concept of message structure, or messaging. It is necessary to associate the information whose integrity is in question with its hash code. We make this association through a concatenation of collections of bits into well defined sequences that we call messages. Messages are subsequently associated together by protocols through which interactions in the digital domain occur.

As noted, we can use a one-way hash code to determine whether information has changed over time. We can use an enhanced version of a one-way hash code, called a **message authentication code** (MAC), to confirm the source of information as well as its integrity over time. As with encryption and decryption, the algorithm in question makes use of a secret key. A MAC allows us to perform an authentication protocol in addition to calculating a hash code.

To calculate a MAC, a secret key is entered into a special one-way hashing algorithm. Some sequence of information bits is then processed through the algorithm resulting in the generation of a one-way hash code. This hash code is essentially an encrypted version of the hash code of the source information that we first considered above. The secret key is a marker for the differential-identity of the source of the information. Now, if we can associate the MAC with the original sequence of information bits, we can confirm at some later time, or in some different location, that the original sequence of information bits has not changed at all.

When we want to re-check the integrity of the information, the same secret key must be entered into the hashing algorithm and a new hash-code generated. If this new hash code matches the old hash code, it establishes both that the information has not changed and it authenticates the differential-identity of the source of the information. Thus, by using a MAC on some collection of information bits, the source of the information and a measure of the information integrity can be transferred between trusted platforms or across some period of time. This transfer does not require an extension of an interaction focus to encompass the source of the information. This forms a trusted process for importing, or exporting, information across the boundary of an interaction focus.

To establish secrecy and information integrity within or among interaction foci, we make use of secret keys. As we considered in the previous chapter, a secret key can be a marker that we use to authenticate the differential-identity of a person. Such authentication is another characteristic of computer and network security. It is the way that we establish who is represented by a deictic center within the interaction focus. So, let's consider in a bit more detail how we authenticate the differential-identity of a person to a computer platform.

Having established a shared zone of secrecy throughout the interaction focus and having established trusted digital processes through which to bring information into the interaction focus and to export information out of the interaction focus, we must also consider communication between a computer platform and an actual person. A person is not able to perform cryptographic operations with the alacrity of a computer platform. To achieve secrecy of user input to the platform and output to the user from the platform, we must resort to stealth as opposed to cryptography. We must shield from external view the information flow between the user and the computer platform. Passwords are not echoed in the clear as they are typed in by the user and the typing itself should be shielded from external view. We need to discourage people from watching us enter our passwords.

Stealth allows us to extend the zone of secrecy to fully encompass a person through the use of physical means to augment the cryptographic means within the computer platform itself. We can make use of this extension to enable a person to authenticate their differential-identity to the computer platform in a trustworthy manner. Of course, this authentication will make use of non-cryptographic protocols. This might involve the use of passwords or it might make use of biometric characteristics of the person.

There are two rather distinct pathways through which the differential-identity of a person can be authenticated within the interaction focus. One pathway involves a person authenticating her identity to the supplicant computer platform through a **user interface** connected directly to that platform. A user interface is that part of a computer's sensory system capable of observing people. It also encompasses that part of the computer's motor response system capable of impacting people in response. Typically, a computer observes people through a keyboard, a mouse, a microphone or a camera. It can typically impact a person through a graphic display, a printer or a speaker.

Once a person authenticates their differential-identity to the supplicant computer platform, it then recursively authenticates to the sentinel platform; first on behalf of itself and then on behalf of the person. A second pathway allows a person to engage an authentication protocol through a user interface connected to the supplicant's computer platform but then terminate that pathway in the sentinel's computer platform. When using this pathway, the supplicant platform authenticates itself to the sentinel platform, but then the person authenticates herself directly to the sentinel platform by using the user interface of the supplicant computer platform. Interestingly enough, it is this latter pathway that is the more common in use in today's Web environment.

When we use a Web browser to access a Web-site's server, we assume the role of supplicant to the server's role as sentinel. A server is able to present a Web page on our browser that will enable the construction of a channel through which information can flow under cover of secrecy between browser and server. One instance where the secret channel is quite useful is when we access a page through which the server allows us to login to some account. This is the process for authenticating a floating persona that we discussed in the previous chapter.

When the login page is displayed on our browser, in one of the corners of the screen display you might see a small lock-icon pop into view. This is an indication that a key exchange between browser and server has been accomplished and the channel is now encrypted. Any information that flows between browser and server is shrouded in secrecy as it makes its way across the Internet. An interaction focus has been established that encompasses two computer platforms connected through an arbitrary, unsecured network. Note that the level of trust for this interaction focus is limited by the intrinsic security of the lesser of the two platforms. Invasive software on either platform can compromise security, and privacy characteristics of the interaction focus. Even if the information transfer is secret, the subsequent composition of the information may not be secret if privacy is so compromised.

In a previous chapter, we recognized engagement in interactions under the guise of different personas. Presenting a persona is an artifact of our personal privacy. Of course, in the arbitration of policy under which a social interaction is to occur, it may be necessary to recognize the type of persona being offered by each participant to an interaction. Since different types of personas offer different trust characteristics, it is certainly within the purview of one person's privacy to only deal with specific types of persona in certain interactions.

We've recognized the typical account offered by various Web servers as illustrative of the floating persona characterized by an account name. The account name is a metaphorical reference to the persona that is the account a person earlier enrolled on the server. In order to login to an account, two pieces of information must be provided: the account name and its corresponding password. The password is the marker through which the differential-identity of the persona is authenticated. By entering the correct password on the login screen, the sentinel establishes a degree of trust that a specific individual is the supplicant in control of the Web browser.

Once a person has logged in and authenticated the differential-identity of a persona, from the perspective of the sentinel's computer any information passed to it from the supplicant's computer through the communication channel can be ascribed to that persona and correspondingly to that supplicant. Secrecy of the channel assures that no eavesdroppers between the Web browser and Web server platforms are able to understand the information being passed between the platforms. Of course, the level of trust in the connection between the persona and the person is heavily dependent on the type of persona.

When the Web server displays a LOGIN page on the supplicant's Web browser, it is initiating an authentication protocol. The supplicant's Web browser sends a response message of this protocol to the Web server that posted the login page. This message includes the account name and password as provided by a person; the supplicant. For this particular protocol, a copy of the account name and password is stored on the Web server that is the source of the login page displayed on the supplicant's browser.

This account and password copy comes from the differential-identity registry maintained by the Web server. Since the Web browser and the Web server are both contained within the same interaction focus, the account and password information is transferred secretly from the browser to the server. On the Web server, the registry's copy of the password and the password obtained from the Web page displayed on the supplicant's browser are compared. If they match, then the differential-identity of the account is authenticated and the supplicant is assumed to be in control of the account.

This approach to an authentication protocol has some perceived deficiencies. Its marker for differential-identity is a password, which is not physiological credential of the person. Transferring the password across the network increases its risk of compromise, even taking into account that the transfer is supposed to be secret. Since secrecy is always problematic, in general it is less of a risk to use authentication protocols in which the marker never leaves the platform. One approach that accomplishes this is to make use of a series of cryptographic operations called challenge-response protocols, using a key rather than a password. For protocols of this type, the secret key that is the marker for the differential-identity of the persona will never be transferred outside the computer platform on which a person is physically authenticating the persona.

A challenge-response protocol involves an exchange of messages in which a challenge is issued by one party and the other party is required to respond with a message appropriate for the specific challenge. Science fiction writer Robert Heinlein made use of such a protocol in his stories about the Howard Families, a particularly long-lived sub-species of *Homo sapiens*. Members of this set of families used a three message protocol to authenticate their membership to one another. One person would say the challenge phrase "Life is short", to which the challenged person would respond "But the years are long", to which the first person would conclude the protocol with the phrase "Not while the evil days come not". One could certainly debate the level of trust conveyed by this protocol given its unchanged use over a couple of millennia, but it does illustrate the genre.

A rather simple digital variant of such a protocol goes like this. All parties agree in advance on the use of a particular encryption algorithm, for example the *Digital Encryption Standard* (DES). They further agree to use a specific length secret key, perhaps 56 bits, to encrypt messages. With these ground rules, two parties can now approach each other. One party, assuming the role of sentinel, can essentially say to the other, who assumes the role of supplicant,

> If you're really Jane Doe, then you possess the same secret key that I have stored in my registry for Jane Doe. You can prove that possession to me by accepting this challenge-message 'Alpha_X1_yz_13-June-2009', encrypting it with Jane Doe's secret key and giving me back the cipher text.

Since the sentinel also possesses Jane Doe's secret key, when the cipher text is returned by Jane Doe, the sentinel can decrypt the cipher text and recover the challenge-message. If the correct challenge-message is thus obtained, then Jane Doe has proven she possesses the correct key and has successfully authenticated her identity to the sentinel. The sentinel can change the challenge-message for every authentication operation as a means to foil certain types of attacks on the protocol.

If Jane Doe wants to authenticate the identity of the first party, the two parties switch roles and repeat the protocol, this time with Jane Doe assuming the role of sentinel and the other party acting as supplicant. Note that the net result of this protocol is to establish a positive authentication state on the computer platform of the sentinel. It is necessary to perform the protocol twice, with each side adopting the role of sentinel, in order to mutually authenticate both parties on both platforms. There are slightly more complex protocols which can establish the mutual authentication of both parties in a single protocol session.

Using the simpler protocol of our example, Jane Doe's secret key has never passed through the communication channel that connects the sentinel's computer platform with the supplicant's computer platform. What did pass across the channel was the result of an operation that made use of the key, but a result from which the key could not be readily determined. This is the heart of digital cryptography. One can't easily discern the key from knowledge of the cipher text.

The encryption and decryption algorithm used in this example is representative of symmetric *key* cryptography. Symmetric refers to the requirement that the same key is used for both encryption and decryption operations. In considering this example, we have begged the question of how the same key came to be present on both the supplicant's and the sentinel's computer platform. We have ignored the issue of complexity if many different parties want to be able to authenticate each other's differential-identity.

If there's only a single key shared by all the parties, then all the protocol does is prove that any particular party possesses that key. It's impossible to tell the various parties apart. Only if each pair of parties possesses a different key from all other pairs can each side of a "pair" authenticate the differential-identity of the other. If any one party wants to be paired with many other parties, we might then wonder how the many different parties come to possess the many different keys. We'll examine this key distribution problem in more detail a bit later.

This brings us to the heart of privacy, both in the physiological world of people as well as in the digital domain; the mechanisms of authority and attribution. These are two different facets of ownership. The exercise of personal privacy entails making the various choices necessary to engage specific interactions; choices involving context, actions and potential consequences. Policy infringes these choices through the concept of authority and it impacts the consequences through attribution of the choices so made and of their ultimate adjudication. Engagement of an interaction may in some fashion be infringed by policy of the state, or of some other social order; most likely of both. Authority attests to an interaction participant's ownership of the necessary facilities for engagement of an interaction within the constraints of policy. Attribution then attests to the ownership of the consequences of the interaction.

Authority can manifest in several forms; among them are **contact**, **capability** and **consent**. In general, contact is a physical facility, capability is a physiological facility and consent is a social facility. Contact refers to bringing a participant within the domain of the interaction focus where they are subject to the constrained forces on which the interaction depends. Capability refers to a participant being able to engage any or all of the available actions within the interaction focus through their (the participant's) physiological motor system. Consent refers to a participant being able to satisfy any policy constraints imposed on the interaction by the sentinel. Once again, we see the frontier between the privacy manifested by contact and capability, and policy, as manifested by consent. Such forms can present individually, or collectively.

If one can establish contact with the sentinel of an interaction, then one might be said to have authority. Contact refers to reaching the point within a specific context where the physiological motor system can evoke actions. Achieving contact requires two subordinate facilities that are referred to as **directory services** and **signaling**. Directory services are the means by which supplicants and sentinels become known to each other. Signaling is the means by which sentinel and supplicant indicate a willingness or desire to engage an interaction.

In the physical ecosystem of predator and prey, directory services are provided as entities indicate their presence by impacting the environment through their physiological motor system, and by other entities detecting that presence through their physiological sensor system. Signaling entails the entities making known to each other the impending interaction. The lion detects the scent of the wildebeest; this is a natural directory mechanism. The lion then attacks and rips the throat out of the wildebeest; this is a natural signaling mechanism. Conversely, the wildebeest might detect the scent of the lion in time to run; an alternate signal. People typically engage social systems in an effort to moderate the extremes of natural directory services and signaling mechanisms.

A more subjective form of authority is found in capability and consent. Once physical contact is achieved, physiological capability comes in to play. Keeping in mind this series of physical ecosystem examples of mechanisms involving authority and non-repudiation, let's now turn to the digital domain. Here, a simple framework that we can use to examine similar mechanisms is that involving a Web-browser communicating with a Web-server and making a purchase from that Web-server. Every person who makes use of the Internet is familiar with this framework. It's the way we make purchases from Amazon or eBay. However, quite often the mechanisms in play are opaque, if not invisible, to the end user. Nevertheless, they attempt to serve the same purposes as the physical, physiological and social mechanisms in the non-computer world.

As one might guess by now, most digital mechanisms involve some form of cryptography. Actually, we've already considered a significant mechanism through which to establish physical contact and physiological capability in the digital domain; authentication protocols. Accessing any Web-site is predicated upon first establishing contact between a Web-browser and a Web-server. This brings us to the facilities of directory services and signaling that we discussed earlier. In the digital domain, search engines such as Google.com and address data-bases are used to obtain directory services through which a Web-browser can find the Internet location of a specific Web-site's server. Standard communication protocols such as the Hyper-Text Transfer Protocol (HTTP) are then used as signaling mechanisms to effect a communication channel between the browser and the server.

In many instances, once the Internet address of a Web-site is known it is possible to access its content without any further authorization. It's an interaction context similar to walking in to a store to browse where the sentinel is physical in nature; a doorway for example. When we enter the Internet address of a Web-site in our browser, we may find that the door is wide open for anyone to enter. On the other hand, we may find that an encrypted channel is put in place between our Web-browser and the Web-site server. The presence of an encrypted connection is sometimes indicated by a lock-icon being displayed on our browser's screen display.

Accessing a Web-server through an encrypted channel is similar to having the store all to ourselves. There is only the sales person behind the counter with whom to engage an interaction, and who can observe our shopping habits. By virtue of the Web-browser, we have presented authority in the form of contact. So, how about authority established by capability and consent? Authority in both domains is going to be dependent on showing credence, usually through the presentation of digital credentials.

Establishing capability in the digital domain makes use of a combination of the mechanisms that we have previously considered as means to authenticate differential-identity and to establish the integrity of information. This typically begins with a person accessing a computer platform through a user interface, and then subsequently making use of digital encryption and decryption through complex protocols. The examples we considered made use of symmetric key cryptography in which multiple parties must possess the same key for the mechanisms to work. This is quite akin to the physiological mechanisms that we use in the non-digital world. They're really only effective when used among a small group of people.

Provisioning Large Social Orders

As we noted earlier, for people to authenticate each other's differential-identity through physiological mechanisms they must engage in provisioning interactions with one another. To use physiological mechanisms within a group requires a number of interactions that grows as the square of the number of people involved. This presents a problem when attempting the same mechanisms in very large groups; a problem we refer to as a **scaling problem**. The mechanism works well if the number of pairs is relatively small. However, as the number of pairs increases the number of pair-wise interactions becomes unwieldy. The mechanism doesn't scale well from small numbers of pairs to large numbers of pairs.

Earlier we discussed a mechanism that two people can use to authenticate each other's differential-identity in a pair-wise interaction. They can share a single key that can be used to encrypt and decrypt a challenge in a challenge-response protocol. If Bob and Alice share a single key, when the other person demonstrates they have the key, then Bob knows it's Alice and Alice knows it's Bob. If Alice and Carol want to authenticate each other, then they must share a different key from Bob and Alice. Thus, any pair of individuals requires that each person shares a common key which is different from the keys of every other pair.

Using symmetric keys to authenticate differential-identity requires some form of direct, trusted communication between pairs of individuals. This trusted communication is necessary to deposit the same key on the computer platforms of each of the individuals. Thus, symmetric key cryptography presents a scaling problem when used among large groups. Key distribution is not impossible; it is simply feasible only under rather special circumstances. For example, when tokens containing keys are prepared *en masse* for distribution, the requisite keys can be deposited on the tokens while they're in a secure manufacturing facility.

This approach is particularly useful if every person always communicates with a single trusted third party. Then, that trusted third party knows all the keys, but each individual only knows the single key she shares with the trusted third party. Of course, for any two people to communicate they always have to go through the trusted third party. So, what we really need is a technology that does scale up well for large, dynamic and dispersed groups in the digital domain. One such technology is called **public key cryptography**.

Public key cryptography is also referred to as **asymmetric key cryptography**. It is an encryption technique that uses different keys for encryption and decryption. Again, we refer you to Bruce Schneier's book *Applied Cryptography* for an excellent explanation of the mathematics involved. Specific to our purposes, it is sufficient to understand that the technique is available. Using different keys for encryption and decryption offers a wealth of facilities through which to convey trust in the digital domain.

Using public key cryptography, two keys are required to perform cryptographic operations on behalf of a single person; one to encrypt information and the other to decrypt information. We can achieve a significant trust facility if we simply designate one of the keys to be a **private key** and the other key to be a **public key**. The private key becomes a marker for the differential-identity of the person. It's the marker used by the person at the supplicant's end of a challenge-response-protocol.

When presented with a challenge-message in plain-text from a sentinel, the private key is used to encrypt it. The resulting cipher-text is then sent to the sentinel's end of the challenge-response-protocol, which must possess the public key. When the sentinel receives the cipher-text of the encrypted challenge-message, it uses the public key to decrypt the cipher-text and recover the plain-text of the original challenge-message. The public key is thus the means of authenticating the differential-identity of the supplicant whom the two keys represent.

The private and the public keys are uniquely related. For any private key there is only one public key. The keys are generated through standard algorithms and are typically several hundred to several thousand bytes in length. The various algorithms used to create keys are based on the generation of large, random prime numbers. Trust is conveyed through these keys due to the computational difficulty in reverse engineering the keys when given any set of cipher-text. Some keys are better than others at making such reverse engineering difficult. There are computationally intensive tests to establish the relative "goodness" of keys, so the generation process is non-trivial, requiring a computer to accomplish.

When keys of several thousand bytes are used, there is only a vanishingly small probability that duplicate keys will be generated. Nevertheless, an enrollment process is generally used to confirm uniqueness of keys. As part of this process, public keys are compared through an identification protocol to a differential-identity registry. This is the same process that we used for the apple example in the previous chapter. This registry subsequently becomes the basis for directory services through which people can learn the public keys of other people and thus be able to communicate with them in a trustworthy manner.

Let's now consider an identification approach where every person in the world generates two such keys. Each person uses a trusted computer platform to perform the key generation algorithm. The private key is kept secret, known only to the computer on which it is generated. The public key is broadcast to the world through some type of directory service. Every person in the world can have access to the public key for every other person in the world. Any person then can engage in a challenge-response-protocol with any other person in the world and thus authenticate their respective differential-identities. In this fashion, it is quite plausible for any two people in the world to engage an interaction, and to know in a highly trustworthy fashion with whom they're dealing. Note that we haven't yet described how to establish the full level of trust for the entire interaction. This will entail means of distributing authority and attribution; essentially, reputation.

A reciprocal operation to differential-identity authentication is quite useful as well. Any public key can be used to encrypt information that can then be decrypted only by its corresponding private key. Since every person in the world knows the public key of every other person in the world, any person can send a secret message to any other person. Thus, encryption with a private key and decryption with a public key enables the authentication of differential-identity. Conversely, encryption with a public key and decryption with a private key is a means of sending secret and therefore trustworthy information to only that differential-identity. We can use both of these operations to enhance the challenge-response protocol.

If the sentinel first encrypts the challenge-message with a specific person's public key and then issues the first message of the protocol, only that person can decrypt the cipher-text of the challenge-message. That person, in the role of supplicant, can decrypt the challenge-message and re-encrypt it with their private key. This cipher-text can then be returned to the sentinel to complete the authentication of the differential-identity of the supplicant.

A slightly more complex protocol can be used to allow mutual authentication. The sentinel uses its private key to encrypt a challenge-message which the supplicant decrypts with the sentinel's public key and then re-encrypts with its own private key before returning the new cipher-text to the sentinel. Of course, the downside to this approach is that anyone who can intercept the information stream between the sentinel and supplicant can decrypt the relevant cipher-text. This doesn't diminish the trust conveyed through the authentication operations, but it does represent a loss of control of the information itself; a diminution of privacy of both the sentinel and the supplicant. By making the protocol just a bit more complex, privacy can actually be maintained through the mutual authentication protocol.

As it happens, asymmetric key cryptography is more computationally intensive than symmetric key cryptography. Thus, it takes longer to encrypt and decrypt messages using public and private keys. Using the same key for both encryption and decryption is much faster. So, if we want to encrypt a billion bytes of information, we would prefer to do it using symmetric key algorithms rather than asymmetric key algorithms. Interestingly enough, using the two systems in tandem makes for much more efficient operation of the overall desired mechanism.

Asymmetric key cryptography solves the scaling problem of symmetric key cryptography. If I want to send a billion bytes of encrypted information to another person, I encrypt the information with a symmetric key algorithm and I simply send the other person the symmetric key in a message encrypted with their public key. That person then is the only person who can decrypt the message and gain access to the symmetric key. That person is the only person who can read the information that was sent in encrypted form.

Using these cryptographic techniques, in the digital domain one can write a message, sign it and send it to someone else. When they receive the message, they can determine who the message came from and that it has not been altered since it was signed. One can send that signed message under a veil of secrecy such that only the person to whom it was sent can read it. Sending and receiving such messages is then a building block for more complex interactions in the digital domain. These complex interactions require both social and digital protocols through which structured messages are associated for specific purposes. For example, by adding this mechanism to the mutual authentication protocol that we previously considered, the information flow can be made opaque, thus retaining control of its further dissemination.

We've already examined the basic mechanisms needed by complex protocols: encryption, decryption, authentication protocols and one-way hash codes. Building on these, we can create well defined message structures allowing us to use these mechanisms in combination. For example, it's deceptively simple to say "I can write a message." However, if I want someone else to be able to read, and understand, that message then we have to agree on a number of things. We reach this agreement through some form of arbitration. Recursion suggests that to engage arbitration, we must be able to refer to standard arbitration protocols.

Obviously, we need to speak the same language. Not just the same natural language such as English or French. Our computers need to speak the same digital language. That is, they must represent English or French in specific patterns of bits and bytes that can be transferred across communication channels. However, let's take these basic definitions for granted and instead concentrate on the arbitration of higher level mechanisms necessary to engage ever more complex interactions.

Message structures allow us to aggregate information and through that aggregation achieve specific purposes. We can use these structures to build complex semantic constructs. Through them, we can then convey messages of credence related to specific ends. Such credentials come in many forms: for example, a driver license, a passport or a pilot certificate. The most common form of credential in the digital domain is an art-form known as a **digital certificate**. This is a message that bears a **digital signature** to attest to its attribution to a specific person. The signature allows the signer to give credence to the message. While originating in the digital domain, digital certificates are extremely relevant to the non-computer world as well.

The digital signature for a person is simply a message encrypted with the private key associated with that person. This forms an association or an attribution back to the differential-identity of that person; a composition representing an experience that can become part of that person's experiential-identity. Anything that can be represented digitally, as a string of bits and bytes if you will, can be digitally signed. While this of course includes text documents of arbitrary length, it also includes images and sounds. It is quite reasonable to sign virtually any composition: a letter, a photograph, a song or a movie. In each case, the signature conveys some level of credence from the person to the thing being signed.

A digital signature performed from a trusted interaction focus allows a person to attest to the thing being signed. This is sometimes achieved through a formal ritual known as a **signing ceremony** that serves to connect sensori-motor reality to the digital domain. The reputation inferred from the person's experiential-identity forms the basis for that attestation. Correspondingly, the assertion made by the signature cannot be readily repudiated by the person. Thus it establishes a formal attribution. What we then need is a means of associating experiential-identity with interaction context and interaction consequences and those back to experiential-identity. This can be accomplished through a digital domain social construct called a **public key infrastructure**, or PKI.

A public key infrastructure is a digital trust infrastructure. It facilitates an identity system grounded in asymmetric key cryptography with a point of causality known as a **root certificate**. The system establishes a differential-identity registry known as a **certificate authority**, or **CA**. A single Root-CA forms the foundation of the entire infrastructure by generating a public key and a private key used to attest to all subordinate key pairs. It associates this seminal key-pair with a metaphorical reference, such as a name, by creating a digital certificate to associate the name with the root public key, plus a few additional pieces of housekeeping information.

To create a digital certificate, information to be associated is aggregated into a single bit stream that is then encrypted with the private key of the Root-CA. This forms a **self-signed certificate**. A digital certificate derives credence or trust from its signer. In the case of the Root-CA, the digital certificate that conveys the basic differential-identity of the Root-CA is signed by the Root-CA. This is an iconic illustration of causality. The Root-CA is trusted because those who will make use of the PKI agree it should be trusted. This trust must then be maintained and conveyed across the full expanse of the desired digital framework by using the mechanisms that we've been considering; the mechanisms of computer and network security that are also the digital mechanisms of privacy. If the Root-CA is compromised, then the entire PKI is compromised.

We should emphasize that a PKI is a trust infrastructure that is subordinate to the policy infrastructure of the state. The most trustworthy PKI is arguably one directly established through policy of the state. A PKI affords the establishment and conveyance of trust by supporting the strong authentication of differential-identity. Based on strongly authenticated differential-identity, trustworthy registries of experiential-identity can also be created and maintained, allowing for the projection of reputation into interactions throughout the digital infrastructure.

Identification allows policy defined by the state to be associated with specific individuals in a trustworthy fashion. The PKI also allows for the creation of subordinate policy infrastructures; for example, the creation of corporate entities. These subordinate policy infrastructures can form networks of **trusted third parties** which might themselves become participants in interactions. Based on PKI identification mechanisms, such trusted third parties can establish credence within interactions; perhaps through direct participation or perhaps through issuance of credentials. This provides an auxiliary approach to solve the scaling problem we noted earlier.

Once the Root-CA is established, people can be enrolled in the PKI. Corporate entities, or even completely generic entities, can also be enrolled. Through their enrollment, they provide a means through which their differential-identity can be authenticated to other people and to a variety of registries. By allowing various policy infrastructures to be put in place under its auspices, interaction specific policy can be established. Complex policy can be defined through semantic constructs conveyed through digital certificates. Based on these constructs, all interactions in the digital domain can be conducted in a trustworthy fashion. The context of any interaction can be formulated, the participants identified, the invocation of action constrained by authority and the consequences adjudicated according to set policy and attributed to the experiential-identity of each participant. Thus, a PKI offers the prospect of a high degree of personal privacy in the digital domain.

Enrollment in a PKI requires a person to generate their own public and private key on a trusted computer platform. This computer platform then forms a component of an interaction focus that includes the CA computer platform. A shroud of secrecy can be put in place over the complete interaction focus. Now, the public key, along with the name of the person to be associated with the public and private keys, can be submitted to the CA. The CA adds the name and public key to its registry and then creates, and signs with its own private key, a digital certificate that associates the public key and the name. This digital certificate forms a calling card for that person. It can be added to a publicly accessible directory, or it can be held by the person and only distributed to people that the person wants to interact with.

A PKI can support many subordinate CAs. Each of these can be the focus of an experiential-identity registry. A registry could be tightly focused; for example, the graduates from a particular university or persons in the State of Texas who have a driver license. By establishing distinguished characteristics conveyed through digital certificates, an experiential-identity registry can define a specific culture. Thus, the experiences of people enrolled in the PKI can be distributed across a number of different domains, all deriving trust from their connection to the Root-CA. Once again, this seems an interesting manifestation of "distributed cognitive-cultural networks".

Within a PKI, it is quite feasible for the consequences of any interaction to be owned in a trustworthy fashion. No matter how insignificant the interaction, it is feasible for all interaction participants to be strongly authenticated and consequently for any person to own the relevant consequences of the interaction and to control the information through that ownership. Consider the accumulation of information about interactions.

For any interaction, even one as simple as observing information on a Web page, it is quite feasible to attribute ownership of the information, and the act of observation, as part of establishing the interaction context. So, if information about a person's participation in an interaction is collected in a large data-base, the ownership of every bit of that information can be properly attributed to the person from whom it came. When anyone views that information, their act of viewing it can be attributed and made part of the data-base. This facility is neither technologically nor operationally onerous. This has profound implications for personal privacy.

Today, tremendous amounts of information are collected about people; information derived from the consequences of interactions. It can subsequently be used for a variety of purposes. In the digital domain, as a facet of personal privacy the ownership of all such information can be readily determined and cast to compositions in a variety of art-forms. Privacy would further suggest that any information thus owned by individuals is subject to the purview of those individuals according to the resultant arbitration of personal privacy for the interactions in which it was obtained.

The act of observing personal information, including the differential-identities of the observer and the observed, can be cast to a composition and made available to the information's owner. This is all contingent on the arbitration of privacy conducted while setting the interaction context, which in turn is influenced by relevant policy. This suggests families of **arbitration protocols** are needed to establish the details of personal privacy afforded each participant to an interaction, much as authentication protocols are used to establish their differential-identities.

In the preceding discussions about privacy, we have omitted any consideration of authenticating differential-identity through biometric markers. Likewise, we have alluded to the necessity of trusted computing platforms, but we haven't considered in detail just how we come to know that a particular platform is trusted. If one platform is a person's laptop and the other is a generic server, why would they be inherently trusted? To arrive at an answer, we can combine the two concepts of biometric authentication with trusted computer platforms in the form of **digital surrogates**. A digital surrogate is an early species along the evolutionary path toward the transcendent personal device.

Digital Surrogates

A digital surrogate is a computer platform provisioned to function under a **fiduciary duty** to its owner; assuming we can apply the term fiduciary duty in a non-financial context. In financial circles, if one has a fiduciary duty to another it means they are obligated to put the other's concerns before their own concerns in handling the other's financial dealings. A digital surrogate exists for the benefit of the person that carries it and effectively owns it; not for the benefit of any corporate entity that provides the device to a person or provides services through the device. While a laptop computer or a server computer might function in this role, their physical structure makes the fiduciary duty constraint difficult for them to satisfy.

The concept of fiduciary duty that we suggest is modeled on the "oath or affirmation" constraint found in the *Constitution*; particularly in *Article VI*. We will come back to this point in greater detail in the final chapter. First, we observe that if policy mandating a fiduciary duty would exist, then an attempt to make use of a digital surrogate for any purpose other than to directly benefit the person that carries it would be contrary to policy. Moreover, what proves a benefit to a person is purely a judgment of that person. This suggests that any attempt to manipulate the device without the explicit consent of its bearer could be considered a crime. Obviously, just stating that a device is trusted does not actually make it trusted. Making it a crime to manipulate a device contrary to the benefit of its bearer will not keep such manipulation from occurring. However, it does help set the context for application of policy.

A digital surrogate is predicated upon a point of causality in the form of an inherently trusted computer platform. An iconic example of such a platform is a **smart card**, or a **trusted program module** (TPM). These platforms encompass dedicated computers, designed and constructed in a fashion to enhance their ability to effect the mechanisms of computer and network security. In general, their characteristics which facilitate these mechanisms include: **monolithic architecture**, **integrated construction**, **limited sensori-motor system**, **small size**, **ability to perform cryptographic operations**, **tamper-resistant** and **tamper-evident**. To personify such devices, they are savants of privacy and identity. It might prove illuminating to briefly review their makeup.

Every computer includes a number of standard elements: a central processing unit, a memory storage facility and a sensori-motor system through which it engages the world outside itself. On most computers with which we're familiar, there are communication channels connecting these various elements; channels that can be relatively easily observed. A monolithic device incorporates all of these elements into a single integrated circuit chip. It is difficult, though not entirely impossible, to observe the distinct, etched layers within such a chip without removing successive layers and thereby making it very evident that the chip has been tampered with.

A complete computer realized through a single integrated circuit chip is the most compact and opaque form of computer currently in use. Most are smaller than the head of a match. To observe the internal structure of the chip generally entails the destruction of the device. For this reason, we refer to them as tamper-evident and tamper-resistant. To compromise the computer, an attacker generally must have possession of it and will usually destroy it while hacking it. This affords opportunities for the owner and bearer of such computers to notice them missing and to institute remedial measures to guard against their future fraudulent use.

The sensori-motor system of these devices is a single, serial channel through which a digital bit stream can be transferred into the device or out of the device. The cognitive facilities of the devices are derived from the primary program that runs on this restricted computer platform. These facilities form a sentinel that is intended to monitor all activity on the device and to protect it against unwarranted intrusion. With only a single channel available, there is a very limited sensori-motor system to guard.

If the digital surrogate is capable of general cryptographic operations, it is able to make use of all the computer and network security mechanisms that we've previously considered. Being very small, and not very expensive, these devices are ideal to be carried by individual people. In fact, they form the trusted core of most cell phones in the world as well as most credit cards; at least, outside the United States.

Since the digital surrogate is highly portable by an individual person, it must also include comprehensive means of establishing a deictic center in both the digital realm as well as the non-computer world. This suggests that a smart card chip alone doesn't fully constitute an effective digital surrogate. Instead, it leads us to consider a portable device with a distinct head and a distinct body; or perhaps a better analogy is an entity with a two-part brain. For example, a rather powerful computer that encompasses a smart card chip in some fashion. In this form, the digital surrogate becomes our avatar on the Web.

The digital surrogate needs some means to establish temporal and spacial location; for example, a clock and a Global Positioning Satellite (GPS) position locator. It needs communication channels through which to connect to other points in both the digital as well as non-computer worlds: for example, wireless-Internet (WiFi), near field communication (NFC), cellular telephony and Bluetooth channels. Biometric sensors are needed to establish a strong bond between the digital surrogate and the person who carries it.

An effective digital surrogate needs a comprehensive user interface through which its bearer can communicate with the device. A user interface is a major component of the sensori-motor system for a computer. It connects the sensori-motor system of a computer with that of a person. The desired interface includes at least a high-resolution display and a text input mechanism such as a keyboard. A graphical input device, a microphone and a speaker would be useful as well. Perhaps of at least equal importance, the digital surrogate needs to be independently powered; it should operate off of long-term, rechargeable batteries, or perhaps a miniaturized fuel cell.

Given the current state of technology, the ideal digital surrogate device looks and acts much like a smart phone; something along the lines of Apple's iPhone. We use the iPhone as the illustration because it is comprised of two main components; a handset and a Subscriber Identity Module (a SIM), which is the same type of computer found in smart cards or TPMs.

The handset encompasses a very powerful computer coupled to a variety of input and output devices. These include a color display, a digital camera, a microphone and a speaker. The handset provides communication channels in a variety of forms such as cellular telephony, WiFi and Bluetooth. If the handset were enhanced with fingerprint sensors, both iris patterns and fingerprints could be used as biometric markers to authenticate to the phone the differential-identity of the person carrying the phone. It is plausible that within the foreseeable future, DNA pattern recognition could be performed on this class of device as well; of course, this is quite speculative at this point.

The SIM card which plugs into the iPhone handset is a trusted computer platform; it's actually a smart card. It's a place to store biometric images, secret encryption and decryption keys, and sensitive experiential-identity credentials, with an expectation that none of this information will be divulged improperly. It's a trusted platform on which to run a variety of secure protocols. Some devices of this class also provide an additional slot in which a standard smart card can be inserted. This enhances the use of the device in non-digital or quasi-digital interactions.

The handset is less trustworthy than the SIM card since it is composed of discrete components that are connected through communication channels that are more readily observed than the connections among logic elements within the integrated circuit chip that comprises the SIM card's computer. However, quite important from a trust standpoint, the handset incorporates a rechargeable battery which can power its operations for relatively long periods of time.

Continuous power means that the computer processors, the one in the handset as well as the one in the SIM card, can always be operating. They can always be on guard against threats. Does this make them tamper-proof? No, but continuous vigilance makes them less susceptible to compromise. In addition, the two computers can serve to protect one another more reliably than either acting alone. Looking to the future a bit, continuous operation makes possible continuous attention to the person who bears the digital surrogate. This would enhance the bonding between person and device, allowing better privacy for the person through health and location monitoring.

Let's now come back to the interplay between biometric characteristics and a PKI facility accessed through a digital surrogate. This is the path to a true Web avatar. The purpose of the device is to project, in a trustworthy fashion, the participation of a person into the digital domain. As we've noted, a number of the digital facilities that we've considered are applicable to the non-computer world as well. Hence, it is useful to consider a number of ways that a person can engage an interaction focus using biometrics and digital surrogates..

Making use of biometrics to authenticate the differential-identity of a person requires consideration of trust on the part of the supplicant as well as the sentinel. A biometric characteristic is a naturally occurring credential of a person. Under the auspices of personal privacy, biometric characteristics are owned by the person. If some characteristic of a supplicant, perhaps a fingerprint or an iris pattern is possessed by the sentinel then there exists a threat to the supplicant since virtually any biometric characteristic can be counterfeited to some degree. By using a biometric prosthesis, the supplicant could be impersonated by someone else. So, to perform an authentication protocol requires special attention to the complete trust environment of the interaction focus. Specifically, the supplicant must be able and willing to trust the biometric sensors and the comparison algorithms.

If biometric sensors are provided on a sentinel's computer, the supplicant might question the trustworthiness of the configuration. There could be surreptitious back-channels capable of intercepting the biometric image as it is acquired. More insidious, the comparison algorithms might be manipulated to incorrectly indicate the authentication of a differential-identity, allowing identity theft to occur. A more satisfactory solution for the supplicant is to use only biometric sensors on the supplicant's own computer platform; a platform that has a fiduciary duty to the supplicant. However, this then poses the question of why should the sentinel find satisfactory trust in this arrangement?

A more mutually satisfactory approach uses biometric markers to authenticate the supplicant to her own personal digital surrogate. This then allows the mechanisms of public key cryptography to use a private key stored in the digital surrogate to further authenticate the differential-identity of the supplicant to the sentinel's computer platform. The supplicant can establish the seed of her perspective of the interaction focus on her digital surrogate and extend that to merge with the interaction focus on the sentinel's computer platform. To use this approach supposes that it is established through a formal protocol subject to external certification that provides explicit technical and policy guarantees to both the sentinel and the supplicant.

This is not to say that a trustworthy interaction focus cannot be based on biometric sensors found on a sentinel's computer platform. However, if a supplicant is going to make use of biometric sensors that are provided by the sentinel, then there should be explicit technical and policy guarantees to the supplicant as evidenced by external certification through formal protocols. This suggests that some agency independent of both sentinel and supplicant must be trusted to establish a point of causality for trust between the two parties and their respective computer platforms.

A corollary to this protocol is one that establishes trust through permanent fixtures, as opposed to transient computer platforms. For example, if a supplicant goes into a well identified office and presents a finger to be printed, or an iris to be scanned, then some level of credence does accrue from the *gravitas* of the environment. The office itself can be a credential of capability and consent. Hence, it becomes quite attractive from a trust perspective to have a broad network of trusted office locations available within an identity system. This suggests at least three points of connection for a person engaging digital transactions: an office with biometric sensors, a simple smart card token using biometric sensors on a sentinel's platform, or a more fully capable digital surrogate.

In the first situation, a person can engage highly trusted interactions simply by showing up in the office and presenting her biometric characteristics. She can sign a document, withdraw money from a bank account, or perhaps vote in an election. All that's required is the trusted office and a highly trustworthy sentinel computer platform, complete with a full range of biometric sensors with access to comparison services from a differential-identity registry. Cursory instances of such facilities are found today in banking and pay-day check cashing facilities.

In the second situation, a smart card can provide a quite useful, albeit very basic, digital surrogate if proper attention is paid to the trustworthiness of the facilities of the interaction focus in which it is used. Since the smart card is not an internally powered device, and since it's user interface is non-existent, its capabilities are limited. However, it can enhance the characteristics of personal privacy on existing systems with limited inherent trust facilities. In particular, it is capable of supporting strong authentication of differential-identity of its bearer and it is capable of performing digital signature operations. This facilitates the participation of a person in interactions in the digital domain. Of course, a more capable digital surrogate offers more enhanced personal privacy facilities.

In the third situation, let's assume that a person carries a powerful digital surrogate that looks like a derivative of a smart phone. Through biometric characteristics detected by sensors that are part of the device, a person can authenticate their differential-identity to the digital surrogate. Thus, only the intended bearer can use the device, or perhaps more appropriately stated, the device can act as a surrogate for only one person. It does so by projecting the biometrically authenticated differential-identity of the bearer to other computer platforms using public key cryptography.

Once authenticated, the intended bearer of the device can communicate in a trusted fashion with the device through its user interface. In an extension, the device can also communicate in a trusted fashion with other computers through complex, untrusted networks. Thus, the bearer is able to engage trusted social interactions involving those computers. If the digital surrogate includes a reader interface for a smart card, then authentication of other parties can use any of the three mechanisms we've noted. That is, other parties can be authenticated purely through presentation of their biometric characteristics, through presentation of a smart card identity token, or through presentation of other digital surrogates. In this manner, a digital surrogate can act either as supplicant or sentinel.

The digital surrogate provides means for a person to assert virtually complete personal privacy in the digital domain and it provides a tool for enhancing the realization of personal privacy in the non-digital world as well. A significant facility provided by the device is the establishment of the initial context of an interaction through the arbitration of privacy infringement, including the determination of relevant policy constraints. It can establish first the type of personas to be engaged in an interaction, and then the authentication of acceptable personas. For example, if one chooses to engage only an anchored persona, this constraint can be established as a requirement before further engagement occurs. This facility alone is a barrier to predators.

The two components of the digital surrogate, the handset and the SIM, together form a more effective avatar than either alone. Both components can be owned by a person with the expectation that they will collectively act as a fiduciary agent for the person. Smart phones don't act in this manner today. In particular, they lack proper provisioning and policy from the state to mandate a fiduciary duty for the device in acting for the person who bears it. Nonetheless, both the technology and the policy infrastructure are available to accommodate such devices. Needed are the specific policies, devices and social protocols tailored for an environment of expansive personal privacy. We might ponder how these goals can be pursued.

Campaign on the Frontier

To address the stated goal of enhancing the environment of expansive personal privacy, a **campaign** seems an appropriate metaphor, suggesting as it does a **structured set of interactions aimed at well defined consequences**. In the second chapter, we briefly considered the effort by the United States to send men to the moon. We could characterize that entire effort as a campaign to achieve the specific consequence suggested by President Kennedy; to send a man to the moon and return him safely to the earth. As we noted, that campaign was waged in all of the domains of interaction forces. It illustrates quite well the complexity that can result from even succinctly stated goals.

A campaign is often an adversarial process. It might involve development of some means to "defeat" a natural process; for example, a campaign to "wage war on cancer." In some situations, it might involve a more literal "war" aimed at achieving victory under the rules of the physical ecosystem; a campaign seeking "survival of the fittest" in a war among nations. In a different guise, a campaign might comprise a concerted effort to effect policy through the infrastructures of a social order; a campaign for public office in order to control governance among the polity.

With this preface to set the context, let's give some thought to a campaign to enhance the assertion of expansive personal privacy within American jurisprudence; a campaign to meld digital technology with social order. While we'll begin the consideration in the technical realm, it will truly reach full voice in the following chapters when we more explicitly examine privacy in the context of law; and, law in the context of privacy. In the end, we will seek to understand at least some aspects of the desired enhanced environment. We really won't be able to state significant details of the requisite campaign, but perhaps we can give some idea of what it will involve.

Earlier, we observed three important facets of this campaign: technology, social protocols, and state policy. We've already reviewed several of the more relevant technologies in some detail. We generally characterize them in the form of **Identity, Authority and Attribution (IAA) Systems**. IAA Systems are social infrastructures that encompass the technology and protocols forming the trusted processes of privacy: opacity, integrity, identity, authority, and attribution. Their full impact is dependent on complementary state policy that constrains the social forces at work between the collective polity and the individual. To gain the greatest enhancement of personal privacy, what is needed is nothing less than an IAA System that buttresses the trust and policy infrastructures of the American Republic.

Lest we withdraw too far into more palatable metaphors, the IAA System that we suggest is, in fact, a national system for personal identity. Many people are quite averse to such a system. They harbor the idea that they have a right, and an ability, to achieve anonymity in their everyday lives. Moreover, through this anonymity they can achieve personal privacy. They believe that a national identity system is a direct threat to achieving the desired anonymity. We suggest, based on our previous discussions, these ideas no longer hold.

Technology provides means to observe people in virtually any activity. More insidious, there are few constraints in law on the acquisition, dissemination and pervasive use of the products of such observations. To the extent that there are constraints, they tend to be haphazardly and ambiguously defined and enforced. Any significant degree of anonymity, and privacy derived from it, is but an illusion. Instead, it is the **lack of an effective means of ubiquitous identity grounded in law** that is the greater threat to the individual.

If this is indeed the case, then the more reasonable campaign aimed at achieving any significant level of personal privacy is one that makes technology work on privacy's behalf rather than as its adversary. Hence, a national system for personal identity is an attractive path forward. The primary *caveat* of such a system is that it must encompass the entire populace in supporting the mechanisms of privacy. To do so, it must be effective in all of the activities of the trust and policy infrastructures of the state. A corollary suggests there is no room under such a system for institutional anonymity on the part of any state or corporate entities. Every institution must have skin in the same game. In an attempt to make that case, let's explore some of the aspects of such a system.

The technologies in play start with the biometric characteristics that allow establishing unique differential-identities of all persons. To exploit the facilities of biometric identification and authentication, Public Key Infrastructures are needed to enable credentials of authority and attribution grounded in differential-identity to be conveyed across the full expanse of the social order. In turn, these technologies depend on computer platforms that can be ubiquitously realized in a trustworthy form. Adopting such platforms as a causal foundation of trust, cryptography can then be used to communicate credentials in the presence of adversaries. Building semantic content into families of credentials enables social protocols through which the mechanisms of privacy can be realized in generic social interactions.

There are a variety of "identity providers" offering services today, particularly for Internet based activities. The most common such systems provide a floating persona capability. In some instances, these systems operate in "confederations", allowing identity to be conveyed among multiple systems with a person being enrolled in only one. The rules under which such federated systems operate typically derive from consensus based standardization with, at best, modest testing and certification to attest to their adherence to the standards. The level of trust conveyed by authentication in such systems is often problematic. Based on the following rationale, we suggest that a more hierarchical approach is preferable.

A foundational IAA System operator provides a focal point for standardization and certification of technology and social protocols. It also provides a point of focus for the development of policy that supports a national identity system. Most equipment and services can be obtained by the operator from private entities through conditional covenants. Using a PKI whose root certificate derives from the seminal system operator, we can implement a fully capable IAA System; in fact, a collection of IAA Systems related as trusted third parties. By "fully capable", we mean the IAA Systems can address all of the mechanisms of privacy and can extend those mechanisms beyond the purely digital domain. The first mechanism to be engaged, actually the first necessary protocol, is the differential-identification of each person.

To put everyone on an equal footing in social interactions, every person should be enrolled in the base IAA System; the national identity system. As we have previously noted, the enrollment process comprises a census of the constituent members of the IAA System. So, for an IAA System to encompass the American populace it will comprise a census of the nation. Moreover, at any point in time it can provide a census count of the current population to some minimal level of uncertainty. This presumes, of course, that included in the IAA Systems are trusted processes through which people are enrolled in the system when they come under its purview and deleted when they are removed from its purview.

To support an anchored persona, the differential-identity of a person should track to a single registry. To avoid a single person being enrolled multiple times, it is preferable there be only a single differential-identity registry. At the very least, all differential-identity registries should be included in the identification search conducted when people enroll. On the other hand, under the auspices of the PKI many experiential-identity registries can be created, all of which can be orthogonal to each other and to the differential-identity registry. This allows for experiential-identity of the individual to be segmented into various personas; an architecture that offers significant facilities for enhancing the personal privacy of individuals.

To achieve the level of trust desired from this system or collection of systems, it needs to be grounded in the police powers of the state. Policy of the state can then make the operation of the system subject to the state's adjudication facilities. This suggests that the basic differential-identity registry be deployed and operated under strict control of a quasi-governmental entity. As a safeguard against unwarranted exploitation by the state to the detriment of individual personal privacy, there must be physical as well as policy firewalls between the IAA System and elements of the state's policy infrastructure; specifically, regulatory authority, the military and the police.

The necessary firewalls are easier to achieve through a quasi-governmental entity, as opposed to a purely state agency or a purely private organization. This claim follows from a presumption that the quasi-governmental entity flows from authority granted by law, as opposed to deriving indirectly from executive or administrative authority. This grounding in law provides a point of causality for trust that we seek from the system. From our perspective, an excellent candidate for such an entity already exists; the United States Postal Service (USPS). Actually, the foundation of the USPS may require modification to meet the previously stated presumption. In our final chapter, we'll give voice to a more detailed proposal in this regards. Hopefully, the intervening discussion will contribute to the justification for that proposal.

When people are enrolled in an IAA System, a marker must be captured to be used to authenticate their differential-identity in future interactions. As we alluded in some detail in the third chapter, only biometric characteristics of a person should be used for markers since these are the only credentials fully suitable for establishing an anchored persona. For the IAA System in question, the biometrics used should specifically include: a facial image, two iris patterns and ten fingerprints. Retina and DNA patterns should be considered as well. If one assumes a rather conservative rate for positive comparisons of one in a thousand, then any four of these characteristics accessed in series should yield an accuracy of identification in the range of one part in 100 billion. It may not be necessary to achieve this same level of accuracy for all future authentication protocols, but it is available when needed.

Enrollment is accomplished by engaging each person in a one-to-one interaction with the identity system's registry. To enhance trust in the enrollment process, this interaction should occur under the auspices of a sentinel from the identity system. This suggests either enrollment within an office of the system operator or enrollment with a trusted agent of the system operator using trusted portable equipment. To enroll everyone suggests a widely dispersed assortment of office locations and many trusted agents from each office interacting with people. If biometrics comprise the basic markers of differential-identity, then the more colloquial markers such as names and addresses comprise the basic experiential-identity compositions that can form a second phase to the enrollment process.

As we've previously observed, the necessary portable equipment for enrollment is functionally equivalent to a slightly enhanced smart phone. Current smart phone architectures have illustrated the power of wide ranging applications (apps) to address a plethora of social situations and services. Embedding such devices and their apps in comprehensive IAA Systems allows them to be grounded in an environment of expansive personal privacy. This is at least one clear path to the realization of an effective digital surrogate.

While enrollment is a crucial protocol for any IAA System, many additional protocols are required if the system is to be useful in generic social interactions. Among the necessary protocols must be at least one that specifies how some arbitrary collection of individuals or entities can engage an interaction. In the extreme, simply signaling a desire for an interaction can be viewed as a threat. Hence, an acceptable protocol should present the minimum threat feasible, consistent with actually effecting an interaction. Once engaged, the protocol should allow extension to an extremely trustworthy interaction; one that supports an expansive level of personal privacy for all concerned.

Subsequent protocols must provide for agreement among participants for mechanisms to achieve all the processes of privacy and for acceptable levels of operation of those mechanisms. These certainly include secrecy, integrity, identity, authority and attribution. Such protocols comprise an art-form that's continually evolving. While it's impossible to present an exhaustive list, there are a number of obvious social protocols that a general IAA System should handle. Many of these are digitally enabled equivalents of protocols that we engage in everyday life. The IAA System operator must provide means for standardizing and certifying such protocols such that their implementations by a variety of entities can interoperate.

The development of general arbitration protocols is a facility in its infancy. Negotiating the effective privacy rights of multiple individuals in generic interactions falls into this category. Most corporate entities provide their own "privacy policy", generally in response to specific legal requirements. There is, however, little in the way of actual arbitration regarding such policies. Currently, virtually all arbitration between sentinel and supplicant occurs in a piecemeal fashion during the course of the interaction. To address the haphazard nature of this approach, the development of interaction oriented protocols expressed through computer processable semantics will allow for complex interactions to be engaged with a high degree of personal privacy.

The digital mechanisms that we have considered are essential to privacy in the digital domain and they also enhance privacy in the purely sensori-motor domain as well. The mechanisms provide for a collection of capabilities that enhance privacy through their aggregate use. They specifically allow trustworthy attribution of the consequences of interactions, allowing for improved trust assessment in the context of subsequent interactions. This, in turn, enhances the level of trust in the application of policy, allowing for greater confidence in the evoking of actions.

We have suggested that a national identity system must be grounded in law. It is highly desirable that a variety of actions and situations be explicitly considered in such law. The operation of the various facilities of the system should be predicated on the privacy of the individual. Equipment, particularly devices to be carried by a person, should be developed and operate under a fiduciary duty to that person. A number of behaviors having obvious fraudulent intent should be proscribed; for example impersonating another or falsely attributing consequences to another. While aspects of many such behaviors are covered by existing policy, the rules should be enhanced to accommodate a comprehensive IAA System.

We have observed that privacy is primarily about control, and control must be accommodated by policy. So, this will be our focus going forward. In the following chapters, we'll first consider how current jurisprudence defines and accommodates what it calls "privacy". Then, we'll look at the foundation of the American Republic to see if we can recognize our more expansive definition of privacy. Finally, we'll conclude with some observations of what the more expansive concept of privacy means to American jurisprudence.

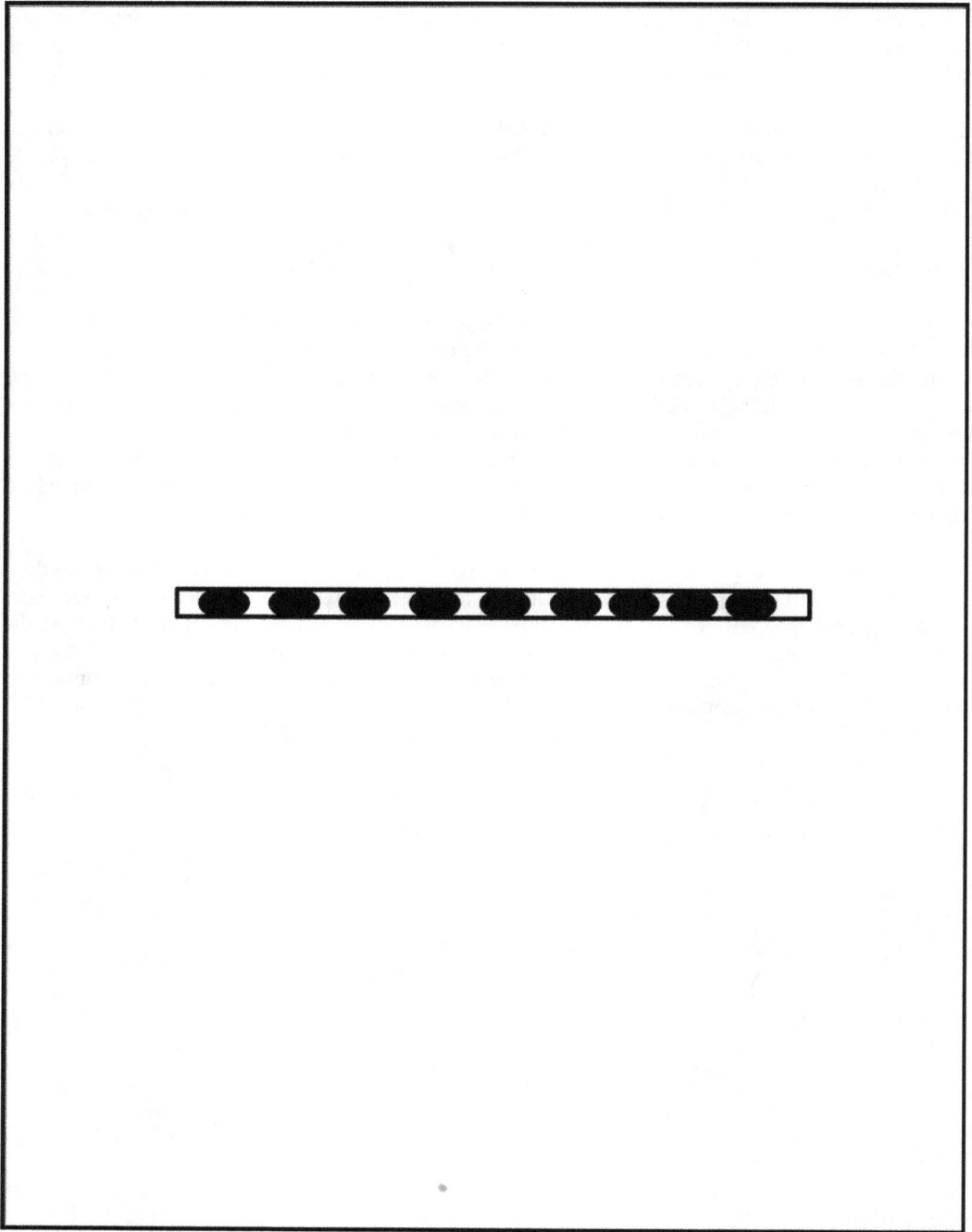

5 *Privacy in Contemporary Jurisprudence*

Privacy in contemporary jurisprudence emerges from a seemingly random walk through case law; a measured journey in search of a unifying concept. Much of the apparent lack of direction results from the haphazard nature of case law itself; appearing as a social equivalent to the concept of punctuated equilibrium in the evolution of species. It requires a special confluence of interaction context, policy, actions and social adjudication to peer through the opacity of court decisions and discern the breadth and depth of a specific legal concept with significant clarity.

Case law is an illustration of the interaction mechanics we've considered in previous chapters. A case is a social interaction. It is bounded by context. A case has a beginning and it has an end. In its course, constrained forces in the form of social policy are applied through actions that result in consequences. These social forces have the property that their consequences can become subject to a legal process pursued within a system of jurisprudence; a process referred to as **adjudication**. Once consequences enter the realm of adjudication, the entire interaction becomes subject to a new set of social forces. This environment is one of recursive application of policy through sequential interactions, and it's often quite onerous to terminate the recursion. We'll look into the details of this process in the next chapter.

There are many distinct domains of adjudication; each an area of law replete with arcane procedures that have evolved over time. Among them are civil law, contract law, administrative law, tort law, and criminal law. Procedures can vary significantly among domains and **jurisdictions**, which are the constraining contexts for legal processes. In the United States, all domains and jurisdictions are ultimately encompassed by the Supreme Court of the United States. As the ultimate arbiter of policy, decisions rendered by the Supreme Court are as close to final consequences as exist within the policy infrastructure of the American incarnation of a nation-state.

To enter adjudication, a case must involve a **justiciable issue**. This means that with respect to an interaction whose consequence is called into question, before a court accepts jurisdiction it must deem it possible to ultimately conclude the interaction through judicial action. For participants to have **standing** to be involved in a case, they must be directly impacted by the interaction. The judicial environment is comprised of a variety of trial courts which are subordinate to hierarchical appellate courts culminating in the Supreme Court. Adjudication typically resolves to a ruling by the Supreme Court for closure. At each level, appellate courts, including the Supreme Court, can choose to render a decision or let stand the ruling of some lower court.

It is the exception rather than the rule that all of the facets of a case line up so as to allow the courts to clearly establish and espouse profound findings that are applicable beyond the case at hand. Hence, there exists a class of **landmark rulings** that serve to reinforce or redirect policy, if not to define it anew. These landmark rulings are illustrative of the metaphorical models which characterize social policy; to a certain extent they represent canonical instances of the models. They are the ecstatic experiences of the polity. The progression of significant issues such as privacy can be followed through the rulings on such profound cases. A case is profound because of the issues of judicial interpretation it raises, not necessarily because of its direct consequences.

Landmarks

The process that we're discussing is generically characterized as **the common law**. This is complementary to statutory law, which comprises the recorded rules and regulations of the policy infrastructure. Judicial decisions aimed at statutory infractions in individual cases form the precedents for future case decisions. A legal principle called *stare decisis* suggests that judges should adhere to these past precedents as their basis for future rulings.

The common law is a provisioning process in a fashion quite analogous to privacy. At any point in time, the common law encompasses the policy of the state. Past provisioning establishes the rationale for future decisions. Just as with the trust infrastructure for interaction mechanics, to alter the direction of the court's assessment of policy requires something like an act of ecstasy; that is, a landmark ruling.

Current case law paints an ambiguous picture of privacy. To adopt a digital perspective, it is a picture in which only random pixels are displayed. As more pixels are shown, the picture becomes clearer. Court rulings say that privacy exists, but it's unclear whether it has always existed within the Republic or whether it came into being at some later point. It is to be expected that new cases will reveal additional pixels. Unfortunately, history has shown that sometimes the courts get a pixel wrong.

Given that the common law is a cumulative process, when the foundation of any court decision is circumspect, the decision tends to propagate the circumspection. To backtrack and correct an errant direction can challenge the entire society. The general approach of the courts is to backtrack only as far as necessary to construct a plausible course correction, not to reconsider the point where a train of court opinions first went off track. In a few, exceedingly profound instances, the Supreme Court did force society in a completely new direction; in some cases, with little to distinguish the result from a train wreck. We will touch on a few such cases.

The meandering path toward privacy has seen several interim course corrections within relevant case law; points of incremental direction change. It begins from a formally specified policy infrastructure that defines government in terms of enumerated powers, and then constrains these powers by defining a number of **rights**. Rights defined through the *Bill of Rights*, the first ten amendments to the *Constitution*, were late additions to the initial policy infrastructure.

A right would appear to be an immutable constraint on policy; a personal characteristic or capability that the state can not infringe. They would seem to represent instances where privacy trumps policy. However, rights have a tendency to intersect and interfere with other rights. Moreover, the state quite often finds reasons why it feels the need to abridge well defined rights. As we've noted, the state feeds off of the privacy of the individual. Thus, the reality is that a right of privacy is subject to abridgment. The issues we want to better understand are why such abridgment is allowed under law, and how is it accomplished?

The first of the direction changes deals with the immutability of a right. American courts have decreed that no right is inviolate. The impetus for this direction change came in regards to the right of **freedom of speech**. A series of cases centered on situations when free speech could be abridged by law. If the state can infringe enumerated rights on a whim, then it doesn't mean much to identify something as a right in the first place. The reasons became something of a moving target, all directly associated with speech. What about other rights?

In time, the courts ruled that any right can be abridged for the correct reasons; specifically, if the state has a **compelling interest** in the abridgement. When the courts establish a more general concept, they sometimes specify a **bright line rule** giving objective criteria for its interpretation. The concept of compelling interest has not been afforded a bright line rule, so it requires subjective interpretation on a law-by-law basis.

As we will see later, the courts have provided somewhat objective criteria for determining whether a law actually satisfies a compelling interest, once the interest is stated. Showing the justification as compelling is a subjective determination. However, if the justification is deemed compelling, the law must be shown narrowly tailored to satisfy this justification and the approach taken must be the most unobtrusive approach relative to the fundamental rights abridged. This was the second course correction on the somewhat meandering route toward privacy.

Finally the question arose whether the only rights subject to constrained infringement are those enumerated in the foundational policy infrastructure, or are there other rights drawn from other sources? A corollary to this issue is whether there are other fundamental rights besides those enumerated as part of the formal policy infrastructure. Well, according to the courts, there are. To better understand the path, and particularly the course corrections, given that we have some idea of where we're headed, let's examine some of the relevant landmark cases.

Young students are not typically taught a lot of constitutional law, but they're forever getting called down for talking in class. When admonished to stop talking, it's not unusual to hear a student respond with something like "It's a free country! I can say what I want!" At this point, most students then hear from the teacher some variant of Justice Oliver Wendel Holmes' observation in the Supreme Court decision in the case of *Schenck v. United States*: "The most stringent protection of free speech would not protect a man in falsely shouting fire in a theatre and causing a panic." This case began a series of decisions through which the court held, and then refined significantly, that policy can infringe the freedom of speech enumerated in the *First Amendment* to the *Constitution of the United States*.

In 1917, Charles Schenck, the general secretary of the Socialist Party, ran afoul of the *Espionage Act* of 1917 when he was accused of circulating pamphlets encouraging men to protest their possible induction into the army. The pamphlets encouraged men to assert their right to oppose the draft, suggesting that the draft was a form of involuntary servitude. Responding to the conspiracy charges against him, a portion of Schenck's defense was his claim to the right of freedom of speech under the *First Amendment* to the *Constitution of the United States*. Found guilty of the charges, the defense appealed to the Supreme Court, claiming that the *Espionage Act* was therefore unconstitutional. Writing the opinion for the court that upheld the constitutionality of the law and affirmed the conviction, Justice Holmes made the famous observation noted above.

It was the opinion of the court that the right of free speech could be abridged if the words uttered presented a **clear and present danger** that they would encourage actions that Congress was duly authorized to forbid. This provided an early illustration that basic rights ostensibly guaranteed by the *Constitution* could be infringed for the correct reasons; that is, if there appeared to be a compelling interest to the state in the infringement. This issue then was, and still is today, what comprises a compelling interest for the state to abridge fundamental rights? The *Schenck* case gave us the **clear and present danger** test which established a rather low threshold for determining what constituted a compelling interest to abridge the right of freedom of speech.

In a later case, Anita Whitney was found in violation of California's 1919 *Criminal Syndicalism Act*. As a member of the Communist Labor party, she was convicted of associating with a group that was devoted to teaching the violent overthrow of government. This act took the rather novel approach of outlawing associations among people through organizations which, it was deemed, would then teach concepts that might bring about consequences inimical to the state.

In 1927, the Supreme Court's decision in the case of *Whitney v. California* established an even lower bar than *Schenck's* clear and present danger test. The court held that the state had the power to sanction those who

> ...abuse this freedom by utterances inimical to the public welfare, tending to incite to crime, disturb the public peace, or endanger the foundations of organized government and threaten its overthrow by unlawful means.

In short, the test for unlawful speech was that it merely had to have a **tendency** to bring about bad consequences; hence, it became known as the **bad tendency** test. Of interest in this case was Justice Louis Brandeis' concurring opinion which essentially took the opposite tack from the opinion of the court regarding the freedom of speech.

Justice Brandeis concurred in the opinion that the California law was valid under the *Fourteenth Amendment*. This was a rather restrictive result because the results that had been appealed to the Supreme Court were themselves restrictive, not requiring the court to address larger constitutional issues. However, in his opinion Brandeis presented a very far-reaching defense of an expansive right to freedom of speech by suggesting:

> Whenever the fundamental rights of free speech and assembly are alleged to have been invaded, it must remain open to a defendant to present the issue whether there actually did exist at the time a clear danger; whether the danger, if any, was imminent; and whether the evil apprehended was one so substantial as to justify the stringent restriction interposed by the legislature.

Continuing, he stressed:

> But even advocacy of violation, however reprehensible morally, is not a justification for denying free speech where the advocacy falls short of incitement ...

A more stringent constraint on speech that can be abridged by the state is found in the Supreme Court's 1969 decision in the case of *Brandenburg v. Ohio*. Clarence Brandenburg was a leader of the Ku Klux Klan in Ohio. At a KKK rally, a film was made showing various speeches giving reference to possible acts against black people and their supporters and announcing plans for a march on Washington, D.C. As a result of the film, Brandenburg was charged with advocating violence under the 1919 *Ohio Criminal Syndicalism* statute. In this case, the court rendered a *per curium* decision; an opinion of a majority of the court that was anonymously authored. The decision overturned the Ohio law, giving rise to what has become known as the **Brandenburg** test which maintains that speech advocating specific acts can be sanctioned only if the advocacy is

> ...directed to inciting or producing imminent lawless action, and is also likely to incite or produce such action.

The *Brandenburg* case contains a concurring opinion by Justice William O. Douglas, in which Justice Hugo Black joined, that suggests in conclusion that, except in very rare circumstances:

> ...speech is, I think, immune from prosecution. Certainly there is no constitutional line between advocacy of abstract ideas..., and advocacy of political action... The quality of advocacy turns on the depth of the conviction and government has no power to invade that sanctuary of belief and conscience.

If we associate the advocacy of abstract ideas with the dissemination of metaphorical models, it might seem that Justice Douglas is addressing in part the concept that we have termed aesthetic expression. Speech can thus be presented in a form that enhances the sensation evoked in the listener; a significant aspect of the act of provisioning.

We've arrived at one of the incremental direction changes. The switch from a right that is inviolate to a right that can be abridged for the correct reason. The concurring opinion voiced by Justice Douglas and Justice Black represents the high water mark for the idea that rights are absolute and cannot be abridged for any reason. Of course, in the three cases we've noted, there are three different court opinions on just what constitutes the correct reason to abridge the freedom of speech. We observe that the direction shift took quite a long time to happen; a period of 50 years between *Schenck* and *Brandenburg*. This brings us to a second incremental direction shift that began in mid-stream of the first; defining a moderately rigorous process for establishing the right reason to abridge a fundamental right.

This shift began with the case of *United States v. Carolene Products Co.* This 1938 case involved a federal law that forbid milk compounds other than milk fat from being shipped in interstate commerce. One manufacturer of such compounds, Carolene Products Co. claimed that the law was unconstitutional based on the *Commerce Clause (Article I Section 8 Clause 3)* and the due process requirement of the *Constitution (Fifth Amendment)*. The Supreme Court ruled that the law was constitutional, and then with something of the subtlety of a hand grenade tossed into the foxhole of constitutional law it included a footnote; *Footnote 4*:

> There may be narrower scope for operation of the presumption of constitutionality when legislation appears on its face to be within a specific prohibition of the Constitution, such as those of the first ten amendments, which are deemed equally specific when held to be embraced within the Fourteenth.
>
> It is unnecessary to consider now whether legislation which restricts those political processes which can ordinarily be expected to bring about repeal of undesirable legislation is to be subjected to more exacting judicial scrutiny under the general prohibitions of the Fourteenth Amendment than are most other types of legislation.
>
> Nor need we enquire whether similar considerations enter into the review of statutes directed at particular religious ... or national ... or racial minorities ... : whether prejudice against discrete and insular minorities may be a special condition, which tends seriously to curtail the operation of those political processes ordinarily to be relied upon to protect minorities, and which may call for a correspondingly more searching judicial inquiry.

This footnote suggested that the court could apply varying standards in determining the validity of a law, depending on the actions which the law affected and who would be impacted by those actions. The footnote specifically calls out the protection of **discrete and insular minorities**; those who might not have the political power to protect themselves. The court was likely referring to minority groups inferred from various constitutional amendments. However, we would suggest that the ultimate discrete and insular minority is the individual claiming a right of personal privacy.

Three standard levels have now been defined under which the courts examine the validity of laws. The most stringent is termed **strict scrutiny**. For laws to be ruled as valid under this rationale, they must meet three constraints:

> The law must be justified by a **compelling state interest**. The concept generally refers to something necessary or crucial, as opposed to something merely preferred.
>
> The law or policy must be **narrowly tailored** to achieve that goal or interest. If the government action encompasses too much or fails to address essential aspects of the compelling interest, then the rule is not considered narrowly tailored.
>
> The law or policy must be the **least restrictive means** for achieving that interest; there cannot be a less restrictive way to effectively achieve the compelling state interest.

Strict scrutiny is generally applied to laws that infringe basic constitutional guarantees; especially the enumerated rights in the *Bill of Rights*. However, as we will see below, it is also applied to laws that infringe unenumerated rights, such as the right of privacy.

A more moderate level of scrutiny is termed **intermediate scrutiny**. To be valid under this basis, the following criteria must be met:

> To pass intermediate scrutiny, the challenged law must further an important government interest by means that are substantially related to that interest. As an example, intermediate scrutiny is used in equal protection challenges to gender classifications, as well as in some *First Amendment* cases.

The most lenient level of scrutiny is **rational basis scrutiny**. Under this test, laws must meet the following criteria:

> The challenged law must be rationally related to a legitimate government interest. Rational basis review is generally used in cases where no fundamental rights or suspect classifications are at issue.

Unfortunately, having established moderately stringent tests for determining when a basic right can be abridged, in its first application of strict scrutiny the Supreme Court created a major controversy. The court used the test to justify the constitutionality of a law that seemed to fly in the face of a number of basic rights; the 1944 decision in *Korematsu v. United States*. The case involved a native born American citizen who happened to have parents born in Japan.

Toyosaburo Korematsu was convicted of evading internment in a detention center based on *Civilian Exclusion Order No. 34* issued during World War II. The order came from a military commander on the west coast, issued under the authority of an *Executive Order* from the President of the United States. The effect of the order was to remove all persons of Japanese ancestry, including native born American citizens such as Korematsu, from certain areas along the west coast of the United States. The stated goal was to thwart espionage and sabotage in advance of a feared Japanese invasion. The crux of the court's application of strict scrutiny appears to be presented in these words from the opinion:

> To cast this case into outlines of racial prejudice, without reference to the real military dangers which were presented, merely confuses the issue. Korematsu was not excluded from the Military Area because of hostility to him or his race. He was excluded because we are at war with the Japanese Empire, because the properly constituted military authorities feared an invasion of our West Coast and felt constrained to take proper security measures, because they decided that the military urgency of the situation demanded that all citizens of Japanese ancestry be segregated from the West Coast temporarily, and finally, because Congress, reposing its confidence in this time of war in our military leaders-as inevitably it must-determined that they should have the power to do just this.

In a dissenting opinion, Justice Robert Jackson suggested that an act of military expedience should not be given the imprimatur of constitutional validity:

> I should hold that a civil court cannot be made to enforce an order which violates constitutional limitations even if it is a reasonable exercise of military authority. The courts can exercise only the judicial power, can apply only law, and must abide by the Constitution, or they cease to be civil courts and become instruments of military policy.

Justice Frank Murphy wrote an even more strident dissent. In it, he raised the prospect of racism as the basis for the order. He specifically noted that American citizens of German and Italian descent were treated quite differently from those of Japanese descent. The court's opinion, including the phrasing noted above, attempted to downplay its racial overtones; obviously, to only limited success.

One point illustrated by the *Korematsu* decision is that the courts sometimes offer positions that give unwarranted deference to the executive and legislative branches of government. We will consider some additional and extreme examples of this in our last chapter. The courts are the guardians against the excesses of government power; the supreme arbiters of policy. It is a difficult task in the best of times; in times of war it is particularly onerous! Nonetheless, the courts are the protectors of last resort for the ultimate, insular minority; the individual.

Foundation of Unenumerated Rights

Having established that the fundamental rights identified in the *Bill of Rights* are subject to abridgement if there is a compelling interest for the state to do so, the remaining issue on the road to privacy is whether other rights might be identified. If so, is it to be assumed that they are subject to abridgement for the same types of reasons as fundamental rights? Or, are they in fact fundamental rights?

In the 1965 case of *Griswold v. Connecticut*, the Supreme Court ruled that there are fundamental yet unenumerated rights. This decision also established the concept of **substantive due process** under which the courts can rule on the substance of a law as well as the procedures under which a law was developed. In considering the Supreme Court's decision in this case, one is reminded of the old adage "When the only tool you have is a hammer, every problem looks like a nail." Writing for the court, Justice William O. Douglas, after citing a number of cases in which the Supreme Court recognized fundamental rights not explicitly stated in the *Constitution*, observes that:

> The foregoing cases suggest that specific guarantees in the Bill of Rights have penumbras, formed by emanations from those guarantees that help give them life and substance.

The biggest shadow is cast by the concept of **liberty**. In the *Constitution*, liberty is one of the justifications found in the *Preamble*; however, the courts have avoided referencing the *Preamble* as a source of law. Instead, the court deemed relevant the reference to liberty found in the due process mandates of the *Fifth Amendment* and the *Fourteenth Amendment*. In our first chapter, we drew a subtle distinction between liberty and rights, suggesting liberty relates to the precipitation of actions, while rights relate to the establishment of policy that constrains the forces that actions enlist. One can see a similar distinction in the words of the court.

Probably the most widely recognized fundamental right is embodied in the *First Amendment's* guarantee of the freedom of speech. Over the course of many court decisions, the concept of speech has been expanded to encompass expression in a variety of forms. Rather obviously, expression is the more expansive concept and it would have simplified matters greatly if the *Bill of Rights* expressed a **freedom of expression**. However, that's not the tool that was provided. The result is the rationale that the enumerated rights, including freedom of speech, in combination cast penumbras that look like other fundamental rights. Somewhat intriguing, the *Griswold* case involves contraception; a rather obtuse form of expression at best.

Estelle Griswold was the executive director of the Planned Parenthood League of Connecticut. Dr. C. Lee Buxton, a medical doctor and professor at Yale Medical School, was the Medical Director of the Planned Parenthood League of Connecticut. In 1961, the two were arrested and charged with violating a Connecticut law that prohibited the use of "any drug, medicinal article or instrument for the purpose of preventing conception." They were found guilty as accessories to providing illegal contraception and fined $100 each. Following appeals in the Connecticut appellate courts, which upheld the convictions, Griswold and Buxton appealed to the U.S. Supreme Court, which issued its decision in 1965.

The finding of the court was almost startling in its succinctness:

> Held:
>
> 1. Appellants have standing to assert the constitutional rights of the married people. Tileston v. Ullman, 318 U. S. 44 , distinguished. P. 381 U.S. 481.
>
> 2. The Connecticut statute forbidding use of contraceptives violates the right of marital privacy which is within the penumbra of specific guarantees of the Bill of Rights. Pp. 381 U. S. 481-486.
>
> 151 Conn. 544, 200 A.2d 479, reversed.

The concepts of contraceptive, marriage and privacy are not found explicitly in the *Bill of Rights*, but their emanations were obviously perceived by the majority of the court; however, just as certainly not by all of the court. In his dissenting opinion, Justice Hugo Black, joined by Justice Potter Stewart writes:

> For these reasons, I get nowhere in this case by talk about a constitutional "right of privacy" as an emanation from one or more constitutional provisions. [Footnote 2/1] I like my privacy

> as well as the next one, but I am nevertheless compelled to admit that government has a
> right to invade it unless prohibited by some specific constitutional provision.

It is, of course, equally difficult to find mentioned contraceptive, marriage and privacy as among those things that the government is empowered by constitutional provision to **invade**. The *Ninth Amendment* and the *Tenth Amendment* would seem to speak more strongly to a general prohibition of government intrusion, with the default appearing to be a lack of government power in a given area rather than an assumption of government power. This is the root dichotomy that the Supreme Court is required to continually address.

From the current legal perspective, privacy emerged as a distinguished concept in the 1890 Harvard Law Review paper *The Right to Privacy* by Louis Brandeis and Samuel Warren. Their work associated the term "privacy" with a variety of the human behaviors that could be discerned through case law. While they were able to recognize the emergence, they couldn't give voice to a coherent, solid form. None-the-less, the term gathered credence from their defining work and it began to be referenced in opinions of the Supreme Court.

Perhaps the greatest epiphany of Brandeis' and Warren's work was the existence of a profound right not explicitly enumerated in the *Constitution*; a right derived from the common law. The *Constitution* recognizes in the *Ninth Amendment* that unenumerated rights do exist. This recognition notwithstanding, Brandeis' and Warren's consideration of a right of privacy was groundbreaking. This suggests that the effective impact of rights, both enumerated and unenumerated, results from a legal discovery process. In the next chapter, we will pursue the possibility that an expansive concept of personal privacy is at the root of this process.

Defining Privacy by Adjudication

We seek to observe a moderately coherent path toward the case of *Roe v. Wade*. As we observed in our first chapter, Justice William O. Douglas wrote a concurring opinion to *Roe* in which he presents a rather detailed roadmap of cases which led to the court's decision. It is a roadmap that shows the building of a substantial foundation for privacy, leading through *Griswold v. Connecticut*, which Justice Douglas authored.

Where we have attempted to present privacy as a single, coherent concept, Justice Douglas shows its piece-by-piece construction in contemporary jurisprudence; at least, from his perspective. His roadmap includes the main pathway, but also a few jogs in the road which he denotes through his dissents. It is illuminating to consider some of the individual pieces as they derived from the cases that he referenced. We must note that this progression of cases is not an exhaustive list relative to an emerging right of privacy. It is however an illustrative list.

In his concurring opinion, Justice Douglas classifies rights protected by the *Bill of Rights* and the *Fourteenth Amendment* in three categories:

> First is the autonomous control over the development and expression of one's intellect interests, tastes and personality; then … freedom of choice in the basic decisions of one's life respecting marriage, divorce, procreation, contraception, and the education and upbringing of children; and finally … the freedom to care for one's health and person, freedom from bodily restraint or compulsion, freedom to walk, stroll and loaf.

All these he perceives to be **fundamental**, yet all are "…subject to regulation on a showing of 'compelling state interest'."

Among the cases suggesting rights protected by the *First Amendment* is *Terminiello v. Chicago*. This was a 1949 case in which a Chicago city ordinance that banned speech that "stirs the public to anger, invites dispute, brings about a condition of unrest, or creates a disturbance" was declared unconstitutional under the *First Amendment* and *Fourteenth Amendment*. The *First Amendment* was applicable because of its guarantee of freedom of speech and the *Fourteenth Amendment* because it applied the *Bill of Rights* to laws of the states as well as laws of the federal government.

The case dealt with Arthur Terminiello who gave a speech to a Christian veterans' organization. During his speech he uttered some inflammatory comments directed at a crowd outside the hall. When some unrest broke out among the crowd, Terminiello was arrested and convicted of **breach of the peace**. Justice Douglas delivered the opinion of the Supreme Court which held the law in question to be unconstitutional in its violation of Terminiello's *First Amendment* rights as applied to the states through the *Fourteenth Amendment*. The ruling rejected the idea that the speech rose to the level of presenting a clear and present danger of inciting unlawful action. Instead, it notes:

> … a function of free speech under our system of government is to invite dispute. It may indeed best serve its high purpose when it induces a condition of unrest, creates dissatisfaction with conditions as they are, or even stirs people to anger. Speech is often provocative and challenging. It may strike at prejudices and preconceptions and have profound unsettling effects as it presses for acceptance of an idea.

The 1957 case of *Roth v. United States* affirmed the constitutionality of various state and federal laws involving **obscenity**, which one might expect to be protected by the *First Amendment* guarantee of freedom of speech. Part of the court's ruling states:

> In summary, then, we hold that these statutes, applied according to the proper standard for judging obscenity, do not offend constitutional safeguards against convictions based upon protected material, or fail to give men in acting adequate notice of what is prohibited.

As to just what constitutes obscenity, the court's ruling says in part that material is obscene if: "… to the average person, applying contemporary community standards, the dominant theme of the material, taken as a whole, appeals to prurient interests." An appeal to prurient interests would seem to fall within the realm of what we have termed aesthetic expression. The issue of obscenity deals with both the definition of what constitutes obscene material and to whom it is distributed.

In the digital realm, using the digital surrogates that we discussed previously, both of these facets of obscenity are impacted. Highly focused communities of interest can be rigorously established. The citizens of such communities can be authenticated through trustworthy processes and communication among the members of these communities can be shielded from general view using digital mechanisms. Authority to present or receive information can be controlled by the policy infrastructure of the community itself, based on the same digital approaches. This might suggest that both the definition of, and the constraints on, obscenity would be altered if personal privacy in the digital domain were fully considered.

Justice Douglas, joined by Justice Hugo Black, dissented in the *Roth* case. His reasoning was firmly grounded in the *First Amendment* and the *Fourteenth Amendment*:

> When we sustain these convictions, we make the legality of a publication turn on the purity of thought which a book or tract instills in the mind of the reader. I do not think we can approve that standard and be faithful to the command of the First Amendment, which, by its terms, is a restraint on Congress and which by the Fourteenth is a restraint on the States.

His dissent also contained a nod to the idea that even if a compelling interest in abridging a fundamental right could be stated, the law through which such abridgment was effected had to actually address the rationale of the compelling interest. In this vein, he questioned the science on which was based the idea that obscenity stimulates unlawful acts:

> If we were certain that impurity of sexual thoughts impelled to action, we would be on less dangerous ground in punishing the distributors of this sex literature. But it is by no means clear that obscene literature, as so defined, is a significant factor in influencing substantial deviations from the community standards.

The court drew an interesting distinction between obscenity and a **novel idea** through the 1959 case of *Kingsley Pictures Corp. v. Regents* involving the State of New York *Education Law*. It required the licensing of individual motion pictures before they could be exhibited in theaters. The film *Lady Chatterley's Lover* was denied a license because, in the words of the New York Education Department, "... the whole theme of this motion picture is immoral under said law, for that theme is the presentation of adultery as a desirable, acceptable and proper pattern of behavior." Justice Potter Stewart delivered the opinion of the court which overturned the denial of license on the grounds that it violated the *First Amendment* and the *Fourteenth Amendment* in their protection of the **freedom to express ideas**.

The decision struck down a ruling by the New York appellate courts with this admonition:

> What New York has done, therefore, is to prevent the exhibition of a motion picture because that picture advocates an idea -- that adultery under certain circumstances may be proper behavior. Yet the First Amendment's basic guarantee is of freedom to advocate ideas. The State, quite simply, has thus struck at the very heart of constitutionally protected liberty.

The *First Amendment* provides a guarantee of freedom of speech, and it also provides a guarantee of freedom of the press. This second freedom is complementary to the first in that together they cover the presentation, distribution and impressions of the personal expressions from others. They suggest that we have a right to express ideas and to disseminate those ideas broadly; and, we also have a right to selectively receive information so disseminated. We might refer to this as a right of selective impression. We will consider this interpretation in more detail in the next chapter.

As we will see a bit later, while these are aspects of a right of privacy, they can be difficult to reconcile in practice. The reconciliation is particularly awkward when one aspect such as expression is viewed asymmetrically with a different aspect such as selective impression. The reconciliation will obviously depend on arbitration that will be sensitive to context. The Supreme Court's decision in the 1964 case of *New York Times Co. v. Sullivan* begins to speak to this issue.

In the midst of civil rights protests in Montgomery, Alabama the *New York Times* ran a full page advertisement with the title "Heed Their Rising Voices". Although he was not mentioned by name in the advertisement, L. B. Sullivan, the Commissioner of Public Affairs and hence the supervision of the Police Department, Fire Department, Department of Cemetery and Department of Scales for the City of Montgomery claimed that he was libeled by the contents of the advertisement. He brought suit under Alabama law and was awarded a significant monetary sum for damages. The judgment was appealed to the Supreme Court of the United States on the grounds that the Alabama law violated the protections of the *First Amendment* and *Fourteenth Amendment*.

In overturning the judgment, the court ruled that for a public official to claim libel there must be proof of actual malice in publishing the offending material:

> The constitutional guarantees require, we think, a federal rule that prohibits a public official from recovering damages for a defamatory falsehood relating to his official conduct unless he proves that the statement was made with "actual malice" -- that is, with knowledge that it was false or with reckless disregard of whether it was false or not.

This has the effect of putting **public officials** in a different context from **private citizens**, at least with respect to questions of libel. Proving actual malice is akin to proving actual motivation; it can be difficult, if not impossible, in any case. We generally assess another's motivation by applying our own provisioning and hence our own motivational processes; a dubious approach in an environment of expansive personal privacy. An earlier case began to speak to this point; that is, the thoughts of people that reveal their motivations of actions, or inaction.

In the 1957 case *Watkins v. United States*, John Watkins was convicted of contempt of congress for failing to answer questions posed to him at a hearing of the House Un-American Activities Committee. The committee hearings were a wide ranging inquiry into the activities of persons thought to be associated with the Communist Party.

Watkins freely testified about his own involvement with communism, but he balked at answering questions about the actions of friends and associates and his thoughts regarding those activities of others. The inquiries appeared to be aimed at exposing peoples' activities purely to expose the activities; perhaps as a form of **shaming**. The Supreme Court overturned this conviction on the grounds that the questioning was not necessarily pertinent to the **question under inquiry**. Delivering the opinion of the court, Chief Justice Earl Warren wrote:

> The power of the Congress to conduct investigations is inherent in the legislative process. That power is broad. ... But, broad as is this power of inquiry, it is not unlimited. There is no general authority to expose the private affairs of individuals without justification in terms of the functions of the Congress. ... Nor is the Congress a law enforcement or trial agency. These are functions of the executive and judicial departments of government. No inquiry is an end in itself; it must be related to, and in furtherance of, a legitimate task of the Congress. Investigations conducted solely for the personal aggrandizement of the investigators or to "punish" those investigated are indefensible.

Having held that one had the right to remain silent in the face of questioning by the state in regards to their beliefs, the courts then addressed the privacy of external extensions of physiological manifestations such as speech. Personal privacy also accrued to the use of external tools such as the United States Mail. This was the subject of the case of *United States v. Van Leeuwen*.

In this 1970 Supreme Court decision, it was found that a proper search warrant was required before a First Class mail package could be opened and examined. Gerritt Van Leeuwen mailed two packages at the post office in a small town in the State of Washington, not too far from the border with Canada. The postal clerk became suspicious and alerted a policeman that the return address on the packages was a vacant area of a local university. The police checked with customs and found that one of the packages was addressed to a person under investigation for trafficking in illegal gold coins. Citing this as probable cause, the police requested search warrants to open the two packages.

Due to the time of day when the warrants were requested, they could not be issued until the following morning. Once the warrants were issued, examination of the packages found gold coins that had been brought across the border without payment of proper customs duties. Once arrested and convicted, Van Leeuwen appealed his conviction on the grounds that when the Post Office detained his packages for more than 24 hours before a search warrant was issued, it constituted unreasonable search and seizure under the *Fourth Amendment*. An appellate court agreed with this argument and reversed the conviction. This reversal was then appealed by the prosecution to the Supreme Court.

Justice Douglas wrote the opinion for the court which reversed the appellate court ruling and let stand the original conviction. The court's finding was that First Class Mail was indeed part of the personal papers protected by the *Fourth Amendment*. However, the court also found that the approximately one day delay in obtaining a valid warrant was acceptable under the circumstances and hence did not constitute unreasonable search and seizure. This is an illustration of the court's subjective assessment of what constitutes **unreasonable** with respect to search and seizure. A similar assessment also comes into play in considering compelling interests.

The 1940 case of *Cantwell v. Connecticut* illustrates the issue of reconciling the personal privacy of one party to freedom of expression and another party's freedom of selective impression. Through a state law, Connecticut enacted an administrative approach to the arbitration of social interactions. The law required that for a person to solicit funds for their religious organization, they must obtain a permit from a state administrator. This administrator was charged with determining that the purpose of the solicitation was for a **valid religious cause**.

Newton Cantwell, a member of the Jehovah's Witness church, went door to door with his two sons in a predominantly Catholic neighborhood of New Haven. At each house, they would seek permission from the householder to play a record that presented a summary introduction to books and pamphlets that they would then provide to the householder as an inducement to solicit a contribution. One such householder, a member of the Catholic Church, listened to a record that was derogatory toward the Catholic faith. He complained, and the Cantwell's were charged and convicted on a variety of counts for improper solicitation. Upheld by the Connecticut courts, the case came before the United States Supreme Court on appeal.

The Supreme Court ruled that the Cantwells' convictions of the common law offense of breach of the peace infringed their constitutional guarantees of religious liberty and freedom of speech. Justice Owen Roberts delivered the opinion of the court, which contains a most interesting reference relevant to the concepts we have been discussing:

> Without doubt, a State may protect its citizens from fraudulent solicitation by requiring a stranger in the community, before permitting him publicly to solicit funds for any purpose, to establish his identity and his authority to act for the cause which he purports to represent. … The State is likewise free to regulate the time and manner of solicitation generally, in the interest of public safety, peace, comfort or convenience. But to condition the solicitation of aid for the perpetuation of religious views or systems upon a license, the grant of which rests in the exercise of a determination by state authority as to what is a religious cause, is to lay a forbidden burden upon the exercise of liberty protected by the Constitution.

If *"state authority"* is forbidden from defining *"a religious cause"*, then motivation of actions is effectively removed from the state's subjective purview. This suggests that while actions may be constrained, specific motivations may not; or, at least not through a purely state administration facility. One might then question the manner by which actions may be so constrained.

In the early 1960's, Adell Sherbert was employed in a textile mill in South Carolina. After converting to the Seventh Day Adventist Church, her working hours at the mill were changed to include work on Saturday. Due her church's recognition of Saturday as its Sabbath Day, she refused to work on that day and was let go by the mill. She refused any other employment that included working on a Saturday. When she applied for unemployment benefits, she was denied on the grounds that she refused available work. She brought suit against the employment commission.

The case of *Sherbert v. Verner* made its way to the United States Supreme Court, which ruled that to deny her benefits infringed her *First Amendment* right to practice her religion. In writing the opinion of the court, Justice William Brennan brought to the table the concept of compelling interest on the part of the state, noting that for her denial of benefits to stand:

> ... it must be either because her disqualification as a beneficiary represents no infringement by the State of her constitutional rights of free exercise, or because any incidental burden on the free exercise of appellant's religion may be justified by a "compelling state interest in the regulation of a subject within the State's constitutional power to regulate . . . ."

The court ruled that neither of these constraints was met. The denial of benefits was set aside as an infringement of her right to practice her religion. Justice John Harlan II wrote a dissenting opinion, with Justice Byron White joining, in which he observed the court's ruling placed the state in a position of actually advocating a specific religious practice:

> The State, in other words, must *single out* for financial assistance those whose behavior is religiously motivated, even though it denies such assistance to others whose identical behavior (in this case, inability to work on Saturdays) is not religiously motivated.

The rationale for demonstration of a compelling state interest in the infringement of a fundamental right was put to the test in the 1969 case of *Kramer v. Union Free School District*. Morris Kramer was an unmarried man living with his parents in the Union School District. The State of New York had a variety of school district types, each with its own means of selecting the governing school board. The Union District was of a type that required voters for the school board to be property owners within the district. Kramer was not a property owner, so he sued to have the property ownership restriction declared unconstitutional as an infringement to his rights of equal protection under the *Fourteenth Amendment*.

The ownership restriction was declared constitutional by the lower courts. The case reached the United States Supreme Court on appeal. At issue before the court was whether the New York law expressed a compelling state interest in its limitations on the franchise of voting in the school board election. In its decision, the court did not consider whether a compelling interest might be recognized, but rather was a compelling interest demonstrated for the law referenced in this particular case. In ruling the law unconstitutional, the opinion delivered by Chief Justice Earl Warren held:

> For, assuming, *arguendo,* that New York legitimately might limit the franchise in these school district elections to those "primarily interested in school affairs," close scrutiny of the

§ 2012 classifications demonstrates that they do not accomplish this purpose with sufficient precision to justify denying appellant the franchise.

The court suggested that there might be compelling reasons for limiting who could vote within a particular election domain, but the specifics of this particular law did not satisfactorily establish that reason. This case dealt with defining the constituency that is allowed to vote within a social aggregate. A separate issue is who within a social aggregate is allowed to receive direct benefits from the social order.

With the emergence of significant entitlement programs, which essentially have no restrictions on the number of people who can received prescribed benefits, ostensibly to address budget concerns several states enacted laws that sought to restrict those who could qualify to avail themselves of such benefits. One approach to this restriction was to place a residency requirement on people who move into a state before they were allowed to apply for benefits. In the 1969 case of *Shapiro v. Thompson* the Supreme Court rejected this approach, ruling unconstitutional state laws in Connecticut, Pennsylvania, and the District of Columbia that mandated a one year residency requirement before a person could collect welfare benefits.

In the *Shapiro* ruling, the court recognized an unenumerated yet fundamental right, the **right to travel**. In subsequent rulings, the court conflated this concept with what might be presumed an orthogonal concept; that of residency. Residency, the act of residing in a place, is explicitly stated as a requirement to serve as President of the United States in *Article II Section 1*:

> No person except a natural born Citizen, or a Citizen of the United States, at the time of the Adoption of this Constitution, shall be eligible to the Office of President; neither shall any Person be eligible to that Office who shall not have attained to the Age of thirty-five Years, and been fourteen Years a Resident within the United States.

If we accept the premise that anyone can grow up to be President, it seems an implicit requirement on the state that the place of residence of any citizen of the United States must be discernable at any point in time; otherwise, it is impossible to objectively assess that a candidate meets this requirement. A more expansive definition is given to the concept of residency in *Section 1* of the *Fourteenth Amendment*:

> All persons born or naturalized in the United States, and subject to the jurisdiction thereof, are citizens of the United States and of the State wherein they reside.

To establish a process through which a person who is not a citizen of the United States can become a citizen, a process called **naturalization**, is a power delegated to Congress in *Article I Section 8*. One implication of these two mandates of the *Constitution* is that to become a citizen of a state in the United States one must first be a citizen of the United States and then must take up residence in a specific state. A further implication is that to be resident is to be physically present; hence, to travel to a place is to take one physically to that place, and therefore to be a resident of that place. This suggests rather profound effects on the various states; ranging from who can vote for the members of the policy infrastructure to who can receive direct benefits from the services provided by a state. The court's *Shapiro* ruling suggests that all that's necessary to be a citizen of a state is to show up.

State's that are home to large military bases tend to be sensitive to the perceived transient nature of those members of the nation's military who are quartered at such bases. The concern often voiced is that these personnel might unduly influence the policies enacted in some fashion as to be unfair to more permanent residents. Cities within a state often have the same concerns with large numbers of students attending university in those cities. A corollary to the concern about students exerting influence through voting in local elections is the desire on the part of state run universities to charge higher tuition for those who are not local residents.

Herbert Carrington was a soldier in the United States Army stationed at White Sands, New Mexico. He entered the army as a resident of Alabama. While serving at White Sands, he bought a home in El Paso, Texas and established his official residence there. When he sought to vote in a Texas election, he was denied a ballot due to a clause in the Texas *State Constitution* that said a member of the military could only vote in the district where he resided when he entered the service.

The end result was that while he was recognized as a resident of Texas, he was denied the vote solely because he was a member of the military. In 1965, the Supreme Court decision in the case of *Ccrrington v. Rash* ruled unconstitutional this aspect of the Texas *State Constitution* as a violation of the *Equal Protection Clause* of the United States *Constitution*. The right to travel on which this ruling is based extends to international travel as well as travel among the various states. This leads to consideration of the mechanisms of such travel; specifically, a passport.

As is obvious from many of the cases thus far considered, government seems to always seek to apply mechanisms beyond their intent. Thus, in the wake of World War II and the advent of the cold war, the passport was thrust into the battle against communism. To that time, passports were issued by the Secretary of State. The only criteria that were assessed in issuing a passport were the citizenship status and any criminal acts attributed to the applicant. These criteria were then extended so as to exclude issuing passports to communists. Rockwell Kent applied for a passport in order to travel to England and was denied because of his communist leanings. He brought suit in an effort to attain a passport.

The Supreme Court ruling in the case of *Kent v. Dulles* includes an overview of the legal basis for a passport. Historically, its function was aimed at foreign governments, representing a "... request to all whom it may concern to permit safely and freely to pass, and, in case of need, to give all lawful aid and protection".

In the 1950's, its purpose changed:

> ... throughout most of our history -- until indeed quite recently -- a passport, though a great convenience in foreign travel, was not a legal requirement for leaving or entering the United States. *See* Jaffe, The Right to Travel: The Passport Problem, 35 Foreign Affairs 17. Apart from minor exceptions to be noted, it was first made a requirement by § 215 of the Act of June 27, 1952, 66 Stat. 190, 8 U.S.C. § 1185, which states that, after a prescribed proclamation by the President, it is "unlawful for any citizen of the United States to depart from or enter, or attempt to depart from or enter, the United States unless he bears a valid passport."
>
> ...
> Its crucial function today is control over exit.

The court's ruling set aside the refusal of the Secretary of State to issue the passport as an improper delegation of power by the legislative branch to the executive branch and an infringement of the applicant's *Fifth Amendment* rights. Given the fundamental nature of the passport's utility,

> The right to travel is a part of the 'liberty' of which the citizen cannot be deprived without due process of law under the Fifth Amendment. . . . Freedom of movement across frontiers in either direction, and inside frontiers as well, was a part of our heritage. Travel abroad, like travel within the country . . . may be as close to the heart of the individual as the choice of what he eats, or wears, or reads. Freedom of movement is basic in our scheme of values.

Taking an alternative tack, through the *Subversive Control Act of 1950* Congress sought to establish a United States Passport as a non-membership credential for communism. Through a ruling in the 1964 case of *Aptheker v. Secretary of State* the Supreme Court declared unconstitutional a clause of the relevant law which said that a member of a communist front organization had to register as such and subsequently could not be issued a passport. This was also ruled a violation of the *Fifth Amendment*

Something of the same approach to addressing membership in organizations unpopular with the state was used by the State of Alabama against the NAACP during the civil rights movement. In the 1958 case of *NAACP v. Alabama*, the Supreme Court held that the NAACP could not be required to disclose its list of members in the State of Alabama. This case was something of a back and forth between the Supreme Court of the State of Alabama and the Supreme Court of the United States. At the very least, the case illustrates the hierarchical order of the judicial system; the United States Supreme Court trumps the State of Alabama Supreme Court.

Attempts by the state to control the actions and movements of citizens occur in the small as well as in the large. In 1972, several convictions of ostensible **vagrants** were consolidated under the case of *Papachristour v. City of Jacksonville* to contest the city's vagrancy laws. One of the cases involved four people convicted of "prowling by auto" and another of "common thief." Setting aside the convictions and invalidating the relevant laws, the Supreme Court raised the issues of ambiguous complexity in the formulation of policy and lack of consistency in its application:

> This ordinance is void for vagueness, both in the sense that it "fails to give a person of ordinary intelligence fair notice that his contemplated conduct is forbidden by the statute," *United States v. Harriss* ... , and because it encourages arbitrary and erratic arrests and convictions. *Thornhill v. Alabama,* ... ; *Herndon v. Lowry,* ... .

As we meander along the path toward privacy, it is perhaps appropriate to at least note the anti-privacy canon; the 1928 case of *Olmstead v. United States*. This case involved the government's un-warranted wiretapping telephone conversations involved in "...a conspiracy of amazing magnitude to import, possess and sell liquor unlawfully." The wiretaps were done on telephone lines external to the direct premises of the conspirators. Conversations were recorded secretly and without obtaining warrants from a court. The Supreme Court ruled that this information was admissible in court and did not represent a violation of the defendants' *Fourth Amendment* and *Fifth Amendment* rights; observing:

> The United States takes no such care of telegraph or telephone messages as of mailed sealed letters. The Amendment does not forbid what was done here. There was no searching. There was no seizure. The evidence was secured by the use of the sense of hearing, and that only. There was no entry of the houses or offices of the defendants.

The opinion for this 5-4 decision was authored by Chief Justice of the United States William Howard Taft, who earlier served as the 27th President of the United States. This highly restrictive interpretation of the *Fourth Amendment* and *Fifth Amendment* was subsequently overturned by the Supreme Court's 1967 decision in the case of *Katz v. United States*; a case involving the act of eavesdropping on telephone booth calls by way of a microphone positioned on the outside of the booth.

The court's opinion in *Katz* continues the consideration of privacy that is observed in contemporaneous decisions. In an effort to frame the constitutional issues before the Supreme Court, the appellant seemed inclined to view privacy more in line with what we've characterized as opacity. They saw the issues in the form of two questions:

> A. Whether a public telephone booth is a constitutionally protected area so that evidence obtained by attaching an electronic listening recording device to the top of such a booth is obtained in violation of the right to privacy of the user of the booth.

> B. Whether physical penetration of a constitutionally protected area is necessary before a search and seizure can be said to be violative of the Fourth Amendment to the United States Constitution.

Declining to debate the salient issues in these terms, the court's ruling presented a perspective on privacy as a more expansive concept, not restricted to a physical area:

> ... the Fourth Amendment cannot be translated into a general constitutional "right to privacy." That Amendment protects individual privacy against certain kinds of governmental intrusion, but its protections go further, and often have nothing to do with privacy at all. ... Other provisions of the Constitution protect personal privacy from other forms of governmental invasion. ... But the protection of a person's *general* right to privacy -- his right to be let alone by other people ... -- is, like the protection of his property and of his very life, left largely to the law of the individual States.

Thus we see progress toward viewing privacy in terms more consistent with the mechanics of interactions that we have been considering. This refocusing continued with a subsequent case which dealt quite explicitly with protocols related to the arbitration of the intersection of personal privacy of multiple individuals involving their dynamic actions when they all met on a street corner. The Supreme Court might not have perceived the case to be about arbitration protocols, but that seems an apt description.

The Supreme Court's decision in the 1968 case of *Terry v. Ohio* affirmed the search for and seizure of weapons conducted by a police detective on three men acting suspiciously for an extended period of time. Based on his observations, he engaged the men on a street corner in front of a store they had apparently been "casing." Concerned for his own safety, he patted their external clothing and detected the presence of pistols. He then detained the men and searched their coats more carefully, finding concealed weapons that were grounds for their arrest. At issue before the Supreme Court was whether this constituted an unreasonable search and seizure and whether the weapons found were admissible as evidence in a subsequent trial.

The opinion of the court written by Chief Justice Earl Warren quite methodically reviewed the distinct steps taken in the course of the street corner encounter. We recognize these steps as forming a protocol that a police officer might follow and which concludes in the legal detention of suspects based on successive steps of observation, interpretation and action. The opinion provides an excellent assessment of the social processes that must be encompassed by such a protocol:

> Street encounters between citizens and police officers are incredibly rich in diversity. They range from wholly friendly exchanges of pleasantries or mutually useful information to hostile confrontations of armed men involving arrests, or injuries, or loss of life. Moreover, hostile confrontations are not all of a piece. Some of them begin in a friendly enough manner, only to take a different turn upon the injection of some unexpected element into the conversation. Encounters are initiated by the police for a wide variety of purposes, some of which are wholly unrelated to a desire to prosecute for crime.

This last observation recognizes the reality that sometimes the police, or those that they encounter, will engage interactions as a means of harassment or intimidation. As we have noted in considering the mechanisms of privacy and identity, motivation is central in establishing context, assessing trust and evoking actions. When motivation is taken into consideration, the remedial actions derived from adjudication become exceedingly complex. Historically, as the court recognized, if searches and seizures are conducted without a warrant, then any evidence gathered is excluded from further consideration. If motivations are aimed at other than making arrests and gathering evidence, then the control mechanism for the interaction process ceases to be effective, as the court further observed:

> Proper adjudication of cases in which the exclusionary rule is invoked demands a constant awareness of these limitations. The wholesale harassment by certain elements of the police community, of which minority groups, particularly Negroes, frequently complain ... will not be stopped by the exclusion of any evidence from any criminal trial. Yet a rigid and unthinking application of the exclusionary rule, in futile protest against practices which it can never be used effectively to control, may exact a high toll in human injury and frustration of efforts to prevent crime.

The end result of the court's ruling was recognition of the concept of a reasonable **stop and frisk protocol**:

> Our evaluation of the proper balance that has to be struck in this type of case leads us to conclude that there must be a narrowly drawn authority to permit a reasonable search for weapons for the protection of the police officer, where he has reason to believe that he is dealing with an armed and dangerous individual, regardless of whether he has probable cause to arrest the individual for a crime. The officer need not be absolutely certain that the individual is armed; the issue is whether a reasonably prudent man, in the circumstances, would be warranted in the belief that his safety or that of others was in danger.

We observed earlier in touching on the case of *Brandenburg v. Ohio* that Justice William Douglas tended to view the fundamental rights expressed in the *Bill of Rights* as absolutes that the state could not infringe. In a dissenting opinion in *Terry*, Justice Douglas strenuously defended the existing concept of **probable cause**:

> The infringement on personal liberty of any "seizure" of a person can only be "reasonable" under the Fourth Amendment if we require the police to possess "probable cause" before they seize him.

We started our trek on the road to privacy with cases dealing with freedom of speech. We'll conclude this part of our journey by observing several cases that deal with "... freedom of choice in the basic decisions of one's life." Perhaps the first case that truly dealt with this aspect of what we're coming to understand as privacy was the 1891 case of *Union Pacific Railroad Company v.*

Botsford that affirmed a person's right to not be required to take an invasive physical examination as part of a civil trial.

Clara L. Botsford was severely injured while traveling on a Union Pacific Railroad Company train. She sued the company seeking damages on the grounds they were negligent in the construction and maintenance of the upper booth in the sleeping car in which she traveled. The company sought an order from the trial court to require her to submit to a surgical examination to assess the degree of her injuries. The trial court refused and the Supreme Court agreed, observing:

> No right is held more sacred or is more carefully guarded by the common law than the right of every individual to the possession and control of his own person, free from all restraint or interference of others unless by clear and unquestionable authority of law. As well said by Judge Cooley: "The right to one's person may be said to be a right of complete immunity; to be let alone."

As we observed earlier, Judge Cooley was the father of Charles Horton Cooley whose book *Human Nature and Social Order* we used as a source for our better understanding of the concept of identity.

In considering the conflict between state policy and fundamental rights expressed through the *Constitution*, the courts always allude to the possibility of their infringement given a compelling interest to the state in so doing. In the early 1900's, the city of Cambridge, Massachusetts was in the throes of a smallpox epidemic. A state law was enacted requiring adults to be vaccinated against the disease. Henning Jacobsen refused to be vaccinated, citing personal bad experiences with vaccinations as a child. He was convicted and fined for his refusal. He appealed the case to the United States Supreme Court on the grounds that his fundamental rights had been violated.

In its ruling in the case of *Jacobsen v. Massachusetts* the Supreme Court affirmed compulsory vaccination of adults as an acceptable application of the police powers of the State of Massachusetts to protect the public health. The opinion cited experiential justification for vaccination against smallpox. The court did recognize that while the fundamental rights of an individual could be infringed through application of the state's police powers, those powers were not themselves inviolate:

> ... the police power of a State, whether exercised by the legislature or by a local body acting under its authority, may be exerted in such circumstances or by regulations so arbitrary and oppressive in particular cases as to justify the interference of the courts to prevent wrong and oppression.

This case is generally perceived to lay the foundation for public health activities in the United States. While justifiable in the case of smallpox vaccinations, using police powers of the state to address other ostensible public health issues is fraught with opportunities for unreasonable exploitation.

In the early 1900's, the concept of eugenics was somewhat in vogue among policy purveyors around the world. The thought was that by removing undesirable individuals from the greater gene pool of society, a proclivity for criminal behavior could be eradicated, thus enhancing the health of the society. One way to pursue this goal was forced sterilization as remedial action for such behavior. In this vein, the State of Oklahoma enacted the *Habitual Criminal Sterilization Act*. Jack Skinner was convicted under this law and sentenced to be sterilized.

In its 1943 ruling in the case of *Skinner v. Oklahoma*, the *Habitual Criminal Sterilization Act* was ruled unconstitutional. While one might have surmised that this law would run afoul of the *Eighth Amendment* restriction on cruel and unusual punishment, this was not the case. Rather, the court primarily based its ruling on the fact that the law did not apply the sterilization punishment equitably across various manners of crimes and that the distinction presented had no basis in scientific or legal fact. Justice Douglas delivered the opinion of the court, including the observation:

> Oklahoma makes no attempt to say that he who commits larceny by trespass or trick or fraud has biologically inheritable traits which he who commits embezzlement lacks. ... We have not the slightest basis for inferring that that line has any significance in eugenics, nor that the inheritability of criminal traits follows the neat legal distinctions which the law has marked between those two offenses.

The court did not rule directly on the suitability of sterilization as a punishment. Rather, the court noted that laws effecting such punishment should be subjected to strict scrutiny:

> We advert to them [the police powers of the state] merely in emphasis of our view that strict scrutiny of the classification which a State makes in a sterilization law is essential, lest unwittingly, or otherwise, invidious discriminations are made against groups or types of individuals in violation of the constitutional guaranty of just and equal laws. The guaranty of "equal protection of the laws is a pledge of the protection of equal laws."

We interpret this last observation as a reference to the concept of **due process**, which we will consider in a bit more detail later in this chapter. This concept figures prominently in the court's consideration of racial constraints on marriage in the 1967 case of *Loving v. Virginia*.

In 1958, Mildred Jeter, a black woman, and Richard Loving, a white man, were married in the District of Columbia. While both people were residents of Virginia, they went to the District to be married since there was no prohibition against interracial marriage there. In Virginia, such marriages were forbidden. After marriage, the couple returned to Virginia to make their home. There they were subsequently indicted by a Grand Jury and convicted of violating the Virginia law. Their appeal made its way to the Supreme Court and Chief Justice Earl Warren delivered the unanimous opinion of the court in 1967.

The gist of the court's opinion is summarized in its final order:

> Marriage is one of the "basic civil rights of man," fundamental to our very existence and survival. Skinner v. Oklahoma, 316 U. S. 535, 316 U. S. 541 (1942). See also Maynard v. Hill, 125 U. S. 190 (1888). To deny this fundamental freedom on so unsupportable a basis as the racial classifications embodied in these statutes, classifications so directly subversive of the principle of equality at the heart of the Fourteenth Amendment, is surely to deprive all the State's citizens of liberty without due process of law. The Fourteenth Amendment requires that the freedom of choice to marry not be restricted by invidious racial discriminations.

> Under our Constitution, the freedom to marry, or not marry, a person of another race resides with the individual, and cannot be infringed by the State.

> These convictions must be reversed.

> It is so ordered.

As we observed earlier in this chapter, the case of *Griswold v. Connecticut* affirmed the right of married couples to use contraceptives. The 1972 case of *Eisenstadt v. Baird* extended this right to unmarried couples by declaring unconstitutional a Massachusetts law that prohibited selling contraceptives to unmarried couples. The court ruled this a violation of the *Equal Protection Clause*. It established the right of unmarried couples to have and use contraceptives on the same basis as married couples, essentially establishing a right for unmarried couples to have non-procreative sex. In delivering the opinion of the court, Justice William Brennan built upon Justice Douglas' allusion in *Griswold v. Connecticut* to "... a right of privacy older than the Bill of Rights -- older than our political parties, older than our school system." with this further admonition:

> If the right of privacy means anything, it is the right of the individual, married or single, to be free from unwarranted governmental intrusion into matters so fundamentally affecting a person as the decision whether to bear or beget a child.

The 1923 case of *Meyer v. Nebraska* addressed perhaps the second most basic aspect of personal privacy; the use of language, which is the most general tool that humans use to engage the sensori-motor world. The case involved a teacher by the name of Robert Meyer. He was brought to task for violation of a State of Nebraska law entitled the *Siman Act*. His crime was teaching in a private school using the German language; more specifically, he was teaching an elementary student from the *Christian Bible* in German.

The Supreme Court overturned this law through its opinion written by Justice James Clark McReynolds. The ruling included one of the more cogent expressions of a general right of privacy found in any ruling that we have considered:

> While this Court has not attempted to define with exactness the liberty thus guaranteed, the term has received much consideration and some of the included things have been definitely stated. Without doubt, it denotes not merely freedom from bodily restraint, but also the right of the individual to contract, to engage in any of the common occupations of life, to acquire useful knowledge, to marry, establish a home and bring up children, to worship God according to the dictates of his own conscience, and generally to enjoy those privileges long recognized at common law as essential to the orderly pursuit of happiness by free men.

The court's ruling in *Meyer* makes a profound point that touches at the nature of the state's infringement of personal privacy in regards to the provisioning of the polity:

> In order to submerge the individual and develop ideal citizens, Sparta assembled the males at seven into barracks and intrusted their subsequent education and training to official guardians. Although such measures have been deliberately approved by men of great genius, their ideas touching the relation between individual and State were wholly different from those upon which our institutions rest, and it hardly will be affirmed that any legislature could impose such restrictions upon the people of a State without doing violence to both letter and spirit of the Constitution.

In 1922, the people of Oregon engaged the most basic aspect of personal privacy; that of provisioning. Through a popular referendum, the *Compulsory Education Law* was enacted. It required all children ages 8 – 16 in Oregon to attend public schools. Its effective purpose was to shut down private education as a means to promote **Americanism** in an effort to force the large and growing immigrant population to adopt the popularly perceived virtues of the **American way of life**. The law was challenged in court by the Society of Sisters, a Catholic Church agency that provided private, parochial schools to approximately 10% of the students in Oregon.

The case made its way to the United State Supreme Court in 1925 as *Pierce v. Society of Sisters*. As he had for the case of *Meyer v. Nebraska*, Justice James Clark McReynolds wrote this opinion of the court which struck down the Oregon law. Extending the concepts noted above derived from *Meyer*, the ruling included this admonition:

> The fundamental theory of liberty upon which all governments in this Union repose excludes any general power of the State to standardize its children by forcing them to accept instruction from public teachers only. The child is not the mere creature of the State; those who nurture him and direct his destiny have the right, coupled with the high duty, to recognize and prepare him for additional obligations.

The provisioning of the polity is at the heart of American jurisprudence. It is the most basic manifestation of American culture. Taken together, the two cases of *Pierce v. Society of Sisters* and *Meyer v. Nebraska* recognize provisioning the young as an assertion of personal privacy. We will come back to this point in the final chapter, but to get to that consideration we need to complete our tour of the evolutionary pathways of privacy and policy.

Canonical Case for Privacy

The current high water mark in understanding and recognizing privacy in the United States is fixed by the case of *Roe v. Wade*. In this 1973 landmark ruling, the Supreme Court recognized a right of privacy under which a woman has the power to decide whether to terminate her pregnancy. Justice Harry Blackmun wrote the opinion of the court which said in part:

> We, therefore, conclude that the right of personal privacy includes the abortion decision, but that this right is not unqualified and must be considered against important state interests in regulation.

The court's finding brings into sharp focus the concept of **compelling interests** of the state as a determining factor in the infringement of any right. While the decision affords a right on the one hand, it recognizes there might be grounds for restricting it through policy on the other:

> ...a State may properly assert important interests in safeguarding health, in maintaining medical standards, and in protecting potential life.

The ruling is then quite rigorous in defining when the power of a woman to make the relevant choices regarding her pregnancy is absolute, versus when the state might abridge the decision power in some way. During the first trimester of pregnancy the power is unfettered; during the last trimester, ostensibly when the fetus reaches a state of viability, the state might offer a compelling interest to intercede in the decision-making process. We have suggested that privacy sits at the frontier of social evolution. In this case, the Supreme Court recognized that the frontier sits at the middle of gestation of a human fetus. It is a frontier fraught with turmoil.

There is compelling logic in the turmoil. Privacy and policy sit astride the boundary between the person and social order. Abortion is exactly positioned at the juncture of the physiological and the social. Some on one side of the divide perceive abortion as a purely medical procedure directed at a woman's body and hence is completely under her purview. Some on the other side perceive the act as an attack on a new person; the fetus that came into being as an embryo at conception and is developing within the woman. Many, including a majority of the Supreme Court, sit astride the divide, recognizing that the salient point is that a woman has the power to decide, not the state. She has that power as a manifestation of her right of privacy.

The court's decision leaves somewhat ambiguous the actual source of this right, deferring to the *Fourteenth Amendment* as opposed to the penumbras suggested in *Griswold*. Where ever the right originates, the court established that it encompasses the abortion decision with the words:

> The right of privacy, whether it be founded in the Fourteenth Amendment's concept of personal liberty and restrictions upon state action, as we feel it is, or, as the District Court determined, in the Ninth Amendment's reservation of rights to the people, is broad enough to encompass a woman's decision whether or not to terminate her pregnancy.

One might observe that among the three possible reasons noted above for the state to abridge a woman's right of privacy, perhaps only the last one listed could prove compelling to the level of infringing a woman's decision to have an abortion; "...protecting potential life." It brings into focus the privacy of the potential adult individual that might ultimately derived from the fetus versus the privacy of an existent adult individual; the woman who is pregnant.

The immediate interest of the state lies in providing a level playing field regarding the state's infringement of the personal privacy of the mother. To forego a termination of her pregnancy is a demand by the state for an altruistic act on the part of the woman. While the fetus may develop into an adult through many years of provisioning, its immediate physiological state is obviously not that of an adult and hence is subject to consideration independent from that of the potential adult.

We're well aware that we've stated this consideration of potential life in terms that some will find pejorative; that a fetus might become an adult person. We do this to draw out the point that members of the human species develop through a variety of stages. While latter stages build upon prior stages, the physiological entity is distinct in each. The point when the entity is due full protection of personal privacy is difficult to discern. Further, as we have noted previously, what constitutes full protection is itself ambiguous.

In current American society, once afforded, even the fundamental rights of any member of the human species are age dependent, capability dependent and policy dependent. The state doesn't give driver licenses to five year olds, nor does it allow them to vote. Adults are charged with the provisioning of the young. At the other end of the age spectrum, when the elderly person reaches a point of severe senility, their rights to make decisions for themselves may be sharply curtailed by the state. They no longer retain the unfettered right of personal privacy. Their driver license is taken away. If a person degenerates to a totally unresponsive condition, the state can deem their quality of life to be so degraded that measures to prolong that life will not be pursued.

In the extreme of adjudication, a person convicted of a crime can have their life terminated. It is to be assumed that all infringements of personal privacy, be it age, capability or policy derived, must be justified through a compelling state interest. In the case of the abortion decision, the courts have considered the prospects of compelling state interest and found them wanting. It's not clear that can yet be said of the other infringements of personal privacy that we've noted.

A progression of cases led to *Roe v. Wade*, a case that ostensibly began when an unmarried young lady who was pregnant filed suit against the State of Texas, seeking to obtain an abortion in a safe medical facility. Texas' anti-abortion statues at the time prohibited the provision of abortion services, not the actual receiving of an abortion on the part of a woman. We say *"ostensibly began"* because the decision to file a legal challenge to Texas law was made by Sarah Weddington, a young attorney from Austin, Texas in 1970, well before a plaintiff for the suit was actually identified.

Weddington recounts the history of the *Roe v. Wade* case in her book *A Question of Choice*, first published in 1992. Beginning with her own experience in obtaining an abortion in Mexico while a college student, she follows the history of consciousness raising among women as a corollary to the civil rights movement of the 1950's and 1960's. Her primary goal was the recognition as a matter of law of a woman's right to make decisions about her own body, including whether or not to bear children.

Through its police powers, the state seeks to impact interactions through laws aimed at three facets of interactions: their context, their constrained actions and the consequences of those actions. The American judicial system attempts to be, and largely is, devoid of emotion. While this is presented as a desirable trait in the administration of justice, it begs the question of how interactions replete with emotional context are to be properly adjudicated. This aspect presented itself rather vividly during the *Roe v. Wade* case. Jane Roe, a pseudonym for the pregnant young lady who was the plaintiff in the law suit, actually carried her baby to term while the case was in process.

In oral arguments before the United States Supreme Court, the State of Texas argued that this fact rendered the case moot. The woman who had been seeking injunctive relief in order to obtain an abortion was no longer pregnant, so she had no need of an abortion. What the State of Texas argued meant that the American system of jurisprudence should be worse than useless for the principal in this case. Not only was she prevented from seeking a safe, medical abortion by the enforcement of an unconstitutional law, but in fact the typical adjudication process would never allow the determination of its unconstitutionality. The gestation period of a human fetus and the timeframe for judicial review are just too different. Nonetheless, the suit was pursued. For others in her foxhole, Jane Roe fell on the grenade. It seems a strange requirement of **due process** under the **rule of law**.

In many instances, an occurrence of this nature is sufficient to have a case dismissed. Even in this particular case the point was in doubt until its ultimate resolution by the Supreme Court. In its final ruling the court found that the case was not moot because the issue was "capable of repetition, yet evading review." The court reasoned that because of the length of time necessary for the normal judicial review process, a pregnant woman would never be able to receive relief from laws making abortion a crime. She would always have had the baby before the final court ruling could be delivered. Hence, a special accommodation in the judicial review process was necessary. The *Roe v. Wade* case took approximately three years from filing to resolution. Not even an elephant could have remained pregnant long enough for the courts to render the final consequence under normal procedures.

This case also illustrates a necessary social aspect of current jurisprudence. Jane Roe filed the law suit with little expectation of resolution. While she sought injunctive relief from the courts, it was not forthcoming. The courts were fully complicit in the enforcement of an unconstitutional law.

However, the filing was made as a class action, enabling the ultimate ruling to be made applicable to a social order; that of pregnant women in the state of Texas. During the oral arguments before the Supreme Court, one of the justices commented, "I suppose we could almost take judicial notice of the fact that there are, at any given time, unmarried, pregnant females in the State of Texas." In social interactions, emotional response to sensory observation gives an indication of the necessary time frame for a motor action response. The judicial system has no such indicator.

The lack of injunctive relief for Jane Roe would seem to present a problem in American jurisprudence that comes into focus with the court's ruling. The case demonstrates a perceived logical inconsistency in the adjudication system that brings it into violation of the requirements of due process as suggested in the *Constitution*. The inconsistency arises when any law subject to strict scrutiny lacks a compelling interest. In this situation, evaluating the compelling interest served by a law is **case independent**.

For example, in the *Roe* decision the court determined that during the first trimester of pregnancy there is no compelling interest under which the state can infringe a woman's right to decide to terminate her pregnancy. To make this determination, there was no need to have an actual appellant. It was more than sufficient for the court to simply observe "... that there are, at any given time, unmarried, pregnant females in the state of Texas." The law itself was suspect; any enforcement of the law referenced an unconstitutional act and it could have been so determined without having any case on which to base the determination. The sticking point is that the courts need a reason to even think about it; an on-switch if you will for the adjudication process.

The rationale for this is found in *Article III Section 2* of the *Constitution* which notes "The judicial Power shall extend to all Cases, in Law and Equity, arising under this Constitution ... ". Its reference to **cases** has been construed as requiring the judicial system to only address issues after the fact of their occurrence. A case can't exist until a controversy exists. This suggests that the judiciary cannot act to assess laws before their enforcement creates a controversy. However, forcing a person to be subject to a law that could be determined as unconstitutional *a priori* would seem to present an interesting problem relative to due process. We'll further explore this inconsistency in the next chapter by taking something of a technical perspective on the adjudication process.

This perceived logical inconsistency can actually become quite pernicious by keeping the adjudication system from presenting finality of consequences. In controversial areas of law, even with Supreme Court decisions derived from judicial review comes continuing ambiguity when policy purveyors enact laws at odds with existent court rulings. The result is that such laws have a chilling effect in the controversial area, particularly if they are enforced while the wheels of justice grind exceedingly slow.

It is interesting to consider this process in light of the oath and affirmation constraints established by *Article VI* of the *Constitution*, an issue we will discuss in more detail in our last chapter. Often deferring to the legislative and executive branches, courts will allow enforcement until the law is adjudicated. It's sometimes unclear whether the legislative and executive branches of government feel at all compelled to understand and adhere to due process.

History suggests that the state pursues a continuing process to subjugate the polity to the will of the legislative and executive majority. There seems to be less dedication to recognize and follow constitutional obligations than to exploit legislative and executive majorities. Rather, it is left to the courts to recognize and restrain excessive behavior. This exploitation by the majority represents a form of recursion in the adjudication system that has no apparent control mechanism save for the courts. This results in a rather awesome mandate for the courts that derives from a seemingly innocuous constitutional constraint; that of **due process**.

Bright Lines and Due Process

Privacy is not mentioned in the *Constitution*. Rather, giving form and substance to privacy in contemporary American jurisprudence has been an evolving process of discovery by the adjudication system. Independent of its profound relationship to privacy, the process itself is a central characteristic of law. It finds a beginning in the *Fifth Amendment*, which says in part:

> No person shall ... be deprived of life, liberty, or property, without due process of law; nor shall private property be taken for public use, without just compensation.

This recognizes two causal principles. First, the protection of what we recognize as facets of privacy, that is, life, liberty and property, forms a basic constraint on policy. In the *Meyer v. Nebraska* case, the court's ruling included the admonition "...a desirable end cannot be promoted by prohibited means." Second, conditional covenants whose consequences are **just compensation** are a basic means through which policy is intended to impact privacy. These aspects of due process are subsequently extended to the laws of the various states through *Section 1* of the *Fourteenth Amendment*, which says in part:

> No State shall make or enforce any law which shall abridge the privileges or immunities of citizens of the United States; nor shall any State deprive any person of life, liberty, or property, without due process of law; nor deny to any person within its jurisdiction the equal protection of the laws.

Based on our previous discussions regarding privacy, identity, policy, society and interactions, we have some insight into what this requirement for due process means. One might construe the *Fifth Amendment* reference to apply primarily to the adjudication of consequences; mandating that a court cannot apply remedial actions unless the rules of adjudication have been correctly followed. However, the *Fourteenth Amendment* reference suggests something more expansive.

This draws into consideration the making and enforcing of laws coupled with "...the privileges and immunities of citizens of the United States." This suggests that in assessing the due process requirement to have been satisfied, the courts have the power and responsibility to examine the entire infrastructure within which laws are enacted and enforced. Due process is obviously about process, and since process proceeds from a point of causality, due process is about the individual receiving the benefit they are due from that causality. We can contrast this more expansive meaning with the concept of a bright line rule that we mentioned a bit earlier

A bright line rule is a test or measure applied by a court to a specific case to objectively assess whether policy has been correctly interpreted and enforced. In the technical domain, a concept known as **derived test requirements** is somewhat synonymous to a bright line rule. These are test protocols used to confirm that specific requirements for complex systems are met in the actual implementations of those systems. In the legal domain, various bright line rules have been defined that apply to specific parts of an interaction; to context, to motivation, to action and to consequence. We suggest that an assessment of due process is metaphorically similar, yet far more extensive.

To examine due process, the courts must pursue an objective process, a protocol if you will, through which they ultimately make a subjective decision regarding the adequacy of all aspects of justifying, enacting and enforcing the law applicable to a specific case. The Supreme Court is the ultimate purveyor of this subjective decision. It might then establish, or accept from a lower court, more rigorous and objective measures in order to convey the results of its subjective decision throughout the judiciary. These objective measures comprise bright line rules.

The concept of due process had its beginnings with the *Magna Carta* a millennium ago. It came to American jurisprudence on the back of British common law, but it is no longer found in British common law. It's most common usage was to assure accessibility of law to the common person. From a number of landmark cases in which it is referenced as justification for the court's rulings, we have come to recognize that due process is concerned with virtually all aspect of jurisprudence, including the form and function of:

- Trust infrastructure
- Policy infrastructure
- Process of policy
- Substance of policy
- Mechanics of adjudication
- Remedial measures

In a recursive act of shaping the policy infrastructure, the United States Supreme Court established itself as the guarantor of due process very early in the life of the nation. The *Constitution* alludes to, but does not explicitly assign the duties of the Supreme Court, other than to invest in it the ultimate power of the judiciary; whatever that might comprise. Through a Supreme Court ruling in the case of *Marbury v. Madison*, the court effectively established itself as the arbiter of policy and the policy infrastructure. Relating this back to the mechanisms of privacy we consider in a previous chapter, this action had all the earmarks of a self-signed certificate; that is, a credential of authority grounded in causality and distributed through trusted processes.

The case involved a procedural issue that ultimately called into question a section of the *Judicial Act of 1789*; at least, that was the stated rationale of the court. The section in question ostensibly changed the domain of jurisdiction for the Supreme Court; an action the court held to be contrary to the domain established in the *Constitution*. The court's ruling invalidated that section, declaring it unconstitutional, thus forcing a reversion to the terms in *Article III* of the *Constitution*. Chief Justice John Marshall, the longest serving Chief Justice of the United States, in writing the opinion of the court recognized the recursive nature of the process:

> The judicial power of the United States is extended to all cases arising under the constitution. [5 U.S. 137, 179] Could it be the intention of those who gave this power, to say that, in using it, the constitution should not be looked into? That a case arising under the constitution should be decided without examining the instrument under which it arises?
>
> This is too extravagant to be maintained.

In some cases then, the constitution must be looked into by the judges. And if they can open it at all, what part of it are they forbidden to read, or to obey?

The decision was not without controversy. In reality, the case was at the center of a clash of constitutional interpretation between the Republicans (more formally, the Democrat-Republicans) led by Thomas Jefferson and the Federalists led by John Adams. At issue in the young republic was the power and function of the courts relative to the executive and legislative branches. The Republicans stressed the subservience of the courts, believing that the executive and legislative branches were each responsible for interpreting the *Constitution* as it pertained to their individual dominions. With a contrary view, the Federalists believe that it was the purpose of a strong, independent judiciary to hold government subject to the constraints of the *Constitution*.

The subject of the case was of little enduring interest. It revolved around the commission for William Marbury to assume the office of Justice of the Peace to serve in the District of Columbia. The position was that of an officer of the federal administration in the newly created district. The commission was issued by the outgoing administration of John Adams, but its actual delivery to Marbury was delayed and subsequently diverted by the incoming administration of Thomas Jefferson.

In a rather obtuse ruling, the Supreme Court held that Marbury would not get his commission through the court's action. However, in rendering this decision the court ruled unconstitutional a part of an act of Congress that had previously modified the procedures of the judiciary; a modification the court held to be in conflict with *Article III* of the *Constitution*. Through this ruling, the court's expression of judicial review comprised a giant step toward establishing the judiciary as a co-equal branch of government. This lay the groundwork for recognizing the Supreme Court as the ultimate arbiter of policy under American jurisprudence.

The *Fifth Amendment* and the *Fourteenth Amendment* translate into procedural form the principles expressed in the *Declaration of Independence*. They make explicit as property the concept of interaction consequences that result from assertions of personal privacy. When applied to the various enumerated rights recognized in the *Bill of Rights*, due process provides the illumination that casts the penumbras recognized by Justice Douglas.

The *Fifth Amendment* incorporates into the concept of due process that of **just compensation** for the state's taking of property from the individual. This suggests that conditional covenants between the state and the individual comprise the basis for the infringement of the consequences of personal privacy; that is, of property. Through a conditional covenant, one party offers consideration to another party in exchange for like consideration.

This further suggests that in assessing the due process of conditional covenants the basis of compensation is subject to due process as well. The value afforded to any means of compensation must be consistent across the timeframe of the conditional covenant, to the extent that the state controls value as it pertains to compensation. This is a crucial component of the concept of altruistic action that the state mandates of the polity. We will consider this in more detail in the next chapter.

Beginning with the ruling that established judicial review, the consideration of due process has extended recursively through the entire trust and policy infrastructures. The last bastion of executive and legislative prerogative that the courts have sought to address is the substance of law;

the concept known as **substantive due process**. However, in their considerations of the *Griswold v. Connecticut* case and subsequently in *Roe v. Wade* the court moved into this domain; ostensibly only in the consideration of fundamental rights. Seeking to limit the area of such consideration, Justice Douglas wrote in the *Griswold* ruling that the court would avoid substantive consideration of "... laws that touch economic problems, business affairs, and social conditions." The implication is that economic, business affairs and social issues do not directly engage fundamental rights. One might wonder at the basis of this exclusion and whether it can continue into the future?

Laws enacted under the police powers of the state can evoke remedial actions that enlist sanctions enforced through the police powers of the state. These remedial actions imposed through the adjudication process inherently result in the infringement of personal privacy; a fundamental right. Many of these sanctions are intended to be punitive in nature; purely punishment with no other social purpose. Thus, it seems difficult to differentiate the domain of laws when their enforcement ultimately resolves to the infringement of fundamental rights in the application of remedial measures.

It is particularly onerous when the mere application of the law, not the remedial actions derived from its enforcement when broken, involves punitive measures. As the Supreme Court ruling in the case of *United States v. Jackson* reasoned:

> If a law has "no other purpose . . . than to chill the assertion of constitutional rights by penalizing those who choose to exercise them, then it [is] patently unconstitutional."

In its imposition of altruistic behavior on the polity, the state resorts to three economic mechanisms: taxation, borrowing and manipulation of the availability, and hence the value, of money. When borrowing by the state is obviously never intended to be repaid in equivalent currency, then it can be considered as taxation against the future polity. This appears to be the prevailing situation; high and increasing public debt coupled to financial policy aimed at inflating the available currency and hence diminishing its value. It has become questionable whether such policies are sustainable over the long term. This would seem to invite consideration by the courts since constitutional protections are eroded by such policies.

The trust and policy infrastructures put in place by the Founders are intended to be enduring. This is emphasized in the *Preamble to the Constitution* with the admonition to "... secure the Blessings of Liberty to ourselves and our Posterity ..." The infrastructures have evolved to the point that it has become the responsibility of the courts to assure this. Hence, they must look to the time dependence of mechanisms, including altruistic requirements and the compelling interests that give rise to them. This would seem to imply that over time the mechanisms derived from the infrastructures cannot be allow to become too complex or too contrived if they are to maintain sustainability. Complexity threatens the control loops on which sustainable operation depends. Other threats to sustainability must be addressed as well.

This suggests that due process requires that the state optimize policy for the long-term. If there are short term excursions, there should be recognized means for coming back to a sustainable process in the longer term. This does not suggest, of course, that the state cannot establish onerous levels of taxation or borrowing. It does, however, suggest that the policies through which taxes are levied and borrowing enacted should present as equitably distributed across the economic spectrum and the multiple generations of the polity.

Thus, two crucial facets of due process are the means of establishing what comprises a compelling interest on the part of the state and the criteria that characterize insular minorities. In particular, it suggests that compelling interest must be differentiated from simply the "will of the majority". Insular minorities can be characterized by economic factors as readily as by race or gender. Chronic oppression of the wealthy is pernicious as is acute oppression of the poor. Due process seeks to avoid the enslavement of insular minorities through the will of the majority as well as the aggregation of power in the hands of subcultures within the social order.

Compelling interests aimed at altruistic behaviors are best addressed through conditional covenants and stochastic processes. In the arbitration of the intersection of personal privacy among interaction participants, the negotiation of consideration offered for consideration received is an explicit manifestation of the compelling interest of each party. If one party is able to assert its own value system on the consideration of the other party, then the infringement of personal privacy will most likely be inequitable. This is the great danger that emerges when the state seeks to enforce its own assessment of perceived value of consideration. The social order becomes asymmetric and compelling interest becomes self-serving to distinct subcultures.

Explicit conditional covenants expressed as contracts generally result in the most equitable infringement of personal privacy. If people could communicate perfectly in establishing contracts, and if the participants brought impeccable trustworthiness to the table when they engage contracts, then there would be little if any need for policy mandates from a higher social order. Unfortunately, neither of these assumptions is completely valid. Consequently, there is ample opportunity for the state to establish policy under which contracts can be developed and their consequences adjudicated when disagreeable consequences ensue.

Each party has an assumption of equality at the engagement of the interaction. In many, if not most cases, the abridgement of privacy will occur through a conditional covenant among parties. We know these conditional covenants as contracts. The purpose of establishing a contract is to recognize an equitable infringement of privacy for each party. Since each party brings their own motivations to the interaction engaged through the contract, the parties are the preeminent arbiters of what constitutes an equitable arrangement.

The constituent aspects of any conditional covenant tend to be quite similar, encompassing some or all of these characteristics:

- Participants to the interaction
- Interaction policy or rules established by the contract
- Consequences desired to result from the interaction
- Adjudication mechanisms in the case of disputed consequences
- Dissolution of the contract on its ultimate completion
- Constraining social order whose policy subsumes the contract's policy

The purpose of a contract is to enhance trust by establishing a structured interaction in which context, motivations, actions and consequences are well defined and understood by all the parties to the interaction. Under a good contract, the relationship of truth to trust should be easy for all to assess. In asserting that contracts are about personal privacy infringement, what we're actually observing is that contracts form the context for social interactions in which individual motivations are voluntarily manipulated by external influences. This often entails the consideration of specific areas where it is necessary to establish the value for dissimilar things.

For any policy established by the state, its model for due process should be the conditional covenant. The assessment of value should derive from motivations of those who engage the covenant. If the state is a party to the covenant, it should not assign its own motivations or assessment of value to other parties. The state is in the unique position to mandate altruistic behavior and to control the availability and value of money; the means through which the value of dissimilar things can be compared. Arbitrary manipulation of both must be tightly constrained; by the courts if necessary. This is the purpose of constitutionally limited government.

A subjective assessment of **fairness** virtually always results in a manifestation of motivation and value manipulation. An asymmetric concept of consideration offered "He has more than I, therefore it is only fair that he contribute more (to the state) than I." under the guise of fairness, rather easily morphs into an asymmetric concept of consideration received: "I have less, therefore it is only fair that I get more (from the state) than he." The compelling interests of the state must always be grounded in an equitable assessment of value from a neutral position relative to motivation. Sometimes the manipulation is presented as a consequence of morality.

Comprising a framework for the evaluation of motivation and value that often derives from religious concepts, we define personal **morality** as a **cognition value system grounded in grace and faith**. Based on this concept definition, we suggest a corollary to prohibition of the manipulation of fairness suggests that a similar concept of public or state morality should never constitute a compelling interest. Rather, the state's motivation and value system is reflected in the aggregate of laws affecting behavior, where the compelling interest of each can be determined according to the precepts of strict scrutiny through the assessment of truth using objective protocols. Thus, public morality should be the effect, not the cause. We will consider this in a bit more detail in the next chapter when we seek to relate due process to altruistic behavior.

6 *Privacy as a Social Mutagen*

Congress shall make no law abridging the privacy of the people.

With *Roe v. Wade,* a fundamental right of personal privacy emerged in American jurisprudence; a right that perhaps had existed since the dawn of the Republic. Were it to be written down in the style of the *Bill of Rights*, it might look like the above. *Roe* still begs the question of precisely what fully constitutes personal privacy. The decision notes that whatever privacy is, and wherever it comes from, it does encompass a pregnant woman's right to decide whether to terminate her pregnancy.

In the fifth chapter, we noted a variety of Supreme Court decisions that recognized, among other behaviors: the freedom to walk, stroll, loaf; the liberty to marry a person of one's choosing; the right of procreation; the privacy of marital relations; the liberty to direct the education of one's children; the freedom to use contraceptives; the right of privacy encompassing the power of a woman to decide to terminate her pregnancy; and, the freedom to advocate ideas. This brings to mind the old parable of the elephant being examined by several blind men. Each felt a different part of its body and thus each perceived the elephant as a quite different animal than the others. Perhaps, as *the wise* in their administration of blind justice feel their way around its various appendages, privacy will ultimately resolve to the elephant standing in the midst of the room and the great beast will be perceived in full measure.

Justice Douglas suggested that the various enumerated rights, in combination, cast penumbras in which could be recognized other, unenumerated rights. We suggest that a more fitting metaphor is that of a hologram; a three dimensional picture. To make a hologram of an object, coherent light is reflected from the object and then captured in static form. Unlike an image captured on film, the static form of a hologram has depth such that it can record the phase differences of light reflected from various parts of the object. Consequently, if you subsequently shine light through the hologram, you can see the original object in three dimensions, allowing you to look at the object from different perspectives.

An interesting feature of a hologram presents itself if you cut the hologram into pieces. You can shine light on any one piece and see the entire original object in a three dimensional perspective. It is in this fashion that the enumerated rights look like pieces of a hologram. When any specific right is illuminated by the consideration of due process, you should be able to discern the entire source from which the hologram was cast; that is, personal privacy.

We've suggested that society feeds off of the personal privacy of its constituent members. It does so in pursuit of the two basic goals of any social order: to arbitrate the intersection of personal privacy among individuals within the social order and to arbitrage the infringement of personal privacy of individual members to benefit the social order. The state addresses these goals through policy enacted under the auspices of its police powers. Experience shows us that social policy is not fixed; it invariably changes over time. Privacy continually emanates not only from the constituent members of a social order, but from the members of its policy infrastructure as well.

Thus, there is an almost organic quality to the evolving tension among the manifestations of privacy and policy.

Classical evolutionary theory suggests that living entities evolve either by genetic adaptation or by induced or spontaneous mutation. Through genetic adaptation, capabilities inherent in the genetic code of organisms can emerge, allowing the organism to thrive in a changing environment. Alternatively, through the action of various mutagens, the genetic code of an organism can be induced to change; to mutate. During the course of an organism's growth, such mutations can impact the capabilities of the whole organism. This has the possibility of introducing completely new capabilities into the organism, which in some cases may allow the organism to thrive in the encompassing environment. When change does occur, natural selection ultimately judges its efficacy.

Privacy is dynamic. Through ongoing personal provisioning, motivations and capabilities evolve and new expressions of privacy emerge; often stimulating social policy to follow suit. In this manner, privacy functions as a mutagen for social order. The ever changing environment for personal interactions sometimes proves to be a fertile ground for new expression but the results can present a challenge for existing policy to accommodate as they issue simultaneously from multiple individuals. Alternatively, the results may offer a compelling interest in potential benefits to the social order from a new policy of altruistic action. Either way might present a compelling interest for the social order to modify its policies of privacy abridgement.

Personal privacy presents a consistent procedural form. When two or more people interact, they comprise at least an impromptu social order. For each of the people engaged in the interaction, their perspective on the interaction derives from the effective policy of that impromptu social order. To determine effective policy some form of negotiation occurs with each person bringing their own personal privacy to the actual or virtual negotiating table. It is part of establishing the context for the interaction to arrive at some arbitration of the infringement of personal privacy of each of the participants.

When the arbitration of privacy infringement conforms to the policy of the state, it forms either a *de facto* or a *de jure* contract. *De facto* contracts are the implied agreements of structured, albeit informal interactions; the subject of generic civil law. *De jure* contracts are formal agreements that establish conditional covenants; the subject of contract law. If the resulting arbitration does not conform to the policy of the state, then it may well constitute a **crime** or a **conspiracy**; or both. We use the term conspiracy under its less pejorative meaning of simply an **agreement for common action**.

As an effective social mutagen, central to the basic trust and policy infrastructures of the emergent republic, it should be possible to discern privacy's influence on current American social structure. By considering the various mechanisms inherent in the personal interactions through which privacy manifests, we should recognize some of the basic form and function of American governance that was put in place by the Founders and which endures today. For example, in considering the state's policy of personal privacy's arbitration and arbitrage we should be able to discern some, if not all, of the enumerated rights found in the foundation documents. We should also find the rationale for unenumerated rights that have emerged over time.

The policy infrastructure defined by the Founders establishes enumerated powers that contrast with enumerated rights. It seems at least plausible that if a right is not absolute then neither is a power of government. There is a constant tension between the rights of the individual and the powers of the state. The state must present a compelling interest to abridge a fundamental right, whether it is enumerated or unenumerated. Given an expansive right of personal privacy, the complementary perspective would suggest that the application of government power, in particular the "police power", must derive from that compelling interest and is strictly limited by that compelling interest. This further suggests a preferential superiority of the rights of the individual over the enumerated and unenumerated powers of government.

Assuming privacy was familiar to the Founders, it should present an organizing principle for the American concept of constitutionally limited government and its rendition of American jurisprudence. With that in mind, let's consider how an expansive right of privacy might manifest in this social environment, thus revealing itself through the fundamental forms of the Republic. For purposes of brevity, we will concentrate on criminal proceedings, since these are most intimately related to the state's assertion of its police powers. The first problem in dealing with criminal acts is to determine that a crime has been committed; to find truth in the allegations of violations of policy.

Truth through Adjudication

Throughout the history of human social orders, processes to extract truth from consequences classified as criminal by the state have taken many forms. In some societies, to be accused was tantamount to being convicted. In particular, to be a common person accused by a person of privilege was particularly onerous. Establishment of truth through the assessment of guilt or innocence might be left to the titular head of the social order. In some societies, the accused were subjected to torture in order to extract confessions of truth. Sometimes, guilt was assumed and innocence had to be proved. Tribunals to assess truth, conducted by members of an aristocracy, clergy or judiciary, often lacked any enduring rules.

Social orders that we characterize as religions usually base their assessment of trust on **faith**. Faith is trust derived from causality, independent of truth. Actions that are predicated on faith can be viewed as deriving from a sense of morality, or a moral code. This establishes a basis of altruistic behavior and forms a bonding mechanism among members of a social order. Faith based actions engaged under the auspices of the police powers of the state are expressly prohibited by the *Constitution*; that is, the state cannot establish a religion. Rather, bringing a systematic and objective approach to relating truth to trust and using this as a measure of policy is the goal of American jurisprudence.

We define **jurisprudence** as a **system of interaction management**. Jurisprudence elicits a specific instantiation of policy infrastructure; the collection of mechanisms enabled under the auspices of an encompassing trust infrastructure on which a social order is grounded. We can then define **justice** as **truth through jurisprudence**. To seek justice is to find truth through a system of interaction management. Viewing jurisprudence as an abstract concept, one expects it to encompass the establishment of policy, the administration of interactions and the adjudication of consequences.

The administration of interactions generally takes two distinct forms. The first is to enforce policy before an action is evoked. The second is to wait until an action is completed and then to adjudicate if its consequences suggest it has not sufficiently conformed to policy. The first uses regulators to enforce policy prior to allowing actions to occur. The second uses police to detect consequences that do not appear to conform to policy and adjudication to determine the truth in this appearance. From a technical perspective, the purpose of the police is to raise an error warning that subjects an interaction to adjudication. In American jurisprudence, the error warning is called a **case**.

Our reference to an error warning comes from the perspective of complex computer systems. In such systems, there are many places where errors can occur. It is virtually impossible to deal with each error at the point or time of its occurrence, often because the error must be understood and dealt with in a larger context than can be discerned at the site of its occurrence. Hence, it is common practice for the system to raise an error warning when an error is suspected. The system then, at what it perceives to be a more opportune moment or perspective, will engage an **exception handler** to deal with the potential error. While manifesting as a social system rather than a purely mechanical system, jurisprudence seems to have similar problems with complexity.

When consequences are alleged to result from a criminal act, which is the equivalent to raising an error warning, the social order engages a process of exception handling called adjudication. Through adjudication, the social order seeks to determine that an interaction consequence is in fact due to a criminal act, and to somehow **make whole** that specific interaction's consequence; to bring the consequence into conformance with policy.

If an interaction cannot be made whole, the adjudication system resorts to punitive measures to punish the criminal actor. A punitive measure might be thought of as a negative conditional covenant; don't commit the crime and the state won't punish you. However, this has the unfortunate connotation of a true conditional covenant in which the consideration from each side should be of comparable value. How does the state place a value on the murder of another? It seems more appropriate to pursue punishment as an asymmetric response to an abrogation of policy. The more important point is that any punitive measures should only be applied as a result of adjudication.

This rigorous approach to justice found in American jurisprudence derives much of its structure from various European traditions; most notably those of British common law. However, the American system features refinements that reflect an analysis by synthesis approach. This has resulted in a formal expression of a metaphorical model for interaction management; a system of jurisprudence if you will. It is a model seemingly constructed around personal privacy.

The primary mechanism of adjudication for this system of interaction management is called a **court**. A court is the instantiation of an analysis by synthesis metaphorical model whose purpose is the evaluation of exceptions and the determination of corrective actions. A court makes use of mechanisms that have much the appearance of simulators and emulators that are found in the more technical world. A simulator is a mechanism or a system that creates an artificial environment, a context if you will, where some distinct process can function as if it were actually in its intended operational environment. Think of a flight simulator.

A flight simulator is a device that can create for a pilot the appearance of being on the flight deck of an airplane and able to fly the airplane without ever leaving the ground. The simulator presents a replica of the flight deck of an airplane. Surrounding this replica are other systems that can present, through the flight deck instrumentation, the dynamic characteristics of the airplane and the air through which it flies. The orientation of the replica flight deck can be manipulated to give the sensation of airplane motion. Images of the surrounding countryside can be projected on the windows of the replica flight deck. An administrator who is actually in control of the entire simulator can control the appearance of various conditions, including error conditions to which the pilot must then respond. In fact, the administrator completely controls what is presented through the simulator.

A separate mechanism used in the technical world is an emulator. This is a mechanism, often a computer of some type, which functions as a different mechanism. In an airplane, there is an auto-pilot that can fly the airplane without significant pilot intervention. The auto-pilot is a computer that emulates a pilot. A flight simulator can be used to train a pilot. It can also be used as a platform on which to operate an auto-pilot. Typically, in the training of a pilot, both components are used, with the replica flight deck also including an auto-pilot. This allows the pilot to be trained and gain experience in flying a plane directly through airplane controls or indirectly through an auto-pilot; or, avionics as the auto-pilot is usually called. The pilot's training can include responding to error conditions that might arise in either situation. A court is something like a flight simulator, with an auto-pilot included.

As a means of establishing truth, courts engage highly constrained processes that synthesize personal interactions through simulation and emulation techniques using an objective social protocol known as a **trial**. This process within a process is an example of recursive social interactions that presents many of the characteristics of privacy. To consider the trial in more detail we first **assume a symmetric court**; a techno-wonk's imperative if ever there was one. A court can invoke a trial, the purpose of which is to evaluate a particular interaction in which a **defendant** is alleged by a **prosecutor** to have broken the law; to have violated policy in the words of the wonk. A symmetric court will treat both the prosecutor and the defendant in a generally equivalent or symmetric fashion.

A trial is a constrained interaction in which all the members of the social order are perceived to participate; it is, in fact, an art-form. It is an expression of **the peoples' right to know** (the truth). This right extends from the police powers of the social order. Obviously, all the people won't fit into a single courtroom, so **the people** are metaphorically represented by the prosecutor. The trial then becomes a very formal interaction involving the defendant and the prosecutor conducted under the auspices of the court. Both parties can assert personal privacy in the interaction.

A symmetric court will arbitrate the intersection of privacy between the defendant and the prosecutor, giving both parties a neutral context for the ensuing interaction; a level playing field if you will. To delve a bit deeper into the metaphor, the objective is a level playing field, not forced equality of the competing teams. The state is ill-equipped to assess **equality** of the aesthetic expression that is a significant aspect of a trial. The arbitration proceeds via policy that abridges to a certain extent the personal privacy of each party as part of a compelling interest of the state to find justice. The trial of a case is a composition that encompasses subordinate compositions by the defendant and the prosecutor. The truth of the case as expressed by each party must ultimately be determined by a subjective measure.

The trial is an interaction simulator whose primary purpose is to allow emulation of the subjective decision-making process involved in a prior interaction; one in which the crime is alleged to have been committed. Through this emulation, truth is extracted from the alleged criminal acts and consequences. As we have previously defined, truth is a probability assessment of whether specific actions resulted in the observed consequences. Once this assessment is made, it can then be determined whether these actions did, or did not, conform to the policy under which the interaction occurred.

If a criminal act is determined to have occurred, then the court can attempt to address the errant consequences by mandating some form of **remedial action**. This remedial action might include restitution of improper consequences, usually a payment of some type for the purpose of attempting to make whole the victim of the criminal act. It also might include punitive fines or incarceration of the errant actor from the original, criminal interaction. An extreme consequence might find the defendant executed by the state as the ultimate remedial action. Since any remedial actions will infringe the privacy of the defendant, they should be subject to strict scrutiny by the courts.

Forcing a person to stand trial is an exercise in the orderly, incremental abridgement of privacy; or, at least it should be. If one person can simply assert that another person has committed a crime and thereby invoke a trial, it's clear that this would be an effective way to thwart the privacy of the other person. It seems a reasonable compelling interest of the social order to mandate that a person submit to trial only if a trustworthy accusation is made against them.

If there is no risk to the accuser, then making false accusations is a good way to infringe another's privacy; forcing them to spend time and money defending themselves and impacting their reputation as a result. There is even a non-negligible probability that they will not be able to defend themselves. The defendant may be convicted and punished even though no crime was actually committed, or at least not one committed by the defendant. So, it really needs to be more difficult to invoke a trial than simply asserting a crime.

It should be noted that the freedom to allege a crime and the freedom to be free from false accusations are both facets of personal privacy. To arbitrate the intersection of these two facets requires a means of establishing a sufficient level of trust that the allegation of a crime will be found to be truthful through a trial. For alleged crimes of a severe nature, usually called **felonies**, the typical approach is to require a seminal tribunal called a Grand Jury to assess the probability of a crime. Testimony and evidence presented to the Grand Jury is done so under oath, averring truth to the testimony and evidence. Lying to a Grand Jury is a crime itself. If warranted, this tribunal can then assert a specific crime by issuing an **indictment** against the ostensibly errant party.

A Grand Jury has strict rules of procedure, and it operates in secret. This means the mere allegations of crime are not widely disseminated and thus are less of an infringement of the privacy of the accused. A Grand Jury assesses truth, but at a significantly lower level of certainty than the truth determined by a trial court. An indictment means that the Grand Jury believes there is enough evidence of a crime to warrant a trial. When an indictment is returned, the accused party is then required to stand at trial for the alleged crime.

As we've previously noted in considering its mechanics, by asserting privacy a person can establish a persona through pair-wise interactions with others. Remember that a persona is an expression of experiential-identity, including physical consequences. It results in the memories of consequences or their expression through compositions. In alleging a criminal act, the prosecution seeks to establish a forensic wake and to then equate this forensic wake to a persona. This ultimately requires a subjective decision of the equivalence of the forensic wake to a persona of the defendant. Establishing this equivalence is the process of finding truth.

A criminal case can be characterized as an alleged persona; again, in the words of the wonk. A single case can involve multiple crimes by encompassing subordinate interactions. In such a case, a Grand Jury will issue an indictment with multiple counts; each count comprising a discrete criminal act. Any criminal act(s) is only alleged, because the truth regarding the actual consequences of the persona must be established through a trial using only evidence and testimony from witnesses; the physical memories related to the specific interaction in question. Within a trial, determining truth is termed **answering questions of fact**. Determining whether the actions to which the truth applies conform to policy is termed **answering questions of law**.

A person cannot typically be convicted of a crime based purely on their reputation. Their guilt must be established for the interaction in question, using only consequences from this interaction. Guilt is an expression of truth. In the pursuit of truth from these consequences, a trial assumes an initial context of **presumption of innocence**. The simulation begins from the perspective either that the alleged consequences did not derive from the alleged actions, or that the alleged actions were not actually crimes. Prior to the invocation of an action we deal in the assessment of **trust**; the probability that a specific consequence **will** result from the action. Through a trial we assess **truth**; the probability that a consequence **did** result from a specific action. The purpose of a trial is to establish a sufficient probability that a criminal consequence derived from an expression of personal privacy by the defendant.

In the course of the simulation that is a trial, the alleged criminal interaction is reconstructed. This allows a judgment to be rendered as to whether in fact an infraction of the law actually occurred. This judgment of truth derives from an evaluation that looks similar to the assessment of trust that a person, the defendant, would have performed during the original, suspect interaction. For a trial to accomplish this evaluation, in addition to establishing the original interaction's context, and its ensuing action and consequence, it is also necessary for the court to replicate the decision making process of the human mind in evoking the action that resulted in the consequence in the first place; this is the emulation part of the trial. Truth is determined through a subjective facility that must be brought into the simulation process. The court accomplishes this through two human components.

As the first of these human components, the court is personified by a **judge** who is responsible for controlling the operations of the simulator; that is, the trial itself. The judge is also responsible for the conduct of the emulation part, the assessment of truth. This is an operational sub-process of the trial. The judge is synonymous with the court and will typically be referred to as **The Court**. The judge serves as the arbiter of policy within the trial and answers all questions of law. The judge also assures that only trustworthy processes intended to respect the rights of all participants are used during the trial. The goal is that the simulation that is the trial presents an objective base from which an emulator can render its verdict in the assessment of the truth.

The emulator part of a court is a **jury**, the other human component of a trial. The jury emulates the subjective decision making facility of an ordinary person. It serves to answer questions of fact. It does so by rendering a **verdict** comprised of subjective decisions as to the truth of what happened during the interaction in question. The significant aspects of this role are to assess the context of the interaction under scrutiny, including the applicable policy (law) as established by the judge, and to then render an evaluation of the probability that specific consequences ensued from the actions indicated. Referring back to the case of *Cantwell v. Connecticut* that we considered in the fifth chapter, a jury is a means of evaluating motivations of actions that is independent of any "state administration facility."

A jury is typically a multi-person panel. It is a social order, subordinate to an encompassing social order, but with significant facilities for establishing the policies under which it effects a decision. For a specific trial, a jury is randomly selected from the peer-group of the defendant. This draws upon a characteristic of stochastic processes; that a random observation selection will mask sensory bias. A randomly drawn group of people are assumed capable of making an unbiased evaluation of truth from the forensic wake established within the trial.

As a peer-group of the defendant, it is assumed that the provisioning of each member of the jury will be qualitatively equivalent to that of the defendant. The mental subjective assessment processes of the jury should then be equivalent to that of the defendant. The members of a jury are expected to subordinate their individual motivations to a common motivation to seek justice by an impartial evaluation of truth. **Jury duty** is an example of the arbitrage of the personal privacy of the jury members in order to benefit the state. It is an altruistic act.

The jury's evaluation of truth in the form of a verdict of **guilt** or **innocence** is complementary to the assessment of trust by the defendant in the original interaction. In the conduct of a trial, questions of law should have objectively determined answers. Questions of fact usually require subjectively determined answers that are dependent on the provisioning of the interaction and of the subjective decision making process. The trial is an attempt to recreate (simulate) the provisioning of the original interaction context using consequences derived from a forensic wake that can be attributed to a high degree of truth to have come from the interaction in question.

In determining the truth, a jury's verdict is an evaluation, under the guidance of the judge, of the probability that the consequence of the alleged criminal interaction actually was the result of criminal actions. In an ordinary personal interaction, both the role of the judge and that of the jury are played by the human mind of the person evoking the interaction. During a trial, the prosecutor attempts to establish the interaction context to some level of objective probability. The jury then serves to emulate the subjective decision making that is central to evoking an action. Correspondingly, a jury verdict is thus a subjective evaluation of truth, generally rendered at one of two levels of certainty: **beyond a reasonable doubt** for cases of criminal law or in accordance with the **preponderance of evidence** for cases of civil law.

The interaction brought before a court for simulation (trial) is termed a case. There are two primary interaction roles: the prosecution that presents the rationale for deeming that the case includes criminal acts, and the defense that seeks to refute the prosecution claims. **Presenting a case** is the process of establishing the context in place when the original interaction occurred and in affirming that the consequences resulting from actions within that context actually broke the law. The defense seeks to tailor the context by presenting rationales that no criminal act can be determined to within the required level of certainty. It is a confrontation between two parties, each asserting their own personal privacy under the strict procedures of the court.

Both the prosecution and the defense are constrained by the court to pursue their goals through the presentation of evidence, including testimony, in open court during the trial. There are strict rules of evidence enforced by the judge. These rules actually speak to the relationship between privacy and identity. Specifically, only the consequences of motor-system actions by the defendant(s), a persona, are allowed as evidence or as testimony offered by witnesses. Assertions of privacy that resulted in that persona are subject to only limited infringement during the trial. For example, as deference to privacy a person cannot be forced to give testimony about her assertions of privacy that resulted in the persona in question; that is, she can't be forced to offer testimony against herself.

An important characteristic of the adjudication system is the concept of making whole the consequences of an interaction found to be in violation of policy of the state. This can be done through remedial actions by the court such as paying a fine or paying damages. The model for such remedial action is a conditional covenant. In some instances, religious concepts have been introduced into state adjudication and a remedial action of **mercy** is put forward. We define mercy as **remedial action independent of adjudication**.

Establishing conditional covenants in general requires some means of assessing value of dissimilar things; a way to make them fungible. The same facility is required in order to make whole the consequences of diverse interactions. The social mechanism through which this is accomplished is money; instantiated as currency. *Article I Section 8* gives the power to the Congress to establish money:

> To coin Money, regulate the Value thereof, and of foreign Coin, and fix the Standard of Weights and Measures;

> To provide for the Punishment of counterfeiting the Securities and current Coin of the United States;

Wealth derives from personal privacy. Based on our individual motivations, we ascribe value to the components of interactions. Referencing money, we place a value on the context of a pending interaction and we place a value on the consequences of the interaction. Any change in value between establishing context and observing consequences, we can ascribe to the intervening action.

In forming conditional covenants, we often seek to compare the values of dissimilar things. For example, what is the value of building a fence compared to the value of a loaf of bread? In the arbitration of personal privacy intersection, we may resort to barter; *"will work for food"* is a very tangible means of comparing value. However, on a larger scale we need a more abstract way to gauge the value of things.

Money provides a means to compare the relative value of dissimilar things. We also need a way to compare like-things. We do this through objective mechanisms of weights and measures. Just as with money, Congress is also empowered to establish standards of weights and measures. This allows policy to be equitably applied to those aspects of conditional covenants that manifest as physical entities. Just as with the system of adjudication, money along with the standards of weights and measures are intended to be equally applied to all. One might assume that while policy may address the value of these standard things, policy should not manipulate their value to favor one over another; to create an uneven playing field if you will.

The foundation documents prescribe instances of such equitable treatment in the words of the *Eighth Amendment*:

> Excessive bail shall not be required, nor excessive fines imposed, nor cruel and unusual punishments inflicted.

Bail is the means through which an accused person is released from incarceration while awaiting trial. Fines are the tools of punitive remedial actions imposed by the court when a guilty verdict is rendered.

Money, like the courts provided by the state, must be stable and equitable in order to truly provide a basis of equality for effecting personal privacy. There seems always a tendency for the state to manipulate the availability and value of money, relative to other goods and services, as a means to effect policy. Any such manipulation should be viewed as an infringement of personal privacy. As a consequence, it is to be anticipated that a compelling interest must be shown to justify such infringement.

So, at this point we have considered a technically stylized description of a court, a case and a trial, including its component parts, along with several of the mechanisms that comprise the trial's processes and its means for remedial actions. While we've used definitions and terminology developed in our discussions of an expansive concept of privacy, the descriptions are qualitatively consistent with actual legal processes. The presentation we've used is relevant if one wants to extend these concepts of legal proceedings into the digital domain. The intent of the relatively formal descriptions is so that one can readily discern the various aspects of privacy and the mechanisms through which it is pursued. These are the manifestations of the Founders' familiarity with an expansive concept of personal privacy.

Privacy's Influence

Within any legal domain, there are many arcane rules and procedures involved in formal proceedings. They have evolved over a long period of time. Our goal in presenting this cursory overview is to offer some context for relating privacy to the mechanisms defined in the founding infrastructures of American jurisprudence. Our suggestion is that the correlation we'll find is not an accident. It seems evident that American jurisprudence is based on a fundamental and expansive right of privacy.

We also suggest that when policy diverges from an appropriate consideration of personal privacy, it is fairly obvious to discern. It then becomes interesting to consider whether this divergence is really in keeping with the limited government initially established. *Article III* of the *Constitution* specifies The Judicial Branch of government. In *Section 2* is made the only mention of a "trial" found in the original body of the *Constitution*:

> The Trial of all Crimes, except in Cases of Impeachment, shall be by Jury; and such Trial shall be held in the State where the said Crimes shall have been committed; but when not committed within any State, the Trial shall be at such Place or Places as the Congress may by Law have directed.

The original *Constitution* is silent on most other aspects of adjudication. It does provide for a hierarchical set of tribunals, or courts, culminating in the Supreme Court. It mandates that courts will be administered by a cadre of professional jurists with life tenure, assuming good behavior. Perhaps most interesting, it does not explicitly consider the abridgement of the rights of a person as a means of punishment within the general system of jurisprudence. With personal privacy as a basis of this system, the concept of making whole the consequences of a criminal act appears as a conditional covenant. Punitive remedial actions are viewed in the same way, giving rise to the concept of **paying one's debt to society** for crimes committed.

The *Bill of Rights*, the first ten amendments adopted shortly after the original *Constitution*, does expand on the required characteristics of trials; specifically, the manner of treatment of those standing accused at trial. In addition, the *Eighth Amendment* prohibits cruel and unusual punishment, but is silent on what would constitute acceptable punishment. One is left to wonder if there are in fact any written constraints on the police powers of the federal government. Indeed, this has been the continuing problem in the development of the common law. The *Constitution* alone does not provide sufficient guidance; something is missing.

It seems clear that the *Constitution*, including the *Bill of Rights*, must be encompassed within some greater context which provides, in the words we used earlier, an organizing principle. One might contend that British common law forms an organizing principle. However, the *Declaration of Independence* is replete with instances where the application of British law is deemed unacceptable. Perhaps, this is where we should look for organizing principles? More than a simple statement of principles, the *Declaration of Independence* also provides a succinct yet structurally sound framework for governance.

Consequently, from our perspective, the *Declaration of Independence* comprises the greater context within which the *Constitution* is constrained. We will consider this assertion in some detail in our last chapter of this book. However, for the moment we want to continue the exercise of examining the policy infrastructure defined by the *Constitution* and observe the points where an expansive right of personal privacy contributes salient organizing principles.

We begin with the *Article III* requirement that crimes will be tried before a jury within the state where the crime occurred, unless the crime was committed outside of a state; in which case, the jury trial will be held at a place designated by Congress. As we noted earlier, even this mandate can be derived largely from a consideration of an expansive concept of personal privacy. The *Bill of Rights* further expands on this concept. In general conversation, we speak in terms of someone getting a **fair** trial. An assumption of personal privacy provides a way to determine what fairness looks like.

Our rationale in this discussion is not that a right of privacy indelibly leads to the existent system of American jurisprudence. Rather, we want to point out that the existent system apparently reflects a profound dedication to personal privacy by those who put it in place. We view this as supporting our suggestion that an expansive concept of privacy is ground into the basic trust and policy infrastructures of the Republic. To continue with the theme of trials, let's consider the *Sixth Amendment* to the *Constitution*:

> In all criminal prosecutions, the accused shall enjoy the right to a speedy and public trial, by an impartial jury of the State and district wherein the crime shall have been committed, which district shall have been previously ascertained by law, and to be informed of the nature and cause of the accusation; to be confronted with the witnesses against him; to have compulsory process for obtaining witnesses in his favor, and to have the Assistance of Counsel for his defense.

One can begin to see in this amendment the basic architecture of the adjudication system that we described earlier in this chapter. It is worth noting that nowhere in the foundation documents is this architecture written down with the level of specificity that we included. However, many of the concepts are mentioned in this amendment, thus indicating that their common understanding is **self-evident**; consider the concepts so noted: **prosecution; defense; accused; impartial jury; nature and cause of the accusation; confront witnesses against; compulsory process for obtaining witnesses; counsel for his defense.**

Article III Section 2 of the *Constitution* required that the trial "...shall be by jury." The *Sixth Amendment* further mandates an "impartial jury." As we noted earlier, a jury selected as a random sample from a peer group of the defendant would normally be viewed as an unbiased arbiter of truth. Through the random selection of the members of a jury, a trial encompasses a stochastic process. This process should be difficult, if not impossible, to manipulate. However, court oversight of the makeup of a jury has the unfortunate aspect of affording just such manipulation; for example through the *voir dire* process of examining and excluding certain members who had been randomly selected.

The concepts noted assume a process of confrontation between the prosecution and the defense; a metaphorical allusion to the process from which derived personal privacy. The trial is obviously intended to present a neutral ground for the confrontation based on an arbitration of the intersection of personal privacy between two equal individuals. This arbitration is a matter of policy that establishes a mandate for the judge of the court. This is important, because the original Constitution does not mention **equality among people**; something of a glaring omission.

The right to have a compulsory process for obtaining witnesses, generally called a **subpoena**, is a further recognition of equality. The prosecutor has this power under the police powers of the state, so giving the same power to the defense is an example of leveling the playing field. The requirement for a *speedy* trial recognizes a crucial aspect of interaction mechanics; memory is an organic process. It is subject to inexact formation of memories and the memories formed are subject to degradation. Evidence has a tendency to degrade over time as well. However, in some cases it takes time to identify and obtain the relevant evidence within the potential forensic wake.

In the abstract, the most conducive environment in which to assess truth is as soon after the suspect interaction as possible. Speedy is a relative term however. Both the prosecution and the defense are generally provided ample opportunity to prepare their specific interpretation of the case. Given the confrontational process that is the trial, each side will typically attempt to game the system to their advantage. This is certainly an expression of their respective privacy. However, it must be noted that attorneys for both the prosecution and the defense are **officers of the court**. This establishes policy in the form of rules of conduct that they are obliged to follow. Coupled with these rules, it is the purpose of the judge to strike the correct balance between having sufficient time to prepare versus an attempt to gain advantage by indefinitely delaying the proceedings.

The requirement for a **public trial** recognizes the privacy of the defendant by providing the most generally appropriate forum for a truly fair process. The state is better positioned to benefit from institutional anonymity than the defense. If the trial is cloaked and hidden from public view, the prospects are greater that the privacy of the defense will be more substantially infringed. Transparency of the interaction that is the trial will tend to benefit the defense. However, if the defendant is found guilty the consequence will be more widely disseminated, resulting in a more severe loss of privacy.

Through personal privacy, one seeks to control the context of interactions. The right to be informed of the nature and cause of accusations gives the accused a better position from which to control both the simulation that is the trial and the interpretation of evidence and testimony regarding the interaction that the trial will simulate. By providing the opportunity to contest information brought into the trial, a further opportunity is afforded to control the context. This also provides the opportunity to present material from the forensic wake of the alleged criminal interaction that might bolster the case for the defense.

The right to confront witnesses against the defense is quite consistent with the assertion of personal privacy. To a certain extent, it provides a means to partially control context in that witnesses can be challenged by the defense if it can be demonstrated that they were not directly impacted by the interaction in question. The ability for the defense to compel witnesses in its favor allows control of context and also provides favorable actions and consequences from the witnesses.

The *Fifth Amendment* establishes required characteristics of the context of a trial, including the trusted precursors that give rise to the trial itself:

> No person shall be held to answer for a capital, or otherwise infamous crime, unless on a presentment or indictment of a Grand Jury, except in cases arising in the land or naval forces, or in the Militia, when in actual service in time of War or public danger; nor shall any person be subject for the same offense to be twice put in jeopardy of life or limb; nor shall be compelled in any criminal case to be a witness against himself, nor be deprived of life, liberty, or property, without due process of law; nor shall private property be taken for public use, without just compensation.

A Grand Jury is a constituent element of the system of adjudication commissioned by the *Constitution*, but left to the Congress for definition and implementation. One assumes it is one of the subordinate tribunals authorized by the *Constitution*. This amendment suggests that many, if not all, of the operational characteristics of a Grand Jury are viewed as self-evident by the Founders.

The constraint against bringing a person to trial on multiple occasions for the same crime is also a pragmatic recognition of equality as well as offering a needed way to guard against an infinite recursion in the adjudication process. Recursion can occur in at least two ways; by bringing a person to trial multiple times for the same crime, continually seeking a conviction after a person has been found not guilty, or through an unending appellate process. The first approach can be abused by the prosecution; the second by the defense. The existence of a Supreme Court provides for a termination of appeals. The *Fifth Amendment* prevents recursion of the initiation of the trial process. Both serve the goal of equality since, without this constraint, superior resources of either the defense or the prosecution can tilt the playing field.

The *Fifth Amendment* is best known for its exclusion of compelled testimony from the accused standing trial. This is easily recognized as deriving from an assertion of personal privacy. Compelled testimony would abridge the accused's ability to control or influence the context of the interaction simulated by the trial. It would subject the defendant to cross examination which would further diminish control. Most important, by not being able to compel testimony from a defendant the prosecution is forced to rely on evidence and testimony from other parties to the criminal infraction; that is, purely from the forensic wake. This provides the jury with a view of the interaction context that is not tinged by sensation derived from the defendant's appearance, thus removing a significant source of subjective bias from the jury's assessment of truth.

The *Fifth Amendment* prohibition against state compelled testimony from a defendant has been specifically ruled to include the gathering of evidence by the police in advance of bringing a criminal charge. This was done through a 1966 decision of the Supreme Court in the case of *Miranda v. Arizona*. This decision was applied to several cases in which confessions were obtained from defendants without their fully understanding their rights against compelled testimony. This case resulted in the specification of the *Miranda Warning* that police are now required to give to any person they suspect of criminal activity before they can obtain any information from that person:

> You have the right to remain silent. Anything you say can and will be used against you in a court of law. You have the right to speak to an attorney, and to have an attorney present during any questioning. If you cannot afford a lawyer, one will be provided for you at government expense.

The *Fifth Amendment* requirement for due process and the protection of private property certainly bring into sharp focus the motivational aspects of personal privacy; perhaps better than any other part of the *Constitution*. The references to life, liberty and property are all central to what we seek in our provisioning of identity. The *Fourth Amendment* serves to extend these provisioning characteristics:

> The right of the people to be secure in their persons, houses, papers, and effects, against unreasonable searches and seizures, shall not be violated, and no Warrants shall issue, but upon probable cause, supported by Oath or affirmation, and particularly describing the place to be searched, and the persons or things to be seized.

The *"right to be secure"* is a reference to one's ability to control the context of interactions. It also refers to the ownership of consequences. This suggests that one has a right to personal security, wherever one might be; at home or on the street. One has a right to the security of one's domicile ("house") and personal possessions ("effects"). One has a right to security and possession of the product of one's labors ("papers"). These rights apply to interactions involving the state as well as other persons.

Fourth Amendment rights form a constraint on the state's power to mandate altruism, a facility we will consider just a bit later. It is also a constraint on the ability of other people to engage in any type of "search and/or seizure". Such actions are subject to the arbitration of personal privacy between the owner and the other people. This arbitration must conform to the policy for inter-personal interactions established by the state.

The state has the implicit power to mandate search and seizure, but only through a warrant. This assumes the supporting adjudication infrastructure such as the court system described earlier. The warrant must be issued by a court or perhaps a Grand Jury. In order to obtain a warrant, the state must sacrifice some level of its own privacy in that it's required to tell the explicit truth about what is to be searched and potentially seized, along with the justification for the search. This implies the gathering of "probable cause" information before a warrant can be affirmed and issued. Such information must be derived from the visible parts of a forensic wake. The courts have held that if these constraints are not met, any evidence gathered through the illegal search will not be allowed into a trial. This amendment is a critical aspect in protecting personal privacy through the trusted procedures under which trials are conducted.

Three other aspects of the adjudication process that serve as a protection of personal privacy can also be identified in *Article I, Section 9* of the *Constitution*.

> The privilege of the Writ of Habeas Corpus shall not be suspended, unless when in Cases of Rebellion or Invasion the public Safety may require it.

> No Bill of Attainder or ex post facto Law shall be passed.

First is a prohibition against suspending the writ of *habeas corpus*; a process through which a person accused or convicted of a crime can seek release from incarceration through the actions of a court. It is a means to recursively demand of the adjudication system confirmation that a person's privacy is being infringed legally. This is another of the characteristics of the adjudication system that is not specified in detail within the *Constitution*. Once again, it suggests the Founders were well in tune with the concept of personal privacy.

Second is an exclusion of any state power to directly legislate a criminal conviction; a facility known as a **Bill of Attainder**. This is important for maintaining a level playing field for all people when it comes to adjudication. The state cannot establish policy directed explicitly at the ultimate insular minority; a specific individual. One might assume that this precludes the state from arbitrarily establishing policy that sanctions any insular minority. This prohibition is also addressed in the First Amendment that we'll consider below. Third is an exclusion of making policy that would render an interaction consequence illegal after the interaction has occurred: a facility known as an *ex post facto* law.

We've considered the *Fourth Amendment*, *Fifth Amendment*, *Sixth Amendment* and *Eighth Amendment* to the *Constitution*. Together with certain mandates found among the articles of the original *Constitution*, these establish characteristics of personal privacy that must be protected within the adjudication system. A separate set of amendments and additional facets of the *Constitution* address other protections of personal privacy. In general, these protections deal with actions or consequences that the state is not allowed to abridge. These are generally characterized as rights. As we've noted earlier, there is always the prospect that even these rights can be abridged if there is a compelling interest on the part of the state in doing so; and, if the Supreme Court accedes to that justification.

It's particularly fascinating that the Founders obviously realized that the structure of an adjudication system needed relatively little specification in the basic trust and policy infrastructures. The mechanisms through which the legislative and executive branches create policy are defined in significant detail; the functions and mechanisms of the judicial system, not so much. In fact, in the foundation documents the Founders simply expressed a need for a means to terminate recursion of the adjudication process, and the rest is pretty much left to be filled in later.

In the *Constitution*, there is a specification for the Supreme Court of the United States, its constituent members and its constraining context; but, otherwise the actual structure of the judicial system is left to be defined by the legislative and executive branches. The details of the relationship between the judicial branch and the other branches are left ambiguous. History suggests this was a result of disagreement among the Founders as to just what this relationship should be. However, enough autonomy was established through the *Constitution* to allow significant nuance to be derived through judicial action as we noted in the fifth chapter with the *Marbury* case.

Privacy in Practice

The enumerated rights noted in the *Constitution* can be recognized as facets of a right of privacy. In the context of social interactions, they become targets for abridgment due to their intersection with the same rights of other people. All inter-personal interactions require the establishment of *de facto* or *de jure* conditional covenants based on arbitration of the conflicting personal privacy of each individual.

A systematic way to achieve this arbitration involves policy from an encompassing social order, most notably the state. The compelling interest for the state to infringe personal privacy of all derives from the principle of maximizing the personal privacy of each.

The *First Amendment* deals with the iconic set of fundamental individual rights:

> Congress shall make no law respecting an establishment of religion, or prohibiting the free exercise thereof; or abridging the freedom of speech, or of the press; or the right of the people peaceably to assemble, and to petition the Government for a redress of grievances.

The *Second Amendment* accentuates this initial set of rights when they are all viewed as deriving from a single concept.

> A well regulated Militia, being necessary to the security of a free State, the right of the people to keep and bear Arms, shall not be infringed.

Speech is a manifestation of the human physiological motor system. At its most basic, speech is achieved when we make coherent sounds through our vocal system thus enabling communication with others. Freedom of speech is congruent with freedom of expression. If we use the metaphor of newspapers or pamphlets, both popular means of expression during the era of the Founders, then freedom of the press means that we are at liberty to manifest our expression in a variety of forms, including through the use of tools.

The same metaphor suggests that freedom of the press also means that we have a right to receive information at our discretion. We might pick up and read a newspaper, or a pamphlet, purely at a time and place of our own choosing. Alternatively, we might buy a newspaper and never read it. Someone might leave a pamphlet on our car's windshield, and we simply take it off and throw it in the trash. Thus, one person's right of expression is tempered by another person's right of impression. Viewed in concert, these two complementary rights clearly signal the need for arbitration in social interactions.

The *"right of the people to keep and bear Arms"* seems very clearly stated; although, long ambiguously interpreted. The reference to *a* "well regulated Militia" has been construed to mean that people could keep and bear arms only within the constraints of a state administered military organization. However, the amendment seems to clearly state that an individual has a right to keep arms and to use them. In the 2008 Supreme Court decision in the case of *District of Columbia v. Heller* the court did hold that the right to bear arms is a fundamental individual right.

An auxiliary interpretation of the Second Amendment considers the right to keep and bear arms in the context of the *First Amendment's* "right of the people peaceably to assemble, and to petition the Government for a redress of grievances." A militia exists at the frontier between the military and the police; an existence both literal as well as metaphoric. In the time of the founders, a standing army and a standing police force were minimal in scope, if they existed at all. Protection of the personal privacy of the individual required a malleable expression of governance. The militia was a means to these ends; finding appropriate form in the individual as well as the social aggregate.

An individual right to keep and bear arms can be understood as a manifestation of a person's right to control the context of an interaction and to pursue actions through the force of arms when personal motivations deem it necessary. This is a direct derivation from the fight or flight response to stress. Hence, when combined, the freedoms of speech, press and arms amplify the right to use tools, to control context and to evoke expressive actions; and, the right to deny any external action or expression from reaching us. Taken together, these all look like parts of a right of privacy as we have expressed it.

What is heard by others is a consequence of actions taken by a person impelled by that person's individual motivation. However, perceiving a freedom of expression that derives from an expansive right of privacy is a much more powerful concept than simply claiming a right to vocalize sounds through the human voice; that is, speech. Even more expansive, language is a tool used to convey complex information and sensation from one person to another through speech, or other motor system manifestations. Language augmented by aesthetic expression is explicitly aimed to convey sensation. Thus, the freedom of speech is encompassed by the right of expression including aesthetic expression, which also encompasses the right to use tools.

In the second chapter, we observed that the brain is structured so as to facilitate the provisioning through which the young acquire language. At about two years of age, the provisioning of the brain to use language goes through a statistical learning phase during which some of the basic characteristics of language processing are acquired through stochastic processes. The brain subsequently learns to augment the basic mechanics of language with the sensation oriented facilities of aesthetic expression. Through language conveyed aesthetic expression, humans acquired the facilities to form social groups, including the means to establish a common basis of trust for a social collective.

Government is one manifestation of our social assembly; one that we grant police powers to provide us security and the privacy through which we pursue happiness. It is not government's role to choose our happiness or the basis of our establishing trust in all interactions. Rather, we imbue limited government with our highest level of trust; the police powers through which we allow it to infringe our personal privacy, but only in situations that present a compelling interest in that infringement.

The *First Amendment* offers a rather complete summary of the fundamental human behaviors necessary to establish social collectives. It emphasizes this collection of behaviors by explicitly noting a right of free assembly, which we can interpret as the formation of social collectives. Through these collectives we can seek to impact policy. It is important to note that such collectives have a right to petition the government for the redress of grievances, but not to unduly become part of the policy infrastructure. This is the caution expressed by the prohibition of state mandated religion.

There are other manifestations of the human physiological motor system. Using our legs we can walk and run. We can jump and dance. Depending on our specific motivations which we recognize generally as our pursuit of happiness, we might choose to walk, stroll or even loaf. Alternatively, we might work to create wealth that we can use to further our pursuit of happiness. While money might not be able to ubiquitously buy happiness, it is certainly within the realm of our personal privacy to give it a try. We might also seek happiness through family.

Our personal privacy offers us the prospect of bonding with someone of our own choosing. Under the auspices of our religious beliefs, which the state can not infringe, we might choose to marry that person of our choosing. Marriage is a religious state. It is not the purview of the state to define what is, or is not, marriage. However, in its guise as guarantor of our individual equality, it is within the purview of the state to provide a basis in policy for contracts that we seek to establish among people. If conditional covenants are implied by the concept of marriage, then it is the purview of the state to enable the expression, impression and enforcement of such contracts, but not to mandate their detailed composition.

In the bonds that we form with people of our own choosing, we might seek to have and provision children. Our personal privacy affords us this right of procreation. Personal privacy affords us the right to use tools, and contraception is one tool that we use to affect our procreation. There are certainly other tools that can enhance the capability to have and provision children. It is not the intrinsic purview of government to infringe this right. Compelling interests have yet to be presented for the government to even consider it. Rather, we suggest that through the diversity derived from personal privacy, the capabilities of social order are strengthened.

The state is prohibited from criminalizing a specific person through legislative action. This is the constitutional restriction on "Bills of Attainder." Extending this prohibition to social aggregates, the state is generally restricted from criminalizing a specific group. If there is a compelling state interest, it can perhaps criminalize behaviors of the aggregate that might be found in other aggregates as well. Actions can be criminalized, not the rationale behind those actions. This was made clear in the series of landmark cases related to the freedom of speech that we considered in the fifth chapter.

The *Bill of Rights* comprised a series of amendments to the *Constitution* enacted shortly after its ratification. The series draws heavily from the complaints against Great Britain in the *Declaration of Independence*. However, it is clear that the Founders did not view this list as exhaustive. They realized that additional fundamental rights could manifest from this same list of complaints, and from the self-evident liberties that were assumed a birthright of American citizenship. To explicitly recognize the existence of a greater collection of rights, the *Ninth Amendment* and the *Tenth Amendment* were enacted.

Ninth Amendment:

> The enumeration in the Constitution, of certain rights, shall not be construed to deny or disparage others retained by the people.

Tenth Amendment:

> The powers not delegated to the United States by the Constitution, nor prohibited by it to the States, are reserved to the States respectively, or to the people.

These amendments make it abundantly clear that the Founders viewed government, both state and federal, as limited in their scope of authority. Thus, the expanding collection of rights that emerged through the landmark cases that we considered in the fifth chapter is really not surprising. That we can derive this collection as projections from an expansive right of privacy suggests the rationale behind the Founders' actions.

Referring to the heuristic model of human motivation that we considered in the second chapter, a social order asserts its policy through manipulation of each individual's perceived needs. The success of this manipulation is a direct measure of the individual's devotion to the social order. Manipulating individual motivation is a means of eliciting altruistic behavior on the part of the individual even when no other person is directly involved in an interaction. This addresses situations when there are perceived threats to the social order that must be dealt with by the person in isolation.

Altruism and the State

Adopting the perspective that individuals function within a social structure through their assertion of personal privacy, we've suggested that any social order must address two areas of policy relative to this assertion. First, the social order must provide for the orderly and equitable arbitration of privacy among the members of the group. This is the central rationale for social aggregates; to sacrifice some amount of privacy in exchange for an environment in which trust is not based on the predator versus prey "law of the jungle." Such rationale is necessary if people are to work in concert to achieve common goals.

Under the auspices of its police powers, state policy must address the forfeiture of select assertions of privacy that manifest as extreme predator versus prey behavior. This is necessary to afford equal protection of the weak and the strong, as well as to protect the individual from the group. Such protection establishes the basis of policy that classifies certain actions as criminal; for example, theft, assault, extortion, murder, etc. It also forms the basis of policy that protects the individual from unwarranted actions of the polity. If the social order with police powers can't manifest such policies, then there's no improvement over simply the "survival of the fittest."

Beyond these basics, more general policies can enhance the environment within which people can reasonably pursue their own happiness; specifically, how we arbitrate the conditional covenants that govern various interactions among people. In many instances, such policies simply comprise standard rules of social etiquette; protocols that allow us to interact with one another in a non-threatening manner. We touched on some of those in the third and fourth chapters. However, as the social order becomes more complex the arbitration can become more involved.

In the abstract, complex arbitration of individual actions to keep them conformant with desired collective consequences suggests a need for policy that provides a level playing field for conditional covenants among people. Since privacy, with its inherent personal motivations, is the primary rationale for social interactions, it is not the function of such policy to mandate the results of the conditional covenants, but rather to facilitate their establishment, and, if necessary, their enforcement.

The second area that must be addressed is the arbitrage of the infringement of personal privacy to benefit the social collective. It arises when the social order must exhibit truly concerted action; for example, protecting the group from competing groups. In such cases, the social order must pursue policy that enlists the infringement of personal privacy of individuals to benefit the group; actions that we would more easily recognize as altruistic. In times of war, the state needs a military capability with personnel willing to literally fall on the grenade. In times of peace, as well as war, the mechanisms of the state require means of their fulfillment.

Many, if not most of these facilities can be obtained by the state through conditional covenants, assuming the state has the means to offer responsive consideration. More simply put, the state needs money to provide basic functionality. As recognized in the *Constitution*, this funding can nominally come from taxation, an altruistic act, or through borrowing by the state, a conditional covenant. There are some additional avenues from which the state acquires funding; for example, fees derived from the state's administrative functions, and also the state's ability to manipulate the availability and the value of money.

In general, there is no direct linkage between funding provided to, and expenditures made by the state. Revenue received by the state has no direct bearing on spending for services by the state save for certain instances of public borrowing. One might anticipate that fees are paid under a conditional covenant. However, this is usually not the case. Fees paid in a given area rarely provide dedicated spending for that area; hence, there is no direct balance between consideration offered and consideration received. Fees are established by the executive through administrative power granted by the legislative branch. Unlike taxes, fees generally result from voluntary acts, or actions that we might observe as deriving from assertions of personal privacy.

The behaviors that we've noted such as paying our taxes and not stealing from our neighbors can be classified as **altruism**, which we define as **policy mandated behavior of the individual to benefit the social order.** Altruism is relevant, and thus effective, only when the polity has sufficient devotion to the basis of trust of the social order. In the second chapter, we briefly considered the heuristic model of motivation for individual behavior developed by Abraham Maslow. This model suggests a number of rationales for devotion to a trust infrastructure; all grounded in individual needs.

At the highest level of Maslow's hierarchy is the need of transcendence, which presents as appetites resulting in behaviors directed beyond the individual; behaviors aimed at satisfying the needs of social order. Among all groups, the state is distinguished by its ability to assert police powers to effect altruistic behavior among its polity. Lower in the individual's hierarchy is the need of safety and security. At the two extremes, we can see that one might be devoted to the state because "it is transcendentally good"; or, one might be devoted to the state because "it is to be physiologically feared!"

History might suggest that the better rationale for behaviors of the polity is the former, while the better rationale for relationships among social orders is the latter. The reason for this observation is that the trust infrastructure for societal relationships is primarily that of the physical ecosystem; survival of the fittest. Personal relationships can be based on privacy and reputation derived from identity. However, even considering interactions freely engaged among the polity, the mechanisms through which "goodness" is assessed must be equitably applied.

In 1887, the historian and moralist Lord Acton expressed an opinion in a letter to Bishop Mandell Creighton: "Power tends to corrupt, and absolute power corrupts absolutely. Great men are almost always bad men." This admonition is particularly pertinent when one considers how the state applies its police powers. Viewing personal privacy as a fundamental right of the individual, great caution should be exercised in its abridgement. If the police powers of the state can be used without limit to infringe personal privacy, then the danger arises that this will lead to corruption of the state. Actually, this is probably a good definition of corruption of the state.

The Founders were familiar with the dangers inherent in the unrestrained power of the state. To that end, the policy infrastructure that they established through the *Constitution* is one of divided government. Various combinations of the branches of government provide a series of checks and balances that constrain the others. Investing the police powers of the state in a republican form of government was a further step toward balancing the power of the state by that of the polity. However, even the power of the polity must be constrained if not to lead to general systemic corruption.

The Founders recognized a threat when specific desires became the focused demands of subcultures within the polity. To this end, the infrastructures they defined attempted to restrain the actions of the state taken against individuals, or less powerful subcultures, by defining fundamental rights which state policies could not abridge. In practice, the greatest threat to fundamental rights arises from state policies; especially those that benefit one subculture at the expense of another.

The courts, as the ultimate arbiters of policy, constrain the power of the state by the balancing of rights versus the policy desires which lead to their abridgement through a cautious consideration of the two. The Supreme Court recognized this need for caution when it ruled that any infringement of a fundamental right can only be done in response to a compelling interest on the part of the state. Even lacking a truly compelling interest, it is not unusual for the state to transform a mere desire into a mandatory need. Hence, one arrives at the rationale for strict scrutiny.

The Supreme Court alluded to the danger inherent in the police powers of the state in one of its early rulings that molded the jurisprudence of the new nation; the case of *McCulloch v. Maryland*. Taxes are an obvious form of altruistic behavior mandated under the police powers of the state. This case involved the issue of whether a state government could tax an entity of the federal government; specifically, a bank chartered by the federal government.

Chief Justice John Marshall, in writing the unanimous opinion of the court, observed "An unlimited power to tax involves, necessarily, a power to destroy; because there is a limit beyond which no institution and no property can bear taxation." There is a corollary to this related to borrowing. We might paraphrase Justice Marshall by noting that an unlimited power to borrow, which is a tax on future activities, involves necessarily a power to destroy; because there is a limit beyond which no institution and no property can bear the cost of borrowing. This raises the aspect of due process that we considered in the fifth chapter; the requirement that state policies enlist only sustainable processes.

At the time of the *McCulloch* decision, *Article I Section 9* of the *Constitution* stated relative to direct taxes on the people, "No Capitation, or other direct, Tax shall be laid unless in Proportion to the Census or Enumeration herein before directed to be taken." This established a concept of equality in the levying of direct taxes on the people and provided a balance against an unlimited power of taxation. This equation of balance was altered somewhat by the *Sixteenth Amendment* that allowed for a direct tax on income.

> The Congress shall have power to lay and collect taxes on incomes, from whatever source derived, without apportionment among the several States, and without regard to any census or enumeration.

A direct tax on the individual obviously represents an infringement of personal privacy. From the perspective of due process, it seems appropriate to consider whether this amendment was an explicit recognition of the power of the government to destroy, or at least to apply punitive measures to, individuals or specific subcultures based on economic characteristics?

Alluding to the words of the Supreme Court in *Footnote 4*, does the *Sixteenth Amendment* allow the state to preferentially address, and in fact punish, "... discrete and insular minorities..." distinguished by economic factors? Does the "...power to lay and collect taxes on income..." allow the state to apply variable punitive sanctioning of an individual or a subculture purely on the basis of the amount of that income? Actually, the more general question is whether taxation can be used to punish? This seems a power more characteristic of adjudication for which there are a variety of protections, including oversight by the courts.

Power sufficiently effective to destroy is also the power to enslave. The Civil War was fought in large part to justify what should have been a proper reading of the *Constitution* as encompassed by the *Declaration of Independence*; that "...all men are created equal." Today's Supreme Court might have no problem dismissing slavery as unconstitutional, regardless of whether the *Thirteenth Amendment*, the *Fourteenth Amendment* and the *Fifteenth Amendment* were in place. They might well find in personal privacy, as they seemed to find in *Roe v. Wade*, revulsion to state sanctioned enslavement for any reason, save for a compelling state interest such as remedial action against those found guilty of criminal acts.

In establishing by law the criminality of various acts, each such law should demonstrate a compelling state interest as well. So, it is interesting to consider the question as to whether the court would accept virtual enslavement on the basis of economic condition. At the present time, people cannot be incarcerated for debts owed, save to the state. One might wonder whether they can be punished for failure to commit altruistic acts when such acts are not grounded in a compelling state interest or symmetric application through sustainable processes.

The point we suggest here is that the courts clearly recognize that when any entity can, without restriction, tax a different entity, then the first has the power to destroy the second. In the case of government-mandated altruistic action in the form of taxation, an infringement of personal privacy, the assessment of any tax should be subject to strict scrutiny by the courts. The purpose of government is to conduce to the happiness of the people, not to enslave or destroy them. Moreover, it is not to provide happiness to one at the direct, punitive expense of another.

A comprehensive right of privacy can be quite inconvenient to those who seek to establish, apply and adjudicate policy. In a republic, the motivations for policy should derive from the perspective of the polity, not the personal motivations of policy purveyors, or the motivations of subcultures to which they subscribe. Following the principles of the *Declaration of Independence*, a necessary characteristic of such motivation is deference to the privacy of the individual.

To those seeking to eradicate the injustice of racial or gender based inequities, privacy was and is a powerful concept. Slavery infringes personal privacy. Not being able to vote because you're a woman infringes privacy. Being denied behaviors protected by the state for others simply because you're gay infringes privacy. These applications of privacy, or rather banning their infringement, are on the ascendance in American jurisprudence.

However, there are other forces aimed at the infringement of privacy that are on the ascendance as well. Some subcultures within the polity seek benefits paid for by other subcultures. A significant problem that contemporary jurisprudence has with an expansive right of privacy derives from issues beyond those influenced by race, gender or sexual orientation. An expansive right of privacy runs head-on into issues that Justice Douglas sought to avoid in his *Griswold v. Connecticut* opinion; "... laws that touch economic problems, business affairs, and social conditions."

As we noted back in the fifth chapter, *Griswold* was a landmark case that recognized unenumerated yet fundamental rights. To rule on the constitutionality of laws that attempted to abridge such rights, the court expressed its power to examine laws according to **substantive due process**. For the court to address the substance of laws, not just the process of their creation, is at the heart of what many view as **judicial activism**.

The argument is that such oversight by the courts infringes on the legislative and executive prerogatives to create and enforce laws as they see fit; where fitness is determined purely by the relevant legislative and executive majorities. A contrary perspective was expressed by Justice Marshall in *Marbury* and in *McCulloch*. There, the court recognized that one purpose of a constitution is to guard against the excesses of legislative and executive majorities. The Supreme Court manifests this guardianship through the ultimate prerogative to assess the constitutionality of laws.

On reflection, it seems impossible for the courts to apply the test of strict scrutiny to any law without resorting to substantive due process. Perhaps more to the point, without substantive due process there is no effective means to constrain within constitutional limits the police powers exercised by the legislature and executive. If an expansive right of privacy does exist, then substantive due process applied by the courts forms its primary protection against legislative and executive excess.

In the early Twentieth Century, the Supreme Court actually started down this path through the case of *Lochner v. New York*. Under the rationale of this ruling, the courts overturned a relatively small number of laws on the basis of oversight of primarily economic and social issues. With the advent of the New Deal of the Franklin Roosevelt administration, a progressive movement came to the fore. This movement comprised a subculture that strongly espoused the concept that the state could pursue policies aimed at a redistribution of wealth among the populace as a manifestation of its police powers. This progressive movement was strongly at odds with the *Lochner* ruling.

In his book *Rehabilitating Lochner*, legal scholar David E. Bernstein opens with this assessment: "If you want to raise eyebrows at a gathering of judges or legal scholars, try praising the Supreme Court's 1905 decision in Lochner v. New York." As evidenced by the title of his book, Bernstein suggests that at least some of the rancor in the discussion might be moderated by a more accurate understanding of the context of the times. If this is so, perhaps we could hope for a mere flaring of the nostrils in attempting to discuss the case in a positive light.

The case dealt with a law to limit how many hours per day and week a bakery employee could work. The rationale for the law was ostensibly to be found in protecting the public health. Overturning the New York law with its ruling, the court recognized an unenumerated right; the **right of contract**. The Supreme Court's decision begins with a concise statement of fact:

> The general right to make a contract in relation to his business is part of the liberty protected by the Fourteenth Amendment, and this includes the right to purchase and sell labor, except as controlled by the State in the legitimate exercise of its police power.

> Liberty of contract relating to labor includes both parties to it; the one has as much right to purchase as the other to sell labor.

As we've observed earlier, the liberties referenced in the *Fourteenth Amendment* are used as justification for many unenumerated rights in subsequent (to Lochner) cases. The court's opinion in *Lochner* includes the following section which certainly looks like a precursor to the concept of strict scrutiny that will arise a few decades after *Lochner*.

> It is a question of which of two powers or rights shall prevail,-the power of the state to legislate or the right of the individual to liberty of person and freedom of contract. The mere assertion that the subject relates, though but in a remote degree, to the public health, does not necessarily render the enactment valid. The act must have a more direct relation, as a means to an end, and the end itself must be appropriate and legitimate, before an act can be held to be valid which interferes [198 U.S. 45, 58] with the general right of an individual to be free in his person and in his power to contract in relation to his own labor.

We have suggested that in any interaction involving two or more people, a necessary aspect of setting the context for the interaction is the arbitration of personal privacy among the participants. This arbitration establishes a contract. Hence, the right of contract recognized by the court in *Lochner* quite reasonably derives from a right of privacy. As with the right of privacy as expressed in *Roe v. Wade*, the holding of the court is not that the right cannot be abridged, but that the state must demonstrate a compelling interest to do so.

The court's ruling in *Lochner* was effectively invalidated through the 1937 case of *West Coast Hotel Co. v. Parrish*. This case considered a State of Washington law mandating a minimum wage for women. The Supreme Court upheld the law, and reinforced the concept that the state could, through its police powers, protect the "health and morals" of a discrete and insular minority; that is, women. The court held that forcing employers to pay a "living wage" relieved the state from having to do so:

> The exploitation of a class of workers who are in an unequal position with respect to bargaining power, and are thus relatively defenceless against the denial of a living wage, is not only detrimental to their health and wellbeing, but casts a direct burden for their support upon the community. What these workers lose in wages, the taxpayers are called upon to pay. The bare cost of living must be met.

This court ruling is one of many delivered during the days of the Great Depression. It fostered the concept that various subcultures could express their specific, often dogmatic economic and social policies using the power of the state. The issue with this approach to governance is the apparent lack of any restraining power on that of the state as enacted by the minimum majority of fifty percent plus one. If a subculture can achieve this simple level of political superiority, it can exert total power over the policy infrastructure.

As we considered in the second chapter, this has the appearance of a positive feedback loop. When a legislative and executive majority has unlimited power over an insular minority, then the path is open to complete abridgement of the personal privacy of that minority. Thus, a danger arises when the court affords protection of minorities identified by characteristics of race and gender but not of minorities characterized on economic or personal motivation grounds.

It seems a good bet the Founders did not intend for government to function as a top predator; to resort to the "law of the jungle" under which government could, by virtue of its physical prowess, simply confiscate the consequences of personal privacy in the name of altruism. This was certainly not the intent of the adjudication system expressed through the *Constitution*. Therefore, we suggest that an expansive right of privacy does require judicial oversight of "... laws that touch economic problems, business affairs, and social conditions"; at least, when they result in infringement of personal privacy. This oversight must encompass the application of strict scrutiny to such laws.

Manipulation of Motivation

When first we began a consideration of society's benefitting from the privacy of the individual, we suggested that success of a social order comes from "...just the right amount of altruism." If a social order achieves too little altruism it may lack the means to compete in the physical ecosystem because no one falls on the grenade and the immediate battle is lost. Given that altruism is counter intuitive relative to natural selection applied to the individual, if a social order demands too much altruism it may lack the requisite motivation of individuals to excel as they seek their true happiness. In essence, everyone falls on the grenade and future battles are lost for want of enhanced capabilities derived from individual exceptionalism.

Behaviors of the individual can be influenced, if not controlled, through manipulation of the motivation that drives action responses to sensory observations. Individuals and social entities, including the state, seek to influence the motivations of others by expression aimed at the mechanics of trust assessment of the individual; in essence, by manipulating an individual's cognitive facilities. We can recognize a spectrum of such expressions that ranges from censorship to propaganda. Viewed metaphorically, this spectrum encompasses not only the context of cognitive models, but also the actions they evoke. Censorship seeks to curtail information and actions that evoke "undesirable" motivations while propaganda seeks to enhance information and actions that evoke "desirable" motivations. Such expressions, in whatever form, are direct assaults on personal privacy.

Motivation is one facet of an individual's assessment of trust. In the second chapter, we briefly considered a heuristic model of motivation first suggested by psychologist Abraham Maslow. Demands for altruism on the part of the polity are expressed through policy that can be aimed to influence personal motivations across the full hierarchy of needs identified in that model. By thus manipulating the trust infrastructure of the individual, a person can be pushed toward the pursuit of altruistic actions as a means of self-fulfillment. If their devotion to the trust infrastructure is sufficient, they can be guided to excessive altruistic acts to the detriment of their otherwise "true" happiness. As we have previously noted, the degree to which policy seeks to impact privacy is a defining characteristic of the culture of the social order.

The *First Amendment* recognizes the importance of enabling the influencing of others through a right of expression. We have previously suggested that an expansive right of personal privacy actually subsumes this right of expression, but tempers it with a constraining right of selective impression. Within the framework of American jurisprudence, mechanisms have been identified through which these competing demands can be addressed. However, in much of current law the right of expression vastly outweighs any contravening characteristics of personal privacy. This has resulted in asymmetric considerations regarding expression versus impression.

In the course of manipulating individual motivations, a variety of issues have stressed the policy infrastructure in its attempts to address activities that bring individuals into structured contention with one another and with the state. Together, these provide a representative sample through which we can consider whether or how policy might be impacted by an expansive right of privacy. As a corollary to this consideration, we can anticipate the utility of a comprehensive, state enacted identification system as a means of providing enhanced mechanisms to support the assertion of personal privacy and its impact on policy formulated by the state. Let's at least introduce a few of the more readily recognized issues.

Advertising

Advertising, and its more expansive corollary known as **marketing,** generally present as expressive campaigns using art-forms aimed at the manipulation of motivation of the individual. They occur along the spectrum from unconditional to conditional covenants; usually somewhere between censorship and propaganda. While such compositions and campaigns have clearly existed since the dawn of recorded history, with the advent of the digital world they have become incredibly pervasive aspects of American culture. In virtually all their forms, they seek to create an artificial metaphorical connection among concepts in order to manipulate the assertion of personal privacy of the individual.

In its most banal form, advertising seeks to motivate a person to "want", and subsequently engage a conditional covenant to "buy" something. The act of advertisement is generally perceived to be a conditional covenant in its own right. It seeks to provide some consideration, typically entertainment, in exchange for which the person being entertained agrees to receive impressions from the advertisement. This is obviously a tenuous covenant since many people channel-surf during the commercials. The advertisement itself aims to manipulate the motivations of the person by invoking an association with "something different" that is already favorably perceived. It seeks to piggy-back a sensation of "desire" on top of a sensation of "happiness"; more accurately, on top of an existing motivation derived from the hierarchy described by Maslow.

In its more pernicious forms, advertising seeks to recalibrate the personal or social trust infrastructure in order to affect how an individual or a social aggregate responds to more general social contexts. In essence, by evoking the sensation of "ecstasy", advertising seeks to manipulate what motivates people to act in a wide variety of situations. At the boundaries of its application, advertising can become propaganda for a changed assessment of truth versus trust, or censorship of contextual information central to that assessment.

Chapter 6 – Privacy as a Social Mutagen

The concept of advertising in its many forms is interesting because it has become as much a science as it has always been an art-form. Through studies of individual and group behaviors, expressive mechanisms to evoke specific impressions in others have become incredibly effective. If the subject being advertised is not truthfully presented, the manipulation of motivations can become quite malevolent. Policy of the state to address this in part differentiates between "commercial" use and "free expression" use of expressive mechanisms. **Truth in advertising law** allows adjudication in instances where fraudulent claims are made.

In any interaction involving multiple individuals, including the use of tools to form compositions, the effective privacy rights of all concerned must be subject to reconciliation as a precursor of the interaction. More to the point, since privacy rights do exist they must be explicitly addressed through interaction processes that we have previously referred to as arbitration protocols. Issues to be arbitrated include recognition of the pending act of advertisement as well all the other aspects of privacy.

If one person can snap a picture of another person on a public street, the subsequent commercial use of that picture is obviously an infringement of personal privacy. When availability of images entices others to look at them, and subsequently expose themselves to additional forms of expression seeking to impact their basic cognitive models, "commercial use" in the form of **advertising** virtually always ensues.

In today's digital world, any public expression can easily morph into commercial use through a derivative composition. This is the typical goal of advertising; to exploit the sensations evoked by one expression in order to enhance some secondary expression. A corollary suggests that since the goal of advertising is manipulation of the personal trust infrastructure, any endeavor supported by advertising is suspect and of questionable trustworthiness. This establishes compelling grounds for the individual to seek control of being subjected to advertising, as well as the subject matter involved. State policy in this regards would seem appropriate.

Surveillance

When Brandeis and Warren wrote their pioneering review paper on privacy, they were particularly concerned about the intrusion into the private lives of the well known by newspapers seeking candid photographs they could publish. This gave impetus to their general reference to privacy as "…the right to be let alone." In the current world, freelance photographers termed **paparazzi** seek out and photograph people in unguarded moments and sell the pictures to various publications. This seems aimed at feeding the desires of people to be vicariously entertained by observing the private lives of those with some degree of celebrity.

A more insidious side to such activity is general surveillance of specific individuals or of collections of people. Sometimes this is done with the clandestine goal of influencing how they and others behave. Sometimes it is with the goal to obtain entertainment fodder to fuel advertising; including personal notoriety. However, entertainment or newsworthy expressions provide raw material for a wider variety of commercial enterprises.

Biometric technology, specifically facial recognition and iris pattern recognition, have evolved to the point of allowing differential-identification of individuals without their being aware of the activity. Photographic mechanisms are able to capture images of people from great distances.

Most smart phones have a camera with video capabilities allowing still pictures and video clips to be captured virtually anywhere. Miniature cameras with WiFi connections allow surreptitious observation with instantaneous transmission. A significant problem arises because of the lack of specific reasons for such surveillance as required by constitutional mandates.

Various subcultures have emerged to exploit these facilities; often as a means to manipulate the motivations of others. It's easy to post pictures or videos and have them go viral across the Internet. Ease of dissemination is complemented by ease of acquisition. The result is that computer networks take on an organic quality which is difficult, if not impossible, to quarantine or control. The admonition is: "Once it's on the Internet, it's there forever." Once there, it influences behaviors of all those it reaches. While the effectiveness of any policy aimed at curtailing such activities is questionable, an entirely distinct consideration is policy regarding the ownership of images and identification of facilities that make them available. Neither of these is technically onerous.

Of similar concern is the truth averred by images. Given the incredible computing power that can be brought to bear on digital material, the unfettered publication of images not only infringes personal privacy, it can easily do so without actual merit. While a picture has long been thought to convey a significant level of trust, in fact the truth derived from pictures is deserving of a good bit of skepticism. The full interaction resulting in such tool aided sensory observations must be addressed through trusted protocols in order to reasonably extract truth with a given level of certainty. Technology can be brought to bear to detect false images, but it is even more capable in assuring the continuing integrity of images; or, of all forms of information for that matter.

While biometric mechanisms give aid to those performing surveillance, they also give aid to those who seek to assert ownership of the images or information gathered. If a person can be reliably authenticated in a photograph, then they should able to claim an ownership interest in that photograph. The extent of this interest is an excellent subject of policy. Hence, policy to address such infringement is certainly in order.

Personal Information

A slightly different perspective on surveillance derives from the remembrance through compositions of interactions, particularly digital interactions. When one engages in an interaction, its consequences become distinct memories and compositions that contribute to the experiential-identity of the person; actually, to each person who engages in a common interaction. As we have noted, personal privacy suggests that each person has an ownership position in these consequences. However, often such consequences are not afforded the privileges of ownership and hence the control that personal privacy would suggest. Many entities can realize value from the compositions of these consequences compiled as **personal information**.

Colleting personal information is not purely an artifact of the digital world. There is a great deal of such data amassed in the non-digital world as well; from purchasing records at stores of all types to the medical records archived by dentists, physicians and hospitals. Perhaps, most insidious is the gathering of personal financial information by **credit bureaus**. Archives of personal information typically surface a variety of issues, not the least of which is that they're always an infringement of personal privacy. A significant consideration then is whether the infringement is allowed through the arbitration of some form of conditional covenant?

A pervasive problem with compositions involving personal information is the integrity of the data. For example, who acquired it? What guarantees are there that the information is correct; that it was reliably attributed with associated means of non-repudiation? Are there any constraints on who can access the information? Perhaps most pertinent, is there a justification for its maintenance? This is an area where state policy is appropriate to establish effective recognition of personal privacy when the process of arbitration is difficult to realize. It is an area where an effective IAA System offers an appropriate means to enhance personal privacy.

Using digital mechanisms, it is quite feasible to realize privacy in the collection of personal information. Strong authentication of identity coupled with a PKI allows proper establishment of authority to collect and archive information, along with the proper attribution to show ownership and the assurance of information integrity. Subsequently, it is quite feasible to identify all those who access these information archives and to record the details of that access. Access to archives by the observed parties could be guaranteed by state policy, if not through conditional covenants. The direct benefit of effective IAA Systems comes from enabling policy that can assure personal privacy for virtually all information observed and archived.

Public Demonstrations

From the Boston Tea Party as a precursor to the American Revolution to the Whiskey Rebellion as an introduction to the difficulties of governance, public demonstrations have become a fixture of American culture. Ostensibly aimed at policy, they sometimes represent a distancing of social aggregates from the trust infrastructure of the state. They are an attempt to influence policy in a manner external to the defined mechanisms found in the *Constitution*. At the extreme end of the spectrum, one finds in them the nascent threads that lead to the terrorists that society must deal with today.

More typical are two types of prevalent public demonstrations; those that innocuously express ideas inimical to the state or other interests and those that forcefully assert those ideas in the venues of the state or other interests. Some demonstrations are meant to simply express ideas. Other demonstrations are intended to force others to pay attention to those expressions. We might recognize either as a form of advertising. There are reactions to both forms and an expansive right of privacy has impact on each.

As observed in the case of *Schenck v. New York*, there are subcultures within the policy infrastructure that seek to silence ideas with which they disagree. During World War I, laws were passed to limit speech perceived as unpatriotic and supportive of ideas contrary to the prosecution of the war. Through the successive cases that we considered, the courts forced the moderation of such policies, deferring to the *First Amendment* guarantee of freedom of speech. When the expression is in a form that others can simply ignore, then privacy infringement is comparable to more common forms of advertising. However, the physical assertion of ideas through demonstrations in venues established for other purposes offers the distinct possibility of greater infringement.

Rather routine today are public demonstrations that seek to raise the awareness of issues that are important to some and yet unpopular, unimportant or unknown to others. Often, demonstrations go well beyond simply raising awareness by actively seeking specific resolutions to the issues in question. Citing deference to the *First Amendment*, the courts have tended to be accepting of such activities. However, an expansive right of privacy suggests a competing rationale for limiting such demonstrations once they cease to be purely about expression of ideas and instead seek to disrupt the activities of others. At such points, the concept of a right to be left alone becomes pertinent.

It is at this juncture, when a right to free expression runs headlong into a right to be left alone, that sorting out the correct policies becomes problematic. As an example, demonstrations by religious groups at the funerals of military personnel killed in action certainly do not warrant unqualified protection as free speech. To the extent that they interfere with a funeral ritual, which is a unique occurrence and an expression of the freedom of religious practice, they certainly do not hold a privileged position as a fundamental right.

This is a place where fundamental rights intersect and which require some level of arbitration among the affecting and affected parties, perhaps established through policy of the state. Ideas can be expressed at many times, in many ways and at many places. A funeral for a person occurs only once. As the confluence of the freedom of speech and the freedom of the press would suggest, a right to expression does not require someone else to listen to what is expressed. An expansive right of privacy suggests a right to control the context of an interaction; for example, a funeral. This illustrates an area where the intersection of two fundamental rights is ripe for an appropriate expression of policy.

Taxation

We have suggested that paying taxes is an altruistic act intended to provide funding to allow the state to function. There is no direct, conditional covenant assumed in the assessment of taxes. Moreover, taxation is not intended to be a means to effect punitive measures through which to coerce behavior of the polity. When viewed as acts of altruism, payment of taxes should either be equitably required across the polity and triggered through stochastic processes, or they should derive from assertions of personal privacy. Taxes paid into the Social Security system are representative of the former and general sales taxes are representative of the latter. At least two types of federal taxes seem questionable from both perspectives; the graduated income tax and inheritance taxes.

An equitable tax on incomes invites an equal level of taxation on all levels of income. This places a comparable demand for altruism on individuals at all income levels. For example, a twenty per cent tax on income means that higher income levels pay a greater tax than lower income levels, but the **tax rate** is equally applied. When higher income levels are assessed a higher tax rate than lower income levels, then the tax is no longer equitably applied; the additional tax is a punitive measure.

Assuming wealth is legally obtained, including the equitable taxation of income from which it derives, to prohibit it being passed to heirs on the death of its owner is certainly a punitive measure. To punish families or others who would inherit wealth is both an abridgment of personal privacy as well as an assault on freedom of association. Both the graduated income tax and inheritance taxes are assessed disproportionally against insular minorities identifiable by economic condition or condition of being; that is, income levels or accumulated wealth. To justify either would require a truly compelling interest on the part of the state.

Beyond the questionable nature of these specific taxes, any use by the state of tax policy to coerce against lawful behaviors among the polity is particularly suspect. The federal income tax code is replete with obtuse considerations of what counts as income, and what expenditures can be discounted as income. By coercing specific behaviors, all of which are appropriate under law, taxation becomes a means of manipulation of motivation outside the purview of policy and its adjudication process. As such, it represents a completely unrestrained exercise of power by the state. It would seem that this falls outside the bounds of due process.

Since income taxes and inheritance taxes are infringements on personal privacy, there must be a compelling interest on the part of the state to assess them. A need for revenue might constitute a compelling interest were the taxes equitably assessed. We say "might" because the current imbalance of revenues versus expenditures of the United States government suggests that money from taxes is not a compelling need. When public borrowing and state control over the availability and value of money are brought into the mix, it is clear that other motivations are at the heart of the state's actions as defined by legislative and executive majorities. Moreover, much of current tax policy and monetary policy is aimed at effecting social consequences based largely on beliefs of faith-based subcultures.

There is a corollary to the non-equitable assessment of taxes based on economic characteristics of the taxpayer. It is discriminatory against those who are taxed less as well as those who are taxed more. The rationale that for one segment of the populace to be taxed less than another is somehow beneficial to that segment infringes the personal privacy of that segment by applying an external assessment of motivation. This infringement strikes at the heart of the feedback control loops built into the policy infrastructure by the *Constitution*.

It was long maintained that laws treating women "preferentially" were a benefit to women in general. In retrospect, such laws clearly put women in an inferior position in provisioning their personal identities. For example, forbidding women in the military from engaging in combat clearly infringes their ability to evoke a reputation as a strong military leader; a reputation that has clear implications in selecting representatives for the policy infrastructure. Thus, notwithstanding some as yet to be demonstrated compelling state interest, the un-equitable assessment of taxes is clearly in conflict with personal privacy.

From *United States v. Jackson*:

> It is no answer to urge, as does the Government, that federal trial judges may be relied upon to reject coerced pleas of guilty and involuntary waivers of jury trial. For the evil in the federal statute is not that it necessarily coerces guilty pleas and jury waivers, but simply that it needlessly encourages them. A procedure need not be inherently coercive in order that it be held to impose an impermissible burden upon the assertion of a constitutional right.

The issue regarding taxation is not the level of taxation. Rather, the greater threat is that policies of taxation are becoming so asymmetric, complex and punitive as to make them unsustainable over the long term. These same asymmetries render constitutional safeguards ineffective unless due process oversight is applied.

Social Safety Net

In considering state mandates for altruism, we alluded to the need for individuals to forego predator versus prey behaviors in order to foster social order under which necessary common goals could be pursued. An extension on this form of altruism is the creation of a social safety net to offer a base level of social support for individuals. A social safety net can take two distinct forms, one providing ubiquitous support and the other providing shared risk with a stochastic selection mechanism that determines who actually receives support.

National defense and national infrastructure such as streets and highways are examples of ubiquitous support facilities. National insurance programs are examples of the other. The Social Security System is an excellent example of a national insurance program. It is designed such that essentially all workers pay an equitably assessed tax to fund the system and longevity provides the selection process that determines who receives a payout benefit. An additional component is a payout for those who become disabled and unable to work. As with any insurance program, the long term viability of social security can be determined actuarially as long as selection mechanisms derive from objective, stochastic processes.

In the case of social security, for decades the program had established tax rates that provided a surplus of funding in the near term in order to provide adequate funding support over the longer term. However, as birth rates have diminished the funding provided by younger workers has become insufficient to support the large numbers of workers who are retiring. The problem that this particular program exhibits is a lack of long term sustainability due to insufficient tax revenues to support the retiring workers.

The danger that has arisen is the lack of political will to bring the system into a sustainable balance. As the crisis looms, potential solutions show a tendency to punish certain minorities of the polity through non-stochastic processes in order to benefit other minorities. This manifests as an infringement of the personal privacy of significant minorities. The question then becomes whether the courts have a role to play in assessing solutions that fit within the constraints of the *Constitution's* mandates of personal privacy based on equality.

Morality

Morality is always presented as a guide to behavior perceived to be **good**. Couched in the terms of our previous discussions, morality derives from a comprehensive metaphorical model that forms the motivation for personal interactions. Motivations consistent across a population result in policy that urges that those motivations be followed. When such motivations are enforced through the police powers of the state, they can go beyond uniformly acceptable motivations and become instead a means of coercion of individuals or insular minorities to engage behaviors that can be uniformly detrimental to those individuals or insular minorities. This is the great danger that is addressed by constitutionally limited government.

A recurring theme of the motivation of state policy that infringes personal privacy is that of **public morality**. The anti-abortion laws overturned through the *Roe v. Wade* decision were premised on a claim of public morality. The separate but equal doctrine affirmed by *Plessy v. Ferguson*, which we will consider in some detail in our final chapter, was predicated upon a claim of public morality. Even much of social safety-net policy such as that referenced in the case of *West Coast Hotel Co. v. Parrish* relies on an assertion of public morality for its basis. Other areas include obscenity laws, marriage laws, general prohibitions against homosexual behavior and anti-suicide laws. Public morality is cast as a motivation for much of tax policy. There are more areas to be sure, and their interpretation results in significant social turmoil.

The decision structure that the courts have erected around the concept of strict scrutiny and compelling interests offers a means to address these areas of turmoil. As with the anti-abortion laws, the courts offer a means to address compelling interests on an issue by issue basis. Laws that can pass muster of this examination will collectively form a specification of public morality. Hence, we suggest morality should be viewed as an effect and not a cause or justification. From our perspective, Justice Douglas' dissent in *Roth V. United States* begins to recognize this distinction when he notes "... it is by no means clear that obscene literature, as so defined, is a significant factor in influencing substantial deviations from the community standards."

When the situation is reversed, and morality is asserted as the justification for public policy, it often results from the faith-based beliefs of religious subcultures. This is a significant threat to the concept of expansive personal privacy. It forms an attempt to arbitrarily manipulate the motivations of individual actions. It often leads to exploitation of one subculture to benefit another. It leads to policy excesses that stifle reasonable assertions of personal privacy; assertions that ultimately benefit the social collective through enhanced action, innovation and social resilience.

Ownership of Self

Privacy sits at the frontier between the individual and the collective; between the self and the polity. Technology has now arrived at this frontier in full force. It manifests at the most basic nuance of policy in the consideration of "Who owns our minds and bodies?" It makes itself known in a variety of forms: the legality of suicide, the selling of organs and body parts, the adoption of children, the incompetence of the individual, and, most recently, the ownership of personal DNA patterns. It is this last consideration that brings technology and privacy into sharp focus.

Over the last several decades, incredible strides have been made in understanding the mechanisms and processes of living material. Congruent with this has been the development of corporate entities that make businesses from this understanding. Indeed, the state is a willing partner in these endeavors. In an effort to exploit natural processes through these businesses, the patenting of organic processes has exploded. Recent forays have been made into patenting DNA sequences directly. This seems to be a direct assault on personal privacy.

Virtually every cell of every person encompasses strands of DNA from which that person is constructed. The mechanisms to interpret these strands are found in every cell as well. Recent advances suggest that DNA from any cell can be used as the starting point for creating clones; genetic duplicates of the individual from whom the DNA is extracted. It seems rather obvious that under an expansive right of privacy, each individual owns their own DNA and the benefit derived from interpreting it and possibly from creating derivative entities from that interpretation. This is certainly one take on the *Roe v. Wade* landmark ruling.

Recalling that Supreme Court decision, during the first trimester of gestation the developing embryo and fetus are viewed as integral elements of the mother's body. It is her sole prerogative to terminate her pregnancy. Once the fetus emerges from her body, when a baby is born, then ownership transfers to the baby. While it is not yet competent to assert personal privacy, its rights must be addressed. The infant becomes a ward of some superior entity charged with, if we can use the term once again, a fiduciary duty to act in the best interests of the infant. The issues are profound.

Public morality is often advanced in the guise of protecting the "sanctity of life." There are discussions throughout society as to "when life begins." The point of the conversation is an attempt to determine when policy protections should be afforded to a new person. The great difficulty is melding technological advances with the historical moral perspective. In fact, "life" is continuous. An objective assessment of truth suggests that while life proceeds in a smooth continuum from "state" to "state", there is great differentiation between the conditions and capabilities of "states." If privacy is a manifestation of cognition, then cognitive capability becomes a defining "characteristic of state."

So, we see in this sampling of policies the potential impact of an expansive right of personal privacy. The potential is profound. How profound? In the final chapter, we will examine the rationales for a new balance between policy and privacy.

7 *Privacy and Policy Redux*

In the course of these pages, we have examined the concept of privacy. We began from the perspective of the individual for whom personal privacy forms the means of interaction within the real world. We found that a discussion of privacy necessitates a discussion of identity since one is cause and the other effect. We then considered the complementary perspective of social aggregates which derive their affect from the personal privacy of their individual members. The manner in which these two perspectives meld is a manifestation of culture.

The historical view of American culture presents a popular image of rugged individualism; a natural outcome of expansive personal privacy. There is significant truth in the picture, but the view is subject to a bit of social myopia as well. There are episodes in the evolution of American culture that don't mesh well with the principles espoused when the nation was established. This is characteristic of evolutionary processes. It requires time for newly emergent characteristics within a population to come to dominate that population. What is striking, however, is the central role of personal privacy in the framework laid down by the Founders of the Republic. It is a tempting, albeit provocative example of the concept of intelligent design, but one couched in objective truth as opposed to religious faith.

Colonial governments were established under the auspices of various European states; most notably Great Britain, France, Spain, Netherlands, Portugal and Belgium. However, in a rather remarkable expression of aesthetic ecstasy, the people of the thirteen colonies along the eastern reach of the North American continent formed a new, independent nation-state. Geography afforded them the isolation for social evolution independent from the main body of European populations, and they did so quite formally through the establishment of new, well defined trust and policy infrastructures. This offers an opportunity to examine the progression of social evolution. It's rare that a nation has been created through such rigorously specified processes. It is a consciously designed culture.

In 1776, meeting in the Second Continental Congress, representatives of the Thirteen Colonies put forward a resolution to dissolve all political ties to Britain, the *Lee Resolution* proposed by the delegation from Virginia. It stated:

> Resolved, That these United Colonies are, and of right ought to be, free and independent States, that they are absolved from all allegiance to the British Crown, and that all political connection between them and the State of Great Britain is, and ought to be, totally dissolved.
>
> That it is expedient forthwith to take the most effectual measures for forming foreign Alliances.
>
> That a plan of confederation be prepared and transmitted to the respective Colonies for their consideration and approbation.

This resolution was approved by the Congress on July 2, 1776. Subsequently, a formal declaration of dissolution was effected and published by the Congress; the *Declaration of Independence* issued on July 4, 1776. This declaration forms the official public act of severing the political bonds with the State of Great Britain.

The people that fomented these processes we refer to as the Founders. In a bit of paternalistic arrogance, they're sometimes referred to as the "Founding Fathers". Hopefully, we now understand that when viewed from a more expansive perspective one sees that the well recognized men were actually the products of provisioning that encompassed women, slaves and a multitude of cultural cross-currents. These Founders thus represent a most interesting confluence of personas. The infrastructures of the nation-state that they created suggest the complexity of the profound expressions of personal privacy that gave rise to their identities.

The trust and policy infrastructures of the new nation-state were social mutations. They presented a form quite unlike any seen before. Certainly they included vestiges of existing social systems. However, that's a bit like saying a Formula One race car has wheels like a buggy or a jet airliner has wings like a Wright biplane. The structures defined by the Founders expressed a deep appreciation for the fundamental processes through which people function within the sensori-motor world. The structures are based on rigorous principles and revisions to them are not undertaken lightly.

In this last chapter, we will consider several areas in which the structures are becoming unwieldy. Briefly considering the risks posed in various areas, we'll conclude with a modest proposal for a technical boost. The areas we will consider include:

- The fundamental role of privacy in American culture
- Provisioning of the American polity as guided by this culture
- Provisioning the policy infrastructure to sustain this culture
- A modest proposal

With respect to each of these points, we suggest looking back to the structure that the Founders originally defined. Many of the mechanisms intended to exert control insuring sustainability have evolved in directions that present significant risk. We will allude to certain course corrections that might serve to buttress the original structures. The design that the Founders created was unique. It forms the construction blueprint for a social structure that today, almost two and a half centuries later, we're still trying to realize. In an iconic act of social provisioning, it began with a formal declaration.

Role of the Declaration of Independence

The United States of America finds its formal beginning in the *Declaration of Independence*; the seminal provisioning of American jurisprudence. In something of a Martin Luther moment, it announces the dissolution of societal ties to Great Britain, states the specific justification for that dissolution, enlists rebellion among the polity of a new social order, asserts the trust basis for that social order and defines the foundational requirements for its ensuing policy infrastructure.

The Revolutionary War, already smoldering for over a year, raged forward in full fury following its signing. People died under the aegis of its words. Their altruistic sacrifice lent credence to its promises among the citizens of the new nation. The *Declaration of Independence* establishes a causal basis of trust for the new social order through its invocation of **equality** of all people and its affirmation of a basic, **unalienable right of privacy** that supersedes all forms of governance.

The *Constitution* is intrinsically subordinate to the basis of trust established through the *Declaration of Independence*. By specifying a comprehensive policy infrastructure for the social order, the *Constitution* propagates this point of causality through trusted processes. To realize the full majesty that is the United States of America, the two documents must be recognized in tandem. The *Constitution* alone leaves too much ambiguity, which has proved to be the bane of judicial interpretation since its inception. It is the ambiguity that too often gives the appearance that the United States is a nation subject to the **rule of men** rather than the aspired **rule of law**.

Simply stated, the *Declaration of Independence* is the social compact that defines America. It establishes the provenance and procedural context for the *Constitution*. Its list of grievances against King George III and the British Parliament is a how-to manual for the future *Bill of Rights*; as if that was needed given the declaration's direct recognition of privacy. Without the *Declaration of Independence*, the *Constitution* is incomplete and in a word, adrift. The *Declaration of Independence* serves as the rudder of the ship of state; necessary, because the executive, legislature and the courts don't always paddle in the same direction, let alone the right direction.

Social compacts often appear tenuous, without detailed form and function; they're rarely written down. They tend to be long on philosophy and short on substance; "all hat and no cattle", as one might say in Texas. The *Declaration of Independence* is not of this ilk. It is an example of an extremely rigorous indenture. It comprises a conditional covenant; consideration offered for consideration received. The covenant established by the *Declaration of Independence* enlists rebellion in exchange for new governance. It establishes the basis of trust in that governance through the definition of acceptable governments "...deriving their just powers from the consent of the governed."

With its opening words, the *Declaration of Independence* states the rationale for governance in general. It is governance supremely grounded in personal privacy:

> ...all men are created equal and they are endowed by their creator with certain unalienable rights ... among these are life, liberty and the pursuit of happiness.

Then, listing grievances against Great Britain in general, and King George III specifically, it states both justification for engaging this specific rebellion as well as the exit strategy for its termination; an exit strategy grounded in the realization that representative government based on universal suffrage offers the best prospect of guaranteeing the security and personal privacy of the people.

In all probability, when the Founders made reference to the "creator" they were expressing an observation grounded in religious faith. However, we note that through the early chapters of this book we presented a rationale that suggests "life, liberty and the pursuit of happiness" can be perceived to derive from evolutionary processes. Whether or not there is some form of deity behind these processes is not terribly important, at least from a policy perspective. If personal privacy encompasses these characteristics, it does not require a religious framework for its recognition. Perhaps an equally good way to phrase it is that privacy derives from the act(s) of creation;

whether the point of causality is a supernatural creator, or natural selection applied to stochastic processes, is pretty much beside the point.

To derive power from the consent of the governed is a strikingly clear definition of suffrage. Indeed, the *Declaration of Independence* is proclaimed "...in the Name, and by the Authority of the good People of these Colonies..." It enlists the polity directly. Thus, the *Declaration of Independence* evokes a common bond for action and a promise of consequences among "the good People." It seeks their engagement of rebellion, and in return the resulting government will derive its authority from their consent. In effect, it says: "You join the struggle, you get a vote!" Further, it defines the individual members of this polity as **citizens.** Thus, suffrage seems clearly an inherent characteristic of citizenship!

The *Declaration of Independence* specifies the acceptable remedial action if the resulting government is not appropriately constituted:

> ...whenever any Form of Government becomes destructive of these ends, it is the Right of the People to alter or to abolish it, and to institute new Government, laying its foundation on such principles and organizing its powers in such form, as to them shall seem most likely to effect their Safety and Happiness.

This phrasing adopts the more expansive term of "the People" as opposed to "all men". This indicates a more expansive and explicit recognition of the polity of the social order; that is, the set of people that comprise its citizens and from whose consent the power of government will derive.

United States jurisprudence is firmly grounded in the *Declaration of Independence*. Judicial review is affirmed through the decision of the Supreme Court in the case of *Marbury v. Madison*. In delivering the court's decision, Chief Justice John Marshall makes clear reference to the foundation formed by the *Declaration of Independence*:

> That the people have an original right to establish, for their future government, such principles as, in their opinion, shall most conduce to their own happiness, is the basis on which the whole American fabric has been erected. The exercise of this original right is a very great exertion; nor can it nor ought it to be frequently repeated. The principles, therefore, so established are deemed fundamental. And as the authority, from which they proceed, is supreme, and can seldom act, they are designed to be permanent.

This phrasing then infers additional facets from the *Declaration of Independence* in the justification of judicial review and the rationale for constitutionally limited government.

The "original right" derives from the successful war engaged under the banner of the *Declaration of Independence*. It establishes the fundamental principles that are subsequently molded into more rigorous procedural form by the *Constitution*. The *Constitution* is subordinate to "the authority, from which they [the principles] proceed." It is the purpose of the *Constitution* not only to give substance to government by defining the mechanisms through which it exerts power through policy, but to place limits on those powers as a means of insuring that the fundamental principles are not abused by the resulting policy.

Although aimed explicitly at the political bonds with Great Britain, the *Declaration of Independence* is clearly recursive in its applicability. It reiterates the rationale for governance in general; "Safety and Happiness". Security and privacy must be the complementary focus of acceptable governance. Once again we see a demand for balance between policy and privacy. If the balance cannot be achieved through a specific government, it is the right of the citizenry to alter its form or to start anew; always adhering to the principles that form the basis of trust of the social order. Thus, the *Declaration of Independence* forms a template for social force of the highest order.

It is sometimes argued that the *Constitution* is not a "suicide pact". The implication being that respecting the rights of individuals can not extend to such a level that the state cannot protect itself. The further implication is that in protecting itself, the state offers protection to the individual. However, the *Declaration of Independence* makes clear that there are limits to even this power of the state. If the state abuses the rights of the individual it is the right, if not the duty of the people to change it.

If the Constitution is not a suicide pact, neither is it a bill of sale into slavery for individuals or subcultures within its polity. As we have noted, there is a spectrum of social policy reactions to personal privacy. The balance between policy and privacy ultimately falls somewhere between a subjective comparison of dangers; human slavery via state policy or state destruction via anarchy, insurrection or foreign aggression. In this regards, American jurisprudence should offer a systematic compromise. Clearly, the compromise cannot be *carte blanche* to the state.

The *Declaration of Independence* presents a masterwork of social structure, melding as it does both liberal and republican concepts. Its rationale for trust in governance, power limited by the consent of the governed, follows well the republican concepts of Jean-Jacques Rousseau. Its guiding principles of policy derived from such governance, equality among the polity, espouse liberalism in the finest traditions of John Locke. Thus is established both the compelling need and the moderating constraint for government power; security and privacy. The Founders came to the game with a healthy suspicion of the unbridled power of government. The Second Continental Congress that gave pen to the *Declaration of Independence* formed only a provisional government whose primary purpose was to prosecute the war. Its charter included defining the foundation of a permanent government, but not to be the permanent government.

The duly designated representatives of that congress acted on behalf of the entire populace of the colonies. "The people" were clearly able to discern a republic from a monarchy, or a pure democracy for that matter, and they did so. The representatives of the people came to forge the means to effectively engage the rebellion; at that point languishing in the throes of haphazard prosecution by the loosely allied colonies. The individual colonies were proving ineffective in waging the war; a truly collective national approach was required.

The *Declaration of Independence* is the basis for a social order that encompasses the people of the former Thirteen Colonies. With its signing, all ties to Great Britain were formally severed and all authority derived from that association, which is to say the entire basis for colonial government including their constraints on suffrage, was dissolved. The remaining basis for trust and common policy among the people of these former colonies was the *Declaration of Independence* itself.

To a lesser extent, the members of the congress were Christians; primarily Protestant Christians. They well understood the concept of covenants, grounded in a written history going back at least three millennia, well before the constructs of English common law. In this case, the covenant is explicitly made effective with "...for the support of this Declaration, with a firm reliance on the protection of

Divine Providence, we mutually pledge to each other our Lives, our Fortunes, and our sacred Honor." This is an iconic illustration of a social compact among people; not among "colonies" or among "states".

One can't help but notice that tossed into the mix of rebellion and new governance with the phrase "...our Fortunes..." are the people imported and enslaved purely under the auspices of colonial rule. Under colonial rule, some people were property. Under the *Declaration of Independence*, not so much! The basis of private property was unalterably changed with the successful outcome of the rebellion. Slavery was abolished with its signing and the successful prosecution of the war.

The *Declaration of Independence* is, unfortunately, the Rodney Dangerfield of American jurisprudence; it "...don't get no respect!" It is the somewhat eccentric aunt that's given a remote seat in the parlor at Thanksgiving; not quite invisible, but far enough removed so she doesn't intrude on polite conversation. Certainly, the *Declaration of Independence* is not in the mainstream of judicial interpretation. It's really not even a backwater. The *Declaration of Independence* is largely ignored in American jurisprudence, despite the obvious reverence for it that Chief Justice Marshall displayed in his *Marbury* opinion on which American jurisprudence is grounded. The ignorance is palpable and to be lamented.

Pursuit of the Covenant

The covenant established through the *Declaration of Independence* was binding upon the populace, not just the signers. More to the point, it was and is binding on those who sought to formally establish government in the wake of war. "The People" engaged rebellion under the banner of the *Declaration of Independence*. They marched in response to its call and covenant; certainly not in anticipation of The *Articles of Confederation*, nor even in anticipation of the *Constitution*. Under the auspices of this declaration, armies were raised and a war was fought. Rich and poor engaged the war. The sacrifices of "The People" were great. Men of many races and women of many races fought and died in response to this covenant. When the victory was won, based on the sacrifice of those who struggled and especially those who died, the survivors each had an expectation of participation in **any** resulting government. It was promised in the covenant. Unfortunately, the covenant went unfulfilled.

Personal expression is the neural circuitry of social order; culture its emotion. A grand composition painted in the art-form of war contributed to the basis of trust for the new social order. It evoked emotional devotion to that trust. If words are ever to have meaning, they should have had meaning then. That those who claimed the victor's spoils continued policy facilities that excluded women, and even more reprehensibly, enabled, with the full concurrence of the judiciary, the enslavement of human beings, calls into question the legitimacy of those facilities. When, in the course of judicial review, the policy facilities are found in conflict with the words, it is the words that are to be trusted; not the suspect facilities nor the intent of their creation. One might assume that this is precisely what is meant by **the rule of law**!

Collectively, those who adopted the mantle of leadership emanating from the successful rebellion failed the covenant when they put forth The *Articles of Confederation*. Likewise, state governments claiming independence, but not in full agreement with the mandates of the *Declaration of Independence* were certainly repugnant to the covenant as well. The *Articles of Confederation*, which espoused the primacy of the states over the national government, were woefully deficient in their ability to effect the principles of the *Declaration of Independence*. It quickly became clear that a national government had been necessary to win independence and a national government was going to be necessary to maintain independence. In recognition of these inequities and ineffectiveness, the *Constitution* was subsequently developed.

The trust infrastructure established through the *Declaration of Independence* remained the focus of the polity's devotion. In order to make amends for the deficiencies of The *Articles of Confederation*, the *Constitution* established a rigorous extension of the principles espoused by the *Declaration of Independence* in order to create a more satisfactory means "to effect their Safety and Happiness." Regrettably, many of its strictures were misinterpreted or simply ignored.

The policy facilities of the states and the nation were flawed, the covenant was not yet fulfilled. Of course, it is both the strength and the weakness of social covenants that they're not terrible sensitive to the passage of time. When established with the rigor found in the *Declaration of Independence*, they are relentless in their perseverance. One might view the history of the nation from its inception to now as a search for truth relative to the trust averred by the *Declaration of Independence*.

From a continuity of process perspective, the trust basis for all state governments dissolved with the execution of the *Declaration of Independence*. Up to that point, they were all grounded in colonial rule granted by Great Britain. With the dissolution of that superior association, the only trust infrastructure under which they collectively endured was the *Declaration of Independence*. It's signing was the beginning of a social transaction.

Should the actions called forth by the *Declaration of Independence* have failed, then the promises that were the other side of the bargain would be called into question. They depended for their validity on the foundation of the declaration. With failure, in all probability the signers and many others would have been hung. Great Britain had a long history replete with stringent measures to address rebellious populations.

Under the *Articles of Confederation*, the colonies, now states, regained a semblance of association. However, the *Articles* themselves were not true to the covenant. The *Declaration of Independence* recognized as a matter of policy the equality of all the people and their suffrage from which power of the new governments, both federal and state, would derive. The *Constitution* subsequently established a framework for the subordination of the states under its auspices, derived from the principles established by the *Declaration of Independence*. The new order was striking in its originality and its formulation is an excellent example of social mutation. Unfortunately, it was more than the old order could or would accept in the short term. Citing a profound disdain for these founding principles, The South rebelled.

Vice President of the Confederate States of America, Alexander Stephens speaking in Savannah, Georgia on March 21, 1861, recounted the Confederate causes for the American Civil War. In his *"Cornerstone"* speech, he laid the root dichotomy between the Confederacy and the Union at the feet of Thomas Jefferson and the *Declaration of Independence*:

> Those ideas, however, were fundamentally wrong. They rested upon the assumption of the equality of races. This was an error. It was a sandy foundation, and the government built upon it fell when the "storm came and the wind blew."

Our new government is founded upon exactly the opposite idea; its foundations are laid, its corner-stone rests, upon the great truth that the negro is not equal to the white man; that slavery subordination to the superior race is his natural and normal condition.

It is testament to, and a condemnation of, the frailty of government institutions when not fully buttressed by all their component parts, that the Supreme Court of the United States largely agreed with Stephens' assertions in its decision in the *Dred Scott* case. It is a decision that is still not repudiated by judicial action. Without the explicit recognition by the court of the *Declaration of Independence* assertion that "...all men are created equal..." the *Constitution* alone proved an insufficient guardian of the principles that Chief Justice Marshall so eloquently called forth in *Marbury*.

Whatever autonomy the individual colonies may have had was totally supplanted with the signing of the *Declaration of Independence*. They were grounded in colonial mandates and when that cord was cut, they ceased as legitimate social structures. It made no logical sense to accede to any of these **states** a level of sovereignty not fully consistent with, and compliant to, the *Declaration of Independence* and subsequently to the *Constitution*. It is to correct this inconsistency in the perceived hierarchical order of the federal and state governments that the Civil War was fought. The covenant still sought fulfillment.

The *Declaration of Independence* started a social interaction. It is an interaction that did not end with the *Treaty of Paris*, or with the *Constitution*. As Abraham Lincoln so eloquently and perceptively dated it, "Four score and seven years..." later, the interaction continued. History may reflect on the rationales of the Civil War, but at Gettysburg Lincoln was quite specific as he drew the line directly back to the *Declaration of Independence*: "...a new nation, conceived in liberty and dedicated to the proposition that all men are created equal."

Citing Lincoln's justification, the most logical rationale for the Civil War is to be found in *Article IV, Section 4* of the *Constitution*: "The United States shall guarantee to every state in This Union a Republican Form of Government..." Lincoln never viewed the struggle as war, which would have bestowed the imprimatur of sovereignty on the Confederacy. Rather, his rationale was always that a rebellion was in process and that it was the duty of The Union to meet its obligations to the United States citizens residing in the southern states. A valid, republican form of government would be restored to those citizens based on the polity established by the *Declaration of Independence*.

A republic obviously begins with the franchise of citizenship. That was established with the *Declaration of Independence*; citizenship that explicitly included universal suffrage. Through force of arms in the fighting of the Civil War, the relevant facilities of the states, improperly addressed at the founding, were substantially corrected. Unfortunately, the covenant was not yet fulfilled; women were still denied the vote. It was a debt not viewed as substantially fulfilled until the *Nineteenth Amendment* was ratified on August 18, 1920. It was a fulfillment long overdue, through a mechanism that was totally unnecessary. It was the ransom that men demanded as payment for their hijacking the proper stewardship of governance following the War of Independence.

Since this resolution, the facilities have endured. But, more important, the words have always endured. The words should certainly evoke meanings in the halls of justice today that they should have evoked at the founding of the nation. The right of personal privacy is the true bedrock of the Republic. The covenant still seeks complete fulfillment. The courts through their often convoluted reasoning are slowly finding their way back to the true foundation of governance; personal privacy.

The *Declaration of Independence* established a very logical progression from one social order to the next. It evoked the transition through the creation of a new trust infrastructure; one based on security and privacy. This firmly defines the relationship of government to the people. It bases this relationship on the right of privacy, encompassing life, liberty and the pursuit of happiness. Privacy is self-evidentially a natural, human characteristic. It is not something granted by the state. Because of this self-evidence, in subsequent defining documents such as the *Constitution*, there's no reason to repeat this justification or rationale for governance.

By and large, the *Bill of Rights* is superfluous. Indeed, the previous chapter was our attempt to illustrate the far reaching projection cast by an expansive right of privacy. Of course, since it's there, the *Ninth Amendment* obviously indicates the Founders were still serious about the rights recognized through the covenant that was and is the *Declaration of Independence*.

If a right is unalienable it is above policy transgression. With concurrence of the court, Chief Justice Marshall recognized this principle explicitly in *Marbury*. Building on this principle, we recognize that privacy is a natural facility that an individual person brings to social order. As we've noted earlier, it is the way that people function; it is the manifestation of their being.

The *Declaration of Independence* recognizes this facility and the *Constitution* affirms this facility as a right within the policy infrastructure. From this perspective, any social order deriving from the *Declaration of Independence* is obligated to accede to this right if the social order is to have legitimacy. The *Declaration of Independence* recognizes the recursive right of individuals to rebel in order to achieve a means to their happiness. In their complementary struggle, we would suggest that privacy is intrinsically superior to policy.

If policy is found wanting, change through physical force is in order; though not to be lightly engaged. As Chief Justice Marshall observed, "The exercise of this original right is a very great exertion; nor can it nor ought it to be frequently repeated." The tragedy and splendor of the Civil War is a testament to this admonition. The standards of citizenship under the *Articles of Confederation* and various state constitutions were explicitly onerous and distant from the *Declaration of Independence*. This was rectified, though not well recognized, in the *Constitution*, but not in the subordinate policy structures of the states. As a result, for some of the states the trust infrastructure collapsed and the social expression that is war was the only means of its restoration; either through the primacy of The Union or of the Confederate States. The Union prevailed.

Thus, the Civil War was actually asymmetric with respect to rationale. The South was fighting to establish a new trust infrastructure. The Union was fighting to enforce policy that derived from the policy infrastructure that was established under the existing trust infrastructure. With the Union victory, the existing trust infrastructure was affirmed, as was the policy of federal superiority over the states.

With the conclusion of the war, there really was no need for a change in the policy infrastructure; states were already subordinate to the federal *Constitution* and people of African descent as well as women were already citizens. However, there seemed a strong feeling that a half-million people had died, so it was necessary to do something. In response, the *Thirteenth Amendment*, the *Fourteenth Amendment* and the *Fifteenth Amendment* to the *Constitution* were ratified; more as an ecstatic ritual than a policy necessity. The somewhat unfortunate result of this is the perspective that the facilities mentioned in these amendments were not already in place through the *Declaration of Independence* and *Constitution*.

In the hierarchy of American jurisprudence, the *Declaration of Independence's* recognition of a right of privacy is superior to the *Constitution's* enumerated rights. The changes to the *Constitution* following the Civil War, ignoring this overarching constraint, actually created a systemic attack on privacy. That is, a potential danger was created by these amendments in that they suggest state protected subcultures based on race and gender that run counter to the concept that the individual is the ultimate state protected minority.

The conclusion of the Civil War through Union supremacy affirmed the original basis of citizenship without the need for these amendments. Specifically, the equality of races along with universal suffrage was established by the trust infrastructure, not the policy infrastructure. Consider whether these amendments could ever be legitimately repealed, even if a sufficiently large majority of the populace enacted the change. An evenly distributed fifty percent plus one, is sufficient to amend the *Constitution*. Without the constraining principles of the *Declaration of Independence*, such a slight majority could ostensibly restore slavery, purely as an act of policy. It is doubtful that the polity is sufficiently devoted to the *Constitution* to allow such a policy; the expected response would address the trust infrastructure through aesthetic expression.

We can recognize in *Section 2* of the *Fourteenth Amendment*, a rather obvious bit of bait and switch relative to gender based suffrage. This section somewhat tenuously relates age and gender to representation; whether to actual suffrage is ambiguous. This affirms the interesting prospect that we noted above of how to deal with properly formed policy stated in the form of an amendment to the *Constitution* that is "...destructive of those ends...".

Finding personal privacy as superior to social policy is a profound rationale on which to base limited government. Exactly this rationale is established pursuant to the mandates of the *Declaration of Independence* and implemented through the policy infrastructure defined by the *Constitution*. Guardianship of this mandate falls to the Supreme Court of the United States. It is a guardianship that has at times been lacking.

Mistakes along the Way

The rationale for limited government introduced in the *Declaration of Independence* was subsequently carried forward into the *Constitution* in the specification of balance between a person and the state as expressed in the *Constitution's Preamble*:

> ...in order to form a more perfect union, establish justice, insure domestic tranquility, provide for the common defense, promote the general welfare and secure the blessings of liberty to ourselves and our posterity...

This language is a carefully measured statement of the principles of limited government originally expressed in the *Declaration of Independence*.

"To form a more perfect union" suggests uniformity of policy across the entire policy infrastructure; federal and state governments. To "establish justice" suggests policy is needed to facilitate the arbitration of personal privacy among individuals and the state and to objectively assess truth. To "insure domestic tranquility", laws are needed to protect prey from predator by equitably addressing the arbitration and arbitrage of personal privacy. To "provide for the common defense" establishes the federal government as the guarantor against foreign transgression and internal rebellion. To "promote the general welfare" suggests support for, not guarantee of, a social infrastructure. To "secure the blessing of liberty" reinforces the primacy of privacy. When the state seeks to define compelling interests, the boundaries on those interests are strongly constrained by these words. This is the origin of any bright line rule on compelling interest.

In the *Marbury v. Madison* decision, the court, through Chief Justice Marshall, recognized the true import of limited government:

> ... The powers of the legislature are defined and limited; and that those limits may not be mistaken or forgotten, the constitution is written. To what purpose are powers limited, and to what purpose is that limitation committed to writing; if these limits may, at any time, be passed by those intended to be restrained? The distinction between a government with limited and unlimited powers is abolished, if those limits do not confine the persons on whom they are imposed, and if acts prohibited and acts allowed are of equal obligation. It is a proposition too plain to be contested, that the constitution controls any legislative act repugnant to it; or, that the legislature may alter the constitution by an ordinary act.

> Between these alternatives there is no middle ground. The constitution is either a superior, paramount law, unchangeable by ordinary means, or it is on a level with ordinary legislative acts, and like other acts, is alterable when the legislature shall please to alter it.

The *Constitution* can be amended through well defined processes. To amend the *Declaration of Independence* requires a more ecstatic event. To change the policy infrastructure requires continuity of trust. To change the trust infrastructure requires aesthetic ecstasy!

Many opinions emanating from Justices of the Supreme Court pay homage to the *Declaration of Independence*. However, rarely do these references find their way into the decisions of the Court. Rather, they're sometimes found in concurring or dissenting opinions, usually as a statement of philosophy (*obiter dicta*), not a substantial basis for law (holding or *ratio decidendi*). On the other hand, a number of decisions by the court were highly questionable to the degree that it's not obvious they even viewed the *Declaration of Independence* as a valid statement of principle.

Over the course of the first two centuries of the Republic, several decisions marked a course that ran rather far afield from the original covenant; either through action or through inaction. Sometimes, one can discern a great deal about concepts and processes by examining situations that don't turn out as we might have expected. These are situations in which the assessments of truth don't seem as consistent to the assessments of trust as one might have anticipated.

The 1849 case of *Luther v. Borden* is a good illustration of apparent court reticence to engage the profound structure of the new nation. The issue really came down to: "What is a republic?" In 1841, some of the good people of Rhode Island finally remembered that there had actually been a Revolutionary War and that all political ties with Great Britain had been severed. It seems that the colonial government of Rhode Island had been established under a charter from King Charles II and was never changed, at least substantially, following the war. Perhaps of greater concern, suffrage in Rhode Island wasn't just limited to men, but rather to men with substantial property; thus omitting much of the common male citizenry.

In an effort to correct this, a constitutional convention was organized and through a process of a few years, a new government for the state was put in place. The existing, charter based government didn't particularly care for this sequence of events and declared the state to be under martial law. It subsequently organized its own constitutional convention that ultimately yielded yet another state government. In due course, a duel between these two governments erupted:

> Martin Luther, a citizen of the State of Massachusetts, brought an action of trespass *quare clausum fregit* against the defendants, citizens of the State of Rhode Island, for breaking and entering the house of Luther, on the 29th of June, 1842. The action was brought in October, 1842.

The irony of the plaintiff's name is almost palpable. At issue in the course of Luther's action was who comprised the legal citizens of the State of Rhode Island and which state government was actually legitimate?

The case ultimately made its way to the Supreme Court of the United States in 1846. Part of the defense of the charter backed government in the case was that, while the charter had indeed ceased to be valid as of July 4, 1776, the date of the signing of the *Declaration of Independence*, delegates from that government continued to participate in the various national congresses and were there accepted as valid. It seems that the legal justification of the state government was that its delegates didn't get thrown out of the hall at the meetings of the national government.

At least one of the issues ultimately posed to the Supreme Court was whether or not the government of Rhode Island was a true "republican form of government" as guaranteed by *Article IV Section 4* of the *Constitution of the United States*. The court's response was that this was a non-justiciable issue. Instead, it was ruled to be a political issue that could only be resolved by the legislative and executive branches of the United States government. In particular, the court held that it could not deal with the issue of citizenship.

It's difficult to reconcile the court's decision in *Luther* with the context of the policy infrastructure of the state. As we noted in the fifth chapter, when the Supreme Court weighs the various aspects of due process, it may well find itself required to render subjective decisions. Subjective decisions are the hallmark of political processes. Actually, the issues posed by *Luther* really tended more toward the objective side of things anyway. However, as we've discussed, subjective decisions are an absolute requirement if the Supreme Court is ever to rule on the compelling interests used to justify abridgment of fundamental rights.

Whether viewed objectively or subjectively, a "republican form of government" is well understood to involve elected officials, comprising a representative democracy. Ruling on the adequacy of an election process is certainly a justiciable issue; the election process is adequate or it's not. An election is quite analogous to a census, and the Supreme Court has no problem in ruling on the adequacy of methodology used in the decennial census.

At issue in the *Luther* situation was whether one or both of the competing state governments were constituted correctly under due process constraints. In particular, since the sitting state government was based on a charter that had ceased to be effective in 1776, there was certainly sufficient cause to consider the legality of its actions. The case had many similarities to the *Marbury v. Madison* case through which the Supreme Court established its power of ultimate judicial review. So, while perhaps somewhat complex, the issues presented by *Luther v. Borden* seem quite justiciable. One has to wonder then, why was the court reticent to offer a judgment? One also has to wonder whether this reticence contributed to the environment that fostered the Civil War a decade or so later.

Perhaps the *Luther* case is an illustration of the early Supreme Court choosing to divorce itself from a fundamental issue of governance, that of the relationship between the national and state governments, because the court was not confident enough in its position relative to the other branches of government. A decision reflecting a federal power to decide the legality of a state government would certainly have impacted the tension between state and federal governments; to what extent is speculative. However, without even a hint of judicial action, the Union Army ultimately had to decide this issue through the Civil War at the loss of a half-million lives. In contrast, a century later the 101st Airborne deployed to Little Rock, Arkansas to assure the integration of the public high school that presaged a sea change in American society at a cost significantly less than civil war; all in response to the Supreme Court's *Brown v. Board of Education* decision regarding equality of public education.

In one of its most infamous opinions, the Supreme Court decision in the case of *Dred Scott v. Sandford* offers a further prelude to the Civil War. The issue at question is the nature of citizenship in a republic. The case involved a slave who took the name Dred Scott. His master was Dr. John Emerson, a physician serving in the United States Army. Traveling extensively with his master, Dred Scott lived for a time in Illinois and then in Wisconsin, both free states.

The prevailing precedent of the common law at the time was "once free, always free". Once having lived in a free state, a slave was held to be free in all states. Some years later, when his master died and Dred Scott learned of this legal doctrine, he filed a lawsuit in the State of Missouri seeking to gain his freedom. Although he won the initial case, it was subsequently overturned by the Missouri Supreme Court, which disavowed the existing precedent and returned Dred Scott to his master's wife; actually to her brother, John F.A. Sanford who was executor of Dr. Emerson's estate.

Since Sanford was a resident of New York, Dred Scott then re-filed his suit in federal court, claiming diverse citizenship. Through appeals, the case found its way to the Supreme Court of the United States. The court ruled on March 6, 1857 with Chief Justice Roger B. Taney writing the majority opinion for the court. The decision said that Dred Scott was still a slave and he was returned to his master. The decision also determined that any person of African descent, whether a slave or free, was not a citizen of the United States, nor could they be a citizen under the *Constitution*. The court also ruled that the *Ordinance of 1787* could not be used to confer either freedom or citizenship to slaves within the Northwest Territory. Finally, the court ruled the *Missouri Compromise Act of 1820* to be unconstitutional. This act was intended to allow slavery to be excluded in the northern sections of the Louisiana Purchase.

The primary rationale behind the Supreme Court's decision was found in the court's assertion of the working definition of the word "men" in the original establishment of the nation:

> It is difficult at this day to realize the state of public opinion in relation to that unfortunate race, which prevailed in the civilized and enlightened portions of the world at the time of the Declaration of Independence, and when the Constitution of the United States was framed and adopted. But the public history of every European nation displays it in a manner too plain to be mistaken.

> They had for more than a century before been regarded as beings of an inferior order, and altogether unfit to associate with the white race, either in social or political relations; and so far inferior, that they had no rights which the white man was bound to respect; and that the negro might justly and lawfully be reduced to slavery for his benefit. He was bought and sold, and treated as an ordinary article of merchandise and traffic, whenever a profit could be made by it. This opinion was at that time fixed and universal in the civilized portion of the white race.

The court in effect ruled that when the *Declaration of Independence* said that "all men are created equal" and when the Constitution referred to "We the people", persons of African descent were intrinsically excluded from the population being referenced. This is not an unusual approach. If the words don't mean what you want, change the meanings of the words. One might assume that's what we're doing in the course of this book, only with the word **privacy**. That's not a totally unfair assessment. However, we would note that our intent is to refine the definition of the word privacy to encompass existing definitions and to place the entire concept on a more rigorous footing. Our intent has not been to exclude commonly accepted definitions from the concept. The court's Dred Scott decision seems a bit more malevolent in this regards.

As we noted earlier, the Founders were largely Protestant Christians. The *Christian Bible* is replete with references to slavery going back at least two or three millennia. It's clear that slavery did not have an explicit racial connotation. People could move in and out of slavery. Thomas Jefferson, the primary author of the *Declaration of Independence* and James Madison, the primary author of the *Constitution* were incredibly skilled at the English language. The language they used was intended to NOT institutionalize slavery. The *Dred Scott* decision explicitly recognized as much with respect to the *Constitution*:

> We need not refer to the mercenary spirit which introduced the infamous traffic in slaves, to show the degradation of negro slavery in our country. This system was imposed upon our colonial settlements by the mother country, and it is due to truth to say that the commercial colonies and States were chiefly engaged in the traffic. But we know as a historical fact, that James Madison, that great and good man, a leading member in the Federal Convention, was solicitous to guard the language of that instrument so as not to convey the idea that there could be property in man.

This ruling also calls out the connection of slavery in the colonies back to Great Britain, the source of colonial rule. Once these ties were severed through the *Declaration of Independence*, slavery in the former colonies no longer had a basis in law. The court's opinion, however, contends that slavery is absolutely a product of the laws of the individual states. It would seem that if slavery derived from the laws of the states, and the governments of the states were circumspect, then slavery would become quite problematic.

The idea voiced in the *Dred Scott* decision that African ancestry would forever bar a person from citizenship in the United States also runs counter to the policy effected in the *Constitution*. Consider the *Article III Section 3* constraint on allowed punishment for treason:

> The Congress shall have power to declare the Punishment of Treason, but no Attainder of Treason shall work Corruption of Blood, or Forfeiture except during the Life of the Person attainted.

The idea that the sins of the parents could be visited upon their children was here made specifically repugnant to the *Constitution*.

One can see in the court's opinion the looming war. The Taney Court displayed an obvious bias toward supremacy of the states over the federal government. The court's decision imbues to the states virtually unlimited power while maintaining strict limitations on the powers of the federal government. The complete lack of deference to the *Declaration of Independence* can be seen in the following excerpt from their ruling:

> Did Chief Justice Marshall, in saying that Congress governed a Territory, by exercising the combined powers of the Federal and State Governments, refer to unlimited discretion? A Government which can make white men slaves? Surely, such a remark in the argument must have been inadvertently uttered. On the contrary, there is no power in the Constitution by which Congress can make either white or black men slaves. In organizing the Government of a Territory, Congress is limited to means appropriate to the attainment of the constitutional object. No powers can be exercised which are prohibited by the Constitution, or which are contrary to its spirit; so that, whether the object may be the protection of the persons and property of purchasers of the public lands, or of communities who have been annexed to the Union by conquest or purchase, they are initiatory to the establishment of State Governments, and no more power can be claimed or exercised than is necessary to the attainment of the end. This is the limitation of all the Federal powers.

The myopic view of the Taney Court is startling in is disingenuous. As we noted earlier regarding the *Luther v. Borden* decision, *Article IV Section 4* of the *Constitution* makes the federal government the guarantor of state governments. This is an explicit recognition of federal power over state power as a policy mandate. If state governments have any power to effect policy not subordinate to federal policy, it would obviously run afoul of this mandate.

The Marshall Court had already recognized as much in their *McColloch v Maryland* decision in disavowing a state's ability to tax a federally chartered bank. If the power to tax is the power to destroy, then equally pernicious is the power to expand policy outside that allowed by the federal infrastructure. This, of course, would seem to counter the concept that state and federal governments are distinct and separate sovereigns.

Examining case law across a relatively wide expanse of time, the reasoning and rationale expressed by the courts in various decisions obviously varies. Descriptions of the development of common law suggest that the reasoning and rationale should be cumulative; the new building upon the old. The concept of *stare decisis* should confer persistence to the cumulative effect.

Considering the clarity of the *Declaration of Independence*, one is left to wonder whether the Founders really put that much nuance into the *Constitution*, or did they perceive it to be extension rather than replacement? One might wonder if the Jerry Bruckheimer movie *National Treasure* has a touch of truth. Did the Founders really speak in riddles? Is the foundation of the Republic actually a puzzle to be explored and solved rather than a primer of trust and policy?

Did they really hide *Footnote 4* somewhere in there like an Easter egg, just waiting for Justice Harlan Stone to find it in *United States v. Carolene Products Co.?* Did they really intend the

Supreme Court to be the sole arbiter of policy; simply relying on Chief Justice John Marshall to tease it out in the form of judicial review in his *Marbury v. Madison* opinion? *Marbury* is a case seemingly having more to do with the authentication protocols and authority credentials than with a fundamental basis of governance.

Did the Founders really intend strict scrutiny? If so, it's unfortunate that it took a string of decisions to find it; barely in time for *Roe v. Wade*. Perhaps, the truth is that none of these points is really nuanced in the first place? We can but observe that much that is incredibly profound was obviously self-evident to the Founders. If one perceives American governance to be fundamentally based on an expansive right of privacy, everything else falls into place rather obviously.

Our suggestion has been that universal suffrage was clearly established in the *Declaration of Independence* as a characteristic of citizenship. The Supreme Court's 1874 decision in the case of *Minor v. Happersett* offers a contrasting perspective on citizenship and suffrage. A lady named Virginia Minor brought suit seeking to be allowed to vote. Her argument was that under the *Fourteenth Amendment*, she was a resident and citizen of the State of Missouri and was therefore a citizen of the United States. As a citizen, she was afforded a right to vote, and the *Constitution's Privileges and Immunities Clause*, buttressed by *Article IV Section 4*, extended this right to the states.

The Court held that in fact Minor was a citizen under the *Constitution*. She was a citizen even before the *Fourteenth Amendment* was enacted. However, the Court held that being a citizen did not grant her the right to vote. The *Constitution*, the Court decided, does not convey suffrage on any person. That, it asserted, is the purview of the individual states. In Missouri, only males were allowed to vote.

In its decision, the Court makes a most interesting observation:

> In this condition of the law in respect of suffrage in the several States it cannot for a moment be doubted that if it had been intended to make all citizens of the United States voters, the framers of the Constitution would not have left it to implication. So important a change in the condition of citizenship as it actually existed, if intended, would have been expressly declared... [88 U.S. 162, 174]

It seems that if it were to be "expressly declared" it might be in a document with "Declaration" in its title. It's curious that the court couldn't find it. One might wonder why, if only white males were intended to have the vote, it was not left ambiguous in the *Declaration of Independence*? One must wonder, if the states were to be the sole purveyors of suffrage, why even mention the rights and immunities of citizens in the *Constitution*?

Perhaps even more perplexing is whether the *Constitution* is excessively vague regarding the abilities of Congress to pass laws against "criminality"? Consider that the recognition of any type of criminality, and its sanctioning by the state, is only implied, and vaguely at that, within the language of the *Constitution*. This language goes to great length to explain how to establish policy, but it leaves unsaid precisely what laws should be enacted. Was the intent to leave policy purely to the unrestrained discretion of the purveyors of policy?

What then of constitutional oversight; of judicial review. What then of suffrage for women? What of privacy? What of strict scrutiny? What acts should be made criminal? Under what rationale are criminal actors punished? None of this appears to be expressly stated in the *Constitution*. We've suggested that none of these "questions" are really questions at all; they were all self-evident truths to the Founders.

The Founders did not leave these issues to implication; they were quite explicit in the *Declaration of Independence*; and, with good cause. To paraphrase the old song, "These were the times that tried men's souls!" The fledgling nation needed all the help it could get, and it offered a powerful covenant to obtain that help. It is, of course, rather common for those in desperate straits to offer up profound payment to the gods in times of direst need. The fact that the fields aren't filled with chapels and churches is a good indicator that once things improve we tend to forget our promises.

In their *Minor* opinion, the Court did observe the existence of a covenant, however they stated it rather self-servingly as "...allegiance for protection and protection for allegiance." This is the fools bargain; "what's mine is mine, what's yours, we'll talk about." This is the statesman's way of averring that the "predator's privacy is the prey's slavery." It's what the extortionists sell on the streets; protection: "Pay us every week and your store probably won't burn down! Grant us your exclusive devotion and we'll keep you from harm, even if we have to enslave you to do it!"

As we observed a bit earlier, the reciprocal obligation is "rebellion for suffrage." Through suffrage should come good government, deriving its powers from the consent of the governed. This is an extremely explicit expression of suffrage as a privilege of citizenship. It then follows that the *Privileges and Immunities Clause* of the *Constitution* mandates suffrage as a privilege of citizenship that conveys to the states as well.

In the *Minor* case, the deficiency lay with the *Constitution of the State of Missouri* in attempting to deny suffrage to women. It was clearly subordinate to the United States *Constitution* as grounded in the *Declaration of Independence* and conveyed to the states through the *Privileges and Immunities Clause*, and therefore was invalid when it denied suffrage to women.

Perhaps the most perplexing aspect of the court's decision was its inability to apply any distinctive characteristics to the concept of citizenship. Indeed, the court was content to view a citizen as simply a member of the collection of people living within a nation-state; consider these words from the opinion:

> For convenience it has been found necessary to give a name to this membership. The object is to designate by a title the person and the relation he bears to the nation. For this purpose the words 'subject,' 'inhabitant,' and 'citizen' have been used, and the choice between them is sometimes made to depend upon the form of the government. Citizen is now more commonly employed, however, and as it has been considered better suited to the description of one living under a republican government, it was adopted by nearly all of the States upon their separation from Great Britain, and was afterwards adopted in the Articles of Confederation and in the Constitution of the United States. When used in this sense it is understood as conveying the idea of membership of a nation, and nothing more.

Among all the questionable Supreme Court decisions that we've considered, perhaps none contains a statement more dubious than this. The equivalence of one who is a "subject" of a nation-state and one who is a "citizen" of a nation-state would seem to go well beyond an ambiguity of understanding; it borders on the intentionally malevolent. For "subject", "inhabitant" and "citizen" to be synonyms whose sole purpose is to convey membership seems a strange observation from the nation's highest court; the place where legal words go for definition and metaphors for disambiguation. We would suggest that a citizen is a member of the polity; a subject or inhabitant is not, but rather is simply subject to policy. Did the court perceive the *Constitution* to establish a stratified social order comparable to ancient Rome, with its subordinate classes of citizenship? If so, could we not assume as the court asserts *"...the framers of the Constitution would not have left it to implication."*

Strict constructionists suggest the *Constitution* is to be read and interpreted literally. It's a very good idea, but it would actually be a significant break with judicial tradition. Also, it would be quite a break from what the strict constructionists probably have in mind as well. During its first hundred years or so, it appears that the courts often interpreted the *Constitution* with a wink and a nod. For example, the *Constitution* certainly does not discuss slavery, much less explicitly authorize it. The Taney court in its *Dred Scott* decision recognized this fact. They explained it by asserting that this simply meant slavery wasn't the purview of the federal government; the power over property, including slaves, resided in the states.

Historians and the Supreme Court note that the Founders went out of their way to avoid mentioning slavery. It's clear that they succeeded beyond their wildest expectations. Interpreting the words "strictly", it is impossible to find either recognition of, or legal justification for, slavery. There is certainly no stated power of one person to own another person; for the privacy of one to be totally infringed by another. Nor is any power granted to any branch of government allowing it to arbitrarily infringe the privacy of an individual and thus deliver them into bondage. If a state government can enact slavery, it could just as easily call everyone a subject and create a monarchy; save for that awkward *Article IV Section 4*.

Taken in concert with the *Declaration of Independence*, it is much simpler to read the *Constitution*, even assuming the language facilities of 1790, as precluding slavery. We have suggested that this, in fact, is the only way to read it. And yet, slavery was obviously a part of the American social order in some states for almost a century following the ratification of the *Constitution* as based upon the *Declaration of Independence*. This is the rather obvious wink and nod.

Only by disregarding the words of the *Constitution* and basing judicial review on the policies of the existing social order could slavery have been procedurally tolerated once the *Constitution* was put in place. Through its ratification it was effectively subsumed by the *Declaration of Independence*, just as it subsumed the existing *Articles of Confederation*. The net result should certainly have nullified any contravening instances of state law

It should be recognized that the *Declaration of Independence* does not establish the unalienable rights that it recognizes as truths. As the document says, the truths are self-evident; a statement of causality, not of process. The truths encompass the *Declaration of Independence*, just as they encompass the *Constitution*. It seems similarly self-evident that they are at least one source of the rights "... retained by the people." that are referenced in the *Ninth Amendment*.

Privacy is congruent with the truths enumerated in the *Declaration of Independence*. These truths are given greater rigor by recognizing their specialization as rights; more to the point, as self-evident rights. It is self-evident that we have the right to live. It is self-evident we have the right to decide for ourselves how we will live. In fact, this is the supreme good evidenced by natural selection. It is self-evident we have the right, as we live according to our own dictates, to pursue happiness as we individually perceive it. It is self-evident that we each have a right to live in a manner so as to impact how others perceive us. It is the purpose of government to support us individually by enabling our enjoyment of these rights. How best does government provide that support? Perhaps it does so by focusing the provisioning of the polity on the concept of personal privacy.

Provisioning the Polity

The limited government defined by the Founders requires a well provisioned polity for its ultimate success. To achieve its purpose, the state relies on the manifestations of personal privacy from its citizens. In turn, it is the purpose of the state to foster an environment in which each citizen can exercise their personal privacy to the fullest. If any aggregate within the polity can unduly infringe the privacy of others using the police powers of the state, then the character of the state will certainly diverge from the principles on which it was established. To guard against the undue influence of such state-based subcultures, the provisioning of the individual should derive from an expression of personal privacy. Unfortunately, that's usually easier said than done.

In the course of their growing up, the young are being continually provisioned. At birth, their provisioning is the purview of their parents. Once a child is a few years old, a major factor in provisioning derives from a more structured approach; an approach which encompasses, but is not limited to what is termed **formal education**. At least four distinct parties come to the fore in an attempt to control the provisioning afforded by formal education:

- the individual,
- the family,
- social subcultures, and
- the state

It is the function of the courts to establish balance among these competing groups. As we saw back in the fifth chapter, the Supreme Court rulings in the cases of *Meyer v. Nebraska* and *Pierce v. Society of Sisters* give superior credence to the individual and to the family in this regards.

Subcultures of greatest concern regarding the protection of personal privacy are social orders that seek to establish policy motivated by certain articles of **faith** of their constituent members. As we noted earlier, faith is an expression of trust that is independent of truth. The history of America is replete with instances where such subcultures have sought to effect their policies under the police powers of the state. The Founders recognized the dangers presented by the most obvious subculture of their era; religion.

To mitigate the danger, the Founders expressly mandated a separation of church from state in the creation and enforcement of policy through police powers. Over the years, similar subcultures have arisen; that of slavery and subsequently of segregation by race, that of public morality and, quite prevalent today, that of social dogma espoused by political parties. Such subcultures have most of the hallmarks of religion as classically understood.

Following the profound aesthetic expression that was the Civil War, entrenched subcultures based on slavery and race were dealt a significant setback. The principle of equality espoused in the *Declaration of Independence* came more into vogue. However, it was a principle that still found resistance throughout many segments of society.

In the 1890's, a State of Louisiana law regarding public transportation facilities was put into effect. The law required that on railway trains, separate passenger cars must be provided in order to divide the riders by race. White people were to have their own cars and people of color were to have separate cars. Ostensibly motivated by a concern for public health and morality, the law claimed to make this segregation palatable to all parties by requiring the separate facilities to be **equal**.

In an effort to mount a challenge to this policy in court, a group dedicated to its repeal, the *Comite des Citoyens* from New Orleans, arranged for Homer Plessy, a man of color, to be arrested and prosecuted under the law. Plessy's defense rested on the rights established under the *Thirteenth Amendment* and the *Fourteenth Amendment*. In 1896, the Supreme Court issued a ruling in the case of *Plessy v. Ferguson*. This ruling affirmed the constitutionality of the Louisiana Law and began a period in which the personal privacy of each individual was subjected to increased assault by policies of the state. The concept of "separate but equal" became a recognized doctrine in law; a doctrine under which both the assessment of **the characteristics of separation** and **the basis of equality** were made by the state, not the individual.

This decision would seem to have a strong parallel to the case of *West Coast Hotel v. Parrish*; the case that effectively overturned *Lochner v. New York*. Its rationale is that the state can, through its police powers, assert its motivations for action in place of an assertion of privacy on the part of individuals. *West Coast Hotel* allowed the state to establish that a "living wage for women" could be mandated to protect the health and morals of women. Moreover, the state could judge what constituted that wage, along with the judgment of what comprised acceptable health and morality. Likewise, *Plessy* afforded the state the power to decide what constituted "separate but equal" facilities as determined by the state's assessment of the impact of those facilities on the health and morality of their users.

In 1906, the National Association for the Advancement of Colored People (NAACP) was formed for the express purpose of seeking equitable **civil rights** for people of color. The inequities of public education for children of color became a strategic focus. The tactical approach to policy pursued by the NAACP was to attack the concept of equality, or rather its obvious lack, with the goal to ultimately disparage the concept of separation by race. Their target was firmly established by Justice John Harlan's dissent in *Plessy*:

> In the eye of the law, there is in this country no superior, dominant, ruling class of citizens. There is no caste here. "Our constitution is colorblind, and neither knows nor tolerates classes among citizens. In respect of civil rights, all citizens are equal before the law. The humblest is the peer of the most powerful . . . The arbitrary separation of citizens on the basis of race, while they are on a public highway, is a badge of servitude wholly inconsistent with the civil freedom and the equality before the law established by the Constitution. It cannot be justified upon any legal grounds.

The tactical campaign was guided by a number of Founders of the Civil Rights Movement. The case was argued by NAACP General Counsel Thurgood Marshall, who would later become an Associate Justice of the United States Supreme Court. Through a systematic approach, in 1952 a consolidation of several law suits arrived before the Supreme Court under the case of *Brown v. Board of Education of Topeka*. Perhaps lacking a unanimous decision, the case was not decided during the court's 1952-53 session. It was re-argued during the 1953-54 session.

At the beginning of the 1953-54 session, a new Chief Justice of the United States was confirmed; Chief Justice Earl Warren. He was able to muster a unanimous decision that ruled public school segregation violated the equal protection and due process guarantees of the *Fourteenth Amendment*. Unlike most segregated school systems, the court actually found in the Topeka, Kansas case that the separate white and black school facilities and faculties were substantially equal. This notwithstanding, the ruling held that separation of schools according to race was harmful to the students so segregated.

In the assessment that facilities and faculties were substantially equal, the courts fell into a rather common trap regarding economic systems. The value of anything, be it an object or an abstract idea, is established through a conditional covenant according to the personal motivations of the person who owns the thing and the person who seeks the thing. This is a natural result of the assertion of personal privacy in social interactions.

The true value of school facilities and faculties cannot be properly assessed by a school board or a school administration. The value can only be judged by the individuals to whom the schools provide provisioning. In the best of situations, a conditional covenant will be established between each student and the school. The goal of the provisioning is personal identity. This is the defining principle of American culture.

The symptom recognized by the court in *Brown* was poor education for children of color. We would suggest that the actual disease was state control of the policies for provisioning the young, which is a direct assault on personal privacy. The solution adopted was to treat the symptom rather than the disease. The courts lowered the fever by overturning "separate but equal" and forcing school boards to discontinue racial segregation of schools. It's not at all obvious that the subsequent forced integration of public schools did not actually constitute a further state affront to personal privacy.

The more direct remedial action, the approach that would address the true compelling interest of the state, would provide funding directly to each student. Students could then select their individual schools as an assertion of personal privacy. Actual implementation of this policy might create social upheaval in the short term, but arguably it would be less than was created in fact by the remedial actions of the courts in *Brown*.

The court's decisions in *Brown v. Board of Education* and *Roe v. Wade* set the level of expectation regarding social upheaval in the face of any finding that provides a more expansive interpretation of privacy. They both afforded tests of the social fabric, suggesting that it is not a sufficient impediment simply to say that the impact on society will be extensive.

The *Brown v. Board of Education* decision was based on the argument that the segregation of the state's education classroom was a matter of bad policy that resulted from an improper application of due process under the *Fourteenth Amendment*. This is simply a recognition that policy is bad, not that the manner of setting policy is bad. This is not a good approach for protecting constitutional guarantees. A significantly stronger basis would be that state run schools as then constituted were an infringement of personal privacy without a compelling interest on the part of the state as discerned through the application of strict scrutiny. Of course, this same problem exists with state run schools today.

While there may be a strong compelling state interest in the provisioning of the young, there is less, if any, in the running of schools. History suggests that provisioning pursued through individual personal privacy offers the greatest and most resilient value to the state. The dictates of diverse, personal motivations regarding provisioning are superior to the centralized assertions of common provisioning for all. The current spectrum of education options would seem to bear this out.

At the present time, in the range of 15-30% of all young people in the United States are educated outside the state's education classrooms. With respect to state run schools, the choice left to the individual student and family is either to accept the services provided by the state or provide their own without state assistance. Those being educated outside the state education classroom have considered an incredibly one-sided covenant, "take it or leave it", and have chosen to leave it.

Any rationale that the state is absolutely necessary to provide exemplary, or even acceptable schools, is obviously suspect. Given an opportunity to take their funding with them, it is likely that an even greater number would opt out of state run schools. Certainly it is the purview of the individual to select home schooling or private schooling for their children. Providing state funding only to state run schools is obviously intended to influence individuals in this decision. Again, this calls to mind the Supreme Court's admonition in *United States v. Jackson*:

> If a law has "no other purpose ... than to chill the assertion of constitutional rights by penalizing those who choose to exercise them, then it [is] patently unconstitutional."

There is a counter rationale that says non-state run schools can provide superior provisioning compared to state run schools because they can be based on conditional covenants between students and schools, thereby recognizing a free market. The state currently serves to certify all schools. Thus, there is a mechanism in place to assure a minimum level of quality in schools; mechanisms that adequately serve the free market. If one further accepts the court's rationale in *Sherbert v. Verner*, then it is actually the duty of the state to provide funding to support non-state school formal education.

In a free market environment for schools, the specific needs of each student can be emphasized, as opposed to monolithic schools which seek to provide some limited access by students to a wide variety of provisioning. The greater number of students that seek a particular school environment, the more capable will be those schools. This seems superior to the approach of having elected school boards set the division of resources for all students among the variety of provisioning approaches. Even religion and other subcultures should get into the act.

Since provisioning includes an aesthetic component, a religious context for education is a valid choice from the perspective of personal privacy. General, formal education within a religious context is certainly the purview of the individual and the family. This was firmly established by the Supreme Court's ruling in the in the 1925 case of *Pierce v. Society of Sisters*. However, the state provides no funding for such education. Thus, current state education policy simply represents a different policy from that pursued under the separate but equal doctrine. It is a policy that infringes personal privacy, but without a compelling state interest.

State run schools are obviously not the sole mechanisms of provisioning. In the realm of formal education, home schooling and private schools are certainly good alternatives. There is substantial evidence that both can actually be superior, particularly if per-student funding levels comparable to state run schools is available. Perhaps more profound, technology offers mechanisms quite distinct from the brick and mortar schools that are currently so prevalent. Through the digital technologies that we considered in the fourth chapter, highly distributed educational approaches offer the prospect of incredibly more cost effective formal education facilities.

Direct funding to students on a large scale is relatively straight-forward to implement. It would be enhanced through more trustworthy identity services; a point we'll consider in our final proposal in this chapter. Viewed from the perspective of strict scrutiny, direct funding is the most narrowly tailored and the least restrictive means to afford good provisioning to the young, which is the ultimate compelling state interest.

Provisioning the Policy Infrastructure

The Founders put in place an exceptional mechanism for provisioning the social order that is the United States of America. As with any finely constructed machine, a bit of tinkering here and there can rather quickly turn a Formula One race car into a street jalopy, if not a wreck sitting on cinder blocks under a tree in the front yard. As the "living *Constitution*" has been continually refined through judicial interpretation, and as the "physical *Constitution*" has been modified through amendment, the nature of the infrastructure itself has evolved.

Particularly important has been the change in the relationship among the polity and the purveyors of policy. Specifically, the means of provisioning the policy infrastructure have evolved to the extent that feedback mechanisms designed into the original set of processes now function in a significantly different way. From the perspective of their intended use, many don't function at all. The result is that there are fewer effective controls in play that can keep the policy infrastructure working in a sustainable way. The system is drifting toward a condition of unstable saturation.

As we observed in the second chapter, for the efficient and effective operation of any process, it typically includes feedback control mechanisms as part of its normal operation. These mechanisms allow for processes to be optimized. An effective feedback loop allows a process to be constrained within some nominal, sustainable operating range. This is generally characterized as a negative feedback loop. As some measureable consequence of a process's operation deviates from optimum, input to some control parameter is changed so as to drive the process back toward optimum. In this discussion, we take the term **optimum** to simply mean **sustainable operation over a long term**.

An alternate form of feedback loop can drive a process into an unsustainable state of **saturation**. This is usually called a positive feedback loop. By saturation, we mean that the process is running at full speed but without sufficient recurring resources to continue indefinitely and no longer subject to effective control. This can occur when a measureable consequence of the process's operation deviates from optimum and changing the control parameter has no affect on the process as it moves even further away from a sustainable optimum.

Positive feedback loops are often the result of asymmetries in the control process. The most obvious such situation results when a control parameter doesn't actually impact the measured consequence of the process. As a result, whatever actually caused the measured consequence to deviate from optimum goes uncorrected. Thus, continuing operation deviates even further from optimum. One might wonder what this has to do with provisioning the policy infrastructure of the state. As is the case with most of the principles and processes defined by the Founders, it seems obvious that they anticipated this failure mode and defined correction mechanisms for it; if we but interpret the mechanisms correctly.

The basic policy mechanism that the Founders put in place is that of a **republic**. In a republic, a citizen of some social aggregate is chosen to make policy decisions for that aggregate; that is, to serve as a representative of the aggregate in formulating policy. The representative chosen is not charged specifically with representing the expressed, cumulative will of the aggregate, but rather with making decisions on behalf of the aggregate. Perhaps most important, the representative acts under authority of the police powers of the state. This establishes a point of causality for the policy infrastructure.

The representative is expected to address the subjective decisions regarding policy according to the metaphors of her own provisioning. However, the motivation for these decisions, the basis of assessing trust and truth, are intended to be the **best interests** of the entire aggregate represented. For the state as a whole, the best interests are defined by the principles and processes found in the Declaration of Independence and the Constitution. In particular, they require an objective assessment of truth, as opposed to faith, in the pursuit of actions to achieve consequences in the best interests of the polity. To the extent that best interests result in the infringement of personal privacy, they should be assessed according to strict scrutiny.

To this end, those who would function as representatives are expected to exhibit a fiduciary duty to these best interests. They are expected to subordinate their personal motivations in deference to the best interests of the polity. They give up a significant degree of their right of privacy in exchange for asserting the police power of the state as the purveyors of policy. They forfeit the predatory role of using policy to further their own interests, including those of the subcultures to which they ascribe. This would suggest that the Founders intended the position of incumbency in a role of public trust as more a curse than a blessing.

The arbitration of the personal privacy of the purveyors of policy is accomplished through the concept of "oath or affirmation", a mechanism that is referenced at a number of points within the *Constitution*. Each occurrence comprises the establishment of a conditional covenant; sacrificing personal privacy in exchange for applying the police powers of the state. Consequently, all those who are entrusted to apply the police powers of the state through positions derived from the policy infrastructure are likewise constrained in their behavior by "oath or affirmation."

Article VI establishes an almost breathtaking constraint on absolutely all of the policy purveyors and arbiters of the federal government, and those of all state governments as well, with this requirement:

> The Senators and Representatives before mentioned, and the Members of the several State Legislatures, and all executive and judicial Officers, both of the United States and of the several States, shall be bound by Oath or Affirmation, to support this Constitution; but no religious Test shall ever be required as a Qualification to any Office or public Trust under the United States.

We characterize this as a breathtaking constraint, because its scope is revealed through the precise oath administered to the President. Interpreting this specific oath as the model for the oaths applied recursively to all those who act under the police powers of the state, it is clear that its requirements are profound! The *Constitution* formalizes the presidential *Oath of Office* in *Article II Section 2*:

> I do solemnly swear (or affirm) that I will faithfully execute the Office of President of the United States, and will to the best of my Ability, preserve, protect and defend the Constitution of the United States.

This oath addresses not just actions, but the allowed motivations for those actions and the sensations through which they mediate conflicting demands for their attention. Execution of any office "to the best of my Ability" mandates a single-mindedness of purpose to that office. To take such an oath of office, one forfeits the right to apply personal motivations to actions. All actions undertaken as part of the execution of office must be subject only to the motivational principles established by the *Constitution* and by its encompassing trust authority and principles formed by the *Declaration of Independence*.

The *Constitution's* demand of the "oath or affirmation" constraint on the subjective elements of adjudication, specifically judges, witnesses and juries, suggests that all members of the policy infrastructure functioning under these constraints are required to accede to the same rules of evidence and "truthfulness" in their utterances as would be found in a courtroom. Accordingly, they may not engage in clandestine activities without a court's warrant and their behavior should at all times conform to a well defined code of ethics. Perhaps most profound, they are expected to tell "the truth, the whole truth, and nothing but the truth" at all times in their public duties.

An oath of office, as iconically illustrated by the presidential oath, places a representative in a different category from a **private citizen**. It is not unreasonable to construe the *Article VI* mandate of "oath or affirmation" as forming the boundary between public and private manifestations of the person. This would place the "expectation of privacy" in quite a different light from that found in much of contemporary jurisprudence. In particular, it would suggest that crossing this boundary is only accomplished through conscious choice and is not to be inferred from any other "legal" actions on the part of a person.

"Oath or affirmation" forms a conditional covenant under which the representative sacrifices a significant degree of personal privacy in exchange for becoming an integral element of the policy infrastructure; including applying the police powers of the state. It signifies that one is, while serving under this constraint, a "public person" as differentiated from a "private person." If the "oath or affirmation" constraint is to have any meaning, then there must be consequences for its abrogation. Thus, a public servant must be subject to sanctions for their acts in public office if they do not adhere to this fiduciary duty. This is a constitutional constraint, not subject to cancellation or moderation through legislative, executive or judicial action. This forms a significant burden for the representative; a burden truly representative of the sacrifices inherent in **public service**.

It seems quite reasonable that the "oath or affirmation" constraint also applies to those who formally seek to become members of the policy infrastructure. The characteristics of age, status of citizenship and place of residence are constraints for those who would serve. Hence, those who seek public office must assert that they meet these requirements in order to seek office. Likewise, it seems reasonable they must also assert that they meet the "oath and affirmation" constraint. This obviously has an impact on the processes of seeking any type of public office. It also has impact on the manner of service in those offices once selected.

We've observed that judging the motivations for the actions of others is difficult. This is obviously true with respect to the "oath or affirmation" requirements of the *Constitution*. However, many policies effected under the police powers of the state seek to assess the motivations of actions. These motivations are then evaluated by courts through trials with questions of the fact of motivations answered by juries. We should therefore be able to make some qualitative observations regarding what the "oath or affirmation" constraint means in the provisioning of the policy infrastructure.

In the *Article VI* statement of the "oath or affirmation" constraints, the *Constitution* specifically notes that the policy assertions of religion cannot be required as qualifications for public office. We suggest that **religion** in this context refers to any subculture that seeks to specify policy applications of the police power of the state based on their own motivations; particularly, their faith based motivations. We further suggest that what we have come to know as political parties fall within this domain of subcultures.

Therefore, it seems quite reasonable that under the "oath or affirmation" constraint, a holder of public office may have no association with a political party. Very specifically, the holder of public office can accept no consideration from a political party nor can they serve in any capacity of policy influence within a political party. Note that this is not a constraint on political parties; it is an expression of personal privacy by one who enters into a conditional covenant to serve as a purveyor or arbiter of policy for the state's policy infrastructure.

The "oath or affirmation" constraint, coupled with recursion in the policy infrastructure derived from due process, suggests that policies applicable external to the policy infrastructure should also be applicable within the policy infrastructure. To do otherwise would result in a non-equitable application of policy. The Supreme Court's ruling in *Skinner v. Oklahoma* speaks directly to this point. "... The guaranty of 'equal protection of the laws is a pledge of the protection of equal laws.' "

The *Marbury* ruling by the Supreme Court rather clearly addresses this concept of equitability in the recursion of policy. Hence, if a policy impacts the Chief Executive Officer (CEO) of a corporate entity, which is a recognized subculture under state policy, an equitable application would suggest it applies to the policy infrastructure itself. If a CEO must personally accept responsibility for actions of the corporate entity, then a member of the executive within the policy infrastructure should be no less accountable.

The "oath or affirmation" constraint should impact the processes throughout the policy infrastructure. A rather clear impact should be the application of the mechanisms of personal privacy to the means of effecting policy. Specifically, much like the deliberations and decisions of a jury, the deliberations and decisions of the policy infrastructure should be subject to the mechanisms of opacity, integrity, identity, authority and attribution. This suggests that no function of the policy infrastructure, including all deliberations related to the development and application of policy, can be guided by the precepts of subcultures such as political parties or caucuses based on restrictive criteria. More specifically, such deliberations should be transparent and subject to rigorous attribution.

The oath of office for public officials has common form and applicability at all levels of the policy infrastructure. A representative within a state legislature is equally constrained compared to the President of the United States. This constraint also has common form with many constraints that have been effected as policy by the federal and state governments. These constraints in policy are often predicated upon concepts such as **conflict of interest** and **corporate responsibility**. The "oath or affirmation" constraint should form the metaphorical boundaries of such concepts. Hence, a conflict of interest for private citizens, for example in the trading of securities, should always be equally or less onerous than the perceived conflict of interest of any public official with respect to the motivations of their public acts.

A rather striking example of such conflict of interest occurs when representatives can foment policy that benefits the subculture(s) that fostered their election. One such policy is the drawing of boundaries on the basis of subcultures for the aggregate charged with selecting representatives; an approach termed **gerrymandering**. Drawing of the boundaries of congressional districts following the decennial census is largely about establishing the dominance of specific subcultures, that is, political parties. In return, the subculture seeks to re-elect the representative(s). This often leads to policy that establishes unconditional covenants for the controlling subculture. Sometimes in such situations, policy is established that penalizes a different subculture in order to benefit the controlling subculture. The "oath or affirmation" constraint of *Article VI* would seem to argue against such behavior.

The truth recognized by the Founders is that when the consequences imposed by social arbitrage of personal privacy become too focused on an individual or subculture, it destroys the basis of trust that is the foundation of the entire social order. This loss of trust first manifests as individual instances of avoiding the rules, or failure to obey the rules when possible. In the end, it results in a breakdown of the social order. It does not take a majority of the polity to cause such a breakdown; it can happen with a much smaller plurality. Consider the examples of prohibition and the current situation with addictive drugs. It seems clear that the Founders recognized this particular threat and established an extremely innovative response.

A far less profound aside, yet still worthy of mention, is that in its present form, the Supreme Court is perhaps too small to represent a good statistical sample for subjective judgment. In addition, the selection process for justices has become embroiled in the same subculture wars that plague the normal election process for representatives. The rather arcane rules of the Senate, which must approve prospective justices nominated by the President, enhance the role of such subcultures. Perhaps a stringent interpretation of the "oath or affirmation" requirements can address this area of concern. Alternatively, perhaps the use of more stochastic mechanisms should be considered in provisioning the court.

The "oath or affirmation" constraint will tend to ensure that those who fill the positions in the policy infrastructure are themselves products of personal privacy. Common law is a system of jurisprudence based on the establishment of consistent precedents through judicial interpretation of the systematic actions of people as applied to specific cases brought before the court. Common law is not grounded purely in statutes; it is grounded in personal interactions. To have legitimacy, privacy must form the basis of the common law.

If personal privacy is not a right of the individual, allowing each person significant, albeit not unlimited control over their individual interactions, then the common law will simply come to reflect the ideology of the prevailing state power structure. It becomes a tautology of the prevailing subculture. If the common law is to truly reflect a consensus based interpretation of justice, then it must be derived from the statistical norms established through acts of personal privacy by the entire polity. To have true meaning as a base for the common law, such acts must be significantly unfettered by state policy.

Going Postal with Privacy

We began with the observation that the concept of privacy arises from the concept of **self**, the manifestation of a unique person. Philosophy suggests two perspectives of self. One gives life to being; "self from the perspective of self." The other gives life to identity; "self from the perspective of others." The first is the actor. The second is the observable consequence. Privacy is the means through which the first provisions the second. At this juncture is the dynamic frontier between the individual and society; "the frontier of social evolution."

Arising as a physiological manifestation, privacy has been well embraced by the foundational trust and policy infrastructures of the United States. The *Declaration of Independence* establishes privacy as the fundamental principle on which is grounded the trust infrastructure of American jurisprudence. The *Constitution* subsequently establishes a policy infrastructure in which the mechanisms of privacy are central to the creation and enforcement of the common law.

The trust and policy infrastructures would be enhanced through the creation of complementary differential-identity and experiential-identity systems based on biometric and digital technologies. A National Identity System encompassing these facilities, if realized through appropriate policy strictures, offers significant enhancement of personal privacy through the mechanisms that we've earlier considered.

In concluding our examination of privacy, we suggest a modest proposal. **Congress should establish a National Identity System under the auspices of the United States Postal Service.** The system should be based on biometric markers for each individual comprising a National Differential-identity Registry coupled to limited National Experiential-identity Registry through a National Public Key Infrastructure. From a metaphorical perspective, a National Identity System is a natural extension of the postal services envisioned by the Founders, as evidenced by the mechanisms they mandated in the *Constitution*.

In *Article I*, three of the powers delegated to the legislative branch of government are to "conduct a periodic census", to "establish Post Offices and Post Roads", and to "establish standards for uniform weights and measures" for the nation. These powers form a framework within which to build an operational National Identity System.

A National Identity System forms the nucleus of Identity, Authority and Attribution System services on which all manner of trusted interactions can be based. The National Public Key Infrastructure affords the means to convey services through well defined authority and attribution facilities. This comprehensive digital infrastructure can be extended through the issuance of basic identity tokens as well as digital surrogates, allowing IAA System services in sensori-motor interactions as well.

As part of this infrastructure, trusted means of location and time determination would allow the establishment of a basic experiential-identity registry that can address identity mandates found in the *Constitution*; place of birth, time of birth, location of residence and status of residence. The entire social structure of the nation is predicated upon being able to establish this information in a manner so as to afford truth to the trust it avers.

An election is an almost trivial application of an IAA system. Consequently, a National Identity System will enhance the trust ascribed to elections for all levels of government. Trusted digital facilities will allow elections to be conducted in a manner dispersed across the polity; not subject to arbitrary time or geographical constraints. The same digital facilities will enhance the assertion of personal privacy in all forms of personal interactions; not just those involving the state directly. By encompassing all those entering and leaving the United States, a National Identity System will allow more flexible policies regarding immigration.

The United States Postal Service is an independent, quasi-governmental organization. As such, it offers a structure through which the National Identity System, including the registries of a National Differential-identity facility and a National Experiential-identity facility, can be maintained at an arm-length relationship to government. The firewall of this relationship can be strengthened through well defined protocols buttressed by appropriate policy. By establishing the root-certificate for a National Public Key Infrastructure, the mechanisms through which privacy is realized would gain substance in policy as well as technology.

The quasi-governmental nature of the United States Postal Service offers a most intriguing opportunity based on its special position in law. Its actions are grounded in the police powers of the state. The services provided are protected by legal sanctions. Material submitted to the postal service for delivery enters a protected context as of the time and location of its submittal. More germane, additional policy and motivational perspective will be required of postal agents regarding identity services. In particular, they must foster a dedication to service like the military and the police as opposed to that of a political patronage organization.

Material submitted to the United States Postal Service is viewed as an extension of the person, requiring a warrant for its seizure and subsequent search. The IAA System services provided by a National Identity System would also be considered as extensions of the individual person. A differential-identity registry containing the biometric characteristics of individuals must be created through pair-wise interactions between the person and the registry. The policies under which such interactions occur are subject to the arbitration of personal privacy and can be viewed in the guise of conditional covenants, altruistic actions or both.

The United States Postal Service is not an agency of common law enforcement, or of national defense; however, it does field its own police force. This force of postal inspectors is charged with enforcing laws related to the services provided and for the equipment used to provide those services. The United States Postal Service also has international scope, providing services world-wide through relationships with similar services in other countries.

In establishing a National Identity System, the necessary first step results from a permanent, continuing census. As we illustrated back in the third chapter, a census is the enrollment process for an identity system. In addition, the *Constitution* mandates a limited set of characteristics of experiential-identity through the qualifications it establishes for members of the policy infrastructure. These qualifications primarily refer to age and geographic location; constraints that translate into a requirement for trusted means to establish time and location.

An extremely profound facility that the United States Postal Service offers relative to a National Identity System is its ubiquitous geographical presence. Post Offices are found in more that 32,000 locations throughout the nation; extending from inner cities to lightly populated rural areas. Mail Carriers, the agents of the postal service, routinely visit virtually every physical location in the country where people are present. They do so in accomplishing their most basic service of mail distribution.

The United States Postal Service is charged with providing delivery services for mail to every person in the nation. As such, it has a basic need to associate names and addresses. Every person can be identified by name and have a mailing address; a physically identifiable location in the country. While the United States Postal Service does not yet provide a general directory system, it does provide a highly redundant and resilient addressing and delivery system. In this sense, it is the direct precursor of the Internet. An experiential-identity registry that relates names and addresses to differential-identity is an important extension of this facility.

These operational characteristics mean that it is relatively easy to put any person in the country in direct physical contact with a postal service facility or employee. This capability is essential to establishing and operating a ubiquitous identification system. The most common services provided by identification systems are identification, authorization and attribution. These can be routinely provided within the trusted context of Post Offices, but they can also be extended throughout society in the form of identification tokens. The source of digital surrogates would be the Post Office.

Today, the United States Postal Service is a social facility. Throughout the country, the local Post Office is a routine aspect of the social life of the community. The Mail Carrier is familiar with many aspects of the individual lives of people and their families through the mail that is distributed. Of all elements of government that might be viewed as a trusted purveyor of identity, the United States Postal Service is easiest to visualize in this role.

It is said that with real-estate, the three crucial factors are "location, location, location". The United States Postal Service occupies an incredibly compelling space relative to identity, and hence to privacy. There will obviously be cultural and policy enhancements required. In particular, all of the functions of the state must be grounded in strongly authenticated identity and trusted interactions, thus supporting policy that gives personal privacy the force of law. The environment of institutional anonymity on the part of the state must be abolished. Of course, this suggests both the promise and the danger.

An effective identity system that does not encompass all facilities of the state is a recipe for "Big Brother" An effective identity system that does encompass the state is a comprehensive menu for the "extreme individuality" we call personal privacy.

Bibliography

Abrams, Paula – *Cross Purposes: Pierce v. Society of Sisters and the Struggle over Compulsory Public Education*, The University of Michigan Press, Ann Arbor, Michigan 2009

Ackerman, Bruce – *We the People: Foundations*, Harvard University Press, Cambridge, Massachusetts 1991

Ackerman, Bruce – *We the People: Transformations*, Harvard University Press, Cambridge, Massachusetts 1998

Balkin, Jack M. editor – *What Brown v. Board of Education Should Have Said*, New York University Press, New York, NY 2002

Balkin, Jack M. editor – *What Roe v. Wade Should Have Said*, New York University Press, New York, NY 2005

Bernstein, David E. – *Rehabilitating Lochner: Defending Individual Rights against Progressive Reform*, The University of Chicago Press, Chicago, Illinois 2011

Bolle, Ruud M. *et al – Guide to Biometrics*, Springer, New York, NY 2004

Cooley, Charles Horton – *Human Nature and the Social Order*, Charles Scribner's Sons, New York, NY 1902

Darwin, Charles – *The Origin of Species by Means of Natural Selection*, J. Murray, London, England 1859

Du Castel, Bertrand & Timothy M. Jurgensen – *Computer Theology: Intelligent Design of the World Wide Web*, Midori Press, Austin, Texas 2008

Ekman, Paul & Richard J. Davidson editors – *The Nature Of Emotion*, Oxford University Press, New York, NY 1994

Feinberg, Todd E., M.D. – *From Axons to Identity*, W.W. Norton & Company, New York, NY 2009

Friston, Karl & James Kilner & Lee Harrison – *A free energy principle for the brain, Journal of Physiology*, Paris, France 2006

Gazzaniga, Michael S. editor-in-chief – *The Cognitive Neurosciences: Fourth Edition*, The MIT Press, Cambridge, Massachusetts 2009

Gerber, Scott Douglas – *First Principles: The Jurisprudence of Clarence Thomas*, New York University Press, New York, NY 1999

Gerber, Scott Douglas editor – *The Declaration of Independence Origins and Impact*, CQ Press, Washington, D.C. 2002

Gerber, Scott Douglas – *To Secure These Rights: The Declaration of Independence and Constitutional Interpretation*, New York University Press, New York, NY 1995

Gould, Stephen Jay – *Rocks of Ages: Science and Religion in the Fullness of Life*, Ballantine Books, New York, NY 1999

Gould, Stephen Jay – *The Structure of Evolutionary Theory*, Harvard University Press, Cambridge, Massachusetts 2002

Kruman, Marc W. – *Between Authority and Liberty: State Constitution Making in Revolutionary America*, The University of North Carolina Press, Chapel Hill, North Carolina 1997

Lakoff, George & Mark Johnson – *Metaphors We Live By*, University of Chicago Press, Chicago, Illinois 1980

LeDoux, Joseph – *The Emotional Brain: The Mysterious Underpinnings of Emotional Life*, Simon & Schuster Paperbacks, New York, NY 1996

LeDoux, Joseph – *Synaptic Self: How Our Brains Become Who We Are*, Penguin Books, New York, NY 2002

Maslow, Abraham H. – *Toward a Psychology of Being, Third Edition*, John Wiley and Sons, Inc, New York, NY 1968, 1999

Mayr, Ernst – *Systematics and the Origin of Species from the Viewpoint of a Zoologist*, Columbia University Press, New York, NY 1947

Neisser, Ulric – *Cognitive Psychology*, Prentice-Hall Inc, Englewood Cliffs, New Jersey 1967

Newton, Michael E. – *Angry Mobs and Founding Fathers*, Elftheria Publishing 2011

Piaget, Jean – *The Psychology of Intelligence*, Routledge, London, England 2001

Post, Robert C. – *Constitutional Domains: Democracy, Community, Management*, Harvard University Press, Cambridge, Massachusetts 1995

Rauls, John – *A Theory of Justice*, Harvard University Press, Cambridge, Massachusetts 1971

Rauls, John – *Lectures on the History of Political Philosophy*, Harvard University Press, Cambridge, Massachusetts 2007

Rees, Dai and Steven Rose, editors – *The New Brain Sciences: Perils and Prospects*, Cambridge University Press, Cambridge, England 2004

Rossiter, Clinton editor – *The Federalist Papers*, Penguin Group, New York, NY 1961

Scalia, Antonin – *A Matter of Interpretation: Federal Courts and the Law*, Princeton University Press, Princeton, New Jersey 1997

Schneier, Bruce – *Applied Cryptography*, John Wiley and Sons, New York, NY 1996

Sinha, Surya Prakash – *Jurisprudence: Legal Philosophy*, West Group, St. Paul, Minnesota 1993

Smith, Janet E. – *The Right To Privacy*, The National Catholic Bioethics Center Ignatius Press, Philadelphia, Pennsylvania 2008

Solove, Daniel J. & Paul M. Schwartz – *Information Privacy Law*, Aspen Publishers, New York, NY 2009

Solove, Daniel J. – *Nothing to Hide: The False Tradeoff between Privacy and Security*, Yale University Press, New Haven, Connecticut 2011

Solove, Daniel J. & Paul M. Schwartz – *Privacy, Information and Technology*, Aspen Publishers, New York, NY 2009

Solove, Daniel J. & Paul M. Schwartz – *Privacy Law Fundamentals*, IAPP Publication, Portsmouth, NH 2011

Solove, Daniel J. – *The Future of Reputation*, Yale University Press, New Haven, Connecticut 2007

Solove, Daniel J. – *Understanding Privacy*, Harvard University Press, Cambridge, Massachusetts 2008

Turner, Jonathan H. editor – *Theory and Research on Human Emotions*, Elsevier Ltd, London 2004

Weddington, Sarah – *A Question of Choice*, Penguin Books, New York, NY 1993

Wood, Gordon S. – *The Creation of the American Republic 1776-1787*, The University of North Carolina Press, Chapel Hill, North Carolina 1969

Wouk, Herman – *The Language God Talks*, Little, Brown and Company, New York, NY 2010

Rulings of the Supreme Court of the United States

YEAR	CASE
(1803)	Marbury v. Madison, 5 U.S. 137
(1819)	McCulloch v. Maryland, 17 U.S. 4 Wheat. 316
(1849)	Luther v. Borden, 48 U.S. 7 How. 1
(1856)	Dred Scott v. Sandford, 60 U.S. 393
(1874)	Minor v. Happersett, 88 U.S. 162
(1878)	Reynolds v. United States, 98 U.S. 145
(1891)	Union Pacific Railway Co. v. Botsford, 141 U.S. 250
(1896)	Plessy v. Ferguson, 163 U.S. 537
(1905)	Jacobson v. Massachusetts, 197 U.S. 11
(1905)	Lochner v. People of State of New York, 198 U.S. 45
(1919)	Schenck v. United States, 249 U.S. 47
(1923)	Meyer v. Nebraska, 262 U.S. 390
(1925)	Pierce v. Society of Sisters, 268 U.S. 510
(1927)	Whitney v. California, 274 U.S. 357
(1928)	Olmstead v. United States, 277 U.S. 438
(1937)	West Coast Hotel Co. v. Parrish, 300 U.S. 379
(1938)	United States v. Carolene Products Company, 304 U.S. 144
(1940)	Cantwell v. Connecticut, 310 U.S. 296
(1942)	Skinner v. Oklahoma ex rel. Williamson, 316 U.S. 535
(1944)	Korematsu v. United States, 323 U.S. 214
(1949)	Terminiello v. Chicago, 337 U.S. 1
(1954)	Brown v. Board of Education of Topeka, 347 U.S. 483
(1957)	Roth v. United States, 354 U.S. 476
(1957)	Watkins v. United States, 354 U.S. 178
(1958)	Kent v. Dulles, 357 U.S. 116
(1959)	Kingsley Int'l Pictures Corp. v. Regents, 360 U.S. 684
(1959)	NAACP v. Alabama, 360 U.S. 240
(1962)	Baker v. Carr, 369 U.S. 186
(1963)	Sherbert v. Verner, 374 U.S. 398

(1964)   Aptheker v. Secretary of State, 378 U.S. 500
(1964)   New York Times Co. v. Sullivan, 376 U.S. 254
(1964)   Reynolds v. Sims, 377 U.S. 533
(1965)   Carrington v. Rash, 380 U.S. 89
(1965)   Griswold v. Connecticut, 381 U.S. 479
(1966)   Miranda v. Arizona, 384 U.S. 436
(1967)   Katz v. United States, 389 U.S. 347
(1967)   Loving v. Virginia, 388 U.S. 1
(1968)   Terry v. Ohio, 392 U.S. 1
(1968)   United States v. Jackson, 390 U.S. 570
(1969)   Brandenburg v. Ohio, 395 U.S. 444
(1969)   Kramer v. Union Free Sch. Dist. No. 15, 395 U.S. 621
(1969)   Shapiro v. Thompson, 394 U.S. 618
(1970)   United States v. Van Leeuwen, 397 U.S. 249
(1972)   Eisenstadt v. Baird, 405 U.S. 438
(1972)   Papachristou v. City of Jacksonville, 405 U.S. 156
(1973)   Roe v. Wade, 410 U.S. 113
(1985)   University of Michigan v. Ewing, 474 U.S. 214
(2008)   District of Columbia *et al* v. Heller – 07-290

Glossary

The symbol ":==" should be interpreted as "is defined as".

- Point :== intersection of the physical and the philosophical
- Source :== point of emanation
- Target :== point of focus
- Deictic center :== source of action and target of observation
- Self :== deictic center of personal awareness
- Polity :== deictic center of social awareness; aggregate self of a social order
- Interaction :== association of independent entities through constrained forces
- Entity :== distinguishable manifestation subject to force within context
- Context :== adiabatic barrier that constrains forces
- Force :== influence the orientation and dynamic characteristics of an entity
  - Domains of Forces:
    - Physical (weak, strong, electromagnetic, gravity)
    - Physiological (biological and physical)
    - Philosophical (social policy)
- Mimesis :== experience sharing
- Metaphor :== concept used as an allusion for a different concept
- Cognition :== application of metaphorical models through neural processing to effect representation of reality through sensory interpretation, motivation formulation, trust assessment, and action invocation
- Sensation :==   consequence of cognition
- Ecstasy :== sensation that recalibrates the trust assessment scale of cognition
- Provisioning :== develop and optimize metaphoric models of cognition encompassing:
  - Trust infrastructure
  - Policy infrastructure
  - Interaction mechanics
  - Initial conditions
  - Measure of consequences
- Identity :== self from the perspective of others
  - Differential-identity :== distinguishing characteristic of an entity
  - Experiential-identity :== art associated with a differential-identity
    - Persona :== subset of experiential-identity
- Action :== application of force
- Observation :== measurement of orientation of an entity
- Consequence :== post-action orientation of an entity
- Identification :== distinguish one entity within a set of entities
- Expression :== convey sensation through the physiological motor system
- Impression :== perceive sensation through the physiological sensory system
- Play :== spontaneous interaction
- Experience :==   persistent sensation
- Memory :== physiological mechanism to convey sensation from the present to the future

- Art-form :== tool used to extend expression beyond its physiological motor system source; external (to the brain) memory
- Composition :== distinguished experience expressed by art-form
- Art :== aggregation of compositions
- Campaign :== structured sequence of interactions aimed at a defined consequence
- Forensic wake :== aggregation of memories and art
- Trust: == probability that a specific action will result in an anticipated consequence
- Truth: == probability that an observed consequence resulted from a specific action
- Faith :== trust independent of truth (*a "religious" concept*)
- Grace :== consequence independent of action (*a "religious" concept*)
- Morality :== cognition value system grounded in grace and faith (*a "religious" concept*)
- Society :== others from the perspective of self
- Social-order :== distinguished society
- Religion :== social order in which trust is grounded in faith and truth in grace
- Consciousness :== instantaneous cognition
- Privacy :== provisioning of identity
- Policy :== provisioning of society
- Culture :== art with a common characteristic; for example, a common social order
- Esteem :== sensation of value on which trust assessment is based
- Reputation :== sensation of value derived from identity
- Devotion :== sensation of value derived from society
- Jurisprudence :== interaction management by the state
- Justice :== truth through jurisprudence
- Adjudication :== exception handling of jurisprudence
- Court :== mechanism for adjudication
- Trial :== interaction simulator used by a court
- Judge :== administrator of a court
- Jury :== subjective decision emulator for a court
- Remedial-action :== consequence correction derived from adjudication
- Mercy :== remedial action independent of adjudication (*a "religious" concept*)
- Suffrage :== means through which the polity conveys authority through consent
- State :== social order with police powers
- Police :== error detection mechanism of jurisprudence
- Police Powers :== exercise force in all domains effecting policy to:
    - Arbitrate privacy among interacting individuals
    - Arbitrage privacy to benefit the social order
    - Apply remedial actions to abrogation of policy
- Altruism :== behavior mandated by policy of a social order
- Stochastic-process : == activity viewed through random observations that reflect recognized probability distributions.
- Right :== behavior precluded from abridgement by the state
- Conspiracy :== *ad hoc* agreement for common action
- Mechanisms of privacy:
    - Opacity :== clarity of sensory observation
    - Integrity :== immutability of sensory observation
    - Identity :== self from the perspective of others

- o Authority :== ability to invoke action
  - Locality :== physical authority for action
  - Capability :== physiological authority for action
  - Consent :== policy authority for action
  - o Attribution :== rigorous association
- Covenant :== policy expressing the arbitration of privacy among entities in an interaction
  - o Unconditional covenant :== consideration offered with no reciprocal requirement for consideration in return
  - o Conditional covenant :== consideration offered for consideration received
- Persistence is achieved either through memory or art-form
- trust is a measure of risk
- truth is a measure of reward

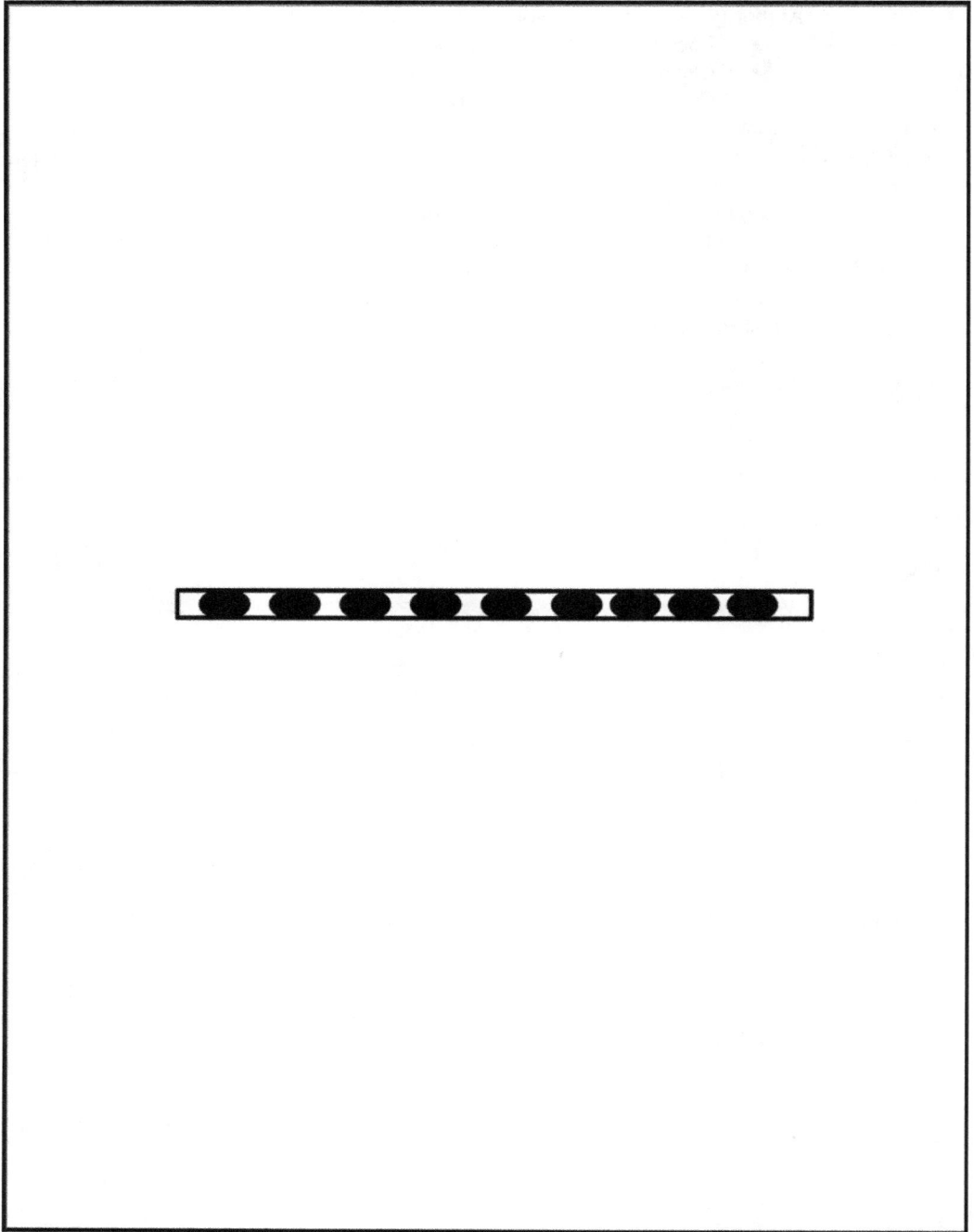

Index

cognitive assessment   46-7, 49, 59
cognitive models   2, 6, 175
colonies   185, 188-91, 198
communication, trusted   95, 103
communication channels   94-5, 99-100,
     102, 105, 109-10
communities   85, 128, 131, 174, 199, 214
compelling interest   25, 121-2, 124-5,
     129, 131-2, 138, 141, 144, 148-50,
     152-3, 155, 160, 165-8, 171, 174,
     180-1, 183, 195-6, 205
compelling state interest   14, 55, 124,
     128, 132, 142, 168, 172, 206-7
compensation   145, 147, 163
compositions   3, 8, 44, 64, 68, 72, 84, 86,
     92, 96-7, 106, 108, 155, 157, 168,
     176, 178-9
computer platforms   74, 81, 92-5, 97-
     100, 102-3, 107-8, 111-12, 114
   sentinel's   98, 100, 111
   trusted   94-6, 104, 107-10
Computer Theology   12, 52, 63, 91
computers   19, 32, 52, 60, 80-1, 85, 91-
     2, 94-6, 98, 104-5, 109-12, 117, 155
   host   80-1
   laptop   35, 108
concept   1-29, 31, 33-4, 42-4, 50-2, 63-4,
     66, 69-70, 85-6, 91, 93, 97, 101,
     108, 119, 121, 123-6, 131-3, 137-9,
     141, 145-8, 159-62, 165, 167-8, 172-
     4, 176-7, 180, 183, 185, 189, 194-5,
     198-9, 201, 203-4, 208, 210-12
   legal   12-13, 119
   orthogonal   62, 133
   reciprocal   4
   religious   150, 159
   republican   189
   subordinate   6, 14
conception   17, 20, 58, 141
conditional covenants   16, 19-21, 43, 86,
     90, 115, 145, 147, 149-50, 152, 159,
     161, 166, 168-70, 176, 178-80, 187,
     205-6, 208-10, 213
Congress   52, 121, 125, 129-30, 133,
     135, 147, 151, 159-61, 163, 166,
     172, 186, 189, 199-200, 212
consent   85-6, 101-2, 112, 187-9, 201
consequences   1, 3, 8-10, 14, 19-20, 22,
     24, 29, 37, 42, 48, 50, 53, 57-9, 62,
     76, 83-4, 86, 91-3, 96, 101, 107,

     113, 119, 143-6, 149-50, 153-4, 156-
     61, 163-5, 167, 178, 188, 208-9, 211
   actual   8, 84, 157
   anticipated   9, 21, 52-3, 83
   desired   8, 29, 47-8, 54-5, 83-4, 87
   interaction's   154
   measureable   207
   measured   207
Constitution   13, 16, 22, 108, 120-3, 125-
     7, 131, 133, 136, 138-40, 144-8,
     153, 160-6, 168-73, 175, 179, 181-2,
     187-202, 204, 208-10, 212-13
constraints   37, 42, 46-7, 51, 61, 83, 88,
     101, 113-14, 124, 128, 132, 147,
     161, 163-6, 179, 182, 189, 198, 209-
     11, 213
   oath or affirmation   108, 209-11
contact   85, 101-2
context   5-9, 20-1, 36-7, 41-3, 47-8, 53,
     55, 57-8, 60, 76-7, 79-80, 83-4, 87-
     9, 91-3, 95, 101, 107, 109, 113, 117,
     119, 129-30, 143, 145, 149, 152,
     154, 158-60, 163, 166-7, 174-5, 180,
     196, 210
   establishing   86-7, 137, 159
   procedural   92, 187
   religious   206
context assessment   87-8
contract
   de facto   152
   de jure   152
contracts   38, 140, 149, 168, 174
control   3, 14, 16, 28, 45, 76, 83-5, 91-2,
     94-5, 99, 105, 107, 117, 134-5, 137-
     8, 150, 155, 163-4, 167, 177-8, 180,
     186, 203
controversy   124, 144, 147
convictions   121, 123, 126, 128-31, 135,
     139, 163
Cooley, Charles Horton   7, 138
Cooley, Thomas   7
counting   61-7, 72
court decisions   119-20, 126
courts   14, 84, 119-22, 124-6, 129-33,
     135-48, 150, 154-60, 162, 164-5,
     167, 171-5, 179, 182-3, 187, 192-3,
     195-205, 210-11
   lower   119, 132, 146
   symmetric   155

Privacy: The Frontier of Social Evolution

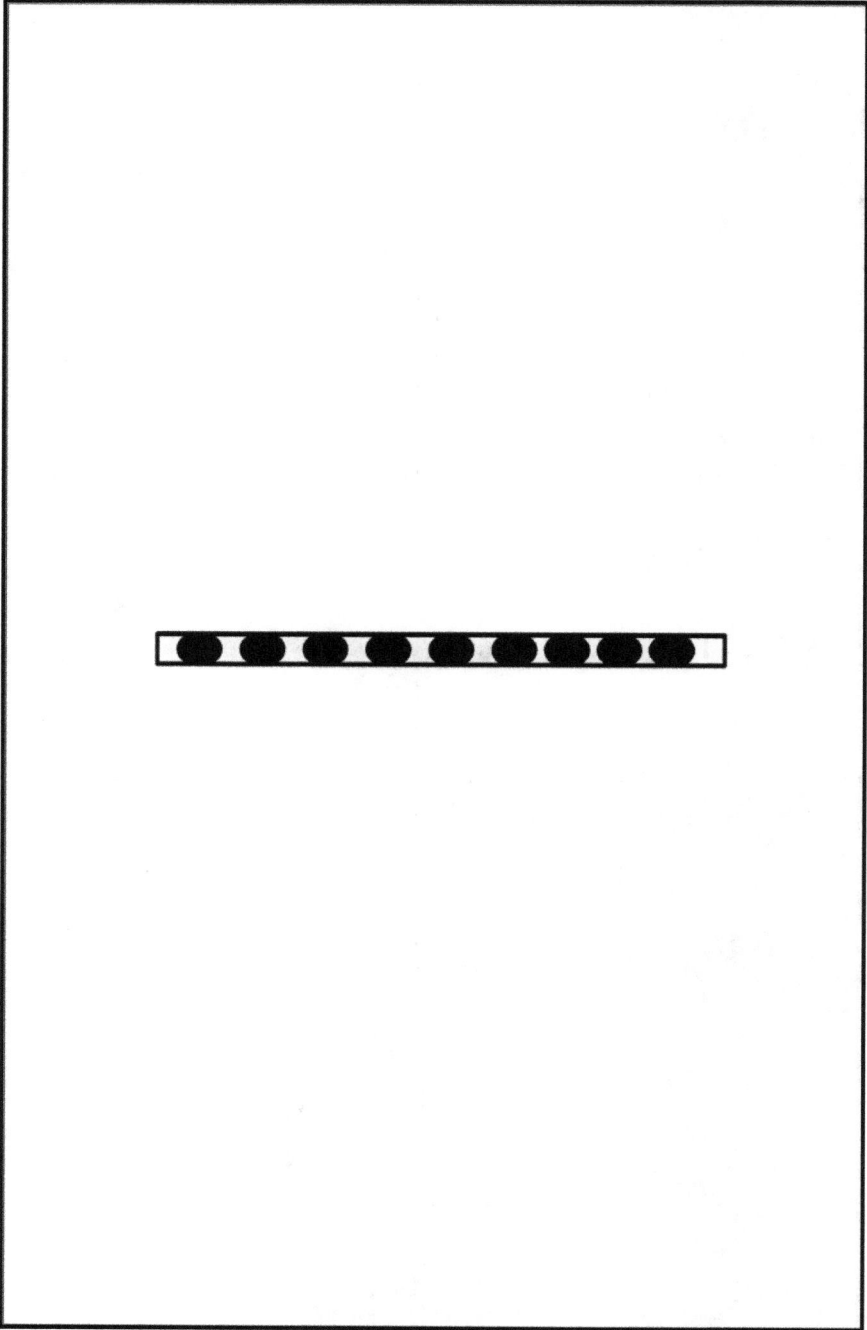

www.ingramcontent.com/pod-product-compliance
Lightning Source LLC
Chambersburg PA
CBHW081147270326
41930CB00014B/3064